The Structure of Folk Models

Association of Social Anthropologists
A Series of Monographs

A.S.A. MONOGRAPH 20

The Structure of Folk Models

Edited by

LADISLAV HOLY

Department of Geography
University of St Andrews
Scotland

and

MILAN STUCHLIK

Department of Social Anthropology
The Queen's University of Belfast
Northern Ireland

1981

ACADEMIC PRESS

A Subsidiary of Harcourt Brace Jovanovich, Publishers

London   New York   Toronto   Sydney   San Francisco

ACADEMIC PRESS INC. (LONDON) LTD.
24/28 Oval Road,
London NW1

United States Edition published by
ACADEMIC PRESS INC.
111 Fifth Avenue
New York, New York 10003

British Library Cataloguing in Publication Data
The structure of folk models – (Association of Social
   Anthropologists of the Commonwealth; Monographs; 20).
   1. Social interaction
   I. Holy, L.   II. Stuchlik, Milan   III. Series
   301.1   HM291   80-41359

   ISBN 0-12-353750-9

Printed in Great Britain by
St Edmundsbury Press, Bury St Edmunds, Suffolk

PREFACE

The essays contained in this volume are revised versions of papers presented at the Annual Conference of the ASA held in Edinburgh from 8-11 April 1980. To circumscribe the area of problems to which the conference might profitably address itself, the working draft of our own paper was sent to the contributors of the conference well in advance and it was suggested that they react to it in their papers, however critically. Most of them did so, although, needless to say, not all of them agreed with all the propositions put forward in it. In this sense, all the papers can be said to cover one, though rather broad, topic of anthropological inquiry; how far they also represent an epistemologically unified approach is not for us to say. The reader has to be his own judge.

The main proposition put forward in our introductory paper is that people's own concepts of their actions, their reasons and explanations for them, and more generally the whole range of their own notions about the social and natural world they live in, form a necessary and indivisible part of the reality we are studying. This might sound like an obvious truism, but in actual fact these notions have often been treated, by anthropologists, simply as descriptive of observable reality and therefore as being the same kind of phenomena as observable reality; or, in a dismissive way, as false representations which should be replaced by the anthropologist's own notions. The point is that people's notions are as much a part of our explanandum as their overt actions. If we do not pay attention to them in our explanatory accounts of that reality, we would be altering that reality itself and, in the last instance, in the process of the explanation modifying, if not directly constructing, the very object of it. This proposition is clearly echoed in Sansom's paper in this volume. He argues that not only is the comprehension of the North Australian Aborigines an indivisible part of their social order, but also that this social order cannot be sociologically explained unless this native comprehension is seen as the basic set of data for such an explanation.

To describe the complex of people's own notions about their world, which is the main focus of attention of all the papers in this volume, we have used a rather loose term "folk model". The term "structure" in the title is not meant to indicate a specific theoretical approach. It merely reflects our assumption that the notions, ideals and concepts which may be collectively called "folk models" are not haphazard or random collections, but are ordered and constitute sets which are interrelated and connected: in other words, they have certain definable properties. Ortiz addresses herself in her paper specifically to the question of how elements of people's knowledge are interrelated, and how specific mental constructs are continually built as parts of decision-making processes. From a different point of view, Strathern demonstrates how one key concept of "self" can be used in accounting for an individual's relations with others and with a collectivity.

Although the assumption about the ordered character of folk models forms an implicit background for most papers, their explicit thrust is more oriented towards the actors' processes of cognition and comprehension than towards the structure of their cognitive systems. One of the most important problems within this broad framework is the problem of the relationship between models and patterns of action. This relationship is the central topic of Jenkins' and Galaty's papers. The relationship between people's models and their actions entails a necessary system of transformation from general to particular contexts, and it raises the fundamental question about the extent to which observed actions can be used as a means of validating or falsifying the model.

One of the specific ways in which folk models of social and cultural reality may be related to social action is by being invoked as its legitimization. Papers by Preston-Whyte and Blacking, the former dealing with a specific model of white South Africans and the latter with a totally different but similarly specific model of black South Africans, both clearly indicate the way in which such models may be used as justifications for taking a certain political position and maintaining specific political aspirations. Both papers taken together have also an added advantage of presenting, so to say, two sides of the same political problem: the relationship between black and white inhabitants of South Africa. Tonkin deals with a similar problem in

Liberia: the dichotomizing ideology as a justification for political action.

Another important aspect of the general problem of the relationship between folk models and observed patterns of actions is the emergence of intersubjectively shared notions as a result of common life experience. Riches' and McFarlane's papers address themselves particularly to this issue.

The notion of folk models is definitely not meant to imply that there exists, in every society, one general or "master" model held by and subscribed to by all its members. Salzman's and Turner's papers take the multiplicity of models co-existing in a given society as their main problem. They both explore the ways in which these various models are interrelated, how far they are complementary and contradictory, and how far they affect each other. Analyzing the co-existence of different folk models in one society enables us not only to understand and explain specific events, as Turner's paper clearly demonstrates, but has important consequences for our conceptualization of culture, a specific problem taken up by Salzman.

The fact that a folk model is necessarily authored, in the last instance, by the anthropologist, raises in a significant way the question of its validity. Only when the anthropologist's research procedures have been clearly specified is it possible to judge to what extent his account of the folk model corresponds to the notions, ideas and concepts held by the actors and to the reasoning processes by which these elements are structured into models. It is obvious that the closer attention we pay to the models and cultural constructs of the people we study, the more crucial our concern with our research procedures and methods of inference has to become. Milton's and McFarlane's papers, which are concerned specifically with this problem, may possibly represent what is likely to become a renewed interest in research methodology in British social anthropology. Strathern's paper represents another aspect of this difficult problem: when presenting a folk model, the anthropologist is basically trying to parallel reasoning processes performed by members of the society. In such an undertaking, the documentation, or presentation of evidence, is one of the main difficulties. Strathern's analysis of the contextual use of the one key folk concept shows a very feasible way of giving such evidence.

Instead of trying to impose some conceptual criteria by grouping the essays into thematic sections, when arranging the volume we have followed, with the exception of our own introductory paper, the simple expedient of alphabetical order.

Finally, we would like to express our thanks to Dr. Anthony

Jackson of the Department of Social Anthropology, University of Edinburgh, for his efficient and impeccable administration of the conference.

CONTENTS

THE STRUCTURE OF FOLK MODELS

LADISLAV HOLY AND MILAN STUCHLIK

Most of the current methodological discussions and disagreements in the social sciences stem, in the last instance, from our uncertainty or confusion about the ontological and epistemological status of the things we study. Yet, the questions of the existential status of social reality and its availability to the observer are rarely addressed directly. In this paper, we wish to point out that one of the essential characteristics of social reality is that it is a constituted reality: a process and result of social life, consisting of intentional performances of members of society. This presents social scientists with considerable methodological difficulties, arising from the necessity of seeing social life as comprising different realms or kinds of reality. In choosing the term "model" for one of them, we are trying to find a broader use for a concept which has been used in anthropology to refer to the analytical or explanatory constructs of the observer. We intend to argue that the study of folk models, far from being a marginal area of anthropology, raises important issues which are central to anthropological analysis and explanation.

Data and Models in Anthropology

The distinction between two different kinds or levels (in a non-hierarchical sense) of phenomena with which anthropologists are concerned has been made many times over; therefore only a very abbreviated argument should suffice in this context. When Durkheim asserted that "sociology does not need to choose between the great hypotheses which divide metaphysicians" (Durkheim 1964: 141), he did not mention that this is so mainly because it has already chosen. The choice is probably best epitomized by the title of one of Radcliffe-Brown's books, *The natural science of society*. The actuality of this choice was recently pointed out by Giddens:

> The wish to establish the natural science of society which would possess the same sort of logical structure and pursue the same achievements as the sciences of nature probably remains, in the English speaking world at least, the dominant standpoint today. (Giddens: 1976: 13)

However, if the science of society has to be built along the lines of the natural sciences, not only the logical structure and achievements, but also its subject matter has to be conceived of as having the same existential status: it must be real, factual, and consisting of empirical phenomena existing "out there" in the world. Also, they must be available to the observer in basically the same way. Typically, participant observation has been seen as giving to the researcher something like sense data, i.e. information about the social world obtained through direct sense experience. Relationships, concepts, etc. that are obviously non-observable have been conceived of as non-problematically following from the proper arrangement of phenomena. All directly observable data, when properly combined, fall into place and reveal "the form of social life" (Radcliffe-Brown 1952: 4). This "jigsaw-puzzle conception" (Levi-Strauss 1960: 52) makes even the non-observable entities, through the empirical availability of their components, a sort of empirical reality.

"Observability", though, is a difficult term. Should we limit it to mean the availability of phenomena to sensory perception, then there is in the whole realm of social life only one kind of thing which is observable: specific actions of concrete individuals (be they "physical" actions or speech actions). Strictly speaking, even actions are not fully observable: what we observe are physical movements. What makes of physical movement an action is its meaning, and, undoubtedly, the same physical movements may have many different meanings (cf. Anscombe 1957: 40ff.). Meaning is given to movements by applying some preconceived criteria known to both actors and observers; applying criteria is not observation. Therefore, even actions are not experienced simply through senses, but simultaneously through senses and thought processes (cf. Gorman 1977: 60).

Since people do not behave in isolated actions but in interactions, with and toward others, their actions must be meaningful to others. And that means that the criteria for ascribing meaning and the ways for interpreting movements must be known and shared by them:

otherwise social life could not exist. To the extent to which members of the society "observe" their mutual actions, i.e. experience the movements and non-problematically or automatically assign meaning to them, their actions are "observable", i.e. non-problematically available, to the observer. The crucial importance of participant observation and long-term fieldwork consists thus mainly in that it permits the anthropologist to learn how and what to "observe".

The epistemological status of interactions in which people actually engage, i.e. their availability through observation, is thus given by their public or shared nature. Their existential status is given by the fact that actions are performed in order to make a visible impact on the physical and social world: to change or maintain the existing state of affairs. By their nature, actions are unique and irrepeatable; once performed, they cease to exist. But, on the other hand, they form a continuous flow of existence in space and time. Furthermore, a state of affairs constituted by an action lasts even after the action has ceased to exist.

The fact that people share criteria, or, more generally, knowledge of how to behave and how to interpret actions, entails the existence of these actions at another level: as "blueprints" or plans for actions in the minds of the members of society. The existence of these plans is perduring: people have and share them even when the actions are not being performed. They also do not refer to a particular action, but to a type. A report on "how it is known that such and such an action is a sacrifice" refers not to a specific action, but to a blueprint or plan for any such action. Even in the above defined sense of observability, plans for actions cannot be directly observed. Neither the observer, nor the actors can, so to say, "witness" them in the same sense as actions. They can be told of their existence or infer it. By holding them, an individual does not directly purpose or intend to maintain or change the existing state of affairs; by themselves, the plans for actions do not "do" anything. They are simply elements of individuals' knowledge, mental constructs, and are part of social life only to the extent to which they are shared among the members of society.

This realm or level of reality contains far more than simple plans for actions. People engage in interactions that are performed in situations, circumstances and environments, both social and physical, that they have to know to be able to perform acceptably. Their notions about all these conditions are mental constructs in the same way as plans for actions, but they differ in the sense that they are not simply descriptions of acts but more complex notions about the relationships between acts, about the way things are, things could be, etc. While a plan for action may contain the answer to the question "what do I need to do so that everybody recognizes that I am performing a sacrifice?", the actor also has the knowledge of when to sacrifice, to whom, how the sacrifice relates to other events of life, etc.

Thus, there are basically two qualitatively different kinds of things which constitute the anthropologist's data: things which exist, so to say, "on the ground" in the sense that they have visible impact on the state of affairs and which are, in the broad sense of the term, observable; and things which exist in people's heads, have no direct visible impact on the state of affairs and are non-observable. This basic distinction has been explicitly recognized for quite some time now, especially by American sociologists and anthropologists who distinguish in their analyses between actions ("social structure") and the ideational system usually called culture (Kroeber and Parsons 1958; Kay 1965; Goodenough 1961, 1964, 1970; Geertz 1966; Keesing 1971, 1975).

It should be understood that what we have said so far is not intended as an essential argument for this dualism (the past and present state of the discussion in philosophy and social sciences alike shows that a conclusive argument for or against it cannot be constructed anyway), but as establishing good reasons for taking it as a basic axiomatic assumption. Once taken, the assumption of differentiated existential and epistemological status of the phenomena which form the subject matter of anthropological analysis has important consequences for the questions of what the anthropologist's explanatory models are models of, and what position folk models, which we consider a convenient term for structured sets of ideas about actions, external states of affairs etc. (perhaps another suitable term could be cultural models), have in relation to explanatory models.

As anthropologists we do not simply describe or report whatever we happen to find during our fieldwork: we construct what are often described as explanatory models. In fact, having explanatory models and being able to "experiment" with them (classify them, compare them etc.) is one of anthropology's main claims to scientific status. As a minimal definition, a model is a construct (mental or otherwise) which is built by somebody and "stands for" something else. Consequently, there are two main questions pertaining to any model: the question of "authorship" and the question of reference. That our explanatory models are our own constructs and that they refer to, or stand for, social life (the reader may substitute "social structure", "social system", "culture", or any other general term referring to our subject matter) is clear to us all. However, it is equally generally known that people we are studying are not mindless subjects; in model-building they are able to hold their own with any anthropologist. This raises an important question: are folk models models of social life in the same sense as anthropologists' models, or are they part of that very social life to be represented in the anthropologists' models? And if the latter, how and to what extent do our models refer to "real" social life or to "modelled" social life? It is our contention that folk models have been often treated inconsistently: in some cases as false or imaginary models, which means as models of the same kind as the anthropologist's ones, only worse. The position has been that there is the same reality beyond folk- and anthropologist's models and both are competing for its explanation or representation. In other cases, folk models have been treated as a part of social life, but often confused with reports on activities, thus denying their proper status. In this paper, we will be concerned to show that folk models are a specific part of social life, and therefore an explanandum, for the anthropologists; we will also try to show, however, that they should not be explained by what they purportedly "stand for", but by their relations to other elements of social life. Perhaps the best starting point can be a short revision of the above mentioned inconsistencies in the treatment of folk models.

The Reference of Anthropologist's Models

Misunderstanding of the relationships between both levels of social reality, i.e. the actions people actually perform and the notions they hold, may lead to a serious distortion of our subject matter. LaPiere, in his research into the racial attitudes on the West Coast of the United States points out exactly this danger. He visited, in the company of a young Chinese couple, a number of hotels, motels and restaurants in that zone. Of the total of 251 establishments visited, they were refused service only in one. Sometime later, LaPiere sent to these and some other establishments a questionnaire containing, hidden among others, the question of whether the establishment would receive Chinese as guests. In 226 out of 276 answers this question was answered negatively. LaPiere explains this apparent discrepancy by suggesting that the knowledge invoked for admitting or not admitting the Chinese is different from the knowledge invoked for answering the questionnaire: the former knowledge cannot be substituted by the latter (cf. LaPiere 1934). This does not mean that both facets of knowledge are not related, but if the observer is trying to ascertain racial attitudes, he has to be aware of whether he is getting data on what people say as answers to leading questions or on what they can actually be seen doing. Many explanatory models are based on the assumption that there is no important difference involved: that if statements refer to actions, generally or specifically, they can replace observation. Radcliffe Brown stressed the concern not for particular events but for general events, kinds of events, leading to an account of the form of the structure (Radcliffe Brown 1952: 192). The form of the structure is obviously a model; but a model of what? It is based on data, but even a cursory look at some monographs will show that these data comprise indiscriminately actually observed behaviour, observer's generalizations, informants' recollections of past events, their statements of what should be or usually is the case, etc. The models resulting from these vastly differing data should also be different (cf. Riches 1979); nevertheless, they very rarely are. The model of structure gives us an illusion that all these possible models are coincident, that one kind of data is an adequate substitute for another. Observed events, events reconstructed by the analyst or by the informants and folk models are taken as informing about the same thing. If a difference is made at all, the levels of reality are considered as homologous.

Probably the most illustrative example of this homologous treatment is the work done on segmentary lineage systems. The segmentary lineage structure is always taken, implicitly or explicitly, as referring to or having substance in behavioural reality (e.g. Evans Pritchard 1940; Fortes 1945; Gellner 1969: 62–3; Salzman 1978; Sahlins 1961: 332). Even though many authors stress that the activities on the ground are not always as clearly organized and structured as when they are expressed in the model (e.g. Evans Pritchard 1940: 144), the structure is still presented as expressing or embodying behaviour. According to Bohannan, "a folk system is a systematization of ethnographic facts for purposes of action. It might well have been called an action system . . . " (Bohannan 1957: 5.) In spite of this, Tiv need perpetually to adjust their genealogies to maintain the fit between existing segments and their political relations (cf. Bohannan 1952). The adaptation of genealogies seems to be rather a common feature of segmentary societies: from the way this problem is usually treated, it is not clear whether this is done to enable people to behave more in accordance with norms, to make norms more in accordance with what people actually do, or, which seems most probable, to make several different folk models more consistent with each other. What does seem to be clear, however, is that genealogies and sets of actions can change independently. Consequently, any model expressing one is not a model expressing the other. This is also implied in Keesing's comment that:

> The gulf between the way Kwaio (and I as their ethnographer) conceptualize their system and the way Fortes and Goody conceptualize African systems seems far wider than the gulf between what the Kwaio and Africans do. And if the gulf is generated more by the model than by the facts, we had better look very carefully at the models. (Keesing 1970: 765)

The controversies relating to the segmentary model are sufficiently known for us not to have to go into any more detail here (for more detailed discussion cf. Holy 1979b). Recent discussion has shown that the use of this model was

> ultimately responsible for neglecting important areas of research into both the actual political processes and notions about them, existing in societies which have been classified as having segmentary lineage systems. (Holy 1979b: 19)

This does not mean to imply that behavioural reality is neglected: structural functional studies provide rich and extensive ethnographic data which often also show discrepancies between notions that people hold and actions they perform. The problem lies in the fact that such data are used as incidental descriptions or illustrations, not as problems to be studied. The problem is how is the society structured; and for this specific data are mainly irrelevant. The proponents of the extended-case method based their main criticism of this style of analysis on the fact that the actual cases of interaction encountered in the field have not been used as the very stuff of the analysis, but merely as apt illustrations for the structural schemata devised by the anthropologists (Gluckman 1961; for a review cf. Van Velsen 1967). The extended-case method has concentrated the analysis on concrete cases of interaction, with the assumption that the regularity of social relationships, i.e. structure, should be both elicited from such cases and demonstrated on them (for an excellent illustration cf. Turner 1957). Though it is a considerable methodological improvement, situational analysis nevertheless still tends to consider "data" as one level of existence and the explanatory model as another, without paying sufficient attention to the fact that the data themselves are "existing" in different ways. Actually, to present the above mentioned views as conflating two levels of existence into one might be somewhat misleading. The problem lies more in that the notions, or more specifically norms, are understood as determining actions. This is derived from the Durkheimian dictum about social facts being external to individuals and exerting pressures on them: they have an internal compelling force of their own to summon actions. They are descriptions and prescriptions, with a direct one-to-one relationship to actions (for the elaboration of these points cf. Stuchlik 1977: 11ff.). In practical terms, it means that once it is established, for instance, that a society practices descent group endogamy — on the basis of what the observer has seen and been told about marriage arrangements (what they are, what they should be, etc.), this society is treated as being endogamous in the behavioural sense, i.e. as if everybody married within his descent group. Even if it is known that the marriages of many people are not endogamous, this is treated as an incidental fact explicable on contingent grounds and does not weaken the classification of the society as an endogamous one. The questions posed then are "why is it endogamous?" or "what function does endogamy have in that particular society or in that type of society?" In actual fact, the category of endogamous societies comprises societies in which some people have been observed to marry within their descent group, those in which some members have stated that this is a proper marital arrangement, etc. Such classification lumps them all together into the category in which, presumably, men marry women of their own descent group.

This has to be understood also in the context of the use of classificatory models. They are not constructed to account for what people actually do (though this is believed to be contained in them) but for ordering societies (in Leach's terms "butterfly collecting", cf. Leach 1961: 2) and comparing them, or, more exactly, comparing their models (cf. Barth 1973). This purpose forces some rather doubtful demands:

> Ethnography impels us to state that a society has lineages whereas it may only have certain values for lineages and tendencies to approximate what we conceive to be a lineage organization. . . . The concept is further hardened when this society is compared to other societies that have somewhat different lineage ideologies, but with which they are lumped because of a further reduction of typological criteria and a growing amorphousness of definition. . . . . . . At the very best, the interrelating units in most functional analyses are norms; in comparative analysis, they are models built upon norms. This is an old and familiar problem in anthropology to which we usually doff our hats as we go on doing just this. (Murphy 1971:59–60)

In other words, what we end up with is an explanatory model which has no actual reference: social life which is presumably represented was so generalized and distorted that there is nothing, save possibly a vague and confused concept like "society", to which we could specifically point and say that this is what is represented in the model.

Though the important difference between the notional and interactional levels of phenomena constituting social life is, as we said above, generally recognized, we suggest that often this is merely an empty concession and that in actual analytical and explanatory work both levels are either conflated or considered as identical. In other words, most explanatory models refer to social life as if it were a simple structure composed of data which have, by and large, the same status and could therefore substitute each other. We have tried to argue that this constitutes a serious mistake which ultimately leads to the deformation of the social life that we claim to study.

Anthropologists' Models and Folk Models

A different kind of misunderstanding derives from treating people's notions about their world, about themselves and their environment, as if they were poorer, simpler or false versions of the analyst's explanatory models and not a part of the reality he is supposed to study. Implicitly, members of society are seen as being, by and large, ignorant of the causes and consequences of their activities, as being able to formulate models which are merely justificatory and not explanatory, and moreover contingent and not general enough, while anthropologist's models are, on all these counts, better (for a more detailed discussion cf. Stuchlik 1976b: 1–2). The net result is that people's explanations are either similar to the anthropologist's explanations, but being more naive and less complete, they should be discarded and replaced by anthropologist's models; or they are different, which means untrue, and should be discarded again.

This is explicitly advocated e.g. by Peters in his comment on Bohannan's discussion of the arrangement of facts relating to Tiv law. Bohannan argues against setting them out as an arrangement of the procedural law of Tiv courts because "the error would be that the arrangement is not part of the Tiv way of looking at it and hence would be false" (Bohannan 1957: 279). Peters asks: "Why? The Tiv are not anthropologists. Is the test of an analytical model its consistency with a folk model?" (Peters 1967: 279). The problem is that an analytical model is not supposed to compete with the folk model, but to take it as data. The Tiv way of looking at their law is a part of that reality the anthropologist is studying, and cannot be discarded for the convenience of having a neater analytical model.

This whole approach is based on the misunderstanding of the nature of folk models. It would be absurd to assume that people behave without any regard to their notions about actions, to their knowledge of the social and physical world. An individual cannot base his behaviour on something he does not know, cannot orient his actions toward something he is fully unaware of, nor react to something he does not even know exists. Consequently, the activities which the anthropologists can observe are what they are because of the notions people have about them and because of the reasons and explanations they have for them. Such notions form an indivisible part of the reality we are studying. To define them as false and thus dismiss them from consideration means to deny the reality even of the observable facts themselves. For a social scientist the very notion of a false folk model is a contradiction in terms, because it means legislating on social life and not studying it. If he does this, he is creating something which does not exist independently of him and his enterprise should not be presented as the study of the actors' reality.

Nowhere else is the procedure of dismissing from consideration as misguided or wrong the people's own knowledge of the significant features of reality more apparent than in the studies of phenomena which, according to our knowledge of the world, simply do not exist. Sorcery and witchcraft are typical examples. We, as members of Western society, know for instance that no one can kill anybody by sorcery, or injure somebody by simply emanating some harmful force. Therefore, we approach the study of sorcery with this knowledge and try to explain it in our terms. Hypothetically, the anthropologist can see the sorcerer performing a ritual intended to kill somebody, but he knows that such action cannot bring about the death. He is therefore faced with the contradiction between the reality of the observable action and the "unreality" of its goal or intention. Therefore, he tries to find a cause or purpose for the action that would be equally real as the action itself. In the case of sorcery, the usual solution lies in asserting that what the sorcery really does is to identify and release structural tensions in society and thus to function, in the last instance, as an integrative force. What is often not realized is that by accepting this view we create a new contradiction: we have found a "real" purpose, but we have made the actions, i.e. the ritual, unreal. It was a ritual performed to kill somebody: we have renamed it a ritual performed to release structural tensions. However, this ritual is not that which was observed, it has no existence. (For a more detailed discussion cf. Stuchlik 1977: 7–8).

Gellner has noted that to pretend that Zande belief in witchcraft is as valid as our rejection of it is "a philosophical affectation which cannot be maintained outside the study" (Gellner 1973: 59). This is an unobjectionable view as far as it goes: the only problem is that we are not dealing with the question of whether or not there are witches; but with the question of whether Zande have witches. Since they can point them out, and since we are studying Zande activities which are based on the existence of witchcraft, it would be far more difficult to discard their belief as false. We would then be studying not Zande activities, but, at best, their physical movements to which we would, ourselves, arbitrarily assign some meanings. Serious methodological and explanatory consequences of such a procedure can be shown, for instance, on Marwick's study of Cewa sorcery (Marwick 1965). Marwick dismisses, as false and imaginary, Cewa beliefs: therefore, he refuses to study the relations between the sorcerers and the victims, since there cannot be victims of sorcery. The only empirical phenomena are alleged sorcerers and their accusers, relations between them, protective measures against sorcery and possibly malevolent rites. This, however, makes it impossible for him to explain not only Cewa beliefs (calling them false and ascribing them to Cewa ignorance is not an explanation) but even facts he sets out to explain, since they exist only as social concomitants of Cewa beliefs. By deciding what part of Cewa social life is "real" and therefore a suitable subject of sociological investigation, he is distinguishing between "true" facts, which should be explained and included in the explanatory model, and "false" facts (or pseudofacts) which, since they must not be included in the explanatory model, do not, for the purpose of study and explanation, practically exist. The ultimate consequence is that the resulting explanatory model has very little, if any, reference to anything outside itself; to put it polemically, the researcher is creating his own world for study (cf. Holy 1976b).

A major approach in anthropology which is specifically concerned with folk models and analytical models is Levi-Strauss' structuralism. Structuralism has been discussed in anthropological writing for many years now: consequently, any detailed discussion here would be largely repetitive, quite apart from being also far beyond the scope of this paper. Therefore, we will limit ourselves to a few comments on the problem of the relationship between anthropologist's models, folk models and what Levi-Strauss calls empirical reality; in other words, again the reference of models. This relationship is not easy to discern, since direct statements and implications in the works of Levi-Strauss and some other authors are sometimes confusing and contradictory. At one point, Levi-Strauss asserts that:

> ... one cannot dispense with studying a culture's "home-made" models for two reasons. First, these models might prove to be accurate, or at least to provide some insight into the structure of the phenomena. ... And second, even if the models are biased and erroneous, the very bias and type of error are a part of the facts under study and probably rank among the most significant ones. ... (Levi-Strauss 1963: 282)

Slightly before formulating this, he proposes that:

> when the structure of a certain type of phenomena does not lie at great depth, it is more likely that some kind of model, standing as a screen to hide it, will exist in the collective consciousness. (*Ibid.*: 130)

It is difficult to elicit from these statements exactly what status folk models have. On the one hand, they may be false, being mere screens hiding the real structure or distorting the real functioning of the society. On the other hand, they may be true, i.e. proper structures, or at least give some insight into the structure, thus presumably doing the same job as the anthropologist's models. The only thing which seems to be clear is that models, anthropologists' or folk ones, may be true or false, which means that they refer to some reality ascertainable independently of them. So, how does the fieldworker go about deciding which of the natives' theories is wrong and which is right? Obviously not on the grounds of what people actually do, because this level of facts has somehow become conceptualized out of existence. This is evident in the two strong areas of structuralist research: kinship and myth.

In the *Elementary structures of kinship* (Levi-Strauss 1969), women are exchanged, alliances struck and solidarity maintained regardless of who actually marries whom. More exactly, who actually marries whom is entailed by marriage rules: by virtue of marriage rules (which are natives' models and therefore can be false or just screens) a society is classified as e.g. being one with preferential matrilateral cross cousin marriage. This means that people are assumed to marry their matrilateral cross cousins: if they don't, it does not matter because the real functioning of the society is based on such marriages anyway. The whole post-Homans-Schneider discussion proceeds at the same level. The discontinuities and discrepancies between the structuring activities of the human mind and empirical reality do not matter, because empirical data are, at the most, only an indication of the direction in which we should look for the explanation of the occurrence of the phenomena (whatever this means; cf. Pouwer 1966: 155). When Ackerman analyzed the actual marriages of the Purum, on the basis of which Needham showed how alliances are maintained by prescriptive matrilateral cross cousin marriages, he found that nothing like such alliances can be derived from the actual data; rather, ". . . the distribution of actual alliances is a function of the marginal distribution among the lineages of the total population of marrying acts. . . " (Ackerman 1964: 64). In other words, people have alliances with whomever they actually marry and not with whomever the rules say they should marry. This is so obvious that it is almost trivial, yet it prompted Maybury-Lewis to a rebuke in which he explains that prescriptive marriage rules are about the division of Ego's conceptual universe and not about the numbers of people who actually marry their MBD (Maybury Lewis 1965: 225).

Thus, folk models are accurate or correct if they are homologous with (or embody) structuring principles of the human mind, and false if they do not, it being by and large irrelevant what the folk in question actually do. However, models, folk- or otherwise, are mental constructs: they cannot but be homologous with (or embody) structuring principles of the human mind. In what sense then can they be accurate or inaccurate, false or correct? A possible answer would be that some of them are better at embodying these structuring principles and some worse, but such a judgment is possible only if we have the structure of the human mind already preconstructed and use models not to find structuring principles, but to illustrate them, which is exactly what structuralism does. In a way, we have returned to a mirror replica of Radcliffe Brown's position, as to the actual doings of Tom, Dick and Harry (Radcliffe Brown 1952: 192): they were just illustrations for his structural devices. The only difference is that for Radcliffe Brown it was all "on the ground" while for Levi-Strauss it is all in the mind.

The problem with the structural analysis of myth is slightly different. What is analyzed are not myths as actually told, but myths reconstituted or abstracted by the analyst from different, often diverging and fragmentary, versions told at different times by different people. The analysis of the contents of myth, which is, according to Yalman, so innovatory for structural analysis (Yalman 1967: 72), is the analysis of contents reconstructed by the researcher and which has no existence independent of him.

Since it was constituted for the purpose of the analysis, there is no wonder that it can be so analyzed (cf. Maybury-Lewis 1970: 156; for a detailed analysis of this problem cf. Milton 1977). But possibly this does not really matter, because, as Levi-Strauss points out:

> ... if the final aim of anthropology is to contribute to a better knowledge of objectified thought and its mechanisms, it is in the last resort immaterial whether ... the thought processes of the South American Indians take place through the medium of my thought, or whether mine takes place through the medium of theirs ... (Levi-Strauss 1970: 13)

However, the objectified thought is quite well known beforehand: otherwise the explanatory models would be impossible to construct. Anthropology simply provides illustrations of how all manner and kind of different things in the world are the same. Their differences are just superficial appearances and do not need to be explained.

Thus, in the final analysis, structuralism does not conflate observable and non-observable reality into one level, nor does it misunderstand the position of folk models in social life; it uses a more drastic measure: it dissolves social life. Social life, whatever its forms and processes, is simply the embodiment of objective thought, it being by and large irrelevant who thinks the objective thought. Since we see the aim of anthropology as making a contribution to a better understanding of social life and not to its dissolution, we have to leave the comment at that.

The Process of Social Life

Though most anthropologists would accept without any hesitation that social life is a process, the majority of problems discussed in the preceding sections stem from the fact that such acceptance is only skin-deep. In analysis and explanation it is treated as an entity which has, above all, a definite form. "The account of the form of structure" is what we need, according to Radcliffe Brown (1952: 192), for our science, and the form of the structure is what we usually get. As Barth points out, most explanatory models are merely translations of one form into another form: "there is indeed no science of social life in this procedure" (Barth 1966: 2). Let us therefore start the argument in this section by taking the proposition "social life is a process" not as an empty phrase, but as a serious basic assumption, and considering some implications of it.

In any process, there are three main aspects which can be studied: its setting (surrounding conditions or environment), its evolvement and its results. Before proceeding further, one anticipatory point has to be raised: we are dealing with a social process, i.e. in the last instance a process carried out by concrete people:

> While not made by any single person, society is created and recreated afresh ... by the participants in every social encounter. The production of society is a skilled performance, sustained and "made to happen" by human beings. (Giddens 1976: 15)

Given that people are intentional and creative performers, the setting of the process and its results are more or less the same thing at different time-points.

If there is something that positivistic and interpretative social science have in common, it is their preoccupation with the externality of physical and social phenomena: positivists because they know the phenomena are there and have problems with locating them, and interpretative sociologists because they know the phenomena are not there and have problems with putting them outside human minds. Hence positivists are preoccupied with external causes or functions:

> ... social life should be explained, not by the notions of those who participate in it, but by more profound causes which are unperceived by consciousness ... (Durkheim 1897)

and interpretative sociologists are preoccupied with the learning or internalization of culture. The favourite starting argument for both is that a man is born into a pre-existing world which exists, therefore, independently of him. This is, of course, an unobjectionable statement as far as it goes: however, while the world we were born into existed before our birth and independently of us, the world in which we die is not the same as that into which we were born. It has changed, and we have, on smaller or greater scale, made the change. The change may be all but imperceptible over a short period of time, but it is always present. Our forefathers were born into a world in which lightning was the expression of the gods' anger; we were born into the world in which lightning is a discharge of static electricity. Somewhere along the line the lightning stopped to be the one and started to be the other. How did it come about? If we take the "natural science of society" stand, we may assume a general suprahuman process of change (e.g. evolution) — but then we are not really studying social life. If we take the "internalization of culture" stand, we are stuck. We can only say that while our forefathers internalized one culture, we internalized another culture. (If we take a structuralist stand, then lightning as the gods' weapon and lightning as an electrical discharge are, on some level, transformations of the same thing, so the problem of change does not even arise.)

The essence of the process of social life is that it is continuous. People did not create their society once and for all, for everybody else born afterwards to be born into a predetermined world. By learning the world into which they were born, and by continually thinking and acting in it, people continually create and change it. Even the fixed in social reality, as Moore aptly noted, "really means the continuously renewed" (Moore 1975: 235). If we accept this, we must also accept the logical corollary that it is a reality or world which is known and familiar to those who inhabit it. They might not fully comprehend it, and they definitely do not exercise full control over it, but in the process of creating their social life they make it intelligible, reasonable and accountable. If it were not, it could hardly be their social world: it would be unintelligible to them, capricious and unpredictable, and they would not have the means to pick their way through it.

Thus, in order for the physical and social world to be a proper setting for their social life, it must be known to people: they must share a 'commonsense knowledge' of it (cf. Schutz 1962, 1964, 1966) so that they can orient their activities. It is in this sense that we can say that it has agreed upon or conventional meaning for them. Obviously, the anthropologist does not have to accept such knowledge as "true", but such judgement derives from his own commonsense knowledge of his own world and is completely irrelevant to his task of analyzing and accounting for the social life of the people he studies. He must, however, share their knowledge:

> Such resources (i.e. people's knowledge and theories) as such are not corrigible in the light of the theories of social scientists, but are routinely drawn upon by them in the course of any researches they may prosecute. That is to say, a grasp of the resources used by members of society to generate social interaction is a condition of the social scientist's understanding of their conduct in just the same way as it is for those members themselves. (Giddens 1976: 16)

The Structure of Folk Models

Every member of the society has a number of notions, conceptions, ideas, etc. which are somehow relevant, actually or potentially, to the conduct of his life. Their totality may be referred to as actor's knowledge or stock of knowledge. Since the expressions of this knowledge, i.e. actions, are observable and understandable to others, this entails that his knowledge is to a large extent shared by others. It is intersubjective or public. However, the stock of knowledge, or any part of it, is not made available to other actors or to the observer in an amorphous or non-organized form: it is presented in more or less coherent structures of different generality, which can usefully be called models, i.e. folk models. Moreover, these structures are not set and fixed, but are continually created and recreated on the basis of probably not a very high number of theoretical principles similar to those on which any philosophical or scientific theorising is based (identity, correspondence, analogy, functionality, etc.).

Insofar as these notions are about the physical and social world, and insofar as we are studying this world as the setting for social life, we are not studying it as it "really", i.e. in some suprasocial or suprahuman sense, exists, but as it is present in folk models; as it is perceived, assigned meanings, explicated and made relevant for people who live in it. In this sense, the knowledge, notions or models can be studied in their own right, as the problem of cognition and theorising of the members of the society. Some works in cognitive anthropology and sociology, ethnoscience and ethnomethodology have made significant progress in this direction (e.g. Tyler 1969; Cicourel 1973; Garfinkel 1967a): it would be beyond the scope of this paper to follow these particular approaches. What is of direct interest to us are some formal properties of folk knowledge which make it possible for the anthropologist to apprehend how it is structured and manipulated by the members of society, i.e. how the folk models are constituted.

The first of these properties derives from the trivial fact that knowledge is something people have in their minds and thus appertains to individuals. Since every individual is different, and since his having a different knowledge is an important part of his being unique, in what sense can we speak about social knowledge, or the knowledge of a society? It has often been assumed that the "knowledge of a society" is the sum total of all the knowledge of all members (Popper holds that, though created by individuals, it became a product and has thus an existence independent of them: this is his 'third world', the world of objective knowledge. Cf. Popper 1972: 106ff., and especially 1973: 20ff.) The problem is that I may be e.g. a member of a society with a long and complicated history, known in detail to a few professional historians, but I individually know only a few selected episodes from it. In other words, though there are things which practically every member of the society knows, it does not follow that everybody knows everything.

We could probably speak about the knowledge of the society in the sense of the minimal knowledge shared by all members in order to be able to behave as members, but this conception would be rather useless. It is difficult to imagine a situation in which an individual would behave simply as an undifferentiated member of society, without any further specification. It seems to us that the only useful way to treat the knowledge of a society is simply as the anthropologist's abstraction, more exactly as denoting the boundaries within which specific items of knowledge are unevenly distributed among the people. This permits us to study problems like the social distribution of knowledge itself, i.e. the fact that individuals, according to their social position, have limited or privileged access to knowledge and consequently different models of the world. At the same time, since a position in society has to be sustained by exhibiting the corresponding knowledge, an individual, by claiming or disclaiming specific bits of knowledge can manipulate his social position: to reinforce it or to change it (cf. Holy 1976a). As an example, we can mention Lapps who deny the knowledge of their language in the presence of Norwegians (Eidheim 1969: 49ff.).

Uneven distribution of knowledge within the society permits us to postulate and distinguish a variety of folk models which accounts for the differential participation of people in social life. Duran has shown the usefulness of such an approach in her comparison of agrarian reform in Chile and Spain. She analyzes the knowledge and intentions of members of governmental agencies, pertaining to the sphere of "administrative reality", and the knowledge of members of agricultural co-operatives, pertaining to the sphere of "local reality", and shows how in both spheres the actions are planned differently: however, it is only in the mutual relations of both spheres that the agrarian reform evolves. (Duran: 1979).

The second important property of folk knowledge is more difficult to define: basically it is the capacity of items of knowledge to be differently combined into structured models. Without claiming anything more than strictly metaphorical status for this, we can imagine knowledge, or a stock of knowledge, as a vast number of bits of information, each of them having, rather like molecules of chemical elements, several or many "valencies", i.e. possibilities of being combined with others into "knowledge in use". Thus the structure of models people construct will depend on ways of combining elements of knowledge so as to represent the things referred to in the model in the best, or most relevant manner.

Presumably, there are many possibilities of kinds of combination, and therefore types of models. The following propositions are not meant to exhaust the list, but merely to indicate the nature of possible combinations.

Though all folk models are, in the last instance, relevant to behaviour, there is a basic difference between models which are directly built to guide behaviour and those which influence it indirectly, as a consequence of being held. This difference parallels to a certain extent the distinction Ryle makes between "knowledge that" and "knowledge how" (Ryle 1949) and has been analytically employed by various anthropologists. Geertz talks about cultural patterns as 'models of' and 'models for' (Geertz 1966: 7). Keesing separates culturally postulated things and relationships from the normative rules (Keesing 1979: 126). Stuchlik distinguishes between formal structure as corresponding to actors' descriptive knowledge, and social organization as corresponding to knowledge employed in concrete social encounters (Stuchlik 1976a). Similarly, Schneider makes a distinction between "a body of definitions, premises, statements, postulates, presumptions, propositions and perceptions about the nature of the universe and man's space in it" which he calls culture and "the more or less complete, detailed and specific instructions for how the culturally significant parts of the act are to be performed, as well as the contexts in which they are proper" which he calls norms (Schneider 1976: 200, 203).

Probably the most explicitly formulated is Caws' distinction between representational and operational models, where the representational model corresponds to the way the individual things things are, and the operational model to the way he practically responds or acts (Caws 1974: 3). There are, however, some problems with Caws' treatment of these models. Some of them are mentioned in detail by Jenkins in his article later in this volume; others are related to the specificity of operational models, in the sense that, as defined by Caws', operational models would simply be "blueprints for action". Moreover, there is some confusion about the relationship between the operational model and action. At one point he talks about the lines of causal determination which go from the model to the behaviour (Caws 1974: 4), while shortly afterwards he says that the mind consciously or unconsciously computes and decides the action in terms of the model. To say that the model causally determines the action is very different from saying that the mind computes and decides in terms of the model. In the first place, the deterministic notion would permit us to replace observed events in our explanations simply by operational models; in the second place, to see operational models as constructs in terms of which the individual decides on actions makes them considerably less situation-specific.

The difference between representational and operational models can be conceived of more usefully in a somewhat changed sense. People do not conceive of their society as being in constant flux, change and movement, they see it as a more or less lasting structure, a more or less lasting distribution of people, tasks, resources, rights and duties, etc., which are ordered according to cultural ties like kinship or class, to space, and other factors. This ordered arrangement, or any part thereof, may be called a representational model. However, this arrangement is general and does not limit or instruct any particular social encounter. For this an operational model is needed. This model permits an instantaneous or short-term rearrangement, or specific choice, from among the elements constituting the order.

Another possibility how folk models can be structured derives from their more or less direct relation with specific social encounters. Folk models can be arranged on a scale according to their specificity or generality. Members of the society may have a model related to a specific type of interactional situation, or to a specific class of phenomena, or one related to a broad range of situations or classes of phenomena. This is a completely different dimension from the above mentioned distinction between operational and representational models. It is this dimension which has usually been employed in the arguments about social change (cf. Leach 1954; Holy 1979a).

Still another dimension along which folk models can be structured is the descriptive or prescriptive nature of their contents. This overlaps to some extent the division into representational and operational models, but is not identical. Most representational models will be largely descriptive, but they may contain prescriptive notions as well. And an operational model may be composed of descriptive notions and still have a direct bearing on behaviour; conversely, there might exist prescriptive notions which are not expressed in behaviour. The Lapps state that a woman after marriage should join her husband's band, but the analysis of actual postmarital residence shows that this happens in only half of the cases, while equally often man joins his wife's band (Pehrson 1964: 292). Moreover, the operational model may simply indicate how to do things and not necessarily whether to do them. In general terms, any notion specifying or directly implying that something should be done is

a prescriptive notion, and any notion specifying or directly implying that such and such is the case is a descriptive notion (even if it
describes a potentiality or a stipulation, it does not prescribe it).
Since prescriptions can be called, in the broadest sense, norms, we
could also say that this way of structuring models matches the
distinction between notions that are norms and notions that are not.

There is still another important category of notions to be mentioned: that of ideal states of affairs, values, etc. These can be
called "ought" models. There is, of course, an "ought" element in
almost every norm, in the sense that for every action there is a right
and a wrong way, an adequate and an inadequate way, etc. of performing it. However, strictly speaking, this relates to the socially
recognized efficiency or inefficiency of the action itself. What we
have in mind here is something different: a distinction between
good and bad which refers not to the action itself but to its intention or goal. To give a primitive example, there is a right and a wrong
way of robbing a bank, but robbing a bank as such is bad: ideally,
one ought not to steal and an ideal society is that in which there is
no stealing. Nobody expects that such a society will exist and nobody orients his activities toward such a society, but the ideal gives
a reference point against which our prescriptive notions may be
measured and found more or less wanting. Notions of values, ideals,
etc. can be seen as general notional reference points for both prescriptions and activities.

There are necessarily many other ways in which individual notions
can be combined and folk models perceived and structured. We have
mentioned those which appear to us to be the most important for
the process of social life as carried out by the members of a society.
A partly overlapping division has been suggested by Ward: models
of the past and present (immediate models), models of what the
world will or should be, models for processes involved in attaining
the embodiment of the second, and ideological models or notions
of the ideal order of things (Ward 1965: 135).

The important thing is that when we speak about the physical
and social world as the setting or surrounding conditions for the
process of social life, we do not define as our problem or subject
matter the relationship between folk models of the world and the
world as it somehow really exists independently of them. Since
we are interested in social life, and since this is carried out by people
in the world as they know it, we consider the question of how it
exists apart from them as irrelevant, or, more exactly, as beyond the
proper field of study of the social sciences, and moreover as imped-
ing our understanding of social life and not furthering it.

Inference of Folk Models

Folk models presented in anthropological works are, of course, authored by the anthropologists: on what grounds can we claim that they are replicas of that which is in people's minds? There are two kinds of data from which the anthropologist derives his conclusions: verbal statements, and observed instances of interactions. (Actually, since observed behaviour may be a speech act, and even if it is not, is often accompanied by statements, the distinction should be between strictly informative statements, or statements of knowledge, and observed instances of behaviour, but we retain the traditional distinction between things we are told and things we observe, since it is simple and does not affect the argument.)

A representational model or descriptive model, since it instructs behaviour only in an indirect way, cannot be learned by observation: it is accessible to the observer only through statements of the members of society, even if it is a very specific and limited model. An example mentioned by Hanson from his study of the Polynesian island of Rapa illustrates this point well. He found that most Rapans do not want more than two or three children, and to limit the size of their families they practice a rhythm method of birth control by abstaining from intercourse for three or four days immediately following menstruation. This practice is derived from their notion of the anatomy and physiology of conception, which Hanson describes in detail (Hanson 1975: 53). Even if he did not specifically mention that his knowledge of their anatomical and physiological notions was obtained through their statements (*Ibid.*: 54), it would be perfectly obvious that no account of observation of their sexual behaviour could have brought this type of information.

Verbal statements are often assumed to be non-problematic: they are seen simply as expressions of notions, or descriptions of models. This is, however, a rather simplistic idea: there are three main problems related to verbal statements as data about folk models. In the first place, a model, especially a more general representational model, will not be expressed in its entirety. People formulate partial statements, situationally relevant statements or direct answers to the researcher's questions. There may be parts of models which can be verbally described only with great difficulty; also, different informants may refer to different parts of the same model.

In the second place, making a statement, even a descriptive one, is in itself a special kind of activity. This holds true irrespective of whether the statements are spontaneous conversational utterances or answers to questions. Unless they are professional theoreticians, people do not go around declaring their knowledge of everyday life: they declare it as a part of their everyday purposive behaviour. Every utterance, every paralinguistic expression, is part of some specific situation, is influenced by the speaker's definition of the situation and represents a part of his participation in it.

In the third place, and related to both preceding points, there is the fact that the verbal statements of the people are highly indexical. The meaning of what is actually said depends on a far broader background knowledge which remains unstated but is shared by other members, and on the "logic in use" which people also share but are often unable specifically to formulate (Kaplan 1964: 8). Typically, the statement that somebody makes may be presented by him as generally true and valid, while it is actually so only under specific conditions and circumstances which are assumed by the actors but not made explicit. His statement, though indexical, is made within a broad framework of background expectations and thus properly understood; because these expectations are taken for granted by the actors, they are not specifically stated. The actor

> is responsive to this background, while at the same time he is at loss to tell us specifically of what the expectancies consist. When we ask him about them, he has little or nothing to say. (Garfinkel 1976b: 36-7; for a further discussion of the problem of indexicality of informants' statements cf. Riches 1977)

Thus, in any given research encounter, be it observation of an event or conversation with an informant, the anthropologist is getting statements which are partial expressions of knowledge, situation-specific, and indexical. His task is to replicate, by combining this information, as precisely as possible the missing parts, the general, nonsituational and taken for granted parts of the models which people construct to make sense of their world and their actions in it. Strictly speaking, it will always be a model of a model, since it can never be " a model in use" but a model as stated by the anthropologist. However, he can put it to the test in a similar way as he can his knowledge of rules, i.e. by formulating statements which would be considered acceptable by the actors.

Operational models, far more closely related to observable events, are obviously also available through statements, insofar as people make references to pragmatic rules which guide their behaviour, and insofar as they make explicit their different goals and strategies for attaining them. However, unlike for representational models, statements are not the only manifestations of operational models. Since actions are rule governed, insofar as it makes sense to say that they can be performed rightly or wrongly (Winch 1958: 64), they are also manifestations or embodiments of rules. The actors may often be unable or uninterested in stating them (cf. Keesing 1971: 125); therefore, it is the anthropologist's task to infer from the observed action (and all the accompanying statements) the rule or rules invoked in acting. This is nicely illustrated by the analyses of folk classification in cognitive anthropology; their object is:

> not only to predict which objects will be referred to by which terms but also to predict what criteria the native speaker will employ in determining the appropriate term in use. (Wallace 1965: 231)

However, this raises an important question of correspondence: how can the observer be sure that he inferred the rules which were, in fact, invoked? The answer lies in Ryle's theory of mind: most mental activities are publicly available since they are overt intelligent and intelligible performances (Ryle 1949). Understanding another culture means sharing the mental activities of its members and that basically means being able to duplicate their overt intelligent performances.

> Understanding is part of knowing how. The knowledge that is required for understanding intelligent performances of a specific kind is some degree of competence in performances of that kind. (*Ibid.:* 54)

As Hanson points out, we operate with such a concept of understanding all the time. If we want to know whether a student understands a theory, we are not interested in whether he went through the same reasoning processes and experience as its proposer, but whether he is able to operate with it, to perform the tasks the theory is supposed to perform (Hanson 1975: 62).

In other words, there is the test by praxis. If, by using the rules he inferred, the anthropologist is able to duplicate actors' performances and make them intelligible, he knows he has inferred the "right" rules or at least the rules which can withstand the test of

> our ability to use the body of custom or system of thought under study. It is to know the correct moves, to know what natives would accept as appropriate responses to particular circumstances. (Hanson 1975: 65)

A possible objection to this is that there may be different sets of rules leading to the same behaviour. For instance, Leach (1958) and Lounsbury (1965) formulated differing rules for Trobriand kinship terminology, and Burling (1965) proposed two sets of rules for generating Burmese kinship terminology. In what sense, however, is one of them "wrong"? Some anthropologists argue that different individuals operate according to different rules, and that rules which are psychologically valid for some are not valid for others (Wallace 1962, 1970: 29–36; Goodenough 1971: 15; Sanday 1968: 522). If the people themselves can invoke different rules and still present an intelligent performance, then in trying to find out the only "correct" rule we may be trying to find something which does not, in any sense, exist.

This point can be illustrated on the criticism Harris makes of what he calls idealist models of social life, in an article with a self-explanatory title: *Why a perfect knowledge of all the rules one must know to act like a native cannot lead to the knowledge of how natives act* (Harris 1974). His position is that since emic rules (i.e. rules people have) are open by their nature, for any rule there is a rule for breaking it, a rule for the rule of breaking it etc., which leads to infinite regress. Therefore, emic rules, though they sometimes might accidentally lead to predictions, must be disregarded and replaced by etic rules, i.e. rules formulated by the anthropologist which are based on a real structuring of events and lead to predictions. Quite apart from the fact that etic rules can hardly be anything more than emic rules of a tribe called anthropologists (cf. Stuchlik 1976b: 11), what Harris is seeking is a one-to-one, strictly deterministic rule of action, or, to put it in other words, a system of rules which would be logically conclusive. Now, we agree with Harris that what he calls emic rules are open-ended, or that practical reasoning is logically inconclusive. However, we take this to be not their defficiency, but an indication of the nature of the reality they embody: it is open and logically inconclusive as well. The infinite regress Harris mentions never occurs because of what could be called the "beyond reasonable doubt" clause: the sequence for breaking the rule for breaking the rule etc. stops at a certain point not because of the logical property of rules, but because by common consent it would be considered unreasonable to continue. There is no logically conclusive procedure for a jury beyond reasonable doubt: and no account of etic studies can find it. The absolute in predictability in social life is simply not the same as in the natural sciences: if the anthropologist can predict with the same degree of efficiency as can adequately informed members of the society, then he has elicited the correct rules, i.e. the rules with which people operate.

Anything above that means that he is trying to read into social life a kind of determinism which simply is not there.

Folk Models and Actions

In general terms, social science legitimately studies the world as it has meaning for the members of the society, i.e. as it exists as the setting for social life. Since this meaning is continuously assigned to the world by the members themselves, and expressed in their folk models, it follows that our interest is in the world as represented in folk models and not as it might exist independently of its inhabitants. Social life in the narrow sense of the word is a continuous flow of activities performed by the members of society, to attain projected or envisaged future states of affairs, i.e. goals. Therefore, it can be said that social life is a process carried out by people in their world, which is destined continually to create and recreate that very world. This makes for a rather complex relationship between the two above mentioned levels of reality, the notions, knowledge or models which, in a sense, constitute the world, and the level of actions which are continuously reconstituting the world.

The distinction between these levels, as we indicated before, is nothing new in anthropology: however, their relationship has been mostly treated as unproblematic. Either the models have been seen as pertaining, somehow, to the society as an entity and determining an individual's actions, or the models have been seen as a naive or false representation of the world, and the activities as determined by some general structuring principles vested in the nature of the universe, nature of the human mind, evolution, etc. Whether the basic assumptions are materialistic or idealistic, man is reduced by them to an agent of external forces, unknown to him and causing his actions, and consequently his whole social life, without his active, willing and conscious participation in the process.

We propose that the social sciences should be based on the concept of man as an autonomous, intentional and skilled agent. This means, among other things, that the relationship between notions and actions, instead of being reduced or treated as non-problematic, should become the main subject of our analysis. In other words, the very manner of the emergence of social life and constitution of the world as its setting should be treated as problematic and therefore the focus of research (cf. Walsh 1972: 20; also Filmer *et al.* 1972, for a fuller discussion of this problem).

In an excellent analysis of the relationship between kinship based norms of land tenure and actual practices on Choiseul Island,

Scheffler asserts that norms as such have no meaning unless they enter into transactions between individuals and groups (Scheffler 1965: 294). This is supported by statements of his informants to the effect that "our customs are not firm. We look only for that which will help us to live well, and the rest is just talk" (*Ibid.* 110). This indicates a point often overlooked in anthropological explanations: people perform activities to attain something, a goal of their interest. It is, therefore, from the viewpoint of this goal that we must analyze the process of social life (for a more detailed argument of this point cf. Stuchlik 1977). Though folk models do not "do" anything by themselves, and though activities are rule governed (i.e. derived from models) but not determined by them, it is only by relating the two in a single analytical framework that the study of social life can proceed.

The relationship between the two levels of reality can best be called a dialectical one (cf. Keesing 1971: 126). This concept, in the first place, denies a unilineal determination or causation and necessary unilineal sequence in time. In the second place, it asserts a mutual dependence on meaning, and a mutual possibility of manipulation in concrete encounters; it postulates changes on one level by presenting "antithesis" on the other, and it indicates that the relationship may be indeterminately sequential in time (feedback effect) in the sense that past and present knowledge may shape present and future actions, present actions may lead to future knowledge, past actions may be reinterpreted by present knowledge etc.

Keesing applies something like this in his analysis of a brideprice contribution among the Kwaio on Malaita (Keesing 1967). The size of contribution is ideally ruled by the kinship distance between the contributor and the groom. Thus, in any particular event of marriage, the meaning of a kinship relation consists in the size of contribution, and the payment of it gives meaning to the kinship relation. However, the size of the contribution is not determined by it, since it can be manipulated: any kinsman can abstain from paying, pay less, or more than ruled, thus presenting an antithesis of the norm, or, more simply, a violation of the norm. There are reasons for this: by abstaining or paying less, a kinsman may express his disapproval of the bride, or sanction the groom for not having fulfilled kinship duties in the past; or, referring to the future, he may want to continue an existing quarrel or assert a greater social distance. By paying more, a kinsman may want to create a stronger obligation for the groom in the future. Whatever the contribution, if it follows the norm, it is reaffirming and recreating the world as it is, while if it violates the norm it changes the world, in the sense that the resulting more restricted or broadened relations will form from now on, till changed, a part of the known and accepted reality.

In a sense, the emergence of a new reality is nowhere as apparent as in a situation perfectly known to all anthropologists: during the beginning stages of his fieldwork, when he is being accepted and defined by the members of the group he is studying. Since both the anthropologist and the people he studies live, at least during the early stages of fieldwork, in different worlds, there is no mutuality of meaning between their actions and their norms, they do not know each other's models. Gradually, by interacting in more obvious encounters, they try to find out as much about how they see the world as possible in order to be able meaningfully to interact (cf. Stuchlik 1976a: 216). If properly taken advantage of, the initial part of the fieldwork can be thus of considerable importance.

Basically, the analysis of social life should consist in studying specific social encounters from the viewpoint of how they are constituted, i.e. what concrete actions they comprise, and why they are so constituted, i.e. on the basis of what publicly available knowledge the decisions are made. Strictly speaking, there is a particular appropriate model for every concrete encounter; however, it is the result of the manipulation of known elements of knowledge. The encounter may be new, in the sense that it was never before realized, but it is composed of known elements and is intelligible to people insofar as the blueprint for it was constituted on intelligible grounds.

This does not mean that the researcher's work consists simply in reporting what people do and what reasons they specifically give for it. As we have argued, both actions and reasons for them are situationally bound, indexical and fragmentary. The anthropologist's explanation is constructed so as to be systematic and nonindexical. People manipulate knowledge with differing degrees of awareness, of functionality (instruction, legitimization, justification, training etc.), often without being able to express the difference directly. The important thing for the anthropologist's explanation is not that it must resemble the folk model or be a duplication of it, but that it must not include any elements not included in fold model and therefore not involved in the shaping of the encounter.

Finally, instead of a conclusion, we would like to make a few comments on a spectre which has haunted the edifice of anthropology for a considerable time now, namely cultural relativism. As happens with all spectres, we have been unable to obtain its exact description since it appears to different people in different shapes; therefore, we have to go by logical consideration.

Obviously, it is something unspeakably bad to be a cultural relativist. However, what constitutes one as such? Not the belief that cultures are different, because we all know that. Not the belief that what is good in one society is bad in some other society, because again, we all know that such is actually the case. We also know that what is rational to us may be irrational to " them" and vice versa. What is usually considered as the basic cultural relativist proposition is that culture has to be understood in its own terms. We are puzzled, because this seems, on the face of it, to be a truism: in what other terms could it possibly be understood? It is also said that understanding a culture in its own terms makes impossible comparative studies: this seems to us a false claim. Whatever one society considers proper in the way of arranging postmarital residence can be compared with whatever another society considers as such, while both ways may be completely different. What one society sees as the right way of solving disputes can be compared with what another society sees as the right way of solving disputes. The fact that the anthropologist constitutes what people are doing and why they are doing it on the basis of their knowledge does not make the comparison impossible.

Obviously, the problem lies not in comparing as such, but in the "why"? of comparative studies. When comparing, anthropologists are trying to do one of two possible operations: either to translate something unknown and puzzling into something known and familiar by pointing out that it is " the same" as some other known and familiar thing, or to reduce two apparently different things to a level on which they are identical. The objective is, in both cases, to show the essential identity of phenomena and events, i.e. of forms. It is assumed that if forms are essentially identical, the processes which generated them must be essentially identical as well and may, therefore, be compared as to their effectiveness. What we are proposing is that the forms should be compared not as to their essential identity but as to the reasons for their difference. What should be compared, then, is the "logic in use" or "situational logic" of those who generate social forms.

The only possible candidate against cultural relativism would be cultural absolutism. This would seem to mean a view that the same actions and institutions (the "sameness" being identified regardless of the people who perform the actions and created the institutions) necessarily have the same causes and the same explanations; that there is only one rational procedure for any given encounter;

that the mother's brother's son in one society is the same as the mother's brother's son in another, regardless of what the society says about it; that Culture has its objective laws in the same sense as Nature has them and that it is our task to find them. In the last instance, it seems to lead necessarily to the view that some cultures, which are nearer to the law of the Culture, are better cultures and some models, being constructed by processes nearer to objective Rationality, are better models. It usually has the corollary that our models are better than "theirs". This might be so. We not only do not know, we also declare a complete lack of interest in such problems. In our view, the study of such problems does not belong to the field of anthropology, since it denies the basic characteristic of our subject matter, i.e. its being social reality (in the sense of being continually created by the people). This probably makes us cultural relativists. Since we conceive of anthropology as being necessarily anthropomorphic, it also has to be relativistic, at least in this sense.

References

Ackerman, C. (1964). Structure and statistics: the Purum case. *American Anthropologist* **66**: 53-65.

Anscombe, G. E. M. (1957). *Intention.* Oxford: Blackwell.

Barth, F. (1966). *Models of Social Organization.* Royal Anthropological Institute Occasional Paper No. 23.

Barth, F. (1973). Descent and marriage reconsidered. In *The Character of Kinship*, (J. Goody, ed.) pp. 3-19. London: Cambridge.

Bohannan, L. (1952). A genealogical charter. *Africa* **22**: 301-15.

Bohannan, P. (1957). *Judgement and Justice among the Tiv.* London: Oxford University Press for International African Institute.

Burling, R. (1965). Cognition and componential analysis: God's truth or hocus-pocus? *American Anthropologist* **66**: 20-28.

Caws, P. (1974). Operational, representational and explanatory models. *American Anthropologist* **76**: 1-10.

Cicourel, A. V. (1973). *Cognitive Sociology.* Penguin Books.

Duran, T. (1979). *Comparative Study of Two Agrarian Co-operatives in Chile and Spain.* Unpublished PhD Thesis. Queen's University of Belfast.

Durkheim, E. (1897). Review of A. Labiola: Essais sur la conception materialiste de l'histoire. *Revue Philosophique* 1897, Dec.

Durkheim, E. (1964). *The Rules of Sociological Method.* 8th edn. Translated by S. A. Solovay and J. H. Mueller, (G. E. G. Catlin, ed). London: Collier-Macmillan, Ltd.

Eidheim, H. (1969). When ethnic identity is a social stigma. In *Ethnic Groups and Boundaries*, (F. Barth, ed.) pp. 39-57. London: Allen and Unwin.

Epstein, A. L. (ed.) (1967). *The Craft of Social Anthropology.* London:

Tavistock Publications.

Evans-Pritchard, E. E. (1940). *The Nuer*. Oxford: Clarendon Press.

Filmer, P., Phillipson, M., Silverman, D., Walsh, D. (1972). *New Directions in Sociological Theory*. London: Collier-Macmillan.

Fortes, M. (1945). *The Dynamics of Clanship among the Tallensi*. London: Oxford University Press.

Garfinkel, H. (1967a). *Studies in Ethnomethodology*. Englewood Cliffs, N. J.: Prentice-Hall.

Garfinkel, H. (1967b). The origin of the term 'Ethnomethodology'. In *Ethnomethodology*, (R. Turner, ed.). Penguin Books 1974.

Geertz, C. (1966). Religion as a cultural system. In *Anthropological Approaches to the Study of Religion*, (M. Banton, ed.). ASA Monographs 3, pp. 1-46. London: Tavistock Publications.

Geertz, C. (1975). *The Interpretation of Cultures*. London: Hutchinson.

Gellner, E. (1969). *Saints of the Atlas*. London: Weidenfeld and Nicholson.

Gellner, E. (1973). *Cause and Meaning in Social Sciences*. London: Routledge and Kegan Paul.

Giddens, A. (1976). *New Rules of Sociological Method*. London: Hutchinson.

Gluckman, M. (1961). Ethnographic data in British social anthropology. *Sociological Review* 9: 5-17.

Goodenough, W. H. (1961). Comments on cultural evolution. *Daedalus* **90**: 521-28.

Goodenough, W. H. (1964). Introduction to W. H. Goodenough (ed.), *Explanations in Cultural Anthropology: Essays in Honour of George Peter Murdock*. New York: McGraw-Hill.

Goodenough, W. H. (1970). *Description and Comparison in Cultural Anthropology*. Chicago: Aldine Publishers.

Goodenough, W. H. (1971). *Culture, Language and Society*. McCaleb Module in Anthropology: Addison-Wesley Publishing Co.

Gorman, R. A. (1977). *The Dual Vision: Alfred Schutz and the Myth of Phenomenological Social Science*. London: Routledge and Kegan Paul.

Hanson, F. A. (1975). *Meaning in Culture*. London: Routledge and Kegan Paul.

Harris, M. (1974). Why a perfect knowledge of all the rules one must know to act like a native cannot lead to the knowledge of how natives act. *Journal of Anthropological Research* **30**: 242-251.

Holy, L. (1976a). Knowledge and behaviour. In *Knowledge and Behaviour*, (L. Holy, ed.). The Queen's University Papers in Social Anthropology 1, pp. 27-45. Belfast: Queen's University.

Holy, L. (1976b). Sorcery and social tensions: the Cewa case. In *Knowledge and Behaviour*, (L. Holy, ed.). The Queen's University Papers in Social Anthropology 1, pp. 47-64. Belfast: Queen's University.

Holy, L. (1979a). Changing norms of inheritance among the Toka of Zambia. In *The Conceptualization and Explanation of Processes of Social Change*. (D. Riches, ed.). Queen's University Papers in Social Anthropology 3, pp. 83-105. Belfast: Queen's University.

Holy, L. (1979b). Segmentary lineage structure and its existential status. In *Segmentary Lineage Systems Reconsidered*, (L. Holy, ed.). Queen's

University Papers in Social Anthropology 4, pp. 1-22. Belfast: Queen's University.

Kaplan, A. (1964). *The Conduct of Enquiry.* San Francisco: Chandler.

Kay, P. (1965). Ethnography and the theory of culture. *Bucknell Review* **19**: 106-13.

Keesing, R. M. (1967). Statistical models and decision models of social structure: a Kwaio case. *Ethnology* **6**: 1-16.

Keesing, R. M. (1970). Shrines, ancestors and cognatic descent: the Kwaio and Tallensi. *American Anthropologist* **71**: 755-75.

Keesing, R. M. (1971). Descent, residence and cultural codes. In *Anthropology in Oceania: Essays Presented to Ian Hogbin,* (L.R. Hiatt and C. Jayawardena, eds.) pp. 121-38. Sydney: Angus and Robertson.

Keesing, R. M. (1975). *Kin Groups and Social Structure.* New York: Holt, Rinehart and Winston.

Kroeber, A. L. and Parsons, T. (1958). The concepts of culture and of social system. *American Sociological Review* **23**: 582-83.

LaPiere, R. (1934). Attitudes vs. actions. *Social Forces* **13**: 230-37.

Leach, E. R. (1954). *Political Systems of Highland Burma.* London: Bell.

Leach, E. R. (1958). Concerning Trobriand clans and the kinship category tabu. In *The Developmental Cycle in Domestic Groups,* (J. Goody, ed.). Cambridge Papers in Social Anthropology 1, pp. 120-45. Cambridge: Cambridge University Press.

Leach, E. R. (1961). *Rethinking Anthropology.* London School of Economics. Monographs on Social Anthropology No. 22. London: The Athlone Press.

Levi-Strauss, C. (1960). On manipulated sociological models. *Bijdragen tot de Taal-, Land- en Volkenkunde* **112**: 45-54.

Levi-Strauss, C. (1963). *Structural Anthropology.* New York – London: Basic Books.

Levi-Strauss, C. (1969). *The Elementary Structures of Kinship.* Boston: Beacon Press.

Levi-Strauss, C. (1970). *The Raw and the Cooked: Introduction to Science of Mythology 1.* London: Jonathan Cape.

Lounsbury, F. (1965). Another view of the Trobriand kinship categories. In *Formal Semantic Analysis,* (E. A. Hammel, ed.). *American Anthropologist* **67**,(5, pt.2).

Marwick, M. G. (1965). *Sorcery in its Social Setting: A Study of the Northern Rhodesian Cewa.* Manchester University Press.

Maybury-Lewis, D. (1965). Prescriptive marriage systems. *Southwestern Journal of Anthropology* **21**: 207-230.

Maybury-Lewis, D. (1970). Science or bricolage? In *Claude Levi-Strauss: The Anthropologist as Hero,* (E. N. Hayes and T. Hayes, eds.) pp. 150-163. Cambridge, Mass.: The M. I. T. Press.

Milton, K. (1977). The myth of King Dutthagamani and its social significance. In *Goals and Behaviour,* (M. Stuchlik, ed.). Queen's University Papers in Social Anthropology 2, pp. 119-130. Belfast: Queen's University.

Moore, S. F. (1975). Epilogue: uncertainties in situations. Indeterminacy in culture. In *Symbol and Politics in Communal Ideology,* (S. F. Moore and B. G. Myerhoff, eds.). Ithaca: Cornell University Press.

Murphy, R. F. (1971). *The Dialectics of Social Life.* London: George Allen and Unwin.;

Pehrson, R. (1964). Bilateral kin groupings. In *Kinship,* (J. Goody, ed.) pp. 290-5. Penguin Modern Sociology Readings.

Peters, E. (1967). Some structural aspects of the feud among the camel-herding Bedouins of Cyrenaica. *Africa* **37**: 261-82.

Popper, K. (1972). *Objective Knowledge.* Oxford: Clarendon Press.

Popper, K. (1973). Indeterminism is not enough. *Encounter* **40**: 10-26.

Pouwer, J. (1966). Referential and inferential reality: a rejoinder. *Bijdragen tot de Taal-, Land- en Volkenkunde* **122**.

Radcliffe-Brown, A. R. (1952). *Structure and Function in Primitive Society.* New York: The Free Press.

Riches, D. (1977). Discerning the goal: some methodological problems exemplified in analyses of hunter-gatherer aggregation and migration. In *Goals and Behaviour,* (M. Stuchlik, ed.). Queen's University Papers in Social Anthropology 2, pp. 131-52. Belfast: Quuen's University.

Riches, D. (1979). On the presentation of the Tiv segmentary lineage system, or, speculations on Tiv social organization. In *Segmentary Lineage Systems Reconsidered,* (L. Holy, ed.). Queen's University Papers in Social Anthropology 4, pp. 69-90. Belfast: Queen's University.

Ryle, G. (1949). *The Concept of Mind.* London: Hutchinson.

Sahlins, M. (1961). The segmentary lineage: an organization of predatory expansion. *American Anthropologist* **63**: 322-45.

Salzman, P. C. (1978). Does complementary opposition exist? *American Anthropologist* **80**: 53-70.

Sanday, R. R. (1968). The 'psychological reality' of American-English kinship terms: an information-processing approach. *American Anthropologist* **70**: 508-23.

Scheffler, H. W. (1965). *Choiseul Island Social Structure.* Berkeley: University of California Press.

Schneider, D. M. (1976). Notes toward a theory of culture. In *Meaning in Anthropology,* (K.H. Basso and H. A. Selby, eds) pp. 197-220. Albuquerque: University of New Mexico Press.

Schutz, A. (1962). *Collected Papers I: The Problem of Social Reality.* The Hague: Nijhoff.

Schutz, A. (1964). *Collected Papers II: Studies in Social Theory.* The Hague: Nijhoff.

Schutz, A. (1966). *Collected Papers III: Studies in Phenomenological Philosophy.* The Hague: Nijhoff.

Stuchlik, M. (1976a). *Life on a Half Share.* London: C. Hurst.

Stuchlik, M. (1976b). Whose knowledge? In *Knowledge and Behaviour,* (L. Holy, ed.). Queen's University Papers in Social Anthropology 1, pp. 1-26. Belfast: Queen's University.

Stuchlik, M. (1977). Goals and behaviour. In *Goals and Behaviour,* (M. Stuchlik, ed.) Queen's University Papers in Social Anthropology 2, pp. 7-47. Belfast: Queen's University.

Turner, V. W. (1957). *Schism and Continuity in an African Society.* Manchester University Press.

Tyler, A. S. (1969). *Cognitive Anthropology*. New York: Holt, Rinehart and Winston.

VanVelsen, J. (1967). The extended-case method and situational analysis. In *The Craft of Social Anthropology*, (A. L. Epstein, ed.) pp. 129-49. London: Tavistock Publications.

Wallace, A. F. C. (1962). Culture and cognition. *Science* 135: 351-57.

Wallace, A. F. C. (1965). The problem of psychological validity of componential analysis. In *Formal Semantic Analysis*, (E. A. Hammel, ed.). *American Anthropologist* 67 (5, pt.2), 229-48.

Wallace, A. F.C. (1970). *Culture and Personality*. 2nd edn. New York: Random House.

Walsh, D. (1972). Sociology and the social world. In *New Directions in Sociological Theory*, (P. Filmer, M. Philipson, D. Silverman and D. Walsh, eds.) pp. 15-35. London: Collier-Macmillan Publishers.

Ward, B. E. (1965). Varieties of conscious model: the fishermen of South China. In *The Relevance of Models for Social Anthropology*, (M. Banton, ed.). ASA Monographs in Social Anthropology 1, pp. 113-37. London: Tavistock Publications.

Winch, P. (1958). *The Idea of Social Science*. London: Routledge and Kegan Paul.

Yalman, N. (1967). 'The raw: the cooked: nature: culture' – observations on *Le cru et le cuit*. In *The Structural Study of Myth and Totemism*, (E. R. Leach, ed.). ASA Monographs in Social Anthropology 5, pp. 71-89. London: Tavistock Publications.

POLITICAL AND MUSICAL FREEDOM IN THE MUSIC OF SOME BLACK SOUTH AFRICAN CHURCHES

JOHN BLACKING

This paper is concerned with relationships between political aspirations and musical performance. Although no current anthropological model would enable us to link musical performance with politics, unless the music were defined in words as political, analysis of the folk model of the independent black Christian churches in the particular social context of South Africa reveals that such links may not only exist but also be an important factor in motivating human action. Music is non-referential and sensuous, and no claim can be made that it is directly political. But some music can become and be used as a symbol of group identity, regardless of its structure; and the structure of music can be such that the conditions required for its performance generate feelings and relationships between people that enable positive thinking and action in fields that are not musical.

The first section of the paper will explore relationships between the sounds of music and conditions of its performance, and political identity and feeling. If the activities of the churches are to be regarded as politically significant, it must be shown that they extend beyond the boundaries of their own group; and so the second section places them in the context of national politics, as part of the Africanist movement. The third section will demonstrate that in South Africa there is an established tradition of expressing political sentiments in eschatological terms. The fourth and fifth sections will describe the notions and actions of the independent churches relating to worship, and the sixth will argue that musical performance is the most important element of worship and that their worship is the most important part of their lives as "Zionists". The seventh section analyses the structure of the music in relation to church members' notions about it and the purposes and effects of its performance. In the final section, I argue that the way in which the Zionists sing, and much of the music that they sing, expresses opposition to white domination and reinforces the Africanist view of the political future of South Africa. Given the tradition of expressing political views in eschatological terms and a folk model of action which links nonverbal to verbal behaviour, spiritual to material, and "this world" to "the other world", the link between musical performance and political aspirations becomes apparent.

Music and Political Consciousness

Models for music and musical performance present special problems of analysis. First, actors' and analysts' concepts of "music" may differ, so that analyses may have to include what one or the other had hitherto regarded as irrelevant. Second, since much music is nonverbal in conception and in execution, analyses with words and the syntax of speech can distort the unique character of music as a mode of thought and action. Even when societies have special technical terms for music, people frequently resort to metaphor, simile, and visual imagery, to describe patterns of sound.

Whether or not we argue that speech must always be the primary modelling system of thought in patterns of social interaction and in the invention of culture (see Blacking 1977: 13ff.; Blacking: In press), and even if we hold that the possession of speech is the crucial distinction between the human and other species, nonverbal modelling systems may sometimes be as important as speech in influencing a course of social action. This is especially true in a country like South Africa, where for the majority of the population freedom of speech is restricted because of a system of repression imposed by a minority and sanctioned by armed force and the financial and moral support of powerful industrial nations.

In the South African context, performances and gramaphone records of modern African music have helped to establish amongst Blacks a new sense of identity and national consciousness, not only by means of overtly political music such as the Freedom Songs of the 1950s (cf. Rhodes 1962: 17ff.), but also through musical styles that have been developed by or are associated with those who have adopted a modern way of life. Thus in 1959, when I was transcribing Venda music on a farm in Kwa-Zulu, unschooled Zulu peasants responded positively to the sounds of Venda "school" songs even though they had no idea what the words meant, whereas they were not interested in the Venda equivalent of their own traditional music.

The sounds of the music, quite regardless of the words, opened up for them a new world to which they aspired but did not fully belong. It was a modern world with cities, industrial technology and, for some, schooling and Christianity. The dark side of this world was white domination, migrant labour and low wages, the police, the pass laws, the Group Areas Act, and the social consequences of these restrictions on living. In such a context, the sounds of new, distinctively Black South African music, enabled people to recall pleasant experiences of weddings and social events at which music and dance predominated, and to contemplate a national, Black solidarity that cut across the tribal divisions which the Whites sought to impose with their system of apartheid.

In rural Venda, and in the predominantly Venda parts of Soweto, where the data discussed in this paper was collected between 1956 and 1966, the sounds of new music were similarly heard and used. As in other parts of South Africa, attitudes to different repertoires and genres, and distinctions between the repertoires used, were related not so much to tribal affiliations as to membership of the new groups that had grown up, especially in the urban areas (see, for example, Wilson and Mafeje 1963; Kuper 1965). One important set of groups which both shared enjoyment or performance of much of the new music, and with which special genres of music were associated, was the independent church movement. Within this broad category were hundreds of Black churches whose membership ranged from thirty or forty people, who were often related members of extended families, to several hundred, and in some cases several thousand.

I shall argue that the music of the churches which I studied expressed and enhanced a Black collective consciousness that members were not able to express in words. Music loomed large in church members' descriptions of the Christian life, but it has been entirely neglected in the many excellent analyses of other independent churches in Southern Africa (e.g. Mqotsi and Mkele 1946; Sundkler 1961; Daneel 1971; West 1975 and Dubb 1976). Since music is a cultural sub-system which emerges only in musical performance, as distinct from notions that are made available through speech acts in any kind of social interaction, it raises the problem of explaining nonverbal behaviour as intentional social interaction and relating it to notions that are verbalized or carried without being verbalized.

In arguing that music had positive political significance, although no specifically political value was assigned to it, I reach very different conclusions from those of Maurice Bloch in his useful contribution to the anthropology of music, *"Symbols, song, dance and features of articulation: is religion an extreme form of traditional authority?"* (1974). My conclusions differ, not because I disagree with Bloch's general thesis relating to the circumcision ceremonies of the Merina of Madagascar, but because much of his argument cannot be applied to *all* song, as he claims (*op. cit.*: 56-57). He contrasts the propositional force of ordinary language with the illocutionary or performative force of song, and concludes: "In a song, therefore, no argument or reasoning can be communicated, no adaptation to the reality of the situation is possible" (*ibid.*). His generalizations do not apply to all musical systems, especially when the folk model of music and its relationship with other activities is taken into account. Some societies' notions of speech and song, for example, conflict with Bloch's analytical model. That is, he reaches the provocative conclusions that art is "an inferior form of communication" (*op. cit.*:72), and that music in particular is characterized by redundancy (*op. cit.*: 76), by way of an assumption which, though common in the ethnomusicological literature, is by no means true of all societies: namely, the view that song is formalized or impassioned speech, and that it is "nothing but the end of the process of transformation from ordinary language which began with formalization" (*op. cit.*: 69-70).

For the Venda of South Africa, however, from whom most of the members of the churches discussed in this paper were recruited, ordinary speech, various types of formalized speech, and song, were sharply distinguished, and the notion of a continuum was ruled out even when I tried to press the point (Blacking 1967: 16; 1973: 27-29.) One of the aims of musical expansion in certain types of song was to escape from the restrictions of words and develop a lively musical argument. Bloch's contention that "you cannot argue with a song" does perhaps apply in specific cases where the accurate repetition of music is the primary aim of the performances (e.g. McClean 1961 and 1978); but it does *not* apply to all music. In musical languages, as in architecture, repetition can be positively constructive, and the core of the "argument": far from being redundant it enhances meaning (cf. Ruwet 1972: 10). The repetitions of the Sonata Form in Western Europe are as much a part of a musical argument as variations in the *Kulingtang* music of Maranao, which is one of many examples of argument in aurally transmitted musical traditions (Cadar 1973: 244 ff).

My argument for a relationship between political aspirations and musical performance will rest on an analysis of the folk model, and will incorporate people's notions of music and musical performance with their notions about religious worship, and social, economic and political life, in the context of social interaction that was outward-looking. Since I claim that the consciousness enhanced by performances of the music was broadly political, and not simply the consciousness of an in-group in South Africa's divided society, the next section will be devoted to a discussion of the kind of social life that church members led and envisaged.

The Social Context of the Independent Churches' Notions and Actions

Many researchers have emphasized the exclusiveness or escapist nature of the independent Black South African churches. Thus, J.P. Kiernan described the Zionists of Kwa Mashu, Natal, as "drawing the line" and "closing off the outside world" in their ritual (Kiernan 1974: 2), and Martin West emphasized the theme of escape in passages such as this:

> In times of crisis many people turn to religion, and it is the integration of religion with healing in the independent churches which makes them attractive and meaningful to many people in Soweto who have difficulty in either solving or coming to terms with various forms of misfortune. (West 1975: 124)

Indeed, the activities of the churches could be regarded as escape from the harsh realities of the South African political system and a classic example of religion being the opiate of oppressed classes and promoting false consciousness of people's situations: they emphasized individual salvation (for those who were treated as chattels and numbers in a system), spiritual healing (for those who lacked proper medical services), seats in heaven (for those who had no resting place on the land that had once been theirs), and hell-fire and damnation for sinners (for those who saw the Whites getting away with all the sins). West argued that the churches "provide important outlets for the poorer and less-educated people in Soweto", and in some respects "satisfy needs which have arisen out of their specific urban situation" (West 1975: 16). He also endorsed Thomas's (1970) more positive argument that people joined for sociability, status, security, and approval.

None of the explanations given by West and others explains why the music of the churches should be consistently different from both mission and traditional musics, or why people were unable to satisfy their needs for sociability, status, security, approval, and so on, *within* the body of the mission churches. West gave an indirect answer in many parts of his book, but he never discussed explicitly the significance of the churches in national politics, even though it may have been impossible to include political questions in his surveys. One reason why mission churches were unsatisfactory is suggested by his observation: "Zionist-type churches will co-operate with Ethiopian-type churches in certain associations, but not with white apostolic missions" (West 1975: 21), even though the white missions also stressed "the influence of the Holy Spirit and divine healing." In other words, dogmatic differences between Zionist- and Ethiopian-type Black South African churches were of less significance than their common desire to build an independent Black society, just as their new church music both transcended traditional ethnic music divisions and broke away from the mission music model. The politics of many Venda Zionists (i.e. referring to Zion City and churches of the Spirit) were Africanist, in so far as they were able to express views openly. They had sensed the futility of building a peaceful South Africa on the terms of the whites: ultimately, South Africa had to be a black, African, country run on Christian and essentially African socialist lines (see Gerhart 1978 and Blacking 1979). The issue of multi-racialism was irrelevant, as that was a consequence of the whites' introduction of racism to people who had hitherto been "colour blind".

These attitudes were not a sign of retreat from confrontation in radical national politics to a mystical tribalism in line with the policy of apartheid, because along with them went the Africanist view of relations between people, and between people and land, and of the spiritual foundations of life. This view was in fact more revolutionary than the Western socialist or liberal multi-racial politics, which politically active members of the African bourgeoisie had pursued, often in company with Whites who were sympathetic towards Black political aspirations, and with members of other oppressed groups (so-called Coloured and Asiatics). The adverse reaction of White socialists and liberals to the formation of the Pan-Africanist Congress in 1959 was a clear sign of the force of the Africanist idea and the unease that people felt about a policy which was less concerned with what the Whites were doing to the Blacks than with what the Blacks would do about the Whites. The comparatively brief and limited success of the PAC at that time belied the undercurrent of feeling about the future of South Africa as a black, African nation, and it was not until the emergence of the national, Black Consciousness movement and the concept of Black Theology in the early 1970s that people began to take seriously the Africanist viewpoint and the kind of theology that Zionists had been pursuing for decades.

Venda Zionists of the 1950s and 1960s saw themselves as more progressive than non-Christians and more enlightened than mission Christians. They did not see themselves as a rural in-group or as exclusively Venda: on the contrary, they moved between rural and urban areas and were particularly active in the latter, and they welcomed contact and worship with Zulu, Sotho, Tswana, and other groups. It is because they saw themselves firstly as Black South African Christians and not as members of a particular ethnic group, that I have not specified in the title of my paper that the majority of the members of the churches studied were Venda.

It seems that Venda Christians began to join and form independent churches around 1912, the year in which the African National Congress was formed and the year before the 1913 Natives' Land Act. Membership received a boost during the 1914-18 War: Venda men travelled more because of military recruitment and labour migration, and the spectacle of warring Christian tribesmen encouraged many to develop a Christianity that was closer to Christ's Gospel of Peace. Moreover, Venda were at the time aware of the activities of the Watch Tower movement to their north in what were then Northern Rhodesia and Nyasaland, and of the growth of Zionism to their south in Natal and the Cape Province, where 117 of Enoch Mgijima's Israelites were killed at Bullhoek on 24 May 1921 (Sundkler 1961: 72-73). Although Venda language and culture are closer to Sotho and Tswana, which predominate in the Transvaal, Venda Zionists tended to stress their church affiliations with Zulu Christians and used Zulu as the second language of their services more often than Sotho or Tswana. One Venda bishop, who had originally been baptized in Venda in 1918, even spoke to his children in Zulu and encouraged them to use the language amongst themselves, because Zulu-speaking Christians frequently visited his home. Zulu seemed to be regarded as the language of the black people of South Africa as a whole: while this is statistically wrong, it is true that the early struggles of the independent churches were accomplished by people whose native languages were Nguni, and that the same languages were native to many contemporary spokesmen of the African people, such as Luthuli, Mandela, Sisulu, Sobukwe, Tambo, and Xuma.

The Zionists acknowledged only God and Christ as their Lord and Master, and so they considered that their activities were above the control of chiefs and headmen. Nevertheless, many ministers were anxious to please rather than antagonize traditional rulers, in the hope that they might become Zionists, and so they both asked chiefs' permission to hold, and paid a portion of the fees received for, their Christian initiation schools (*vhusha ha vhatendi*). This was considered to be less an acceptance of chiefly authority than a demonstration of Venda solidarity and recognition of the rulers' task as administrators of the land; mission churches never gave any thing to traditional rulers, although they operated on the land held in trust by them.

Eschatology and Politics in Church Services

The politics to which the activities of the churches referred, were therefore national politics, and the identity that was stressed through their music was a black Christian identity in the context of South African society as a whole. The theology was a reinterpretation of the dualistic Christianity that had been learnt from the missionaries, but in the light of traditional African beliefs, with an emphasis on salvation, judgement, and the importance of following the guidance of the Holy Spirit. Links between eschatology and national politics were frequently made in South Africa. For example, the symbolic significance of the words of Enoch Sontonga's famous hymn, *Nkosi sikelel'i Afrika,* is without question: it has been accepted for decades by all black political parties as the Black South African National Anthem (Rhodes 1962: 16-17). It is the last hymn, No. 119, in the Venda Zionist Hymnal, *Nyimbo dza Pesaleme,* and a translation of the Venda version reads:

> God Bless Africa!
> Let thy name be praised;
> Let our prayers be heard!
> God bless us; thou only art to be respected.
> Come Spirit!
> Come Spirit!
> Come, Holy Spirit!
> God bless us, thou only art to be respected.

Its basic themes were stressed again and again in Zionist services in the choice of Bible texts, hymns, psalms, and sermons. The following summary of the themes of a service could be described as an elaboration of the Black South African National Anthem. The sequence of ideas was expressed in the words of hymns chosen, in the improvized verses of "psalms", and in the topics of sermons. Sermon themes are placed in brackets:

Jesus is coming — our country is dying; (communal prayer); God is our leader who will help us fight our enemies, (our country is dying – the Day of Judgement will come – believers will be saved and have seats in heaven – the Day of Judgement is coming) the great Day of Judgement is coming; those who are saved are going home to Jerusalem; have pity on our poverty, Jesus! (The Day of Judgement is coming – seats are prepared in heaven for you – God will save you) Christ died so that we may go to heaven; (Christ died for our sins). He was born again, as He promised; Christ's death on the cross saved us and enabled us to take unto us the Word of God; we are taking the Word of God to the leaders of our country – people praise God with words but deny Him with deeds – weep for our people; there is no salvation except through Jesus – let us not be afraid to stand up and declare our faith in the face of our rulers.

Sermons and hymns about "rising up again" in Christ and "living on the earth again" could be and were interpreted in terms of the South African situation. Within a few minutes of each other, one preacher on November 11th, 1956, said "Empires will fall, but we shall rise again. When Christ rules this world, there will be pleasure and peace, and there will be no bribery"; and another said:

Today we are pleased because of Christ's resurrection. Christianity was unknown before Christ. The Jews were the only people who worshipped God. Black people and the Samaritan woman began worshipping God after the birth of Christ. The Samaritan woman was found at the well by Christ, and she believed that He was the Messiah. Philip of Ethiopia then preached the word to the black people. I was a soldier during the War. Black and White are all together as worshippers of God. When I was in uniform, though, a child referred to me as a donkey. This surprised me, because I was in uniform . . .

In heaven, black and white people are equal . . . People believe that we are worshipping the white man's God. This is a pity, because you might not have many things if you do that . . . . God's Empire overwhelms all Empires . . . . And then on earth there will be peace and pleasure. I look forward to the coming of heaven.

The Ideal Structure of Church Life

I use Firth's (1951) terms "ideal structure" and "social organization" both to recognize his comparatively early and important contribution to the anthropological debate on representational and operational models, and because it happens to describe best what follows. Research into Black South African Churches and their music was marginal to my main interests both in Venda and in Soweto, and I never made a specific study of them. I was involved with them insofar as there were several churches and members in the area of

Venda which I studied intensively, and my friend and field assistant, Mr Alfred Tshibalanganda, was an active and enthusiastic member. As a result, I often attended services and meetings with him as a relaxation from my more formal fieldwork and as an involved participant rather than as a researcher, and I noted only things that were unusual in terms of previous experience, once I had become accustomed to the beliefs and practices of the churches. I knew most of the members of congregations in other social contexts, so that I was able to relate church activities, and especially music and healing, to those social contexts and actions.

Because of a shortage of funds and magnetic tape, I recorded only extracts and three complete services: but I recorded others on tape which I subsequently used again after I had discussed the recordings of the music and the service with church members and made notes on the themes of the music and sermons.

All the rural churches that I attended were Zionist churches of the Spirit, and were described as such by the participants. They had the six features specified by West (1975: 19): healing, river baptism, dancing, prophets, night communion, and drums. Their members abstained from smoking and drinking alcohol, and most of them attended short evening services on Wednesdays, and Fridays or Saturdays, and one or two services on Sundays. Their size ranged from twenty to over a hundred regular members; but on an occasion such as an all-night service for the opening of a new shop in Sambandou on 28 November 1958, there were nearly four hundred people present, as well as leading ministers of Venda-based independent churches, such as Bishop L.T. Marole.

Church structure and activities were modelled with reference to two main sources of authority: the Holy Bible, which contained evidence of the Word of God, and the Power of the Holy Spirit, through which the Word of God might be interpreted and applied to every situation. Although every right and acceptable action, such as the decision to form a new church or congregation, had to be inspired by the Holy Spirit, knowledge of the Bible was necessary for its justification and execution. Moreover, oral testimony was not sufficient: the leader of a church had to be able to read the Bible. Thus an illiterate prophet might inspire decisions, but he would not be accepted as the established founder and leader of a church. During the 1920s and 1930s, when primary schooling was not as common as in the 1950s and 1960s, some church members worked hard to improve their reading and understanding of the Bible, so that they could realize their call to the ministry.

There were recognized officers in every church, but the exercise of authority was flexible and the general principle seemed to be that as many members as possible should have an opportunity of holding positions, except those of bishop and *mufunzi* (ordained minister). Leadership was far from authoritarian, especially during worship, when it was expected that the Holy Spirit would lead the proceedings.

The regular services of the churches, and all worship in general, were referred to as *Mushumo wa Mudzimu,* or Work for God, and the amount of time and effort devoted to this kind of work was considered to be as important as any other kind of work. Many argued that it was more important, maintaining that the spiritual welfare of church members and of the community was of supreme importance, and that material welfare flowed from it. All services were expected to include Bible readings, sermons, hymns and psalms, communal prayer in which everyone gave themselves to the Spirit and spoke with tongues, the Lord's Prayer, and probably some healing at the end of the service and occasionally some dancing. The hymns and psalms were generally taken from the Zionist hymn books, and the difference between them was that hymns followed a verse and strophe format similar to European hymns, whilst psalms followed a call-response system similar to traditional African music, and were accompanied by the double-sided *tshigubu,* modelled on the European bass drum. Zionists insisted, though, that the psalms were not modelled on traditional Venda music, and that when they sung European hymns taken from mission books, they sang them in the Zionist way. In comparing their services with mission services, Zionists said that they were "better because people are allowed to lead in prayer and hymns", and that mission services were "dull and send you to sleep". This does not mean that their music was disorganized or that their singing was necessarily fast and rhythmical. The model for performance was not external, in the sense of being an ideal musical reproduction of a given score; and there was no attempt to sing European hymns like, or as well as, Europeans, or even in the way that the mission churches sang them. Though most psalms were sung at a lively tempo, hymns were often sung very slowly. But this did not make them any less lively in the truly Christian sense of the word, because it provided individuals with opportunities to "catch" the Holy Spirit by worshipful elaboration of melodies and embellishment of single tones.

There were different kinds of services that were specified by members, such as all-night services (*milindelo, sing. mulindelo*) for deceased or for sick members of the congregation; for opening a new church; for concluding the initiation of girls; for welcoming back a member of the congregation who had "become weary" of the Word of God for a while; for Holy Communion; for the coming out and blessing of a child; for the departure of a minister or officer of the church to another parish; for the opening of a shop belonging to a member; for raising church funds; or for any other good reason that should be suggested by the minister or a member of the congregation. Baptisms and the laying on of hands were a common feature of regular services.

In discussion, people were vague about the precise order of service, but they were adamant that services were orderly. First, if there was a church building for the congregation, they expected that there would be a table or an altar on a raised platform at the east end of the church, and that the elders would sit there with the minister and any distinguished visitors. There might be a pulpit and a cross behind the altar or table; but these were not essential. There should be benches in the body of the church, and the women and children of the congregation would be expected to sit on one side and the men and youths on the other. Services were supposed to open with a Bible reading, which would provide a theme for a hymn and a sermon. Elders who were moved by the Spirit would come forward, read some verses from the Bible and then preach about them. While they preached, members of the congregation were expected to encourage them with cries of "Hallelujah!" "Amen", and so on. Some members said that the Bible passages ought to be selected by opening the Bible at random, but this did not often happen. On the other hand, all members expected a period of communal prayer to follow the singing of certain psalms, and the laying on of hands to be accompanied by other psalms, with or without dancing.

Preachers and worshippers often said quite explicitly that the hymns and psalms were meant to "remind us all of Jesus", and that worship of God, together with love of neighbours and pursuit of a Christian life, was the main task of the Christian. The music, which was for all the most emotional and expressive element of worship, was meant to help each individual member to find his/her inner self in the presence of and with the help of others, and to achieve experience of the Holy Spirit through participation in collective counterpoint. The form of the services and the style of singing cannot be understood without taking into account the specific social situations in which the general principles of worship were put into effect.

The Social Organization of Worship

In both Venda and Soweto, the order of services and the topics of hymns and sermons varied on every occasion, depending on the purpose of the service and the pattern of decision-making that emerged among the congregation. Some ministers tended to lead hymns and preach more than others, but not for the same reasons. For example, the young and zealous Reverend N. held more services per week than anyone else in the district, he favoured psalms with drum accompaniment to hymns in the proportion of approximately 3 : 1, and he intoned almost every hymn and psalm in the service himself. He was anxious to attract large congregations to the church, and was convinced that vital, directed musical performances were the key to success. In comparison, many much more successful, older ministers of the church were often the quietest of preachers and encouraged others to lead hymns and psalms.

The order of services was supposed to be influenced by the Holy Spirit, who would bring the Word of God in the form of Bible texts, ideas for sermons, hymn themes, prophecies and communal prayer. Nevertheless, Venda ministers seemed to feel the need to exert a little more control over services in the urban area when congregations from different churches and ethnic groups were gathered, although they did not do so either at similar services in Venda or at small gatherings in Chiawelo, the Venda-Tsonga township in Soweto.

In my experience, ministers' attempts to control services sprang from their desire to please rather than to wield power, and were generally an unpremeditated consequence of their perception of situations. Events at two all-night services (*milindelo*) held six months apart, on 9 September 1961 and 24 March 1962, at the Reverend M's home in Chiawelo, illustrate this point.

Congregations from different churches were invited to both services, and several prophets turned up at the first service. Because there were also other ministers and some good preachers, the Reverend M. asked the prophets to do their work early in the service, on the grounds that prophets interfere with preaching. Later, when the Reverend M. noted that some members of the congregation were beginning to complain openly about the length of sermons, he interrupted a sermon with the popular psalm No. 116 on the Transfiguration, from the Zionists' own hymnal. Sermons were often interrupted by someone intoning a hymn, which was then taken up by the congregation. But the interruption was generally inspired by an idea expressed in the sermon, and the hymn was intended to encourage the preacher rather than break off his/her discourse.

When the Reverend M. was faced with another large congregation at the second service, he declared that there should be a five-minute limit on all sermons. Several preachers complained about this restriction, but accepted the house rules. One read from Mathew 5:1, the beginning of the Sermon on the Mount, to show that there had been no five-minute rule for Jesus, and another summed up his objections with a pointed reading from Ephesians 4: 1-6, which begins: "I therefore, the prisoner of the Lord, beseech you that ye walk worthy of the vocation wherewith ye are called." At the end of the service, when they had danced and had breakfast, the Reverend M. asked pardon for imposing the five-minute rule, which he had done with the best of intentions. The objections to the rule, which was never imposed in that church again, were that it interfered with the work of the Holy Spirit, it contradicted the Bible, it was not an African notion, and it would never be done back home in Venda.

There were indeed no restrictions on the length of sermons at similar meetings in rural Venda, and nobody complained when a middle-aged minister carried on preaching for forty minutes at 2.00 a.m., with only a five-minute break for a psalm. He held people's attention not only by the force and drama of his delivery, and by an amusing story, but also by the content of his sermon. The occasion was a shop-opening at Sambandou, on 28 November, 1958. He warned that people should not do ritual murder to get rich, that the owner must not keep beer or brandy in the shop (which was, at that time, forbidden by South African law to all blacks), and that prayer and worship would bring freedom and good fortune. A previous preacher, who had continued for thirty minutes with only two short hymns as contrast, had given an even more remarkable performance, but one less directly related to the occasion. He was followed by a businessman who had come from across the mountains and who, in explaining his actions, said he had wanted a good sing and pray. After a short sermon on the subject of being lost without Jehovah, he launched what turned out to be a magnificent performance of the popular Transfiguration psalm, and then initiated ten minutes of communal prayer.

When, therefore, the organization of events at services in rural Venda was "left to the workings of the Holy Spirit", it was remarkable how good a balance was struck between preaching and singing, and how satisfied and moved the members of the congregations were by the proceedings. The principles of sharing, of accepting equality before God, and of seeking collective experience of the Holy Spirit, were upheld, though thematic coherence was less evident than in smaller gatherings. That is, members brought their own collection of favourite texts, hymns, and even partially prepared sermons; and when the Spirit moved one to act, he/she tended to make a very personal contribution to the service, rather than follow on from the previous idea. At the same time, there were universally popular hymns and psalms, such as hymn no. 37 and psalm no. 116 in the Zionist hymnal, and "We are going home to Jerusalem", which different people might launch for a second or third time in a single *mulindelo*.

In this kind of situation, the themes of a service were not as coherent as at the meetings of smaller groups of thirty to ninety people, where most of the congregation knew each other, or at the regular services of congregations of about fifteen to thirty people. The Reverend Petrus Muthengwe was a quiet, gentle, devout man who held regular services and maintained a thriving congregation in his Church (his daily task was running a refreshment stall at the Sibasa market, by the Post Office): he and his elders liked to establish a continuity of ideas in their services, so that a hymn would be followed by the Bible reading on which it was based, and then by a sermon on the same theme. He also used what might be described as a musical technique of expanding an idea: first, two popular hymns were sung, followed by a reading and a psalm, all of which were led by the Reverend Muthengwe, and then two of his elders repeated the hymns with additions. Thus one service began:

Muthengwe leads
Hymn No. 11   About the Lion of Juda, the opening of
                                the book, and people in white robes
                                washed in the Blood of the Lamb.
Hymn No. 37   The great Day of Judgement is coming.
Reading: Psalm 137   By the rivers of Babylon . . . . .
Psalm: *We are going home to Jerusalem*

Elders follow
Hymn No. 11 + Bible reading on same text (Revelation 5:5) + Sermon.
Hymn No. 37 + words of related Bible text (Revelation 20:12) read in
    a loud voice while the hymn was hummed + Communal prayer.
Psalm: *We are going home to Jerusalem.*
Reading: Psalm 137.
Psalm: *We are going home to Jerusalem* (continued) + sermon on St John
    Ch. 14, about seats being prepared in heaven.

Musical modes of thought were also used in the organization of words in Zionist hymns and in the delivery of sermons. The words of, or words related to, the key texts of hymns were repeated as would be a musical phrase (e.g. Hymn No. 11 in *Nyimbo dza*

Pesaleme), though the vocal melodies followed the sequences of four, six, or eight verses to a strophe that are common in European hymns. When sermons were interpreted into or from Zulu or Sotho in the urban area, preacher and interpreter often created greater intensity of expression by antiphonal delivery, so that sermons often merged almost imperceptibly into hymn-singing.

The Importance of Music in Worship and in Zionists' Lives

In spite of their detail on many matters, studies of the black churches do not always make clear how much of their members' time was taken up by music and church activities and how much by other activities.

Even the most enthusiastic churchgoers in Venda and in Soweto saw themselves in a variety of other social roles, and it was generally only the wives and close relatives of church leaders who devoted most of their time to church work, while their husbands were often busy with other matters, such as running or working in a shop. Thus it seems that many of the explanations of membership given in the literature, and extended to account for the very existence of the churches, are inferred from actors' representational models of the churches and church activities in general rather than from specific social situations that were part of church life or from their general life-style, of which church life was a part. For example, West reported that 83% of the members of two churches studied in depth joined because of the faith-healing (*op. cit.*: 80). But, unless they were chronic invalids, was that why they stayed in the church? I met church members who had joined because of faith-healing, but who had stayed because they had been attracted by a church's fellowship or its prevailing doctrine, and especially by its worships, in which music played the dominant role. Moreover, leadership, which West and others claim was an important attraction that the churches offered (e.g. West 1975: 20, 48-75) was synonymous with *musical* expertise.

Few members of the churches objected to traditional ritual music and its associated rites, but usually they did not perform it after joining a church. Nor did they share the missionaries' objections to traditional drums, although they used a European-style bass drum (*tshigubu*) at their services. Several men, in fact, played and danced *tshikona,* the most important traditional music for reed-pipes and drums, and youths often played traditional instruments. Zionist children sang and danced traditional music, as well as modern school and urban songs in four-part harmony and the European songs and hymns that were taught at school.

Women recited traditional stories and sang story-songs to their children and grandchildren, and several Zionists sang in mission churches or at school-based functions such as fêtes and sport days. When they attended weddings and parties, younger members in particular joined with mission Christians in singing popular urban part-songs, and perhaps dancing jive or *Kwela*. Thus, many Zionists had a working knowledge of the principles of traditional, mission, school, and urban music, as well as their own church music.

Performance of their church music was the chief sign of their commitment to the Zionist way of life, and it occupied much of their spare time; but their appreciation and performance of other musical styles reflected their view that they were not an exclusive in-group so much as a community that encompassed all walks of black African life. They were probably less sharply distinguished from other Christians than might have been expected, because most Venda mission Christians were not as exclusive as a group as were some mission Christians in other parts of South Africa. On the other hand, very few Zionists had any dealings with Europeans except in their official capacities as civil servants, policemen, employers, storekeepers, or labour recruiters. In this respect, they differed from mission Christians, who often had friendships with "liberal" Europeans.

Maurice Bloch pointed out that in the Merina circumcision ceremony, "nine-tenths of the time is taken up singing" (1974: 70); but he also argued that this time was marked by the suspension of rational decision-making and creative action. In the worship of the South African independent churches that I studied, almost as much time was devoted to music; but I claim that singing required constantly creative decision-making, as congregations adapted their model for performance to the unique character of every social situation, and that it enhanced rather than anaesthetized political consciousness.

The key to understanding this lies not so much in what people sang, but *how* they sang, and in particular how they sang hymns of European origin. Several tunes were taken from the Lutheran or Presbyterian hymnals which had been introduced by the missions, together with translations into Venda of the accompanying words. The Zionist method of singing such hymns differed from both the mission and European methods. But this was *not* because of musical incompetence or lack of schooling of members of the independent churches, as even some black members of mission churches suggested. Several Zionists were perfectly capable of singing in the mission style, *when they attended a mission church service;* but when singing with their own congregations they adopted the Zionist style. The Zionist style of singing hymns of European origin was as much a consequence of rational decision-making as their composition and performance of new Zionist psalms and hymns. They made no attempt to sing in the same way as Europeans, but they accepted hymns of European origin as models for performance, because they were *Christian* hymns. There was no contradiction in opposing white Christianity and at the same time using the Christian materials that the whites had brought: the hymns were considered to be an expression of the Holy Spirit through the medium of certain Europeans who had been true Christians, but the Whites' and missions' ways of performing them were symbols of a parochial, racist interpretation of Christianity that was a distortion of the Christian message (cf. Biko 1973: 42 ff.). As the Nigerian theologian Dr Akin J. Omoyajowo, wrote: "The Holy Spirit descended and called out Africans to express Christianity in language that would be understandable and meaningful to the people. Thus came into existence the phenomenon of the African Independent Churches (Omoyajowo 1973: 85). And, as in traditional African societies, musical performance was the major feature of worship, and worship was the most important collective action in people's lives.

The Analysis of Zionist Music

An analysis of musical performance can be concerned with the assignation of meanings that are largely independent of the structure of the music, and also with the processes of decision-making by which certain patterns of sound are produced. The general argument of this paper is that the sounds of the music are as crucial to its analysis as the meanings that are given to or associated with it.

But the problem is that the Venda had no terminology with which to describe what they did, especially in singing European hymns, though their performances provided ample evidence of a systematic model for music-making.

The only ways in which the musical parameters could be assessed was by aesthetic evaluation of muscial events when church members and anthropologist sat down and together analysed tape recordings of services they had attended, or church members commented on recordings of services they had not attended; and through the correction of musical mistakes made accidentally by church members and sometimes deliberately by the anthropologist. This was not easy, because church members were inclined to deny that a musical mistake had been made, since it could have been a special variation inspired by the Holy Spirit. On the other hand, people had less inhibitions about comparing good and bad performances, since they recognized that some services, and some moments in a service, were more inspired by the Holy Spirit than others.

One problem in explaining the music of the services was: how, when, and why were decisions made about what to sing, and to what extent did musical factors influence choice? How was the music ordered thematically and tonally? Did one melody or rhythm suggest its successor? Were there favourite tunes that had to be sung, regardless of occasion and congregation? How did people achieve a balance between psalms and hymns, and between sermons and music? A particularly lively and richly polyphonic rendering of a psalm could be explained by the fact that the congregation was relieved to have a chance to sing after so much preaching; or a faster performance of a hymn by the fact that the leader of the singing at that point wanted to rouse a sleepy congregation before he preached. The particular way (the Zionist style) in which people sang was designed to get the right feeling and bring the Holy Spirit to the congregation; but also the coming of the Spirit gave people feelings which affected the musical product, particularly by sobs, cries, shrieks, or an increase in volume and/or melodic ornamentation. Thus the coming of the Holy Spirit, induced by music, could influence a person to change the quality of musical performance; but it did not change the music chosen, and the singing of a particular hymn or psalm would continue.

The psalms were an original creation of the churches. Some of them might be called syncretic, since they had a superficial resemblance to traditional Venda *malende* and *tshikona* (see Blacking 1973: *passim*). All psalms had call-response structure, with drum accompaniment, and the response was repeated by the congregation with contrapuntal and harmonic additions as long as a soloist or soloists continued to sing the call, with different word patterns modifying the melody as in the traditional system (cf. Blacking 1967: 166-171). Church members emphasized that their music was different and progressive: they generally compared the social context of music rather than its sounds, so that they argued that there was no connection between psalms and *malende* on the grounds that Zionists never drank beer but preferred tea, soft drinks and *mabundu*. The most striking musical characteristics of the Zionist style of hymn-singing were:

1) The tempo was generally slow, except at points in a service where faster singing was needed. This would be accompanied by

handclaps.

2) The general pitch of a melody rose with performance.

3) There was highly ornamented, slurred singing in which the pitch of tones was deliberately varied in order to heighten expressive feeling. (This was a characteristic of Nguni traditional song, which may well have been brought into the singing of church members in the early days of the movement, when it flourished in Natal and the Cape Province. On the other hand, Professor Olly Wilson of the University of California, Berkeley, was struck by the similarities with a style of Black American Church singing that was developed in the 19th Century. No suggestion of diffusion was raised, although the Black AME spread to South Africa: rather, it seemed as if similar backgrounds, religious ideas and hymn models might have given rise to similar music).

4) There was a thick harmonic texture, with frequent parallelism, and a preference for unambiguous shifts of tonality within a diatonic framework.

5) There was a call and response form both in the presentation of whole verses and in the hocket-like use of parts of verses to maintain a constant stream of sound. *Notes were held over phrases, to avoid rests.*

The polyphonic texture of the hymns would seem to require careful social organization, but because the aim of church members was that worship should be guided by the Holy Spirit, the organization of singing developed by consensus. In theory, anyone could preach or inaugurate a hymn at any moment of the service; in practice, the minister or leader of the congregation tended to do this more often than others, though officials of one church were less prominent when attending the churches of others, and preferred to be invited to take the lead. Once a hymn had been intoned, others took it up by singing the part most appropriate to their voices. At the beginning of services, and especially when there were many strangers, the first few phrases of a hymn were often uncertain, as people listened to the texture of the singing. If there was a shortage of an alto part, for example, a singer might switch from singing soprano in order to improve the balance of parts. The most adaptable singers were those who might also be described as the most able, though ministers and leaders of singing generally held to the melody. When a hymn was under way, people felt free to "let go" with slurs, glissandi, ornaments, and short phrases in double time. Different contexts, different stages in a long service, and different social situations, all generated different degrees of participation and correspondingly different musical products. For example, the speed of two performances of the same hymn by the same people at early and middle stages of an all-night varied by as much as $\flat = 54$ M.M. and $\flat = 92$ M.M.; and individuals' performances within the same hymn varied according to their perception of what was expected of them in given social situations: i.e. how much self-expression and variation could the ensemble tolerate.

Political and Musical Freedom

The purpose of this paper has been to relate political aspirations to musical performance in the activities of some black South African churches. By emphasizing the political significance of Zionist styles of music, and in particular their unique way of singing hymns of European origin, I am not trying to reduce music or religion to the political, or vice versa, because people clearly can, and unfortunately do, pursue full and satisfying "musical" or "religious" lives without any concern whatsoever for what is happening to themselves and their fellowmen, and politically conscious people can be quite indifferent to music. Nor am I suggesting that music-making is in itself an alternative form of political action, though it can be used with great effect in a political context.

A basic assumption in my argument is that neither verbal language nor any particular field of action (e.g. economic, religious, or political) is in all cases a primary modelling system or an infrastructure of human thought and action, but that the emphasis varies according to the decisions that individuals make collectively in community: prime importance may be given to one or other field of action, or equal importance to several fields, as in traditional Venda society and in the life-style of some independent Venda churches. Related to this assumption is the claim that in certain social contexts important ideas can be expressed and fundamental changes of direction enacted through the practice of the nonverbal performing arts, before these notions and actions are clearly articulated in words or translated into other fields of action. The performing arts are an expression of what is often termed "affective culture", and the importance of affect in motivating decision-making is widely accepted. The Ghanaian musician, Papa Oyeah MacKenzie, has described this process in words that were frequently echoed by South African blacks: "we feel before we understand"; and the argument of this paper is that the *way* in which members of Venda independent churches sang hymns and psalms was their most potent means of expressing their understanding of the predicament of Blacks in South Africa.

In *The homeless mind: modernization and consciousness,*
Peter Berger writes (1974: 176): "people will be able to liberate
themselves from social and political oppression only if they first
liberate themselves from the patterns of thought imposed by the
oppressors", Black South Africans have no political freedom, and
one aspect of political oppression which was thrust on them was
European mission and school music, which were part of the colonial
package that was compulsory for all who wanted to read, write,
count, and take up new kinds of employment. In South Africa in the
1960s, politics and music were inversely related to each other; ideas
of political freedom could not be expressed but could have been
stated in words, while musical freedom could not be explained in
words but could be expressed in performance.

The Zionist style of singing hymns and the corpus of Zionist
music were seen by many Venda as a *new, Christian, but truly
African* way of acting in community, and their musical meanings
could not be separated from the other ideas and activities that went
with them. At the beginning of this paper, I argued that the analysis
of music and musical performance is problematic because of
different societies' classification of music and non-music, and
because verbal language can distort the intrinsic meanings of music
as symbolic discourse in its own right. Zionist concepts of music-
making were such that outsiders could judge their performances of
hymns as chaotic, or fail to realize that the sobs of a singer "taken"
by the Holy Spirit were not non-music but the epitome of music.
The freedom of individuals to sing as the Spirit moved them was,
however, restrained by the desire to act in concert as a united
Christian community, and the evidence of the quality of the singing
and people's clear recollections of their spiritual experiences showed
that they sought neither trance nor ecstasy, as defined by Rouget
(1980), but a state of heightened consciousness in which each
person's potential was realized and harnessed for the benefit of all.

Thus performances of hymns were generally far from chaotic,
and the way in which diverse groups of people achieved coordinated
polyphony was in itself a politically significant experience as well
as a demonstraction of the Venda principle that the ideal structure
of musical performance should express the maximum of individuality
in the largest possible community of people (cf. Blacking 1973: 28,
51). This principle was frequently expressed by the saying, *muthu
ndi muthu nga vhaṅwe,* "a human being becomes (fully) human
through association with fellow human beings", which has its
counterpart in several other Southern African languages (e.g. the
Zulu *umuntu ungumuntu ngabantu*).

In their common rejection of a European musical aesthetic and European models of worship, the members of Venda independent churches were transmitting messages to each other: their hymns were not protest songs, but nevertheless they protested; and they also asserted different values and a different identity from that generally required of black Christians in South Africa. People said that their singing should express the meanings of the words, but they also said that because they were songs one should not necessarily expect words to mean exactly what they stated.

Even if they did not, for obvious reasons, state their political views openly, the outlook of most members of the churches was Africanist: their music, their ritual, and their life-style expressed Africanist aspirations, confidence in African values, and a desire to be free of European political and cultural domination. These aims had inspired the early independent churches and their leaders at the beginning of the century and have always been an important feature of their existence. Only in the last ten years or so have the same aims come to be accepted more readily by members of mission churches and been given greater force and legitimacy by being gathered together within the imported American title of Black Theology (cf. Moore 1973; Gerhart 1978: 290 ff.). They have for much longer been a powerful influence in the struggle for black freedom in South Africa, because they have been a focus for the social life and aspirations of the industrial proletariat and of peasants who have had a taste of urban life as migrants or have worked on white-owned farms. In the services that I attended, the comparative lack of education and of sophistication of members of the churches was often highlighted by a very moving contrast between the vigour, fluency and creativity of the many ex tempore sermons on the Christian life and the Word of God, and the halting, staccato reading of passages from the Bible.

J.P. Kiernan (1977) suggested that the Zionist movement could better be understood "in relation to conditions of poverty and to the social depression which is their inevitable concomitant", and he presented a convincing argument from evidence of Zulu Zionists in Kwa Mashu. There is no doubt that the poverty of urban blacks in South Africa was acute, especially in relation to white standards of living, and that there were enough problems and general disorder in townships to encourage people to cope with life by "closing off the outside world" (Kiernan 1974), not as an escape but rather as an effort to find a Zionist solution to problems of living. Kiernan argues that the Zulu Zionists of Kwa Mashu "limit themselves to social problems and appear to have no political axe to grind", and that an "us" (Zionists) versus "them" (others, black *and* white) model would be more in keeping with the evidence from the Venda churches. (Kiernan: personal communication).

My interpretation may differ because of personal bias and a smaller body of data than Kiernan and other researchers; but I claim that my conclusions are rather consequences of the particular social make-up of Venda churches, and of the structure of their folk model of the interrelationship of worship, music, politics, and social life. On the whole, Venda Zionists were by no means the poorest members of their communities, rural or urban, and many of them were involved in running small businesses or earning rather more than the average low wage. Their schooling, however, had rarely extended beyond Standard III or IV, and this conflicted with the high value placed on formal education in both traditional and progressive Venda communities. Furthermore, most of them had experienced or were aware of the fact that members of the more numerous ethnic groups such as Zulu, Sotho, and Tswana, looked down on their society and culture. Thus, although their ordinary social networks tended to be predominantly Venda, they were keen to show that they were not backward tribesmen from the north and to share with other blacks a modern, Christian way of life. The most appropriate social situations for expressing publicly such ideas and feelings were the various types of worship, and particularly the all-night service which was followed by a communal breakfast. Although members of other ethnic groups were acquainted with the musical styles of the hymns and psalms and were happy to sing in their own languages or in English while others sung in Venda, few of the hymns and psalms composed by Venda were introduced at urban services.

Another objection to my argument is that it does not make sense when compared with similar evidence from other parts of Africa (cf. Barrett 1971): for instance, if this particular form of musical freedom is an expression of the desire for political freedom, why did not independent churches in West, Central and East Africa abandon similar types of music when their countries became independent? First, I do not see why a comparison with Christian churches in other parts of Africa should be necessary for understanding the South African situation: the common denominator of Christianity does not ensure easy comparison of, say, Catholic and Protestant churches in Lesotho, Uganda, white South Africa, Holland, and Ireland. Second, we must not suppose that similar sounding, or even similarly created, music has the same meanings to those who perform and listen to it. The sounds of music, like the syntax of speech, are consequences of intentions to mean something, and although the immediate aim of musical performance may be the attainment of spiritual experience, the significance of such experiences may extend into many other facets of individual and communal life. I have not heard the music of the Church of John Maranke, in Zaire, but Bennetta Jules-Rosette's detailed account (1975: especially 128-154) suggests that it would not sound like the Venda church music, because there are as many differences in the ideas and actions of the church members as there are striking similarities. Third, if the music of other independent churches in Africa did have Africanist political significance, there is no reason why people should have lost interest in those aims when political independence was achieved, though they might have been redefined more in terms of class than colour.

Studies of independent churches in other parts of Africa have been helpful in highlighting problems of analysis, and authors have given different reasons for the emergence of different movements. But the transfer of conclusions from one area to another can be misleading. For instance, West adopted Peel's (1969) teminology and suggested that the emphasis of the independent churches in Soweto was "this worldly" in contrast with the "other worldly" orientation of mission Christianity. In Venda, this dichotomy could not be applied. First, the Venda saw mission Christianity as completely "this worldly" and concerned with power over black people, black land, and black minds. Second, in traditional Venda cosmology, most of which Zionists had no difficulty in reconciling with the teachings of the Bible, "this world" and the "other world" were but the material and spiritual aspects of the same life experience, and all ritual was designed to maintain or restore a balance between the two in the face of the changing situations of daily life. What caused trouble in "this world" was not change or that some people took the lead, but actions that were selfish and not for the good of the community as a whole. Notions of "this world" and "the other world" were intertwined, and actions in "this world" could not be fully explained without reference to actions in "the other".

Several problems in the analysis of the music of some black South African Churches are clarified when the structure of the folk model is taken as the key to interpretation. The significance of musical freedom in the context of religious worship becomes apparent, and the difficulty of explaining nonverbal action with concepts derived from other modelling systems dissolves in the face of a system that relates feelings and bodily experiences to material realities without any sense of contradiction. There was a systematic folk model of musical performance that was invented in response to changing social formations, but the only real evidence of the actors' notions of its structure was in their musical behaviour, which transcended different social situations. Although all other "folk" data relating to its meaning was, strictly speaking, peripheral to its intrinsic meaning as a unique musical system, it was, in fact, essential for understanding its value in the lives of those who used it - *because that was the way they themselves understood it.*

There was no doubt that the majority of Zionists whom I met felt socially and politically oppressed, and that their Christianity and their music constituted a radical departure from the patterns of thought imposed by their oppressors. To give priority to one or other of these four means of communication (social, political, religious, and musical), or to say that one was an epiphenomenon of another, would have imposed on the folk model categories and distinctions that were foreign to its users: they were all parts of a system of notions and actions in which the affairs of "this world" and "the other world" were supposed to be integrated by careful use of the Life Force, and the structure of feeling cultivated as the source of harmonious action.

Acknowledgements

I am most grateful for the friendship and cooperation of Mr Alfred Tshibalanganda of Gaba, who as an active Zionist member, preacher and singer accompanied me to services both in Venda and in Soweto, and also to Bishop Philip Nebulu, of the Remnant of the New Apostolic Covenant Church of Christ in Africa. Others who contributed to my understanding of the work of the churches were the Reverends Petrus Muthengwe and Elias Makhuvha, and Dr Victor Ralushai and Mr Baldwin Mudau, who were members of mission churches.

Thanks are due to many who made helpful comments on earlier drafts of this article: colleagues in the Department of Social Anthropology at the Queen's University of Belfast and at the ASA Conference at Edinburgh; Judith Becker, Jim Kiernan, Roberta Carradine, David Brooks, Barbara Hudson, Simha Arom, Bernard Lortat-Jacob, Gilbert Rouget, and Hugo Zemp. I take full responsibilities for deficiencies in the paper.

I am particularly grateful to Ladislav Holy and Milan Stuchlik for many seminars in which their repeated insistence on intentionality encouraged me to be much more explicit in analyses of motivation and decision-making in musical performance.

References

Barrett, D. B. ed. (1971). *African Initiatives in Religion: Twenty-one Studies from Eastern and Central Africa*. Nairobi: East African Publishing House.

Berger, P. *et al.* (1973). *The Homeless Mind: Modernization and Consciousness*. New York: Random House.

Biko, S. (1973). Black consciousness and the quest for true humanity. In *Black Theology*, (Basil Moore, ed.) pp. 36-47.

Blacking, J. (1967). *Venda Children's Songs: A Study in Ethnomusicological Analysis*. Johannesburg: Witwatersrand University Press.

Blacking, J. (1971). Music and the historical process in Vendaland. In *Essays on Music and History in Africa*, (K.P. Wachsmann, ed.). Evanston: Northwestern University Press.

Blacking, J. (1973). *How Musical is Man?* Seattle: University of Washington Press. (2nd. edn. Faber and Faber, London, 1976).

Blacking, J. (1977). Towards an anthropology of the body. In *The Anthropology of the body*, (J. Blacking, ed.). ASA Monograph No. 15; pp. 1-28. London: Academic Press.

Blacking, J. (1979). The power of ideas in social change: the growth of the Africanist idea in South Africa. In *The Conceptualisation and Explanation of Processes of Social Change*, (David Riches, ed.). QUPSA, Vol 3, pp. 107-140.

Blacking, J. The problem of ethnic perceptions in the semiotics of music. In *Proceedings of Conference on the Semiotics of Culture, Michigan 1978*. Austin: University of Texas Press. (In press).

Bloch, M. (1974). Symbols, song, dance and features of articulation: is religion an extreme form of traditional authority? *Archi. europ. sociol.* 14: 55-81.

Cadar, U. H. (1973). The role of Kulintang music in Maranao Society. *Ethnomusicology* 2: 234-49.

Daneel, M. L. (1971). *Old and New in Southern Shona Independent Churches*. Vol. 1. The Hague: Mouton.

Dubb, A. A. (1976). *Community of the Saved: an African Revivalist Church in the Eastern Cape*. Johannesburg: Witwatersrand University Press for the African Studies Institute.

Firth, R. (1951). *Elements of Social Organization*. London: Watts.

Gerhart, G. M. (1978). *Black Power in South Africa: the Evolution of an Ideology*. Berkeley, Los Angeles, London: University of California Press.

Jules-Rosette, B. (1975). *African Apostles: Ritual and Conversion in the Church of John Maranke*. Ithaca and London: Cornell University Press.

Kiernan, J. P. (1974). Where Zionists draw the line: a study of religious exclusiveness in an African township. *African Studies* 33: 79-90;

Kiernan, J. P. (1977). Poor and puritan; an attempt to view Zionism as a collective response to urban poverty. *African Studies* 36: 31-41.

Kuper, L. (1965). *An African Bourgeoisie: Race, Class and Politics in South Africa*. New Haven and London: Yale University Press.

McLean, M. (1961). Oral transmission in Maori music. *Journal of the International Folk Music Council* 13: 59-62.

McLean, M. (1978). Innovations in *Waiata* style. *Yearbook of the International Folk Music Council* 9: 27-37.

Moore, B. ed. (1973). *Black Theology: the South African Voice.* London: C. Hurst.

Mqotsi, L. and Mkele, N. (1946). A separatist church: Ibandla like-Krestu. *African Studies* 5: 106-25.

Omoyajowo, A. J. (1973). An African expression of Christianity. In *Black Theology.* (Basil Moore, ed.) pp. 81-92.

Peel, J. D. Y. (1968). *Aladura: a Religious Movement Among the Yoruba.* Oxford University Press.

Rhodes, W. (1962). Music as an agent of political expression. In *Arts, Human behaviour and Africa, African Studies Bulletin* 5: 14-22.

Rouget, G. (1980). *La Musique et la Transe: Esquisse d'une Théorie générale des Relations de la Musique et de la Possession.* Paris: Gallimard.

Ruwet, N. (1972). *Langage, Musique, Poésie.* Paris: Seuil.

Sundkler, B. (1961). *Bantu Prophets in South Africa.* 2nd edn. London: Oxford University Press. (1st edn. 1948.)

Thomas, N. E. (1970). Functions of religious institutions in the adjustment of African women to life in a Rhodesian township. In *Focus on Cities,* (H. L. Watts, ed.). Durban: University of Natal Institute of Social Research.

West, M. (1975). *Bishops and Prophets in a Black City: African Independent Churches in Soweto, Johannesburg.* Cape Town: David Philip.

Wilson, M. and Mafeje, A. (1963). *Langa: a Study of Social Groups in an African Township.* Cape Town: Oxford University Press.

MODELS AND METAPHORS

On the Semiotic Explanation of Segmentary Systems

JOHN G. GALATY

Introduction

The notion of the "symbol"[1] has been vigorously put forth as providing specific content and theoretical rigor to, while retaining the distinctively human and historically encompassing properties of, the general notion of culture (Sahlins 1976; McKinley 1977). I would maintain, however, that the theoretical potential of a "symbolic" or "semiotic" paradigm for anthropology has been consistently subverted by the tendency to reconstitute through its form the tedious dichotomy of the mental and the material which it has promised to overcome. Two dominant trends in anthropology emphasize the study of either symbolic structures or action systems, each to the detriment of the other. In this paper, it is my intention to trace various paths of these two opposing tendencies, and to develop the possibility of a semiotic theory of culture which would provide a unified framework for the explanation of both human action and the coherence of symbolic systems.

Part 1

I will begin by reviewing two approaches to the study of segmentary lineage systems which exemplify the larger issue I have posed. In the classic account by Evans-Pritchard, the segmentary model is taken to be like a "promise" which generates appropriate and meaningful action. In this "normative" theory, behaviour fulfills and is explained by the model. In the second approach, the model is explained by the action to which it refers. In this "reductionist" theory, models are seen to express various parameters of action, albeit in simplified or distorted form. While each approach purports to provide a unitary account of both meaning and action, in actuality the program of each diminishes the role of one of these two poles of human culture, and thus rests on a truncated social theory. Indeed, I will suggest that the apparent holism of these two approaches merely disguises an implicit dualism, the extreme form of which will be reviewed in other theoretical contributions. Out of a critique of dualism in anthropology, I will attempt to develop a more inclusive and explanatory perspective on the complementary analysis of models and action, or structures and events, which will avoid facile conjunctions between the two, while overcoming sterile disjunctions between notions of the subjective and objective, and the intentional and extentional, through a semiotic account of segmentary models.

In his earliest formulation of the Nuer case, Evans-Pritchard stated that the "tribe":

> . . . has a name which is the symbol of its distinction. The tribesmen *have a sense* of patriotism; they are *proud* to be members of their tribe and they *consider* it superior to other tribes. (1940a: 278, my emphasis)

Similarly, he described the logic of segmentation from the perspective of Nuer themselves, using indigenous symbolic forms:

> A member of Z^2 tertiary division of tribe B *sees himself* as a member of Z^2 community in relation to Z^1, but he *regards himself* as a member of Y^2 and not Z^2 in relation to Y^1. Likewise, he *regards himself* as a member of Y, and not of Y^2 in relation to X. He *regards himself* as a member of tribe B, and not of its primary section Y, in relation to tribe A. (*Ibid.:* 281; my emphasis)

The theoretical import of Evans-Pritchard's model lay not only in its identification of the structural principle of complementary opposition by which to explicate a type of political system (of wider relevance than the lineage-based case), but in its use of the same units or terms by which the Nuer "regards himself" to represent and analyze that system. This account of segmentary organization in the terms by which Nuer identity is signified established Evans-Pritchard as a founder of a symbolic anthropology.

His account, however, was rapidly transformed from a cultural model into a statement of the analytical principles of relative group membership, in *actual* settings:

> Hence a man counts as a member of a political group in one situation and not as a member of it in a different situation, e.g. he is a member of a tribe in relation to other tribes and he is not a member of it in so far as his segment of the tribe is opposed to other segments (*Ibid.:* 282)

The absence, here, of the terms of Nuer perception within a

description of attributions of membership in specific contexts fore-
shadows a sociologically objective account of the dynamics of the
feud:

> Feuds frequently break out between sections of the same tribe and they
> are often of long duration. They are more difficult to settle the larger the
> sections involved. Within a village feuds are easily settled and within a
> tertiary tribal section they are concluded sooner or later, but when still
> larger groups are involved they may never be settled, especially if many
> persons on either side have been killed in a big fight. (*Ibid.:* 283)

Implicitly, Evans-Pritchard has moved from the domain of Nuer conceptions of group identity, through the domain of group
membership, to the domain of *relations,* under the assumption that
the former provide the explanatory ingredients for the latter, a
cultural model, analytically expressed in symbolic terms, serving as
the basis for a sociological model of actual social relations and
activity.

Taking exception with this view, Peters maintained that the
orderly regularities of the feud among the Bedouin of Cyrenaica were
inconsistent with a "lineage model" of alliances, for he found that
hostilities were often found between more closely related (and
adjacent) tertiary segments, each of which formed alliances with
genealogically (and spatially) more distant segments. Rather than the
feud rising out of, and expressing, the complementary opposition of
territorial segments ordered through rough correspondence to a lineage structure, Peters asserted that the feud was:

> . . . a violent form of hostility between corporations which has its source
> in the competition for proprietory rights in land and water. This
> competition makes it necessary for groups to combine to prevent the
> encroachments of others in similar combinations and also to expand their
> resources whenever the opportunity arises. (1967: 279)

While Evans-Pritchard, in the quote above, discussed the *structure* of
the feud, Peters concerned himself with the *content* of the feud, the
issues of competition for pastoral resources. However, by
emphasizing the "corporation" as the primary repository for group
"interests", Peters decisively breaks with Evans-Pritchard's relativistic
notion of identity and social structure, for alliances are seen as
resulting from corporate calculations rather than a determinate
political order.

Taking Peters' logic one step further, Emmanuel Marx has recently
suggested that not only do "tribal" level corporations of Sinai
Bedouin form alliances in relation to subsistence needs and resource

competition, but that those processes underlie genealogical relations between them.

> When a group considers some neighboring groups to be genealogically closer to it than others, this may indicate either that these groups are linked by joint interests over and above proximity and common use of territory, or that the topographical boundaries between them are not as clearly demarcated as those with other groups. (Marx 1977: 353)

And, just as interests are conceived to underpin relations between "tribal" corporations, so do they underpin the "tribe" itself, conceived as a *network* of social relations:

> The tribe is then the cumulative end result of the efforts made by individuals and small corporate groups to enlist the cooperation of others, in order to cope with problems of pasture, water, and self-defense. (*Ibid.*: 358)

The segmentary model is, for Peters, a "kind of ideology" (1967: 270), while for Marx it becomes a precipitate of interests, a sort of social map of Sinai topography.

As previously suggested, these two views of the segmentary system represent opposite errors with respect to the relation between models and social action. Evans-Pritchard's great insight was into the meaningful nature of social forms, and as a result of this perceived continuity, he interwove material on the symbols and perceptions of identity and action, and activities themselves. In his assumed continuity between the implications of a model and the domain of events, we can perhaps see the core of a "normative" theory by which the significance of action is attributed to a cultural model, consisting of symbolic units and norms. If I can depict the naive expectations of this "normative" fallacy as a type-one error, perhaps the sceptical views of Peters and Marx can be characterized as involving a type-two error, which categorically asserts the derivative character of the domain of models and its subservience to the domain of events. In this second view, the segmentary model is thought to exist within the domain of ideology, explaining to a group its own social universe, the determinants of which lie elsewhere, such as in the ongoing processes of competition within which production occurs. Here, the meaningful nature of social action, and most importantly productive action, is lost, and the dynamic and directive role of symbolic constructs misplaced within the peripheral functions of ideology and religion. The type-two "reductionist" fallacy not only impoverishes the contents of the models it purports to explain, but yields the tools they offer for the explanation of other domains of social life.

What I have called the type-one "normative" error represents the grounds on which much "symbolic" anthropology is discredited by empirically minded colleagues, who sceptically, though accurately, point out the discontinuity between what people say and what people do, between what is often characterized as "ideals" and the actual state of affairs. In a paper presented to an A.S.A. conference, and published some fifteen years ago, David Schneider pointed out this type-one error as interjecting "muddles in the models", primarily in the work of British alliance theorists. Schneider maintained that Needham confounded the structural principles and rules of kinship classification with the concrete, manifest institutions of real societies (1965: 70), thus misunderstanding the implications of his own theory of kinship (*Ibid.:* 43). With respect to Leach's analysis of segmentary systems, and not irrelevant to Evans-Pritchard's original conception, he further suggested that

> . . . the muddled part of that model is the notion that somehow the seg-ment is not only a conceptual segment, but also in some way a physically distinct and concrete segment. (*Ibid.:* 63)

In Schneider's reading, Lévi-Strauss had demonstrated a more subtle notion of a kinship system which avoided type-one error, it being an "order of ideas, and categories, concepts and rules all 'ordered' by their logical relations" (*Ibid.:* 40). This system of model

> . . . exists and it is real. But its existence is only roughly manifest in the concrete categories and the socially institutionalized rules for relating these categories. Time, ecology, and a variety of factors affect the con-crete manifestation of the principle. (*Ibid.:* 70)

Several elements of Lévi-Strauss' thought, identified here, were later developed by Schneider into an approach to the study of culture (1968; 1976). The most crucial distinction is between the level of symbols and categories, organized in systems, and the level of observ-able behaviour, or, in Levi-Strauss' terms, between levels of *structure* and *event*.

Such a distinction between two *levels* of analysis should not be identified with one outgrowth of the type-two "reductionist" error, which asserts that human societies are divided into two *types* of institutions, those concerned with concrete economic and political activities and the pursuit of "objective" interests, and those con-cerned with abstract logic-meaningful relations and the construction of "subjective" orientations within symbolic systems. This, indeed, is the argument presented by Cohen, whose "two-dimensional man" relates to two distinct kinds of institution, the politico-economic and the religio-symbolic, representing, respectively, the functional and meaningful imperatives of human life, to subsist (in a quite broad sense) and to understand (Cohen 1974). Here, as for Peters, models are forms of ideology serving functions of pattern-integration, reflexive explanation, and religious assertion, and are inappropriately juxtaposed to concrete action of a political and economic sort. In this view, the segmentary lineage model has been misunderstood as a political model, while in actuality it is a symbolic model, not about feuds and fusion, but about definitions of decency and descent, relating man to society and God through ideology. The segmentary system has the *appearance* of a political model, explaining political alliance through principles of genealogically-based complementary opposition, but *in actuality* represents an institution of discourse and thought which only roughly interacts with the contingencies of politics. As a cultural model, the segmentary system is an institution deserving of analytical attention in itself, but should not be confused with a proper sociological model, constructed by the trained observer, whose aim is to account for socio-political forms and behaviour. In this view, Evans-Pritchard's great contribution was the analysis of a Nuer folk model, which unfortunately was confused with a sociological account.

In a modification of this position, Salzman has addressed the question of whether complementary opposition, the core of the segmentary model, really exists. Contrary to Peters' dismissal of the segmentary model as ideology and irrelevant to explanation of such political behaviour as the feud, Salzman maintains that although it is indeed ideology, it is a *political* ideology concerned with its manifest content. But unlike Marx, who would see features of the genealogical representations of existing economic and ecological relationships between individuals and groups, Salzman sees the model neither as a mirror of existing conditions nor as a necessary guide for present political action; rather, he states:

> This folk model is a model of what has been required in the past and is a model for what might be needed in the future. It is a social structure in reserve. (1978: 68-69)

For Salzman, such models and ideologies are symbolic institutions in having "lives of their own, independent of direct and immediate ties to behavior" (*Ibid.*), but are, however, political in nature, though "in reserve". Such folk models and ideologies represent "institution-alized alternatives", which are maintained outside of the behavioural realm through various mechanisms, such as "literary validation", "ritual enactment", and "asserted ideology" (Salzman, this volume). Presumably the segmentary lineage model as depicted by Peters represents an "asserted ideology", which may be activated as a con-crete social structure given a future situation of greater mobility and social instability (1978: 68).

Salzman appears to avoid the pitfalls of either of the two extreme errors, while reflecting the assumptions of both. He appears to accept the distinction between the two institutional "dimensions", the symbolic and the political, but mitigates the dualist disjunction by asserting a reasonable relation between the two, illustrating how the segmentary model is an ideology of political functions. Thus, while he seems to accept the normative promise that behaviour follows from the model, he mitigates the type-one error by maintaining that its implications are for past or future behaviour, rather than necessarily for the more immediate and complex case of the present. In relation to his type-one assumptions, Salzman follows the very useful route of asking questions regarding the forms and contexts of action partinent to complementary opposition, thus establishing ground for a theory of transformations of models into events. The essential problem with respect to type-two position remains, how-ever. Salzman, as well as both Peters and Marx, is left without a sufficient explanation for the socio-political domain, once the model is divorced from it. Peters and Marx both defer to the general nature of "interests" to explain political action, and Salzman concurs, that "the discrepancy between obvious interests and actual behavior, on the one hand, and the folk model, on the other hand, cannot be denied" (Salzman 1978: 68). For Salzman, as for Marx, the apparent continuity between "conditions" and behaviour is established via "interests", and only when the folk model corresponds to conditions and interests does it apparently come out of the reserve into the conceptual front-line. The fundamental weakness of the type-two position, and the ground of its error, lies here: without a symbolic model for political behaviour, whence a theory of interests?

With regard to groups practicing different forms of pastoral pro-duction, one need not go far to identify the fundamental resources for which pastoralists compete: water and pasture. But knowledge of which means are scarce does not imply knowledge of which ends are alternative, that is, of which groups *share* and which groups *conflict* over scarcity. Both Peters and Marx make assumptions about maximization of resources by *individuals,* following on a

formalist economic model: but groups, at various levels of segmentation, rather than individuals are the units which come to conflict
over resources, and with respect to the feud. The segmentary lineage
model originally described by Evans-Pritchard never claimed to
represent a theory of individual behaviour in relation to any rigid
territorial structure of genealogical relations, but was based on the
assumption that individuals of *many* descent groups combined,
through affinal, matrilateral and client ties, as well as the ideal
patrilineal links, to constitute a political segment which would act
together through the *leadership* of a lineage to which the majority
did not belong (Evans-Pritchard 1940b). It appears that for Peters
and Marx, the identification of the ground of a conflict represents a
sufficient explanation for it, that is, in ecological and economic
competition. But the *content* of conflict is not in question, since, in
a given society, persons and groups tend to repeatedly fight over the
same mundane yet essential issues and resources. Rather, it is the
structure of conflict which is crucial, and to which Evans-Pritchard's
model was addressed.

Part 2

I have suggested that the holistic stances of both the "normative"
and "reductionist" theories represent pretensions behind which can
be detected various forms of dualism. In recent contributions to
anthropological theory, we can find more pronounced expressions of
philosophical and methodological dualism, the doctrine of the
irreducible difference between mental and material phenomena.
Harris has recently reasserted his conviction that there are "two
radically different kinds of phenomena", behavioural and mental,
which demand qualitatively different programs of inquiry (1979: 31).
Curiously, this assertion within the framework of cultural
materialism virtually echoes similar statements within the framework
of phenomenology, by Holy and Stuchlik (this volume):

> There are basically two qualitatively different kinds of things that
> constitute the anthropologist's data: – things which exist "on the ground"
> and which are (at least partly) observable, and – things which exist in
> people's heads and are, therefore, unobservable.

Despite their divergent foci of analytical interest, cultural
materialism and phenomenology appear to share a common
epistemological framework, articulated through a common metaphorical currency. The imagery used to signify the "two kinds of

things" is concrete, evoking order in its proper place: "on the ground" and "in people's heads", of course, mixes the metaphor. "On-the-ground" appears to connote concreteness and stability as opposed to the intangible flighty associations of the unspoken "above-the-ground". But, "inside-people's-heads" connotes privacy, hiddeness, and inaccessibility, as opposed to the implicit "outside-people's-heads", which evokes the public, accessible and objective. The unity of the two metaphors can be demonstrated, however, if the internal relation between symbols of the body and symbols of the earth is examined. For if "on" is to "above" the ground, as "outside" is to "inside" people's heads, heads lie "above" feet, which stand securely "on" the ground. In both cases, stable and objective reality is contrasted to individual, unpredictable and subjective reality, and the metaphors are one.

The metaphor contains at once an objectivist and a subjectivist bias. As opposed to the subjectivist bias that a "subjective phenomenon" exists which may represent an object of anthropological inquiry, one must insist that it is by necessity objectively mediated if it is to be an object of inquiry! This is the essence of Derrida's critique of Husserl's notion of the "solitary mental life", in which one finds the "presence" of "pure expression" which:

> . . . is present not in nature, since only indication takes place in nature and across space, but is consciousness. Thus it is present to an "inner" intuition or perception. (Derrida 1973: 40)

Derrida insists not only that

> The lived experience of another is made known to me only insofar as it is mediately indicated by signs involving a physical side. The very idea of "physical", "physical side" is conceivable in its specific differences only on the basis of this movement of indication. (*Ibid.:* 39),

but that there is no "solitary mental life" without the process of "indication" or actual discourse, that there is no "primordial perception" for the "difference involved in 'signs' " is introduced "at the core of what is 'primordial' " (*Ibid.:* 45-46). "Intentions" are not inaccessible and private affairs, secrets hiding behind acts, but the forms which signs adopt as acts.

This critique of a type of phenomenological absolutism, which is indeed vulnerable to such criticisms as Harris' (1979), draws from a half-century of commentary on dualistic theories of mind in the philosophy of language. In an important demonstration, Wittgenstein denied the possibility of a truly "private language" which would appear to be necessary for a non-social mental life:

> Now, what about the language which describes my inner experiences and which only I myself understand? *How* do I use words to stand for my sensations? – as we ordinarily do? Then are my words for sensations tied up with my natural expressions of sensations? In that case my language is not a "private" one.(1958: 256)

This approach, like Derrida's, reveals the dependence of private on public knowledge. To understand human discourse does not require knowledge of private intentions of the speaker; on the contrary, an account of "inner" experience does require an understanding of the nature of the shared cultural "language" which makes it possible. Pertinent to our inquiry is Strawson's account of Wittgenstein's hostility to "the doctrine of privacy":

> For the worn and dangerous "outward" and "inner" we may substitute "shared" and "unshared" . . . a common language for describing and reporting requires general agreement in judgements. So for a (descriptive) word or phrase to belong to a common language, it is essential that *the occasions on which it is right to apply it should provide shared experiences of a certain kind,* the existence of which is connected with the rightness of applying the word.(1954: 41)

In short, most of the things which are tritely said to be "in people's heads" either are *not* in any meaningful sense "in people's heads" since we use mentalistic phraseology to depict the intellectual aspect of overt acts (cf. Ryle 1949), or when they *are* in an obvious sense "in people's heads", such as in the case of images, mental arithmetic, talking to oneself, etc., they are *not* "different kinds of things" from observable acts, as was asserted by both Harris and Holy-Stuchlik.

Side by side with the subjectivist bias is the objectivist bias, most prominent in cultural materialism. If an account of inner experience requires public meaning, is an account of "observable" entities, or "bodily motions", in Harris' description of behavioral phenomena (1979: 31), possible, independent of such meaning? The radical objectivist view would assert that the "on-the-ground" reality of "observables" is self-evident, and exists independent of the significance given to that data by actors or by scientific observers. Both Harris and Holy-Stuchlik distance themselves from this naive inductionist model of scientific observation, and discuss the role of scientific theory and expectation in generating "observable" data. (Harris 1979: 12; Holy and Stuchlik, this volume). Harris, however, ignores the implications of this insight for a theory of activity itself, which represents by necessity an admixture of interdependent intentions and expectations (that is, meaning), on the one hand, and observable vehicles or signals, on the other hand. The self-evident notion of "behaviour" is vulnerable in prescisely the same way that the nominalist theory of language is vulnerable, in the assumption that the external referent *is* the meaning, while the critical question is always "what *aspect* of the referent is the meaning?" which presupposes a prior concept of the *sense* (or concept) of which the behaviour is a manifestation. Wittgenstein discussed the problem of ostensive definition:

> The definition of the number two, "That is called 'two' " — pointing to two nuts — is perfectly exact. —But how can two be defined like that? The person one gives the definition to doesn't know what one wants to call two; he will suppose that "two" is the name given to *this* group of nuts! . . . He might make the opposite mistake; when I want to assign a name to this group of nuts, he might understand it as a numeral. And he might equally well take the name of a person, of which I give an ostensive definition, as that of a colour, of a race, or even of a point of the compass. That is to say: an ostensive definition can be variously interpreted in *every* case. (1958: 14e)

As a comparative discipline, anthropology is especially vulnerable to the objectivist fallacy, since it can easily misappropriate exotic behavioral patterns to its Western standard if it remains outside the symbolic universe of those non-Western societies under consideration. There is nothing "given" in the strictly "observable", for the observer must always define the significance of the observed object, before it is "given"; in cultural studies, the assertion of the observer's viewpoint over that of the culture under study represents not a difference of objective over subjective, but a dogmatic (and tautological) postulate of observer's subjectivity as objectivity rather than pursuing an objective account of the cultural subjectivity. From such a vantage, the issue of whether the analysis is right or wrong is lost, for apart from objective cultural subjectivity, any standard of accuracy or adequacy is lost.

In short, I deny that there are two "kinds of things" that constitute the anthropologist's data, for there is only one source of data: observation.[2] And, although modes of observation and modes of manifestation are far from being identical, they are divided by no simple duality of the mental and the material, or even the verbal and the non-verbal. The notion "objective" and "on-the-ground" data either is inadequate, in positing a "behaviour flow" independent of its significance, or is redundant, in asserting that an observed activity has indeed occurred. Obversely, the notion "subjective" and "internal" data is either a contradiction, in positing a non-observable data, or an impossibility, in referring to a strictly individual interpretation of meaning (for meaning is by definition shared), which, were it possible, would not constitute *anthropological* data, for it would be irrelevant to an understanding of social and cultural forms. While neither objectivist nor subjectivist *stances* are methodologically impossible, alone or in combination one can maintain that both objective and subjective *aspects* are entailed by the nature of the social phenomenon. The source of anthropological data is *strictly* "objective", being external, public, reiterative and replicable, and necessarily observable; it is, as well, *strictly* "subjective", being constituted through the culturally defined intentions of actors, referring by necessity to levels of signification not given in the form of physical sign vehicles, and reflecting the subjective processes of observation. In short, the subjects and objects of anthropological inquiry are "symbols", cultural unions of physical and material vehicles (often words) with meaningful and conceptual referents. Such cultural symbols represent admixtures of the objective and subjective, if so can be described signifiers and signifieds, each of which depends upon the other for its specific existence.

The anthropologist encounters, through the experience of a novel field setting, a welter of words and activities, objects and things, which only gradually become well-defined and meaningful, as well as related to intellectually conceived issues and hypotheses. Wittgenstein reflected on problems of language in a way which speaks directly to the anthropological concern with the phenomenology of field work:

> We also say of some people that they are transparent to us. It is, however, important as regards this observation that one human being can be a complete enigma to another. We learn this when we come into a strange country with entirely strange traditions; and, what is more, even given a mastery of the country's language. We do not *understand* the people. (And not because of not knowing what they are saying to themselves). We cannot find our feet with them, (1958: 223e)

Unlike the objectivist definition of anthropology in *terms* of transparency (c.f. Harris 1979: 44-45), the task of anthropology might be better conceptualized in Wittgenstein's terms, as the transformation of enigma *into* transparency. That is to say, observations must be rendered as events in terms of some order of models, rendered as meaningful structures combined with rules of use.

In Maasailand, one may initially be struck by the apparently formless comings-and-goings of young men, initially indistinguishable because of similarity of dress, demeanor and decorum. It is by "objective" observation, simply being told, or a combination of the two, that one learns that they are *Il-murran,* literally "the-circumcised-ones", often glossed in English (by Maasai anglophones) as "warriors", or that they are distinguished from other age-grades by the long growth of their hair, which is bound in the back in a single braid and lacquered with red ochre, and the wearing of a single one-piece garment, thrown toga-like over the left shoulder? Only by being told did I know when I met the young men known as the *Ilaiguenak,* the age-set "spokesmen", defined by the British — with great satisfaction — as "chiefs", a name which lasts as an English rendering to today. Later, I learned that they alone could carry smooth, polished black clubs, functioning as sceptres, as opposed to ordinary men who carried ordinary but functional clubs and sticks, and ritual officers, who carried long bamboo poles, surmounted by ostrich feathers.

Across Maasai sections, it takes a trained eye to detect the subtle but intentional shifts of apparel, a different tint of red ochre, a slightly thicker bead or a changing pattern of decoration. When one Maasai meets another who is unknown to him, they very quickly share knowledge of their names, their families of origin, their lineages (which most often entails their clans), their age-set, and the immediate locus of departure and destination. With a bit of information, the knowledgeable one can reconstruct the remainder. Often, family name implies lineage and clan, and perhaps section, location and sub-location; if not, then a few questions regarding domicile fills in the rest. Somewhat more laborious is the process of gathering anthropological knowledge, for inevitably the anthropologist lacks a high degree of implicit knowledge which can be evoked by a simple bit of information; but the process is not qualitatively different in nature. One meets individual young men, but gradually transforms them into "warriors" of such-and-such a section, location, sub-location and neighbourhood, or such-and-such a lineage, and of such-and-such an age-set.

What represents the "observable", "on-the-ground" reality of anthropological encounters? Sensory stimuli of vision, sound and touch, or the perceptual realizations of form, color and voice? Does one witness human bodies and wood sticks, or "warriors" and "sceptres" of office? Similarly, does one meet individuals, persons, or members of specific political descent and age-groups? As in the more limited case of "interests", "observable reality" cannot be identified prior to the definition of the meaningful context in which the object of analysis is placed. Given the appropriate knowledge, one observes *at the same time,* and in the same objects, "persons", "warriors", "spokesmen" and "individuals", as well as "sticks-in-general", "sticks-in-particular", "clubs", "emblems of office" and "sceptres". Only for the naive observer are "sticks" more transparent than "emblems", or "spokesmen" more enigmatic than "persons" or "warriors", and research involves, hopefully, the progressive loss of observational innocence, as the enigmas of gross observation are transformed into the transparencies of identity, through the analytical construction of mediating cultural models.

If a semiotic perspective grants a certain precedent to the informants' judgements in construing patterns of signification in action, this should not imply either that other means of observation and inference are not also to be used, or that the semiotic model of the cultural system is the same as a conscious model founded on informant discourse. Indeed, the discontent of type-two theories with the use of informant's statements to construct simple normative models, by which action is generated and explained, is sustained by a semiotic anthropology which recognizes that people inadequately render their own grammars. However, the type-two epistemological rupture between thought and action is not upheld, for what we observe is not thought but speech, which is itself the most appropriate prototype of human *action.* Accepting the type-one program of accounting for the meaning of action, a semiotic perspective must explain the variety of verbal to non-verbal modalities of symbolic action (most actions being a unitary combination of the two) taking informant discourse as a form to be explained rather than an exclusively privileged domain of explanation. In the last assessment, type-one theories appear motivated to explain the comprehensibility, cohesion and stability of social life, while type-two theories rebut with emphasis on the unpredictable, actor-inflected and unique character of action. If analysis is to accept the charge of accounting for both these simultaneously valid aspects of human action, perhaps it is through the contrast of codes and events that a semiotic anthropology can define its program.

In a cultural code, a system of categories, representing units of identity, and a system of norms, representing predicates of identity, may be inter-related, and *generally* related to the domain of events. One analytical enterprise would investigate the various relationships between symbolic categories and predicates, under the assumption that the significance of any one construct can only be revealed through its placement in a symbolic *system* of contrasts with other similar constructs. In the segmentary lineage case, a series of lineages may be placed within a hierarchical structure and related to norms of relative solidarity and military consolidation, to form a segmentary code.

But symbolic identities and norms are invariably ascribed to and embodied in persons, for whom identities and norms are never singular or unambiguous, but rather combined in *sets,* of varying degrees of compatibility. Evans-Pritchard's models depicted a compromise formation between lineage and residential codes, and such compromises are the inevitable ingredients of the domain of events. In order to interpret the significance of a given act, one must invariably parcel out the categories and norms which may relate to several different codes. But if, by definition, codes are general and events are specific, the relation between the two must entail a system of *transformations* between them, which combine symbolic units and norms, and ascribe them to particular individuals in certain contexts. In observation or action, such transformations may be described in terms of rules-of-use. "Constitutive" rules indicate when an individual or object stands for or is an instantiation of a certain symbolic category, in the Maasai case when an individual is a *moran,* or when a certain *moran* is a "spokesman". Analytically separate are "prescriptive" rules, which indicate what such persons may be expected to do, and when and to what end. The classic segmentary model is an articulation of constituents and prescriptions of a particular sort, but includes very few of the rules by which these are combined with codes of other sorts, such as those of military strategy or ecology, and transformed into action. But without such analysis, it is difficult to see how events can be interpreted, codes constructed, and models assessed.

Much of type-two analysis involved the attempt to empirically refute models born out of discourse by reference to the observation of events. But the valid denial, by type-two theory, of a determinant continuity between *conscious* models or articulated norms and specific actions, as proposed by type-one theory, has often been unjustifiably extended to the relationship between meaning and action in general, or between *cultural* models and events. It is a human predicament continually faced by anthropology, that models are produced in self-conscious commentary on other domains of events, but are never sufficient to explain those events, while more adequate models must use precisely such cultural implements as those commentaries represent. In short, there is a necessarily continuous hermeneutical re-cycling of symbolic elements and con-figurations between conscious models and cultural models, which broaden and objectify the self-fulfilling perspective of the former, and narrow and render culturally valid and subjective the analytical aridity of the latter.

In the final section of this paper, I will attempt to demonstrate the value of a semiotic anthropology for the analysis of events, with reference to a specific occurrence in Maasailand, and by appeal to a segmentary model of the Maasai political system. After a discussion of the intransigence of symbolic models before empiricist assessment, I will address the question of the symbolic constituents of both codes and events, and demonstrate the programs by which they can be investigated.

Part 3

In 1972, members of the Purko section of Maasai descended the Western Rift Valley escarpment from Narok District, in Kenya, and crossed into the north-western side of the Lodokilani section in Kajiado District. It was the dry season, and their immediate aim was to gain access to the pasture and water near the Uaso Ng'iro river. But during this ingression of livestock and people, the Purko military force over-ran several Lodokilani villages, and reportedly killed around 15 persons of the Keramatian sub-location, threatening to run members of the section out of the entire area. At the next assault, a consolidated force involving several age-sets from the Shompole location of the Lodokilani, of which Keramatian is a part, met the Purko and reportedly routed them, killing around 45 of the aggressors by using bows-and-arrows, in addition to spears and swords. Government forces prevented any further combat.

Based on quite different data gained through inquiry regarding patterns of sectional affinities and alliances, I developed a model of the territorial and political order of the Maasai, which assumed a segmentary form (Galaty 1977). Unlike the segmentary lineage system, the Maasai system involves descent groups which are to a significant degree dispersed and do *not* form the basis for the exercise of territorially-based political functions. Maasai political segments are constituted through a segmentarily organized system of age-set regimental units, and processes of higher-order decision-making and social control are exercised through age-set relationships by age-set leaders or "spokesmen" (*illaiguenak*).[4]

While "sections" (*iloshon*) such as Purko or Lodokilani represent the highest level of formal political organization, the "central Maasai" sections are grouped into two great clusters of political moieties. Included in the Enaiposha cluster are the Purko, Damat, Keekonyokie and Dalalekutuk, all but the last primarily found in

Narok District, while included in the Kaputie cluster are the Kaputie-proper, the Lodokilani and the Matapato sections, all found in Kajiado District. Consolidating to form a section such as the Lodokilani are lower-level locations, sub-locations and neighbourhoods. Each segment in the Maasai system is named, associated with a territory, related to other segments in a determinate order, and is, linguistically, culturally and socially, signified. Each is, in short, a symbolic unit. (See Fig. 1).

Categories				Levels
Maa People	Other People			"Ethnicity" (?)
Central Maasai	Peripheral Maasai			"Nation" (?)
Kaputie		Enaiposha		Sectional Cluster
Lodokilani	Kaputie-Proper	Purko	Others	Section
Shompole	Kikonito			Location
Keramatian	Shompole-Proper			Sub-Location
Uaso Ng'iro		(Invaders)		Neighbourhood

Fig. 1 The Maasai Segmentary Structure

Our questions are these: To what extent can the pattern of conflict demonstrated in the reported event be explained by the segmentary model, and to what extent can that event be used to assess the model? Although the threatened territory was that of the Keramatian sub-location, the actual combatants were the warriors of the entire Shompole location. Massing occurred to the locational level between two adjacent sub-locations, although the structural model would have predicated that the significant level of complementary opposition should have been that of the super-sections, between the Enaiposha and Kaputie clusters, engaging the entire Central Maasai.

Such evidence led Peters to reject the segmentary model for the Bedouin, since it appeared to fail the empirical test. His type-two theory represents the disillusionment that there was no mechanical fit between generalized norms and specific actions, leading him to the conclusion that if models do not determine, they must ideologically express reality. Of course with such high expectations the model can only fail; conversely, with low expectations, the model can only succeed. In response to Peters, Salzman asks not whether the model fails but whether it succeeds in manifesting itself in any way. He suggests that:

> . . . if ideology is not the sole determining force in actual patterns of behavior, it may nonetheless play an important guiding and constraining role (Salzman 1978: 67)

and he investigates subtle influences of segmentary ideology on behaviour such as restraining conflict, encouraging mediation, modulating commitments, etc. Not considered as *just* ideology, the model is justified through *some* role in action, albeit limited.

Salzman shares the empiricist assumption of Peters, however, that the legitimacy of the symbolic model can be ascertained through the measure of the behavioural reality, in terms of which it may be falsified or verified. Subtle manifestations are seen as no less significant than the grand and unambiguous manifestations which eluded Peters' inquiry, though the strength of the hypothesis of efficacy is weakened. While Peters appears to implicitly assume the principle of falsification, which holds that a single good empirical refutation falsifies the hypothetical model, Salzman appears to assume the less stringent principle of verification, which holds that a single valid instance confirms the model. This latter opinion seems to indicate that socio-cultural phenomena may be fundamentally intractable with respect to falsification, since *any* case of verification validates the model. Indeed, if models are conceived to exist in strictly ideological form the lack of *any* empirical verification may not necessarily falsify it (c.f. Salzman, this volume).

More subtle evidence than the fact of military massing can be adduced for the test of the efficacy of the segmentary model for the Maasai. While massing *did* occur up to the level of the Shompole location, massing *would* have occurred up to the Lodokilani section if the warriors of the complementarily opposed Kilonito location had been able to arrive at the battle site before governmental intervention, for they were *on their way*. This fact alone supports the notion that the defence was not just of a material strip of peripheral land, but of that land conceived as the Lodokilani section itself. While members of the Keramatian and Shompole-proper sub-locations actually fought, we must ask "As *who* did they fight?" By virtue of their consolidation, it would appear that they fought *as* the Shompole location; but by virtue of the salience of the section, calls for assistance and the rapid response of the Kilonito location, it would appear that they fought *as* the Lodokilani section, despite circumstances which prevented sectional massing.

The significance of the super-sectional cluster is more elusive than that of the section. While to my knowledge it was never suggested that other sections of the Kaputie cluster would consolidate with the Lodokilani for the purpose of the battle, in the 19th century such consolidation by warrior batallions occurred, not only to the super-sectional level, but also the level of all Central Maasai, including the Kisongo cluster, who joined to oppose the northern Ilaikipiak Maasai, whom they jointly defeated and dispersed (Thomson 1883). One could conclude that such high level of massing does not occur today because of state-influence on the system itself (super-sectional clusters largely represented by "districts"), or because the level of threats experienced today, with rapid government intervention, is not adjudged to warrant that level of force. However, the significance of these high levels of structure may lie elsewhere. For instance, to my knowledge no significant conflict has been reported between the Lodokilani section and other adjacent sections of the same super-sectional cluster, although from Peters' perspective they would experience greater competition for resources due to increased proximity. Clashes occur, of course, at all levels of segmentation, but it would appear that the normal use of deadly force (i.e. spears, swords, bows-and-arrows) is sanctioned only at the super-sectional level. Thus, it would appear that despite the failure of massing to that level, the Uaso Ng'iro battle was fought *as* a super-sectional encounter.

A more complex code of symbols, involving implicit attributions of identity and levels of force, attests to the relevance of a segmentary structure, despite the empirical absence of any mechanical massing to the appropriate level. Indeed, one must ask *when* particular events do indeed represent, in fact, instances of the general segmentary code, *before* they can be used to empirically assess it, clearly an analytical paradox. Cultural rules-of-use may explain away apparent failures, by qualifying that massing only takes place when militarily necessary and strategically possible, or simply that the model entails the applicability of levels of identity and means of force, but not actual combat. Without appeal to such rules, it is difficult to see how generalized models can be used to explicate events, or events used to assess models. In effect, empiricism is itself radically qualified, for such an approach must rely on non-observable codes of significance in order to even begin its task.

This discussion has assumed, however, the intrinsic referential link between the model and action, rather than considering the model *itself* as a form of action. Indigenous respondents may cast doubt on empiricist construct validation in several ways, such as by making excuses that massing wasn't necessary, that massing would have happened if there had been time, or simply that massing was not appropriate for several possible reasons of a contextual nature. Further, respondents could express indignation that massing did not occur, thus verifying the hypothesis of the reality of the model, while at the same time verifying its non-instantiation! As a form of discourse, the segmentary model may represent a pervasive and significant reality, even beyond any function as a blueprint for action. The model may be "performative" (c.f. Austin 1962), by acting through the rhetorical prediction of massing, the use in verbal address of labels which presuppose segmentary identity, implicit restraint on the use of force, or even the protest of failed alliances. But *even* if such performative manifestations do not occur, the model is thus not proven false, but rather non-relevant, as other models assume greater prominence in establishing frameworks of thought and action. The relevance of another model need not necessarily exclude the first, however, for analytically and culturally separable codes may well be combined to form specific events, as codes of segmentation, age-relations, seasonal-cycles, ethno-ecology and state/local relations surely inter-twined to constitute the Maasai event in question.

The program of anthropology can focus on the problems of systemic models or cultural codes, each leading to a *variety* of performative manifestations, or on problems of action and events, each leading from its own unique combination back to a *variety* of cultural models (c.f. Schneider 1976). As will be seen the semiotic key to the analysis of cultural codes, such as the segmentary model, lies in the mechanism of metaphor, while the key to the understanding of events lies with the mechanism of metonymy, operating through constitutive and prescriptive rules. Rather than representing exclusive claims to the same terrain, as do type-one and type-two theories, these two orientations to the study of codes and events represent complementary and inter-dependent programs, each of which provides the content for the other.

Insofar as events may be interpreted to be instances of a norm of complementary opposition and to involve persons with respect to their segmentarily defined identities, they may be seen as "metonymically" related to those principles and identities, in two respects. First, the event − or an aspect of the event − represents a sign of the larger principle or segment as a part to a whole. That is to say that persons are living "synecdoches", to use a narrower class of metonymical relations, (cf. Sapir 1977) when they adopt a collective identities and act as *representatives* of that whole. Human identity being a complex melange of ascriptions, this semiotic dimension clearly depends on context for its specification. For instance, when a warrior in battle is in mortal danger, he calls not for his age-mates — who invariably surround him as both allies and foes — but for his clan-mates, shifting to the foreground the larger whole to which he calls and thereby signifies as a part at that precise moment. Second, an aspect of the event may be interpreted as an outcome or an effect of a cause bound to the segmentary model being evoked. That is, actions may represent living metonyms, when they emanate from norms which they signify as effects to their causes. The choice of weapons or willingness to use mortal force in a particular conflict thus metonymically signifies, if so interpreted, a special level of segmentary identity and its normative entailments, in the Maasai case the section. From this perspective, the process of analyzing an event involves the interpretation of signs and symbols of a metonymical order, of establishing — by use of contextual rules of constitutive and prescriptive sorts — just what aspect of which model should be invoked to account for the message being conveyed. The interpretive question becomes, what symbolic whole does this observed part signify, and what symbolic cause does this observed effect signify? The answer may well include several symbolic models, which, as previously developed, combine to form the specific case.

It has been here asserted that the 1972 event near the Uaso Ng'iro was constituted through a cultural code for political segmentation, and that this order cannot itself be explained by the material conditions which existed at the time of the event. This view runs contrary to the perspective of Peters and Marx, for whom our instance of Maasai combat, involving dry-season movement, could be explained by competition over the pastoral resources of the west bank of the Uaso Ng'iro river, conflict by a few neighbourhood corporate groups who had the most to gain or lose by the incident. But, clearly, community interests are inadequate to explain either the germination or full-flowering of the conflict into warfare, since proximity alone is never sufficient to define opposing interests. Communities are never contiguous in themselves, for they are always communities or villages *of* such-and-such a group. In my experience, and in recent Maasai history, significant conflict has followed systematic ingression of territory of one section by members of another *only* when they were members of the opposed sectional clusters! The question of when pastoral ingression leads to an offer of hospitality, with general acceptance of the obligation to share scarce pastoral resources, and when it leads to defence of resources and violence, appears answerable only in terms of a model of political structure which defines the terms of relationship, together with an account of the context of group negotiations and interactions, by which the terms are applied. The conflict under consideration involved an encounter by opposing sectional clusters at the farthest reaches of segmental distance, not simply an encounter by contiguous communities, and involved rapid and unmitigated aggression, preceded by threats rather than negotiations over access to resources.

Rather than assert, with Peters and Marx, and ultimately Salzman, that "interests" determine patterns of conflict and cooperation, and eventually political and kinship structures, I would, to the contrary, maintain that interests operate according to a logic of structures which define the interplay of cultural ends and social means. To say, as does Marx, that the "tribe" is a unit of subsistence is only a truism, since the network of relations considered by him to underpin the use of resources and lines of exchange invariably presuppose higher level units such as the "tribe" (Marx 1977). The type-two theory lacks the symbolic ingredients for defining just when scarce resources are *ours,* to be mutually defended and reciprocally used, or *mine,* to be protected from all comers.

But if the segmentary models represents a necessary condition for the explanation of our instance of combat, it is clear that it does not represent a sufficient condition. Indeed, no model of *general* obligations, such as for segmentary solidarity, is sufficient to account for the manifestations of *specific* obligations and actions, such as consolidating under certain conditions. Clearly, what is needed is an appeal to a cultural code of interests, which would represent the needs, motives and ends influencing action. Clearly, the structure of bovine pastoralism defines Maasai interest in certain types of pasture, water and salt resources but does not define the structure of competition over these resources, which we have found in the segmentary model. But it is inadequate, I would maintain, to argue that either the competition over resources or the norms of segmentary solidarity represents the proximate or efficient cause of the event, the other representing an ultimate or final cause (cf. Dyson-Hudson 1979). In the present case, it would be very difficult to state whether the proximate cause of combat was concern for protecting resources (or appropriating them) or generally defending a group by fighting together, for both aspects were clearly part of the conscious symbolic definition of the situation. But the two "aspects" are not equivalent, for the demands of competition always push to the fore, but are always generated by a specific appropriation of situational conditions by the more general principles of identity. And, in the extreme case, the nature of opposed identity appears to represent in itself sufficient motivation for conflict, while other opposed interests defined by the structure of identity move to the background. The segmentary model appears to represent a central nexus in which aspects of the historical situation are ordered and accorded valuation by a specific calculus of complementarities. Whether one factor of the situation formulates a more conscious calculus than another, that is, may be "foregrounded", seems of little relevance in determining the range of significant factors and their pervasive structuring.

A sufficient condition for explanation of the event would necessarily look to the historical factors which supplied the specific content for the conflict as segmentarily defined. Competition for dry-season resources may seem sufficient, but the intensity of combat may well relate to several other factors which heightened concern over what may have been a minor and temporary occupation, rather than an expropriation of territory.

First, the dry-season was exacerbated by the longer term drought, which penetrated southward from the Sahel through the Rift Valley corridor. Not only were pastoral resources thus more in demand, but the unseasonal nature of this general impoverishment of pasture suggested that incursion might well result in long-term claims rather than short-term use. Secondly, in line with this final point, the Purko section was widely known as the most expansionary of Maasai groups, and friction already existed between sections of the Kaputie cluster and a Purko fragment which, together with other fragments of the Enaiposha cluster, occupied certain areas of Kajiado District. The colonial demarcation of the boundary between Kajiado and Narok Districts had in effect straightened the irregular line between the Purko and Lodokilani sections, so the Purko considered themselves not to be invading foreign pastures, but occupying territory they claimed. Thirdly, the issue of land claims was in the early 1970s becoming of great consequence, since the global Maasai reserve system was in the first stages of transformation to a system of individual and group free-hold. In this setting, disputes over the legally informal frontiers between different territorial segments, in particular the sections, assumed significance beyond the conventional shifting uses of certain areas, for legal title in perpetuity was at stake (cf. Galaty 1980).

Emphasis on the structural and hence symbolic underpinnings of conflict need not imply a dismissal of material factors and consequences such as these just discussed, but neither should such factors be conceived as the underlying, hidden and sufficient causes of conflict for they invariably are well-conceptualized and play a role in the conscious calculus of political tactics and strategies. It is only within an underlying organizational structure, such as the segmentary model, that such factors are constituted as interests and serve to mobilize collective action of a specific order. The fact that the pattern of loyalties and alliances may, in a process of escalation of conflict, be projected forward as the most salient ground of individual motivations, in apparent submergence and disguise of material issues, need not lead to the conclusion that those patterns are ideological while the underlying interests are real, for in probing the structure of those interests, it is to the segmentary structure that we return.

If events involve metonymical relations of instantiation, representation, and causality, such as have just been described (though analysis of events is rarely pursued with awareness of their semiotic dimensions), they can be shown to draw their content from a metaphorical grounding within a field of cultural codes. And, though codes are often best considered as relatively bounded systems, I would suggest that they may be usefully conceived, as well as interconnected in chains, for in answer to the question of the specific properties of one code, another code responds through metaphor.

The Maasai segmentary code is based on age-set rather than descent-group solidarity, and the key to the model is the symbol of the age-mate and commonality based on the shared blood of circumcision, rather than the symbol of the agnate and commonality based on the shared blood of kinship and descent, as is true in such segmentary lineage systems as that of the Nuer. The Maasai model adjoins temporally adjacent age-sets to core warrior sets, rather than adjoining secondary kin through marriage to core or "aristocratic" lineages. At the same time, the temporal sequence of age-sets and grades is structured by the alignment of alternate sets into two great atemporal "streams" (c.f. Spencer 1976), which serve to establish lines of authority and leadership between generations; these "streams" may be contrasted to the two great moieties which operate at the apex of the clanship system but which *generally* serve no specific political function.

But although the age-set system largely supplants the lineage-clanship system in political importance, the domain of kinship and clanship offers an elaborated symbolic system by which the domain of age-sets is defined and organized. Circumcision is explicitly seen as a re-birth, by which an individual is recruited to a specific age-set; age-set affiliation is determined when age-set sponsors of the preceding alternative set (*Olpiron,* lit. the fire-stick), make fire over the spot of the circumcision re-birth and thus claim their age-set paternity. The kinship terminology and rules of incest which obtain between the two alternate groups signify a relationship of paternity and filiation, while adjacent age-sets of the opposing "stream" are conceived as in-laws, as relatives by marriage. Just as the patrilineal group appropriates the idiom of fertility and birth from the in-marrying mother, so the age-set system appropriates the symbolic complex of generativity, birth and filiation from the descent system in order to define relations within a given "stream", and from the symbolic complex of marriage and exchange to define relations between "streams". Appropriately, the age-set system feeds back upon the kinship and lineage system by serving as the mechanism by which generational relations within the family and lineage are defined. (See Fig. 2).

Age-Groups			Age-Grades
Stream 1		Stream 2	
"Fa/Son"	"In-Law"	"Fa/Son"	
		Age-Class$_4$	Elders$_2$
Age-Class$_3$			Elders$_1$
		Age-Class$_2$	Warriors$_2$
Age-Class$_1$	(Right-Hand Age-Set		Initiated "Warriors"$_1$
	Left-Hand Age-Set		
		Next Age-Set	Initiation Uninitiated Boys

Fig. 2   The Maasai Age-Set System

In spite of this reciprocal dialectic, the age-set system decisively supercedes and encompasses the descent system by providing the basis for the constitution of the political order. The symbols of "one blood" (*O-sarge obo*) and "birth" (*a-isho*, lit. to bear or to calve) best express the solidarity of descent-groups, while the blood-inflected symbols of "circumcision" (*E-murrata*) and "rebirth" express the solidarity of age-groups. Similarly, the symbol of "pasture" (*Shoo*, lit. herding, pasturing) captures the solidarity of political segments (*Ol-osho*, lit. country; denotes segmentary levels, especially sections or locations; *Ol-chore*, friend; *Shoreisho*,' friend-ship), and at each level of segmentation there exists notions of a-kinship, for it is recognized that segments are "one people", and that opposed segments were "once one", but were "later divided". Through cultural dialectics, the symbolism of one domain is reformulated and used to define the content of another domain, the solidarity of "pasture" interacting with forms of solidarity defined by "birth", "blood", "rebirth", and "circumcision" (c.f. Galaty 1979)[5].

As part of a critique of two approaches to the study of cultural models, I have tried in this paper to demonstrate the difficulty of accounting for social action — for historical events in this case — without the assistance of models, and the intransigence of models to refutation by events alone, due to their often elusive manifestation in diverse cultural performatives. In the Maasai case, I have analyzed the continuing relevance of a segmentary order not only in the determination of patterns of military conflict but in the structuring of material interests relevant not only to pastoralism but to political dynamics in the context of the state. I have not stated that the segmentary model is the only factor determining Maasai political action, but on the contrary, that it invariably combines with other relevant systems in determining specific events. While one can see a tendency for innovations and other elements of social change to be assimilated according to the logic of various Maasai models, I have not suggested that this fact represents a denial of the modern world by Maasai, or its impact on the Maasai by myself. Rather, I am denying a social theory which uses a naive notion of the timeless and unmediated efficacy of models to deny the relevance of cultural frameworks altogether, and to find the explanation for social action and change in a pre-cultural domain of material forces and implications. My suggestion is that when one model appears inadequate, after context is considered, to explain a set of events, one might more fruitfully look to another relevant model than away from the matrix of symbolic forms altogether.

In the dialectic of structure and event, the segmentary order served to render meaningful the colonial division between districts and states within Maasailand, but those legal distinctions have themselves inflected the segmentary order to the point that Kajiado versus Narok Maasai is a more salient distinction than that between Kaputie versus Enaiposha Maasai, and the distinction between Kenya and Tanzanian Maasai more significant (in some respects) than that between those two clusters and the Kisongo cluster. It is likely that as land adjudication is completed, symbols of "pasture" will be less salient than symbols of "land", the latter inscribed on deeds, and that units of "Group Ranches" may become more significant than units of sub-locations and locations, on which they are partially based. But such outcomes of social change will not prove to refute the segmentary model but to transform it, or perhaps to marginalize it. We should beware of contrasting "tradition" to "change" as ossified "folk models" are to political and economic forces emanating from national and international settings, culturally-defined responses as non-progressive, rational responses based on material calculations as progressive. To account for the action of Maasai in changing context will require, in the same fashion, an account of cultural models of modernity, which might embody aspects of a segmentary structure, elements of a more global Kenyan and African outlook, and increased emphasis on the individual. But the predicament of anthropology will remain the same, neither to deduce events from models without concern for context and symbolic combinations, nor to analyze events apart from models, as if situations and interests were sufficient to determine and explain the complex activities produced by cultural beings.

Acknowledgements

An earlier draft of this paper was presented to the Department of Anthropology at McGill University. For useful comments I am indebted to Lee Drumond, Philip Salzman, Ole Sena Sarone, Don Attwood and Peter Gutkind, but have made selective use of their advice and so must accept full responsibility for the form of the present paper.

Unless otherwise cited, the ethnographic information related here was acquired during field research in Kenyan Maasailand in 1974-75, supported by a NSF Doctoral Dissertation research grant (# 74-24627). I would like to express appreciation for the hospitality and assistance provided by the Bureau of Educational Research of the University of Nairobi and the Department of Anthropology of the University of Chicago, as well as for the generosity of so many members of the Ilodokilani section who gave me help and support during my stay with them. Thanks are also due to Thea Pawlikowska and Anna Verilli at the Department of Anthropology at McGill University for assistance in the typing of the manuscript.

Notes

1. My use of the term "symbol" follows the American semiotic tradition, exemplified by Peirce, which defines it as a sign based on a link of convention to its referent (Peirce 1955: 102). The usage is closer to that of the notion of the "sign" in French semiology, in which the signifier and signified

are arbitrarily linked, than to the complex and ineffable units of condensed meaning called symbols in certain traditions of literary criticism and studies of ritual. As will be seen, I conceive of culture itself as semiotic, and society as the process of symbol use rather than extra-symbolic strata.

2. We might usefully distinguish between *"data"*, which is anthropologically processed information (notes, census material, photographs, etc), the *sources* of data, which are various modes of observation (visual and auditory channels, recording of discourse, formal and informal interviews, narrative records, etc.), and the theoretically constructed *objects* of analysis and observation (which may be conceptualized as individual events, human motivations, cultural models, folk models, biological types, etc.). I would maintain that in all three cases of the forms of data, the sources of data, and the objects of analysis, the categories are multiple and resist dualistic classification as either "physical" or "mental".

3. I have elsewhere criticized the view that apparently "ethnic" terms such as "Maasai" represent, in a narrowly referential sense, the highest levels of a segmentary order; such references are — just as the term "country" (*Olosho*) — often applied at various levels, and embody wholly independent meaningful senses, such as — in this case — the practice of pastoralism, the sharing of a language and culture, and a common descent, all of which may be independent of a system of political units (c.f. Galaty 1978).

4. I have described at more length the process by which the age-set organization "constitutes" to segmentary political order (c.f. Galaty 1979).

5. It is clear that such an analysis of the symbolic constituents of a segmentary system does not account for its historical genesis or social reproduction. The first question has been answered in terms of the political necessity of invading groups (Sahlins 1961), environmental factors (Newcomer 1972; Glickman 1972), or the conditions of economic growth and concomitant expansion (Bonte 1979). Since such systems as an age-set based segmentary model represent institutional wholes with an over-determined coherence, I would suggest that their emergence cannot be explained by the functional adaptation of any one component, and their historical nature should not be avoided. While the model may be reproduced through the performative mechanisms already discussed, I would maintain that the key to the intensity of the Maasai age-based system lies in the age-set ritual cycle, through which individual statuses and age-groups are created and promoted, and thus the economic, political and social order reproduced. This process, and its implications for warfare and expansion, have been developed elsewhere (Galaty 1979).

References

Austin, J. L. (1962). *How To Do Things With Words.* Oxford: Clarendon Press.

Bonte, P. (1979). Pastoral production, territorial organisation and kinship in segmentary lineage societies. In *Social and Ecological Systems* (P.C. Burnham and R.F. Ellen, eds). ASA Monograph No. 18, New York: Academic Press.

Cohen, R. (1974). *Two Dimensional Man.* Berkeley and Los Angeles: University of California Press.

Derrida, J. (1973). *Speech, Phenomena, and Other Essays on Husserl's Theory of Signs.* Evanston: Northwestern University Press.

Dyson-Hudson, R. (1980). Review of: Warfare among East African herders. (K. Fukui and D. Turton, eds). *Science* **207**, 170-71.

Evans-Pritchard, E. E. (1940a). *The Nuer.* Oxford: Clarendon Press.

Evans-Pritchard, E. E. (1940b). The Nuer of the Southern Sudan. In *African Political Systems,* (M. Fortes and E. E. Evans-Pritchard, eds). Oxford University Press.

Galaty, J. G. (1977). *In the Pastoral Image: The Dialectic of Maasai Identity.* Ph.D. Dissertation. University of Chicago.

Galaty, J. G. (1978). *Being "Maasai", Being "Under Cows": Ethnic Shifters in East Africa.* American Anthropology Association Meetings, Los Angeles.

Galaty, J. G. (1979). Pollution and pastoral anti-praxis: the issue of Maasai inequality. *American Ethnologist* **6**, 803-16.

Galaty, J. G. (1979). *Ritual Performatives and Performative Rituals: The Ceremonial Cycle of the Maasai Age-Group System.* The "Great Feast Cycle" Seminar. Michigan State University.

Galaty, J. G. (1980). The Maasai group ranch: politics and development in an African pastoral society. In *When Nomads Settle: Processes of Sedentarization as Adaptation and Response,* (P. Salzman, ed.). Brooklyn: Praeger (Bergin).

Glickman, M. (1972). The Nuer and the Dinka: a further note. *Man* (N.S.) **7**, 586-94.

Harris, M. (1979). *Cultural Materialism: The Struggle for a Science of Culture.* New York: Random House.

Marx, E. (1977). The tribe as a unit of subsistence: nomadic pastoralism in the Middle East. *American Anthropologist* **79**, 343-63.

McKinley, R. (1977). The place of the symbol in the practice of anthropological reasoning. *Reviews in Anthropology* **4**, 414-39.

Newcomer, P. (1972). The Nuer are Dinka: an essay on origins and environmental determinism. *Man* (N.S.) **7**, 5-11.

Peirce, C. S. (1955). *Philosophical Writings of Peirce,* (J. Buchler, ed.). New York: Dover.

Peters, E. (1967). Some structural aspects of the feud among the camel-herding Bedouin of Cyrenaica. *Africa* **37**, 261-82.

Ryle, G. (1949). *The Concept of Mind.* London: Hutchison's University Library.

Sahlins, M. (1961). The segmentary lineage: an organization of predatory expansion. *American Anthropologist* **63**, 322-45.

Sahlins, M. (1976). *Culture and Practical Reason.* The University of Chicago Press.

Salzman, P. C. (1978). Does complementary opposition exist? *American Anthropologist* **80**, 53-70.

Sapir, J. D. (1977). The anatomy of metaphor. In *Social Use of Metaphor: Essays on the Anthropology of Rhetoric,* (J.C. Crocker and J.D. Sapir, eds). Philadelphia: University of Pennsylvania Press.

Schneider, D. (1965). Some muddles in the models: or, how the system really works. In *The Relevance of Models for Social Anthropology,* (M. Banton, ed).

London: Tavistock.

Schneider, D. (1968). *American Kinship: A Cultural Account.* Englewood Cliffs (N.J.): Prentice-Hall, Inc.

Schneider, D. (1976). Notes toward a theory of culture. In *Meaning in Anthropology*, (K. Basso and H. Selby, eds). Albuquerque: University of New Mexico Press.

Spencer, P. (1976). Opposing streams and the gerontocratic ladder: two models of age organisation in East Africa. *Man* (N.S.) **11**, 153-74.

Strawson, P. F. (1954). Critical notice of Wittgenstein's Philosophical Investigations, In *Wittgenstein and the Problem of Other Minds,* (H. Morick, ed.). New York: McGraw-Hill Book Co. (1967).

Thomson, J. (1883). *Through Masailand.* London : Sampson Low, Marston, Searle, and Rivington.

Wittgenstein, L. (1950). *Philosophical Investigations.* London: Basil Blackwell.

THINKING AND DOING: TOWARDS A MODEL OF COGNITIVE PRACTICE

RICHARD JENKINS

The ideas expressed in this paper arise from my long-felt dissatisfaction with many sociological and anthropological accounts of why and, more to the point, *how* people actually *do* things. Such accounts characteristically depict either "cultural dopes", who appear not to know their own culture as well as the ethnographer does, or ethnomethodologically rule-governed zombies, paragons of conformity. Either way, it seems to me that these accounts bear little relationship to my experience of my own life or my perceptions of the lives of those around me. There is no attempt to deal with that mixture of knowledge of the world, goals and ambitions, constraints and contingencies, imaginative "shots in the dark", emotion and ignorance, to enumerate only some of the factors involved, which combine in the human experience. Instead we find theoretical elegance substituted for the complexity of social life through recourse to either a *deus ex machina* or a "ghost in the machine".

In the following discussion, decisions and behaviour and the constraints which influence the formulation and implementation of such decisions and actions are viewed as of equal explanatory importance, in an attempt to examine critically the analytical distinction between what people think (or are assumed to think), and what they do. That distinction lies at the heart of the empiricist-rationalist divide and, ultimately, at the root of much analytical confusion. This paper forms part of a much more ambitious enterprise, the eventual transcendence of that divide and the incorporation of thought and action into one unified conceptual framework, the *cognitive practice* of the title.[1].

What are models? In the context of a conference dedicated to the "structure of folk models", such a question may appear to be redundant. After all, "everybody knows" what models are. But do they? In order to clear up whatever muddles there may be, it will be useful to decide exactly what models are, both in everyday speech and in social science.

Going to the dictionary, we may summarise the minimal essence of the word's everyday meaning as follows: a model is something which either represents or "stands for" the structure of something else. Physical scale is not important, it is the *structure* of the object of the modelling, "the proportion and arrangements of its component parts", which is significant (O. E. D. 1971: 1827).

However, this is not all there is to a model. When we examine the detailed meanings listed under the dictionary sub-headings we find, for example, engineers' small-scale models or a human model who sits in order that an artist may create an art-work based on his/her form; a model may act as an archetype upon which a series of reproductions can be based. In other words, a model always refers to a future event. This event need not *necessarily* take place but the model creates the possibility that it *can* do.

When we come to examine the current usage of the word in sociology and social anthropology, I would submit that we find not one meaning, but two competing meanings, only one of which is congruent with the above definition. In this sense, a model is

> any representation that provides a "rough draft" around which to organise inquiry . . . . To be useful, models. . . must permit us to test the goodness of fit with existing general theory, devise hypotheses for empirical testing, and should also suggest directions of fruitful research design. (Pelto and Pelto 1978: 256)

Thus, models are, in Abraham Kaplan's words, "scientific metaphors" (Pelto and Pelto 1978: 11). It must be stressed, however, that the use of such models is not considered to be confined to the domain of scientific discourse (*Ibid.:* 256).

To summarise: a model in this sense is a construct which represents or stands for the structure of something else in order to facilitate the performance of particular operations upon or with the model, in this case, theoretical or projective thinking or certain types of experiment. In other words, what we have is a specialised case of the everyday meaning outlined above; (for approximately similar usages of the word see Barth 1966 and Schneider 1965).

This brings us to the second way in which the word is used, that sense in which a model is simply a "construct (mental or otherwise) which is built by somebody and "stands for" something else" (Holy and Stuchlik, this volume). In this sense, a good case could be argued that all cognitive categories or constructs and most material artefacts are, by definition, models. I shall call this the *all-encompassing definition of models.*

Holy and Stuchlik's work represents a methodological individualist version of this all-encompassing definition, and stems in part from a laudable desire to assert the epistemological equality of the mental activity of ethnographer and subject (Stuchlik 1976). However, having once granted this epistemological equality, we then find a distinction being drawn between *folk models* and *explanatory models* (and, in order to avoid confusion, a very necessary distinction it is too; Holy and Stuchlik, this volume), with explanatory models being regarded, by some people, as in some sense superior (Caws 1974: 10).

The all-encompassing definition of models can, however, also be isolated at the opposite end of the theoretical spectrum, structuralist analyses in which overt activity appears to be viewed as the visible manifestation, albeit a "transformed" one, of unconscious elementary cognitive structures which are assumed to be pan-human in their scope. Within the framework of this particular orthodoxy, *conscious models* are the typically misguided "false knowledge" held by people about their own behaviour and that of their fellows, while *unconscious models* are the models of the "real" structure underlying that behaviour, models which are, needless to say, only accessible via the observing outsider (Levi-Strauss 1968: 281).

Thus, both the above usages of the word model share, in addition to the all-encompassing definition, a distinction between folk (or conscious) models and explanatory (or unconscious) models. It is implicit that the latter will be regarded as in some sense superior.

To conclude this part of the paper, I would argue for a more rigorous analytical usage of the concept *model,* a usage in line with the first meaning outlined above. Thus a model is something which represents or stands for the perceived *structure* of something else *in order that particular operations of a projective or imaginative nature may be performed on it or with it.* This definition has two, equally important, components:

1) a model is a representation of, or homologous with, the structure of something, and

2) modelling is carried out in order to enable the performance of particular types of operations or actions.

I am not for one moment arguing that modelling, in this sense, is peculiar to the scientific domain in any way. What I am arguing, however, is that not all cognitive constructs or categories are models.

White does not exist "on its own", and whether it is a *white wall,* a *white horse* or *white paint* we are talking about, three examples of simple linguistic models, will very much affect the nature of the operations, immediate or projected, we can perform on or with it. *White* on its own we can do nothing with.

There are two reasons for my insistence upon what may seem to many readers an unnecessary and carping definitional rigour. Firstly, my insistence on this particular usage is aimed at collapsing the conceptual distinction between thinking and doing; thus modelling is seen as a basic element in cognitive process, but one which combines elements of thought and action. As I hope will become apparent as the argument unfolds, once the implications of this definition of models are seriously appreciated it becomes impossible to draw a distinction between *models of* and *models for.*

Secondly, it must be realised that this definition allows us to conceptualise the relationships between the signs and symbols which constitute the basic "building blocks" of cultural universes and the models which those signs and symbols are combined to construct, models which themselves function as signs or symbols at a higher level of particularisation. However, brevity precludes the discussion of this theoretical area and I shall not deal with it further here.

An Intellectual Dual-organisation: Thinking and Doing.

One of the more ubiquitous features of social anthropology and sociology, practised from whatever theoretical position, is the taken-for-granted assumption that the socio-cultural world can be divided along an axis between two poles, thought and action. Culture, we are told, is made up of "shared categories and plans for action" (Bock 1969: 27), Schneider distinguishes between culture as "a system of symbols and meanings" and norms as "patterns for action which apply to some culturally defined unit" (1976: 198-199) and Fox evokes a distinction between "social structure" and "culture" (1978: ix). Similarly Goffman talks about "parts" and "routines", as opposed to "performances" (1971: 26-27), while Goodenough's " 'vocabularies of different kinds of forms' operationalised by a 'syntax' or set of rules for their composition into meaningful sequences of social events", is clearly an expression of the same intellectual dualism (1965: 1).

In a more general way, this dichotomy is also apparent in Raymond Firth's classic formulations of structure and organisation (1963: 28), while Berger and Luckman's distinction between "society as objective reality" and "society as subjective reality" is clearly a homologous opposition (1967), as, I would argue, are the linked Marxian concepts of base and superstructure.[2]

However, although all of these approaches share the taken-for-granted central distinction between *knowing how* and *knowing that* (Ryle 1949: 26-61), there are too many major differences of opinion between them in other areas to make a generalised critique either desirable or possible. Instead, I intend to develop a critique of one of the more recent and most explicit formulations of this conceptual dichotomy, Peter Caws' paper *Operational, Representational and Explanatory Models* (1974). Caws is a typical representative of this ubiquitous world-view who expresses his ideas both clearly and concisely and for these reasons I have chosen to concentrate my attention upon him. I shall begin with a brief summary of what he says.

First of all, what does he mean by models? In his own words

> an abstract structure is a model if it stands for a homologous concrete structure, a concrete structure is a model if it stands for a homologous concrete structure differently embodied. By "stands for" I mean that features of the model are substituted for features of the structure whose model it is, *for purposes of presentation, or instruction, or explanation, or imaginative variation, or computation, or prediction. (Ibid.: 1, my italics)*

Thus it would appear that Caws is working with the first of the two definitions discussed above, the definition whose adoption I am advocating. However, as he continues it becomes apparent that he does not appreciate the implications of his own definition; he then tells us that these models, which are in both the natives' and the analyst's heads, may be, as the first step in their analysis, conceptualised as *operational* and *representational* models:

> the representational model corresponds to the way the individual thinks things are, the operational model is the way he practically responds or acts. *(Ibid.: 3)*

Although it need not necessarily be so, it is frequently the case, according to Caws, that, in view of the incompatibility or poor fit which he assumes will obtain between them, representational models are conscious and operational models unconscious.

Coming now to the anthropologist's view of the situation, we see that it is a representational model which Caws designates an *explanatory* model. It is a scientific representation model — as opposed to "folk" or "common-sense" models — encompassing the ethnographic data, observations of behaviour and the verbal statements of informants, and the relationships between that data and the folk representational and operational models.

From his diagram (*Ibid.:* 6) it appears as though Caws conceives of social structure as something "real" which the anthropologist can somehow "see" and incorporate into his explanatory model. This is not the case, however:

> It is the scientist's representational (i.e. explanatory) model, the theory he constructs to account for the data and their inter-relation, that confers objective structure on the system. And the use of "confers" is deliberate, since it would be quite accurate to say that until the explanatory model was constructed the system had no objective structure. (*Ibid.:* 7)

That Caws himself turns out to be unsure of the epistemological status of his own concept of social structure becomes apparent at the end of the paper:

> To summarize: the social structure is not identical with the explanatory model, since the latter is in the scientist's head and *the former is out there among the people* who belong to the society in question. Nor is it identical with the representational or operational models in the natives' heads . . . But the structure is dependent in one way or another on these models, since without them the relations that constitute it would not exist. Priority goes, in the end, to the explanatory model, as the only one that is in a position to reflect all the relevant relations and to get them right. (*Ibid.:* 10, my italics)

Before proceeding to develop a critique of Caws, I would ask the reader to observe that although Caws appears to be working within an explicitly individualist framework, he embodies in his thinking notions which would be more at home in the structuralist scheme discussed briefly above. For example, representational models are what the natives *think* is going on (Levi-Strauss's conscious models?), while the operational models, what *really* happens, smack of unconscious models. The similarity between the two models of models is underlined when we consider the superior explanatory status accorded to the analyst's model in both. Now this in itself need not be a bad thing but, as I hope to show, if Caws is to be taken at face value and operational models are characteristically held unconsciously, then they are either models constructed by the analyst or they are not models at all.

Now I shall address myself more directly to Caws' scheme. I intend to do this in two steps: first I shall examine the detailed concepts he develops in the course of his argument and then I shall briefly discuss the general approach of which I take him to be representative. First then, I shall take the notions of operational and representational models as he presents them.

The distinction as he formulates it makes no allowance at all for the possibility of interaction between the two models; that is to say, there is no scope for feedback between them. Indeed his diagram would appear to expressly preclude the possibility for reciprocal feedback; the scheme seems only to allow for a uni-directional path of effective causality, i.e. operational models $\longrightarrow$ actor's behaviour $\longrightarrow$ actor's perception of his/her own behaviour and that of significant others $\longrightarrow$ representational models held by the actor.

There are two points to be noted here:

1) if, as Caws says, the actor's behaviour is the result of the holding of typically unconscious operational models, and if representational models are, so to speak, the actor's view of that behaviour, there can be no *necessary* reason for one to differ from or contradict the other, unless we revert to viewing social actors as cultural dopes or zombies who don't *really* know what they are doing, and

2) there is no possibility, within Caws' scheme as it stands, for representational models to influence the operational level, either by influencing the mobilisation of the appropriate operational model for a particular situation or by influencing the actual content and meaning of the operational models.

In other words, it is difficult to imagine any criteria according to which operational models could be related by the actor to the needs of the situation and evoked to meet those needs. The model of models which Caws develops is not an affirmation, but a denial, of the dialectical relationship presumed to obtain between the "cognitive level" and the "level of activities".

Operational models, by his definition, merit closer attention in their own right. The notion can be criticised on three counts: either

1) it is crudely tautological in the sense that operational models are simply what people do and thus could not be models *for* action (or *of* anything else), except inasmuch as they are the analyst's models of his subjects' behaviour, and this interpretation is ruled out by his own definition;

2) if, as Caws suggests, operational models are typically held unconsciously, it is difficult to see how they can be models of any sort since models have, by his own initial definition, a purposive aspect; *or*

3) the notion implicitly assumes that which Caws appears to explicitly deny, a mechanistically causal relationship between rules or norms (in this cause operational models) and behaviour, a relation-

ship that has, at best, been shown to be problematic (Stuchlik 1977: 13).

The latter interpretation is the only one open to us if, on the one hand, we are *not* to see models as tautological and, on the other, we are unable, within his framework, to invoke a dialectical relationship between operational models, representational models and behaviour. Either way, the notion poses problems. If it is simply tautological then clearly it can have no explanatory power, if operational models are unconscious then it is hard to imagine what practical significance they can have for either actor or observer, and if the notion is predicated upon a causal relationship between norms and behaviour we should have to conceptualise a patently absurd situation in which individuals either hold "on tap" a potentially infinite number of rules and norms to match the potentially infinite number of situations possible in a lifetime or, as in Goffman's dramaturgical model (1971), act out or perform somehow preconstituted "parts" or "routines" on a set, and according to a script, the source and origins of which are difficult to discern (cf. Bourdieu 1977: 29, 73, and Cicourel 1973: 30, for these criticisms in a more developed form).

Finally, it is obvious that the scheme makes no allowances for the fact, alluded to by Holy and Stuchlik (this volume), that many so-called "representational" models have an operational aspect. This can be so insofar as they have a prescriptive element attached either directly, e.g. in wartime the representational category *enemy soldier* carries a mandatory prescriptive load for an individual who wishes to validate his own identity as *soldier*, although this prescriptive load may be multiplex, giving the soldier a choice between attempting to kill the enemy soldier, attempting to capture him, attempting to evade him or surrendering to him, or indirectly, insofar as the assignation of identity to something, i.e. by subsuming it under a particular model, introduces a prescriptive element into the situation by foreclosing particular behavioural options. For example, one thing the soldier in the above example cannot do is treat his opponent as a friend or comrade without, as happened on the famous Christmas Day on the Western Front, setting aside his own identity as *soldier*.

In the above examples it is not just the assignation of identity to objects or persons in the actor's social world that is of significance, but the actor's assumption and interpretation of his/her own identity. Both of these considerations are of particular relevance when we consider the topic of status and role. As Nadel points out (1957: 29) status and role cannot be sensibly differentiated as being "operational" or "representational", with one as the dynamic aspect of the other, as in Linton's initial formulation of the concepts (1936). Not only is this the case insofar as their categorical content is concerned, but it is also true for the mobilisation of these identities during interaction. Nadel refers to a "principle of *linked options* . . . a *mutual steering process* whereby the performance of one role guides or conditions the performance of another" (1957: 44, italics in the original).

Similarly, "operational" categories may include a descriptive or representational element, if only via a conditional clause, "do X if situation Y pertains". This descriptive aspect of operational categories is underlined by the fact that most operations, even the most generalised or abstract, of necessity imply the context in which they are to be performed. Finally, operational categories are, by definition, descriptive or representational in another sense, inasmuch as they depict or typify the performance of particular actions and the manner of their performance, for enactment either immediately or at some time in the future.

The above discussion has hopefully highlighted my basic objections to any analytical framework that conceptualises thinking and doing as ontologically distinct. Such theoretical schema fails to grasp that, on the one hand, the assignation of meaning, via "representational" categories, is itself an action, in the sense that it is something which people do. What is more, it is usually an action with some significance for the particular social context in which it occurs. On the other hand, "operational" categories, however conceived of, are representations of possible kinds of behaviour and, either explicitly or implicitly, of the future state of affairs which the performance of a particular action may be expected to bring about under anticipated conditions. This is not to say that "operational" models or categories are of necessity goal-oriented, but simply a recognition that people usually have some idea of at least some of the consequences of their actions.

The Proof of the Pudding: the Transition from School to Work in Ballyhightown[3]

In order to thus test the operational strength of Caws' scheme (for even the most problematic of theoretical propositions may be of heuristic value), we must first decide what its operational implications are. We must decide how Caws' analytical categories would help us to encode the data from a particular ethnographic context and, having done that, we must attempt to use the data so encoded to tackle a particular theoretical question. Let us, then, consider that context and that question.

"Ballyhightown" is a large, post-war public housing estate on the fringe of the Belfast urban area in Northern Ireland which provides homes for over four thousand families, about fourteen to fifteen thousand people. Although it is *of* Belfast inasmuch as the majority of the residents identify with and orientate themselves towards the city in their working lives and leisure time, it is also something of a "no-man's-land", sprawled between the city proper and the older village-suburbs further out towards the countryside, bounded on all sides by major roads and owing administrative allegiance to Castleowen borough council.

Working-class, and almost wholly protestant, the population, in the absence of large-scale employment opportunities in or near the estate itself, travels to work, either in Belfast, in the large industrial estates of Castleowen or further afield. The poor local availability of employment is just one aspect of a depressed labour market of long standing; in the Belfast travel-to-work-area (as defined by the Northern Ireland Department of Manpower Services) in July 1979, the overall unemployment figure was 10.5% of the workforce. The corresponding figure for Ballyhightown is undoubtedly higher, though in the absence of detailed local level statistics it is impossible to estimate just how much higher.

Even so, the majority of young people who leave school each year will find a job eventually and it is this aspect of life in Ballyhightown which I intend to examine: the experiences of its young people upon leaving school and entering the labour market. In this context, the specific problem we will examine is why and how some of these young people find work while others do not.

Returning to Caws, how would his scheme serve as an analytical framework for encoding the ethnographic data about this situation? If the scheme is to be regarded as either correct or useful, we may expect that,

1) these young people will hold readily discernible representational models depicting the social world they inhabit, models which identify people and things, jobs and places and, more generally, the social world as they perceive it, and

2) the observer will be able to identify a degree of disagreement between these representational models, available to him as what people say, and what actually happens, what people do.

The ethnographer should then be able to identify the operational models which, usually unconsciously, provide the real motivation for this behaviour. These operational models will be models *for* behaviour, will be deducible *from* behaviour and, while probably unconscious, will be in the young people's heads, they will not be constructs of the analyst.

Leaving aside for the moment the methodological difficulties involved in attempting to operationalise this concept of operational models, I intend to examine the representational models, as defined by Caws, of the young people of Ballyhightown. I obviously don't intend to attempt to prove or disprove that they do in some way possess knowledge of the social world whose daily production and reproduction they participate in: I take that to be axiomatic. What I shall do, by way of illustration, is to examine that knowledge in respect of the kind of jobs which are available, where they are available and how they can be obtained.

First of all, what do our young hopefuls know about the world of work? What is their knowledge of jobs and careers? Most immediately, we can identify that part of their knowledge which derives from their own experience: part-time jobs while still at school, school-based work experience programmes and careers education and their own observations of other people's public work situations, such as those of bin-men, shop assistants or the police. Although such direct experience is at first only likely to provide them with a very incomplete knowledge of work, it becomes more significant as their own working lives unfold and they acquire more experiential knowledge upon which to draw.

Next we have what is probably the most important source of knowledge about work for the school leavers — the experience of their family members and friends who are working or who have worked in the past. Mothers, for example, will tell their daughters that, "It's no life for a girl nowadays, being a stitcher," and fathers will extol the advantages of "serving your time" as an apprentice tradesman. More generally, and outside the sphere of specific advice, all kinds of information about the nature of particular occupations and the experience of working for particular employers will be acquired second-hand in the course of day-to-day social life.

A further source of information, less immediate but nonetheless of some importance, may be identified in the communications and entertainment media. Television programmes such as the BBC's *Angels* (about nursing) and *Sailor* (about the Royal Navy) or Independent Television's long-running soap opera *Crossroads* (about the catering and hotel industry) provide readily accessible stereotyped knowledge about working life, as do magazines and advertising of all kinds.

Finally we come to those official agencies whose function it is to disseminate knowledge about "careers" to young job seekers. In the

Belfast context, this is the Careers Office of the N.I. Department of
Manpower Services, whose officers see young people both in school
and after they have left school, (it is a necessary precondition for
obtaining benefits that an unemployed school-leaver, or any young
worker under eighteen years, register with the Careers Office). Here
the young person can, ideally, obtain information about the nature
of particular occupations, his or her eligibility for them and how to
apply for them.

The first two categories of knowledge about work are the most
important in Ballyhightown. Working-class young people are most
immediately aware of working-class jobs, the typical jobs of their
family and peer group; they will know more about them than they
will know, for example, about the occupations to which their
middle-class equivalents will aspire. Furthermore, one can say with
some certainty that the knowledge they do acquire of occupations
outside the experiential immediacy of their network will:

1) be incomplete, inasmuch as it will not encompass even a
majority of the occupational niches available "out there";

2) be of a particular kind and partial, for example, advertisements
for air travel will display its pleasurable aspects and *ergo* the positive
aspects of an air hostess's or steward's job; and

3) tend, particularly in the case of "higher status" occupations
than those to which working-class school leavers would either aspire
or be formally qualified for, to accentuate their inaccessibility and
"otherness".

For instance, the televised image of a university lecturer is either
of an "egg head" who talks in a highly stylised academic language on
BBC2, or a caricatured clown in a gown in a re-run of an Ealing
comedy. This distance is also due to the lack of direct experience,
either personally or in the more abstract public sense, of such
occupations. None of this, of course, explains *why* it is that such
school leavers don't become academics; what it does explain, however, is *how* their model of the occupational structure of their
society is built up and maintained.

The next aspect of the representational models of the world of
work which our young subjects hold that I shall consider, is the
spatial location of perceived job opportunities. Here we must distinguish between jobs which they see as geographically relevant to
themselves in Ballyhightown, and those they do not. There are
several ways in which this distinction becomes apparent. In the first
place, one may differentiate between jobs which are within travelling
distance and those which are not. The definition of "within travelling
distance" will vary according to personal circumstances and

preferences and may also be affected by the attitude of the Careers Officer concerned if the job has been offered through official channels.

The second distinction, between known and unknown areas, regardless of distance, is important for two reasons. Firstly, young people looking for work will be more inclined to walk around an area they are familiar with, even if only slightly, "asking about" at building sites, factory gates or shops, than they would in an unfamiliar area. Secondly, they will be more likely to answer a "Situations Vacant" advertisement if the address is in an area they know and they are similarly more likely to find a particular address once they have started looking for it if they already possess some knowledge of the area.

Lastly we have a distinction which may be peculiar to Belfast or Northern Ireland, although I imagine it will be relevant anywhere with well-defined ethnic areas or gang "territories". Since Belfast is a city with marked and well-known residential segregation along the lines of religious ethnicity, segregation of which Ballyhightown itself is a good example, there are many districts to which youngsters will not go to work or travel through to get to work. As it happens, due to many years of protestant pre-eminence in, and control over, the labour market (Barritt and Carter 1972: 93-108), this does not affect our school leavers to the same degree that it would their peers in Roman Catholic areas. Nevertheless, it can, on occasion, mean the difference between working and not working.

Finally, we come to these young people's knowledge of how jobs may be obtained. At its most basic, they know, obviously, that in order for a job to be taken it must first be either offered or asked for. The asking may be done by the applicant or by his/her representative – a relative, a friend, a teacher, a Careers Officer etc. What is more, the manner of its being offered, i.e. in the newspaper with a box number, by an employer 'phoning up the Careers Office or through a shopkeeper asking some of his regular customers if they know "any wee girls that's looking for work", will affect the way in which an application ought to be made.

Thus I have painted a very generalised picture of the representational models, in Caws' sense, that the young people of Ballyhightown have about work. Using this ethnography as a basis for discussion, I should like to make some equally general points concerning representational models.

My first point may seem obvious, but it is nonetheless important. These representational models are not homogenous. They are hierarchical and not of equal weight insofar as they, of necessity, embody assessments, valuations and preferences with which their holders distinguish between the desirability of one situation and the desirability of another or the possibility or accessibility of one situation as compared with another. In other words, "representational" models are not neutral in their relationship to action; they are truly models in the sense of the word for which I am arguing. Because they embody an evaluative component they may form part of the process whereby alternative courses of action are adjudicated between, although they need not necessarily effecitvely do so if they are considered to be irrelevant or insignificant.

As I have shown then, the young people of Ballyhightown distinguish between those jobs that are "for them" and those that are not, between those jobs that they consider to be accessible and those they do not. These distinctions are presented here as gross simplifications drawn for the purposes of explanation – there is no invisible border separating the acceptable from the unacceptable. What is satisfactory or possible for one person is unsatisfactory or impossible for another.

My second point is perhaps a little less obvious: with respect to these "representational" models, what is important is not only what is known but what is *not* known. This becomes more obvious if we consider the Ballyhightown ethnography above. Jobs which are not known about cannot, obviously, be applied for. The reason they cannot be applied for is not because there is an absence of the appropriate "operational" model, be it conscious or otherwise, governing the making of such an application (which is what a literal reading of Caws might suggest). The reason such jobs are inaccessible is the absence of the knowledge of those particular job vacancies in the job-seeker's repertoire of knowledge of the sphere of work.

Furthermore, if our young hopeful's knowledge of *how* to apply for jobs is either incomplete or lacking, they may find themselves making an inappropriate application for a particular job. This point is important with respect to Caws' view of the relationship between operational models, representational models and the subsequently occurring action. In such a situation we may imagine a youngster who sees a job advertisement in the *Belfast Telegraph* for builders' labourers. Such advertisements often do not specify how the job should be applied for – it is taken for granted that anyone applying for a labourer's job on a building site will know to apply in person to the site foreman. The telephone numbers of the site office are given in order that hopeful applicants can arrange when to come or can 'phone up in advance, thus saving themselves a wasted journey if the jobs are already filled. Most young people would in fact know this and, if they didn't, there would certainly be no shortage of people to let them know. However, it is by no means beyond the bounds of possibility that they might not know, might not consult anyone else and might apply in writing. In fact, were the young person concerned respecting the conventional wisdom of much formal careers education that is exactly what would happen. In this case, not only would the applicant not get the job (by the time the letter reached the site forman the jobs would probably be filled) but they very possibly wouldn't receive a reply at all.

The point I am trying to make here is this: the behaviour of our imaginary erstwhile labourer and his failure to get a job must be viewed as the result of the pursuit of a particular goal on the basis of inappropriate knowledge. There is no way that the presence or importance of a conscious or unconscious operational model, differing somehow from this goal or knowledge, a model of "what really goes on" as opposed to the disappointed job seeker's inaccurate knowledge of what goes on, can be discerned, at least not in the research subject's head. It must be stressed here that I do not regard *goals,* as defined, for example, by Stuchlik (1977), as being "operational" models in any sense. They are models *of* a desired future state of affairs which, even if only implicitly, include some information as to how the desired end may be achieved. They are, in fact, good examples of a model in my preferred sense.

My final point *vis-à-vis* so-called representational models is, as yet, ill thought out. Nevertheless, I present it here without apologies as pointing out a further area for discussion and research in the future. In the context of the spatial location of job opportunities, most young people from Ballyhightown do not find their way about using a street-map. They either know how to get where they are going, from personal experience or the personal experience of others as embodied in directions, or they don't. They know the territory — which buses to catch, at which church to turn left, the short cut to the flats over the field behind the school — not the map. Unfortunately, I have no detailed ethnography with which to support this assertion. I take some comfort, however, from the research of other people into the ways in which we all find our way about and the kinds of environmental models we appear to use in doing so (Jorion 1978, Ward 1979: 22-31).

Thus, in order for an individual to be able successfully to find his/her way from place A to place B, without a map, he/she must have either a practical mastery of how to do so, based on their own experience, or be able to draw, via directions, upon someone else's similar practical mastery. I would further insist that in a culturally familiar built environment a *detailed* practical mastery is not essential, given the individual's general idea where he/she is going and a "sense of direction". The man-made or man-modified environment encodes the accumulated practical mastery of the culture concerned; Pierre Bourdieu has called this kind of decoding and practical ability, "the 'art' of *necessary improvisation* which defines excellence", (1977: 8). It is obvious from these examples that knowledge may be inextricably grounded in practice, to the degree that to talk about operational or representational models makes very little sense indeed. What is more, such knowledge will, due to its practical indexicality, its necessary continuity with particular tasks or interaction contexts, often be less structured, more improvisatory, than other kinds of knowledge.

When we turn our attention to Caws' "operational" models and try to use them, the problem is this: if operational models are the way in which the individual "practically responds or acts" (Caws 1974: 3), then they cannot under any circumstances be held unconsciously (unless we are dealing with somnambulists). Caws' position becomes more complex and less clear as his argument proceeds:

> As to the operational case [of models], while *representational* "standing for" clearly cannot be expected of it, there is a much stronger sense of this relation that amounts to virtual *constitution:* it is in terms of this model that the mind consciously or unconsciously computes the situation and decides between actions, projecting their alternative consequences; to the extent that the actions are effective, the situation tends to behave as if things are in fact as the model assumes, whether or not it is objectively accurate. (*Ibid.:* 4)

Having observed the existence of two different types of data, what people say and what they do (*Ibid.:* 5), he goes on to designate what they say as expressions and indicators of their representational models, and what they do as expressions and indicators of the operational models, the internal motivators of their actions (*Ibid.:* 5-6). While the first procedure may be methodologically defensible, the second certainly is not.

The contradiction may be stated thus: the way an individual practically responds or acts is his/her behaviour, it cannot be described as a model *of* or *for* his/her behaviour. If, however, this operational model is to be defined as some kind of *internal* model governing behaviour and finding its only expression in behaviour, then its existence and nature can only be inferred by the anthropologist. Caws' operational model, if in fact it is to be regarded as a model at all, is an explanatory model and hence not to be sought after in the social reality under examination.

Having thus examined some of the implications for anthropological practice of the taken-for-granted division of the social world into discrete realms of thought and action, I would assert that the distinction between the two must be put aside if we are to comprehend what I have termed *cognitive practice,* i.e. thinking as doing and doing as thinking. We must recognise, as argued above, that all models, by their very nature, are composed of "representational" and "operational" elements. If they were not they would not be models. It is this recognition of the concept of model as the mediating concept between the spheres of thought and action that may enable us to eventually proceed to more sophisticated analyses of how people actually do things.

Cognitive Practice: An Alternative Scheme.

It would be tempting to call a halt here and conclude with a few general remarks. More useful, however, would be a tentative attempt to develop a theory of cognitive practice, to show the usefulness of my concept of models in transcending the taken-for-granted intellectual dualism outlined above.

I intend to take the first steps towards such a theory through further expansion of the Ballyhightown ethnography. Having outlined a general picture of the situation which young job-seekers find themselves in, we may proceed to examine an individual case in some detail.

Let us look at *Sandra* then, a quiet girl who had enjoyed school but was nonetheless glad to leave. With her she took two "O" Levels, C.S.E. (Certificate of Secondary Education) passes in four subjects and some secretarial qualifications. The eldest of five children, her father is an unskilled process operator in a synthetic fibres plant and her mother a part-time patrolwoman, or "lollypop lady", at Ballyhightown Secondary School.

Before leaving school, Sandra had applied to join the Royal Ulster Constabulary Cadets unsuccessfully, and she had also been turned down for a trainee dark-room technician's job in a hospital in Belfast. She had seen both jobs advertised in the paper, although joining the police was her long-standing ambition. While waiting for her eighteenth birthday to come along so that she could apply for conventional entry into the police, she intended to work as a typist because she liked what she knew of the work, and thought that she would be paid quite well. She wasn't happy about working anywhere in the Belfast area and didn't think she would enjoy factory work; she also mentioned that she didn't want to be a prison warden, perhaps because of the public identification between the jobs of the police and the prison service. When I interviewed her in school in April 1978 she told me that she was engaged, but by January 1979, when I saw her next, that affair had ended.

Upon leaving school in May 1978, she "signed on the brue", remaining unemployed for about two months, after which time she found a job in the office of a large plumbing and central heating contractors, a couple of miles from home. Paying about twenty pounds a week "in your hand", the job involved general office duties and had been found through the good offices of "a woman across the road who worked there" and had advised her to apply.

> It was only temporary. I told them I wanted to join the R.U.C. when I was eighteen, so they only gave me temporary employment. I'd tried twice for the R.U.C. Cadets but I was too old. I liked it very much . . . the people there were very nice and you were always meeting people even when you were in the office doing typing. There were always business-men coming in and out. I enjoyed it most when I was doing the switchboard and reception. And there was no bus fares. I walked down there and got a lift back in the evenings with one of the directors. And there were more people of your own age, young plumbers and all.

Six weeks later Sandra was on the dole again, this time for two and a half months, during which period she applied for several jobs she saw advertised in the newspapers. Early in November she rang up a local printing firm about their advertisement for a junior clerk-typist in the *Belfast Telegraph* and they told her to come up and see them. She got the job and started work on November 13th at a net wage of £23 per week. It only lasted five days:

> I couldn't stand the work, it was mostly clerical. You were sitting at a desk all day doing timesheets, there was no typing. I couldn't stand the work.

However, she did not leave that job facing the prospect of an indefinite period of unemployment. She had already been offered a place in a government sponsored Work Experience Scheme by her Careers Officer; this was another office job, this time in the local College of Further Education, starting in January 1979. Also, there being now only ten months to go until her eighteenth birthday in August 1979, the prospect of finally joining the R.U.C. seemed close enough for her to put up with a spell of unemployment, much as she disliked being "on the brue".

> I get very depressed . . . not having enough money to go out places and things like that . . . and having to sit in the house all day listening to your mum going on at you. I like a change of scenery now and again.

When I interviewed her, on a Wednesday afternoon in January 1979, she was due to start work in the College the following Monday. Since November she had not been idle, however, and she had recently applied for a full-time post in the College which she had seen advertised in the paper; the interview had been arranged for three days after she started. Her ambition was still to join the police but she had added shorthand typing to the list of jobs she wouldn't do if she could avoid it, because "I don't like it." She seemed happier with the idea of working in the city but she still set herself geographical limits: "I wouldn't work anywhere you'd have to take two buses to."

After January 1979 I lost contact with Sandra but since I do know, from inquiries made in the Careers Office, that her name didn't appear again on the "live" unemployment register between then and June 1979, it seems likely that she remained in her College job. I left the estate in June so I do not know whether or not she eventually did apply for the R.U.C. Looking at this case, I would tentatively suggest that we may usefully identify four types of model, as follows:[4]

1) *Subject models:* these are the individual's definition or image of self. Such definitions may be plural inasmuch as ego may *know*, for example, that she is an unemployed female sixteen year old from Ballyhightown who has recently left school, but she may have an alternative subject model available insofar as she may *see* herself as someone who would make a good policewoman. It is also possible, or even likely, that she may define herself differently in different situations. Thus, while maintaining her ambition to be a policewoman Sandra took a clerical job, a job which she preferred to others.

2) *Object models:* ego's models of the persons and things in his/ her environment. In Sandra's case, she knew not only about some of the kinds of jobs available in the abstract, but she knew in more detail about which jobs she did and didn't want to do; she also knew something about which occupations she was qualified to do and which she was not.

3) *Situational models:* these define the relationships between ego

and the persons and things in his/her environment, and the relationships between those persons and things. Thus, Sandra can be said to hold topographical models of her socially relevant physical environment, she knows how to make the journey from Ballyhightown to Belfast city centre, for example. This is not to say that she has a precise inch-by-inch knowledge of the various routes into the city centre, of the minutiae of the environment of those routes or that she possesses clearly formulated blow-by-blow plans of where to cross the road etc. She is, however, on the basis of the topographical models she does hold, as discussed above, practically competent to make the journey successfully.

She has as well situational models which mediate her relationships with her social world, family, members of her peer-group network etc. Such models do not simply represent what is perceived as reality, they are a fundamental part of social action.

It might be asked what the difference between these three kinds of model really is, particularly between the object models and the situational models. The difference between the two lies both at the level of abstraction and the degree of complexity; the situational model is made up of the subject and object models *in relationship to each other*, it encompasses *the subject model(s), the object models and the perceived relationships between them*.

4) *Action models:* models of potential courses of action and their expected or likely outcome(s). For example, Sandra knows that if she is unemployed, she can, by registering with the Careers Office in Belfast as unemployed and then making a formal claim for benefit at the local Social Security Office, receive regular money from the state in the shape of a weekly giro-cheque. The knowledge that she can do so does not make her do so; it does, however, make it possible for her so to do.

Furthermore, I must stress, a propos of Bourdieu's remark about "necessary improvisation" cited above, that it would obviously be wrong to imply that *all* actions are governed by specific action models. In the first place, action models, as I conceive them, are general models of courses of action and their expected consequences and, as such, are not models of discrete items in any particular individual's behavioural repertoire.

Secondly, while specifying, in general terms, *what* to do and even *how* to do it, action models obviously can, at best, only make limited allowances for changes which may occur in the situation. Action is continuously evolved, on the basis of the above models and at least partly in response to the contingencies and unexpected happenings of normal participation in social life.

Conclusion

Before finishing, there are several other matters I would like to discuss. To start with, it may be argued that, because of the positive relationship to behaviour of the first three types of model discussed above, that they imply courses of action related to the particular model and hence could be called action models. What I mean here is that models of these types may be,

1) models of what is, or of what is regarded as possible or impossible, i.e. *knowledge*, or

2) models of what ought to be or is hoped for, i.e. *goals*.

Furthermore, it is not difficult to imagine a model which embodies both simultaneously. For example, should young man A decide that he wants to marry his *girlfriend* and should she accept when he proposes to her, she then, given parental blessing etc., becomes defined both publicly and in his mind as his *fiancee*. This is, from his point of view, an object model of someone whom he *knows* that it is possible to marry (and also likely) and whom he *hopes* that he eventually will marry (and expects to). The first part is knowledge and the second part a goal, but they are both bound up in one object model. It is also obvious, I hope, that the definition of his girlfriend as "fiancee" alters the situational model, *vis-à-vis* his relationships with his future in-laws, the legitimacy of sexual intercourse with his fiancee etc.

Nevertheless, I take the general point. I have, however, itemised action models separately because it is possible to imagine courses of action, action models, which are not implied in subject, object or situational models and which are presumed to be "available" to actors in their own right. All models of the first three kinds routinely imply the practice of culturally appropriate courses of behaviour if their validity is to be maintained.

Not all action models are closely implicated in other models, however. For example, the typical Ballyhightown action model *going into town*, i.e. travelling from the estate into Belfast, can be mobilised for a great many reasons, in a huge number of circumstances and in a number of ways. It is independent of other models.

For the sake of illustration, I would ask the reader to conceptualise the above notions in terms of, for any particular individual, an egocentric *cognitive network* composed of a theoretical infinity of cognitive models. That is to say, in any given cultural context ego has available to him a number of personal identities or subject models. Which one he/she assumes will depend on various factors, i.e. the influence of his/her socialisation upon his/her personality, his/her personal history, present situation etc.

In the next "zone" of this cognitive network, to borrow a term from Barnes (1969: 112), ego has available a large repertoire of object models which enable him/her to render the environment meaningful. Going "further out", to continue the metaphor, there is an equally large repertoire of situational models with which to analyse and render meaningful the social and physical situation.

A matter of particular importance in the context of job-seeking, is that the choice and imposition upon ego by another person or persons, more powerful than ego in the situational model of a particular social and cultural context, of a particular model, particularly when the other's object model of ego *dominates*, for practical purposes, ego's subject model, will feed-back and after the models mobilised or developed by ego in the past and limit the range of options available for mobilisation or development in the next stage, making some of them inappropriate or unacceptable.[5]   In other words, the successful mobilisation or assumption of subject models in particular is not always something that ego does for him or herself. Depending on the situation, he or she may not have a choice.

Returning to the cognitive network metaphor, we may recapitulate thus: the definition of subject, object and situation will, either by the impact of the "operational" and evaluative components of the models, or the mobilisation of habitual and/or culturally recognised connections between these models and particular action models, lead to decisions whether or not to take action and, if action is to be taken, which model(s) ought to be invoked as guidelines. It is here that the "likely or anticipated outcome" component of the action model can be seen as significant; by comparing this anticipated outcome with other situationally relevant models and their evaluative aspects (which, by evaluating the present state of affairs, include, if only by implication, a judgement as to the desired future state of affairs) or with more explicitly goal-like models, a principle governing the choice of action can be discerned.

Thus, in my model of cognitive practice, should an action or situation be regarded by the actors as unsatisfactory there is always the *theoretical* possibility that they may retrace their steps, try "something new", redefine the situation, reformulate their subject and object models etc. However, we must not lose sight of the fact that there may be, and often will be, culturally given factors in any situation, or other, more directly influential, factors such as the exercise of physical power or violence (open or covert), which will limit the possibilities for return and reformulation in the manner described. Such factors, particularly the power to inflict successfully one's own definition of the situation on others, will be of vital importance in any explanation.

Acknowledgements

This paper derives from fieldwork in Northern Ireland carried out under the supervision of Professor Jack Goody. In addition, it has benefited from comments made upon various drafts of it by Jenny Craik, Judith Ennew, Anthony Giddens, Ladislav Holy, Alan Macfarlane, Milan Stuchlik, the participants in the writing up seminar at Cambridge and those who attended the 1980 ASA Conference. All of these people will recognise that many of their criticisms went unheeded: responsibility for the paper's shortcomings remains my own. I am grateful to Clare Hall, Cambridge, the Fortes Fund of the University of Cambridge and the Northern Ireland Department of Education for their various contributions to the cost of presenting this paper at the conference.

Notes

1. In many ways my position has much in common with that of Layder (1979). I must also admit, if it is not sufficiently obvious, that I am heavily in debt to the work of Pierre Bourdieu, although I fear that his distinction between *habitus* and *practice,* i.e. "the habitus is a system of durable, transposable dispositions which functions as the generative basis of structured, objectively unified practices" (1979: vii), is the same taken-for-granted division of the world into the realms of thought and action which I am directly confronting in this paper.
2. Regarding the work of Holy and Stuchlik, their distinction between knowledge and goals is not the distinction I am here attacking. This distinction is exemplified in their work by the dichotomy between knowledge and goals on the one hand, and behaviour on the other (Holy 1976; Stuchlik 1977).
3. In this account all personal and place names have been fictionalised with the exception of Belfast itself. The fieldwork spanned twenty-two months from August 1976 to June 1979, first of all while working for the local education authority as a detached youth worker and subsequently whilst in receipt of a scholarship from the Department of Education, Northern Ireland. I am grateful to both bodies for their support.
4. Since formulating these concepts I have read Davis's lucid exposition of Touraine's theory of social action (1974: 34-47). Touraine's view of workers' consciousness as made up of a *principle of unity,* a *principle of opposition* and a *principle of totality,* all of which find expression in the field of social action, seems to be broadly similar to my view of subject, object and situational models, although my concepts are more general than his. His ideas are further developed in his discussion of social movements (Touraine 1977: 313-317).
5. See Nadel's principle of "linked options" referred to earlier (1957: 44-60).

References

Banton, M. ed. (1965). *The Relevance of Models for Social Anthropology.* London: Tavistock.

Barritt, D. P. and Carter, C. F. (1972). *The Northern Ireland Problem.* London: Oxford University Press.

Barnes, J. A. (1969). Network and political process. In *Local Level Politics,* (Marc J. Swartz, ed.) pp. 107-30. London: University of London Press.

Barth, F. (1966). Models of social organisation. *Royal Anthropological Institute Occasional Paper* No. 23.

Berger, P. L. and Luckman, T. (1967). *The Social Construction of Reality.* London: The Allen Lane Press.

Bock, P. K. (1969). *Modern Cultural Anthropology.* New York: Knopf.

Bourdieu, P. (1977). *Outline of a Theory of Practice.* Cambridge University Press.

Bourdieu, P. (1979). *Algeria 1960.* Cambridge University Press and Paris: Maison des Science de l'Homme.

Caws, P. (1974). Operational, representational and explanatory models. *American Anthropologist* 76, 1-10.

Cicourel, A. V. (1973). *Cognitive Sociology.* Harmondsworth: Penguin.

Davis, H. H. (1979). *Beyond Class Images.* London: Croom Helm.

Firth, R. (1963). *Elements of Social Organisation.* 3rd ed. Boston: Beacon Press.

Fox, R. (1978). *The Tory Islanders.* Cambridge University Press.

Goffman, E. (1971). *The Presentation of Self in Everyday Life.* Harmondsworth: Pelican.

Goodenough, W. H. (1965). Rethinking 'status' and 'role'. In *The Relevance of Models in Social Anthropology,* (Banton, ed.) pp. 1-24. London: Tavistock

Holy, L. ed. (1976). Knowledge and behaviour. *Queen's University Papers in Social Anthropology* No. 1.

Jorion, P. (1978). Marks and rabbit furs. *Peasant Studies* 7, 86-100.

Layder, D. (1979). Problems in accounting for the individual in marxist-rationalist theoretical discourse. *Brit. J. Sociol.* 30, 149-63.

Linton, R. (1936). *The Study of Man.* New York: Appleton and Century.

Levi-Strauss, C. (1968). *Structural Anthropology.* London: The Allen Lane Press.

Nadel, S. F. (1957). *The Theory of Social Structure.* London: Cohen and West.

O.E.D. (1971). *The Compact Edition of the Oxford English Dictionary.* London: Oxford University Press.

Pelto, P. J. and Pelto, G. H. (1978). *Anthropological Research.* 2nd edn. Cambridge University Press.

Ryle, G. (1949). *The Concept of Mind.* London: Hutchinson.

Schneider, D. M. (1965). Some muddles in the moddels. In *The Relevance of Models in Social Anthropology,* (Banton, ed.) pp. 25-86. London: Tavistock.

Schneider, D. M. (1976). Notes towards a theory of culture. In *Meaning in Anthropology,* (Keith H. Basso and Henry A. Selby, eds). pp. 197-220. Albuquerque: University of New Mexico Press.

Stuchlik, M. (1976). Whose knowledge? In *Queen's University Papers in Social Anthropology* Volume 1. (L. Holy, ed.) pp. 1-26. Queen's University: Belfast.

Stuchlik, M. ed. (1977). Goals and behaviour. *Queen's University Papers in Social Anthropology* Volume 2. Queen's University: Belfast.

Touraine, A. (1977). *The Self-Production of Society*. Chicago: University of Chicago Press.

Ward, C. (1979). *The Child in the City*. Harmondsworth: Penguin.

SHETLANDERS AND INCOMERS: CHANGE, CONFLICT AND EMPHASIS IN SOCIAL PERSPECTIVES

GRAHAM McFARLANE

This paper attempts to unravel the social factors which have generated, and which therefore account for, an aspect of the models of local society held by the native population of Dunrossness, an area in the South mainland of Shetland. In these models of the local society, considerable stress is placed on a social dichotomy between, on the one hand, Shetlanders and, on the other, "incomers". That Shetlanders should view the difference between Shetlanders and incomers as a social dichotomy (i.e. as indicating a real, fundamental division of local society) is a relatively new phenomenon, as is the fact that emphasis is placed on it. I argue that both are emergent products primarily of events which have taken place during the first stages of the so called "oil era" in Shetland (1971-1979). In other words, events relating to oil developments have created changes in the structure of Shetlanders' perspectives on society.

I should emphasize here that I am not trying to explain or account for the existence of the categories incomer and Shetlander. That would be a nonsense: these two categories have been part of Shetlanders' language of social identities for as long as anyone can remember or even imagine. The two identities can be thought of as relatively enduring elements, whose place in the folk models might vary over time. What I am trying to explain is why Shetlanders and incomers are presumed to stand in the relationship they do and, at the same time, why this relationship is given over-riding importance in Shetlanders' sociological perspectives.

People's perspectives on the social world[1] can be thought of as comprising a large but finite number of social categories or groups, standing in various kinds of relationships with each other: distant/ close, above/below, inclusive/exclusive and so on. Usually members of different categories or groups are thought to share certain attributes or characteristics. These are the behavioural, attitudinal and mental characteristics which we usually call stereotypes. I will not (and indeed cannot) attempt to give anything like a complete description of all aspects of Shetlanders' sociological perspectives. However, since I must show why I think greatest stress is placed on the dichotomy Shetlander/incomer, it is necessary to set the relationship incomer/Shetlander into some sort of broader framework. Hence a few general words about Shetlanders' sociological perspectives will be presented. These few words should also provide a background and setting for my analysis.

Background and Setting

Dunrossness is the part of Shetland which was, and still is, expected to bear the most immediate social and economic changes relating to North Sea Oil developments. It is the zone demarcated by the local administration as a growth, development and potential problem area. Changes which are identified here are thought to be suggestive of changes which might take place in other areas of Shetland as the construction phase of the oil era winds down, and the oil production phase takes off in earnest. To date, Dunrossness has received by far the largest proportion of the immigration of young professionals associated with various oil-rig servicing industries, based at Shetland's major airport. The overwhelming majority of these immigrants are pilots, engineers, air-traffic controllers and administrative staff associated with their activities. The population in the area increased from 1,141 in 1971 (March) to 1,599 in 1978 (June), and the total number of inhabited dwellings increased from 385 in 1968 to 541 in 1978, an increase of 40.5%.

Housing for oil related workers is considered to be a critical problem for the local administration: the suddenness of demand for housing has necessitated various policies constraining its dispersal, concentration and, most recently, its direction northwards away from the immediate vicinity of the airport. The "traditional" settlement pattern in the area is varied and developed out of topographical constraint, patterns of land tenure and the exigencies of agriculture. To this original settlement pattern have been added new housing estates (both local authority and company owned) and ribbon development of privately owned deluxe housing.

Today the chief employer in the area is the airport. Recent figures from the local council show that there are 529 people currently employed at the airport: 358 immigrants and 171 natives of

Shetland. This represents massive expansion: the labour force in 1968 totalled 9 individuals (7 of whom were classified as natives of the area). The overwhelming majority of Shetlanders employed at the airport are unskilled, semi-skilled or skilled "blue collar" workers. While the airport is the economic hub of the area, agriculture is still an important part of the local economy. In fact, Dunrossness has long been considered to be the most fertile and agriculturally productive area in the whole of Shetland. Most of the agricultural sector is taken up by part-time crofting but, unusual for Shetland, there are tracts of fertile land sufficiently extensive to allow for some full time farming. The most extensive tracts are taken up by 5 dairy farms.

I do not want to go on elaborating on these "objective" features of social setting. It would be more useful, I think, to let Shetlanders help provide the setting; that is, it would be more useful for me to outline briefly how Shetlanders in the area describe and theorize about Dunrossness. "Talk" is the source of this information: such descriptions and theorizing are integral parts of much of "natural", everyday conversations, as well as the result of researchers' efforts during formal or informal interviews. For instance, explicit or implicit reference to various social collectivities (and their supposed attributes) is part of the general process of gossiping about or commenting upon the doings and characteristics of others (see for instance, Cohen 1978, McFarlane 1978). Obviously, therefore, people's ideas about the general makeup of their social environment can be teased out of or inferred from everyday conversation. My outline draws upon such natural conversation as well as on a more restricted amount of interview material.

Now I am aware that interviews are somewhat unnatural events for most individuals, and I am aware that they are particularly problematic sources of information if one is interested in the stress given to particular areas of folk models. In interviews, as in any other interaction, the amount of stress given to various items of information is almost certain to reflect various problematic factors: first, how the researcher is typified by the interviewee for the purposes of dealing with the interaction (there is no reason why typification should always be "researcher"); second, the interests which are attributed to the researcher; and third, the various interests which people themselves might have, for which the researcher might be conveniently used. The interests brought into interviews need not be reducible simply to a desire to create scientific truth. There is nothing new in all this: probably every methodology text-book pays some attention to the problems of "researcher effect". However, these problems do not mean that interviews are a useless source of information, especially if we mean by "interview" simply an organised conversation between researchers and informants. There is no reason why similar information to that obtainable in "natural" everyday conversations should not flow from interviews; and there is no reason why the information from the interviews should not coincide with that found in information exchanged outside the interviews, either between the natives or between the researcher and the natives. There are no reasons for rejecting interviews provided the interview is handled in a certain way: that is, questions should not be derived from some sort of etic series of prompts or questionnaire, and the interview should not be directed by the researcher alone.

All the interviews undertaken by myself, and by other research staff, tended towards the more open-minded, informal end of the naturalistic to artificial scale of conversations. They were relatively freewheeling in content, only being anchored to a common structure by a loosely defined interview schedule, listing only general topics of conversation. In other words, the interviews were like improvisations, created both by the interviewer and by the interviewee (c.f. Davis 1979: Chapter 3): as such, they were almost like natural conversations. Since both interviews and conversations with inform-ants were somewhat similar in format, I feel justified in deriving the generalisations outlined below from both sources: except where indicated in the text, this is the case. I will now describe the setting in Shetlanders' terms.

The word "community" appeared time and time again in discussion. What is meant by it? Perhaps not surprisingly, the term community is used by ordinary Shetlanders in much the same way as it is used by politicians and social scientists. Community can have an occupational referent: for example, the pilot community, the crofting community or the community of airport workers. Community can also be used to refer to various collectivities of people supposedly characterised by distinct ways of life: for example, the Shetlander community, the churchgoing community, the incomer community. However, perhaps the most important referent of community is geographical: a community is a social whole which is usually anchored in space; the members of a community live and do various things together within some (at least vaguely) definable geographical area.

The study area, Dunrossness, as defined by the local administration is *not* such an area. As demarcated by the local authority for planning and research purposes, Dunrossness is not a geographical base for any socially identifiable collectivity. The term

Dunrossness has numerous geographical referents, only one of which, a narrow zone in the centre of the research area, has community characteristics in Shetlands' eyes. As far as I could discover, there is no suggestion that the residents in the defined area for our research see themselves as constituting a socially relevant or meaningful whole.

However, within the study area there are a number of small villages, hamlets or neighbourhoods, all of which are attributed community status by Shetlanders. They are communities in the sense that one has a sense of "belonging" to them, and in the sense that Shetlanders belonging to each are said to be distinguishable by special characteristics in dialect or, less often (and more humourously), by differences in mentality and general attitudes. Belonging to these communities is different from living within their borders. "Belonging" to these communities is to have been born in them; and/or to have close kin in the area; and/or to have a reputation in them (i.e. to be known as having a certain character, certain skills and certain beliefs). If one does not belong one is an incomer. Here there is room for negotiation. One can be attributed incomer status in any local community because one does not have close kin in the area, because one was not born there or, simply, because one has not become known in them. One can also claim membership in terms of any of these attributes. Moreover, claims for membership in terms of one criterion can be, and often are, denied in terms of another. This all applies to Shetlanders as well as non-Shetlanders.

There is a more inclusive meaning to the term "incomer": this is used in relation to both these small, local communities and, more important, in relation to Shetland as a whole. The distinction is between those who are natives of Shetland and those who are not: these latter are, in a sense, "real" incomers. They are often labelled "soothmoothers" for the sake of clarification. It is here that the ambiguity about the application of the term "incomer" comes to an end. As one might expect, these "real incomers" are not all the same to Shetlanders. They have numerous subdivisions, defined along various dimensions. Incomers are differentiated along a scale of what looks like respectability, along a scale relating to relative permanence of residence and, associated with this latter, along a scale which relates to (something like) social investment in the locality in which they live. According to each of these criteria, the new residents in Dunrossness clearly stand apart, in Shetlanders' eyes, from all other incomers. First, the new residents in Dunrossness are different from the construction workers who live in camps situated in various parts of Shetland (including a camp at the airport): these latter are only temporary residents whose residence in Shetland, and whose supposed commitment to Shetland, will end with the end of the construction phase of the oil era. Second, both these latter people and the so-called "oilies" who pass through the local airport on the way to the oil rigs, are much less respectable than the more permanent residents in Dunrossness. Indeed, both construction workers and "oilies" are usually seen by Shetlanders as potential troublemakers who need to be amused, policed and, above all, contained. Shetlanders would point to the names and addresses of those mentioned in press reports of local court cases to provide evidence for their viewpoint.

Shetlanders in the area do divide up "their" incomers, i.e. those incomers who reside in the area. As applied to the population in Dunrossness, the gross category "incomer" is subdivided along various dimensions. For example, incomers are differentiated by age, by sex, according to occupational prestige (pilots stand above engineers and air traffic controllers), and according to place of residence (estate dwellers are supposed to stand apart as more distant from those who live interspersed with Shetlanders). Nevertheless, the gross categories "incomers" and Shetlanders are most often on people's lips whenever they are discussing events which occur in the area, and these gross categories seem to be the implicit (i.e. unspoken) backdrop to a lot of discussions about individuals' behaviour and personality traits.

That the gross distinction incomer/Shetlander is more important in people's perceptions than the finer distinctions which can be made is reflected or indicated in another way. The stereotypes which characterise, or are said to characterise, incomers do not differ in kind between the subdivisions of the incomer category. That is, pilots, or those who live in estates, do not seem to have specific stereotypes associated with them. Rather, pilots, or estate dwellers, differ in the degree to which a given stereotype is applicable to them. The attribute is associated with the category: any differences in stereotypes which exist within the category are differences in degree of applicability.

It is the general character or quality of the stereotypes of incomers volunteered by Shetlanders which point to perceived social distance. As a preliminary to an investigation of social change in the area, a series of 199 interviews were carried out, in order to sensitize research staff to the local society. These interviews involved 168 Shetlanders and 126 incomers: the interviews with Shetlanders provide a finite set of data on which to base my argument. Out of

these interviews it is possible to extract a limited repertoire of incomer stereotypes: these are presented in Table 1. I have taken the
step of reducing the multivarious statements made by informants to
these 14; i.e. I have had to translate their words into my own. I will
admit that this is a difficult (and risky) procedure but, generally
speaking, I do not think that I have made a nonsense of any
informant's statements about incomers. On the list is the number of
people who volunteered each stereotype. Since neither I, nor my

TABLE 1

Shetlanders on Incomers

Stereotype			Number of Shetlanders Volunteering Stereotype (T=168)	
1.	Nice People	Positive	43	
2.	Welcome "new blood"		18	
				61
3.	Transient		32	
4.	Unknown quantity but seem all right	Ambiguous/ Neutral	36	68
5.	Haughty		68	
6.	Ostentatious		9	
7.	Overconcerned with status or prestige		24	
8.	Cliquish	Negative	53	
9.	Standoffish		15	
10.	Inhospitable		3	
11.	Mercenary		27	
12.	Complainers		21	
13.	Silly or naive		17	
14.	Hedonistic		10	
				247
		Total Number of Volunteered Stereotypes	376	

colleagues, inquired whether any given informant agreed or disagreed
with a given stereotype, these figures should be treated with proper
caution: they do not give any clear indication of how many people
might or might not agree with any given stereotype; all they indicate
are the number of people who thought it convenient to volunteer
each stereotype. As such, they provide only vague indications of the
degree to which a given stereotype is shared by Shetlanders.

I have made qualitative distinctions among these stereotypes. I
think that it would be reasonable to suggest that stereotypes 1 and 2
are more positive than stereotypes 5 to 14. Stereotypes 3 and 4 are
rather more ambiguous — the fact that incomers might be only trans-
ient can be construed both positively or negatively by Shetlanders,

while the "unknown quality" stereotype is impossible to place in either category. One can now make a crude qualitative breakdown of statements of stereotype: Shetlanders' statements of negative stereotypes outweigh statements of positive stereotypes by a ratio of more than 6 to 1. This should at least point to a perceived degree of social distance from incomers.

From the interviews with Shetlanders one can also tease out Shetlanders' stereotypes of themselves. Perhaps it is hardly surprising that these are somewhat more positive in nature. These stereotypes are set out in Table 2, broken down in the same way. It can be seen

TABLE 2

Shetlanders on Shetlanders

Stereotype		Number of Shetlanders Volunteering Stereotype (T=168)	
1.	Versatile, self-sufficient and hard working	80	
2.	Close knit, mutually supportive	47	
3.	Easy going, little concern for time	Positive	14	
		Stereotypes	
4.	Friendly, open	45	
5.	Egalitarian	73	
6.	Modest, quiet	26	
7.	Family centred	27	
8.	Religious	8	
			320
9.	Fishermen and Crofters	68	
10.	Part Norse	Ambiguous/ Neutral	9	
11.	Ordinary country people	31	108
12.	Clannish (in non-kinship sense)	5	
13.	Clannish (in kinship sense)	Negative	5	
14.	Unsophisticated	Stereotypes	16	
15.	Fatalistic/Apathetic	20	
16.	Gullible	7	
			53
	Total Number of Volunteered Stereotypes	481	

that statements of positive stereotypes outnumber statements of negative statements by a ratio of 6 to 1. Shetlanders presented a rather cosy image of themselves. However, more direct evidence for the idea that Shetlanders have a dualistic perspective on the social environment lies in the fact that there are fundamental contrasts to be found is some of the stereotypes. Shetlanders stress what I have translated as egalitarianism among themselves: this stands in contrast to incomer haughtiness and concern for prestige. Shetlanders stress their openness: this stands in contrast to incomer standoffishness and cliquishness.

I will not go on labouring my point — I think that I have provided enough information to suggest that a dichotomy incomer/Shetlander exists in Shetlanders' eyes. This dichotomy is a newly emergent phenomenon. How do I know?

Change

As we all know research into social change is fraught with inherent difficulties, especially if one does not have an earlier base line study of the area under investigation or even an earlier study of an area comparable in economic and social characteristics. If one has neither of these, one has to rely on people's reports of their past behaviour and attitudes, and on their recollections of what their society was like in the past. Usually such data is an over-romanticised view of the actual state of affairs (for various reasons). However, if handled with care, one can use individual life histories to ascertain general trends.

It would seem that up until recently (usually this is specified as up to between 2 and 5 years ago) individual incomers (the "sooth-moother' type) were assimilated with relative ease into individual social networks centred in neighbourhoods or villages. There were comparatively few incomers and they were dispersed among the native population (estate building for incomers did not peak until 1976 and none existed before 1974). Most relations were created out of simple necessity — the need for advice, help with building, renovations and so forth. Furthermore, many of the first incomers had (and still have) a rather cosy view of life in Shetland, they pursued the meaningful "community"; as a consequence, these individuals tended to establish their closest relations with the bearers of Shetland tradition, the older Shetlanders. These older Shetlanders seemed to create the incomers' links to the community, in the sense that it was they who helped to forge the reputations attributed to the incomers. Having a reputation, these incomers came to "belong" to different local communities.

Increased immigration militated against the absorption of new arrivals in existing Shetlander networks: while at the same time it was accompanied by the creation of new networks composed of incomers — incomers found shared interests in what they saw as a frontier zone. Incomer networks were forged out of relationships created at work, in the new estates and in the local social club, an institution established to help airport workers obtain some of the benefits of urban civilization. Shift work added to the tenuous links between incomer men and their Shetlander neighbours.

Shetlanders would maintain that in the past individual incomers had to become part of the local community: now they no longer need to. In the past, they were willing to participate in local events, stand about and chat with the neighbours and generally act like good neighbours. The incomers depended upon Shetlanders for socializing and favours, and they had no exclusive networks of their own. To Shetlanders, the division of local society emerged from the creation of incomer networks.

The scene is set — the problem now is to account for changes in Shetlanders' perspectives on the local environment.

Why Dualism?

A superficial view of the situation might see the dichotomy in Shetlanders' views of society as simply a result of the presence of increased numbers of incomers in the area. Hence any more discussion is unnecessary. However, there is no automatic link between the presence of increased numbers of incomers, the Shetlanders' drawing of mental boundaries around themselves and around incomers, the stress put on these categories and the nature of the relationship which is supposed to exist between them. Certainly it would be logical for Shetlanders to cope intellectually with the new arrivals in terms of these gross boundaries. However, pointing out that categories seem to be logical is not the same as accounting for them. Why should the boundaries be drawn where they are? Furthermore, such an argument does not take us very far in understanding why Shetlanders view their relationship with incomers so negatively.

If one wanted to be more sophisticated, as some Shetlanders are, one might stress that the drawing of a boundary around Shetlanders is a simple consequence of the drawing of a boundary around incomers: a boundary which is drawn to cope with incomers' anonymity. The theory is as follows. Newly arrived incomers are absorbed into ever expanding incomer networks. The growing number of incomers in these networks leads to increased anonymity, an aspect of society which is exacerbated by the high level of turnover among incomers, due to occupational and hence geographical mobility and by the clustering of most incomers into housing estates set well apart from Shetlanders. The gross category "incomer" helps cope intellectually with this increased anonymity. As a logical corollary of the increased relevance of the gross category "incomer", the gross category Shetlander is re-emphasised.

As an account of the importance of the social dichotomy, this is quite sophisticated. However, unless it also accounts for the negative nature of the relationship between Shetlanders and incomers, it does not take one very far. The theory can, of course, account for the social distance between Shetlanders and incomers if one adds a rather nebulous and taken for granted psychological assumption – "people do not like people they do not know" or "anonymity leads to increased social distance". One can of course reverse this– increased social distance leads to anonymity. Either way, one is explaining one aspect of Shetlanders' general view of the local society (division between incomers and Shetlanders) in terms of another aspect of that general perspective (increased anonymity). One is in a sense only making more articulate the theoretical assumptions of the local population.

It seems to me, however, that greater explanatory value might be derived from trying to account for *both* the perceived social distance *and* its supposed cause, result of corollary, anonymity. That is, it might be better to step outside this circle of cause and effect. What is it which might account for both? I look for conflicts in the local society: conflicts which are at a lower level of articulation in Shetlanders' perceptions. They are aware of these conflicts: I could not find them if they did not give me direction. They are simply less clearly defined than their most abstract theories: any theorizing in which I could encourage Shetlanders to engage was ad hoc, and designed simply to cope with individual events (why the two types of theory have different levels of articulation will not be discussed here). Where do conflicts lie? They exist in two main areas – in the consideration of social rank and over land and housing.

Social Rank

It can be seen on Table 1 that Shetlanders' stereotypes of incomers include a number which relate to ideas about social ranking (see stereotypes 5, 6, and 7 on Table 1). Shetlanders stressed most the haughtiness of incomers and their morbid concern with status and prestige. Also, linked to these indirectly are other stereotypes: cliquishness and standoffishness. Incomers are cliquish and standoffish presumably because they are haughty. This at least suggests that the question of social ranking is perceived as a stress point by Shetlanders.

Among Shetlanders the ideal, acceptable or usual ways of ranking individuals (and families) seem to be multivarious. Numerous different scales are apparent, e.g. productive skills, industriousness, intelligence, helpfulness, friendliness, modesty, wit, and especially for women, religiosity. Assessment of individuals along any of these scales is an element of the shared local knowledge which develops out of living in face to face (or often back to back) communities. Despite differences in wealth, or in occupation, Shetlanders assume that evaluations of a person's worth should be a result of his or her behaviour, not according to what an individual "has " or "is".

Apparent claims for superiority made in terms of wealth or occupation are invariably countered (in gossip) by negative assessments along one or more of the other scales. The "toffee nosed" person might be useless with his hands or her hands! Nevertheless, most Shetlanders are perfectly aware of what social "class" means. Shetlanders see classes as aggregates of people who are ranked or arranged like layers on a cake. They are distinguished by various combinations of attributes – occupation, money, manners, education, power, jobs, standard of living, possession of material items. There is no doubt that Shetlanders' images of social class vary extensively from individual to individual (typically in relation to the "things" which are thought to "give" people their class, and the elements which are thought to be a consequence of class membership). However, all Shetlanders seem to agree that classes are tied up with wealth and occupation; and most Shetlanders agree that class is a concept which has greater salience in life outside Shetland and therefore among incomers.

Both incomers and Shetlanders make a basic occupational distinction between pilots on the one hand, and engineers and air traffic controllers on the other. Incomers tend to see this in "class" terms as well – pilots are generaly upper crust, while engineers are down to earth (socially as well as literally!). Since many incomer workers are ex-military the distinction is often phrased in military terms: officers and other ranks.

Those incomers with whom I discussed class agreed that awareness of class is a typically British trait. They also agreed that classes are aggregates of people who are distinguishable by one or by a combination of the following: wealth, occupation, manners, standard of living, power, material possessions. As one would expect, incomers took a greater interest in discussing class – class is supposed to go a long way in explaining the membership of given social networks, and of the scope of such networks.

For Shetlanders, it seems that a "new" set of universalistic measures for assessing individuals' social rank has been brought into play in the study area. While Shetlanders seem to cling to ranking schemes based on individual reputations, they believe that they are being judged by incomers in terms of "class" (hence the nature of their stereotypes). In terms of the features which are used to assess "class" most Shetlanders seem to recognise that they lag behind. Such notions are manifest in demonstrations of defence in interaction with incomers – especially with pilots.

Not all sections of the Shetland population cling to traditional measures of ranking with equal tenacity. The younger age group have taken up conspicuous consumption, presumably as a means of recouping some esteem in terms of the apparently dominant and universalistic class criteria. However, in perhaps the most important field, employment, Shetlanders (excluding *older* Shetlanders), do not, and as yet cannot, compete with incomers. Shetlanders seem to assess the "good job" in much the same way as incomers. It is defined in terms of wages/salaries, number of perks, capacity for initiative, amount and nature of skills involved, security and the community esteem which might come from obtaining such jobs. However, the overwhelming majority of recruits to the best jobs at the airport are recruited, unavoidably, outside Shetland (as yet the Shetland workforce does not have the relevant training or skills). Not only have the rules of the game been changed, but Shetlanders are handicapped for it.

There is therefore a sense of relative deprivation among Shetlanders. The general consequence of this is outlined in the literature on urban to rural migration by the middle class. The natives in the area assert that social worth is not to be defined in terms of such universalistic notions as class, but rather in terms of length of residence, i.e. they make a "rank" distinction between the established and the outsiders (see, for example Newby 1977; Pahl 1968).

Land and Housing

As I have mentioned above, the amount of immigration into the area has necessitated the passing over of land for new housing. The general literature on migration indicates that conflict is likely to be engendered here. In what ways has it been engendered in Dunrossness?

The image which most Shetlanders present is of new housing springing up everywhere, without any apparent pattern. Despite the supposed safeguard of a detailed District Plan, development of housing is presumed to be either totally out of control or else subject to inconsistent or ever changing planning policies. At the time of our research, Shetlanders seemed to share the view that the area was either in a state of supersaturation with new housing, or else nearing that state. Those held responsible for this general state of affairs range from the big "companies" to the local administration.

At the time of our research one of the two most widely acknow-ledged and apparent problems for Shetlanders was one which was formulated in public and private discussion as good agricultural land going for new (incomers') housing. One could argue that such com-plaints constitute some kind of rationale for a general feeling that there are too many incomers in the area. There is no reason to refute this argument: undoubtedly this is a sentiment seemingly shared by many Shetlanders. However there is more to it than that. The issue also revolves around a conflict between Shetlanders' "traditional" attitudes to land, and attitudes characteristic of non-Shetlanders which are also shared by some Shetlanders (especially some of the young). Many Shetlanders expressed concern (usually implicitly) about land being considered not as a resource for production, but as a resource to be treated simply as a kind of non-agricultural commodity i.e. something to be surrendered up from agriculture merely for money. This antagonism towards the idea that land is a kind of commodity is linked up to a particular view of history: older and middle-aged Shetlanders, especially, emphasize the importance of safeguarding agricultural land. Many older Shetlanders lay great stress on a boom and bust theory of history: according to this theory, Shetland and Dunrossness have experienced booms in the past, but they have always had to revert to traditional lifestyles and industries when they pass. Although present developments are seen as both quantitatively and qualitatively different, they too will pass: what will happen to the land on which housing is built? Objections that most of the land in question is relatively poor quality land might be accepted, but often the classification on which such estimates are based are challenged. The argument is often that a classification designed in the South (no matter what alterations exist for Shetland) does not take specifically local conditions and local interests into account. Local knowledge of the quality of land and its potential is thought to be more important.

Shetlanders see a conflict among themselves over land, a conflict generated by "incomers" almost by the very fact of their presence. In short, Shetlanders are criticised for selling land. People are quick to articulate such criticisms in gossip but even here there are constraints. Given that Dunrossness is experiencing a boom, it is entirely reasonable to make the most of the boom by selling individual plots of land, if that is the only way one can take advantage of it. People are rarely castigated in public for selling individual plots because such complaints would be counterproductive. However, it would seem that selling sizeable tracts of reasonable quality land (by local standards) is considered to be the behaviour of speculators and/or simple shortsighted. Thus it is a reasonable thing to complain about.

The relation between land and housing has generated conflicts in other ways. Competition between incomers and Shetlanders over house sites seems to be an important factor. House sites are seen to be a scarce resource, by both Shetlanders and incomers, basically because the number of sites given planning permission by the local authority is ever decreasing. Shetlanders are afraid that the majority of Shetlanders might be excluded from this market — with their higher salaries and various company safeguards, incomers are thought to be willing to make higher bids for scarce pieces of land. The conflict between Shetlanders and incomers is presumed in turn to cause friction between Shetlanders. It is not invariably the case that Shetlanders who are selling land will exhibit loyalty and give preference to other Shetlanders, especially if the other Shetlanders are not related. Here the behaviour is discussed as behaviour not reasonable for a Shetlander.

Even rented accommodation has been taken up almost exclusively by incomers: company allowances and incomers' higher salaries generally have meant that rents have increased and that incomers tend to be given preference as tenants. As a consequence, young Shetland married couples seem to presume that their best options are to await council housing or build houses on one or other spouses' kinfolks' land. In general, the ideal of forming a joint household with one or other spouses' parents is not seen to be a serious option.

The provision of council housing can be linked in turn to another source of conflict between Shetlanders and incomers (and to a lesser extent between Shetlanders). The provision of council housing threatens the interests of many private residents, both Shetlander and incomer. Generally speaking, however, incomers seem to be more vociferous about the threat which such housing presents to the peace and quiet of their area. Many incomers have a fixed image of rural life which does not include council estates, no matter how small. Moreover, their image of the countryside often excludes even new private housing as well. I have scant evidence to suggest that the problem for incomers is seen as much more than this — there may be a threat to house prices on behalf of non oil-related incomers (who have no guarantees) but oil-related workers seem to be assured of recovering their costs if they decide to sell up. What is important is that also here is the fact that even shared opposition to council housing (manifest in petitions) is usually blamed on incomers to an area. To many Shetlanders this is often seen to be part of a more general shortcoming of incomers — their overriding desire to maintain the status quo in local communities as soon as they are established there.

The conflicts which have developed over land and housing can be also linked up to the very mobility of incomers. Many of the incomers in resident private housing are still occupationally mobile (they are still mostly young): many have moved out of their adoptive communities, usually with a sizeable profit, after selling their houses. The very mobility of incomers is seen as another example of speculation. Incomers are "mercenary" not least in the sense that they use Shetland land to line their pockets.

That conflicts underly the dualism prevalent in Shetlanders' perspectives on their local society is supported by other more indirect evidence. It can be argued that most (though not all) of the important areas of conflict between "Shetlanders" and "incomers" will involve younger Shetlanders. If one sums the number of statements of negative stereotypes by age set, and expresses these as a percentage of the total number of statements expressed by those in each set, one comes up with the following figures:

TABLE 3

Shetlanders on Incomers

Age Set	20–39	40–59	60+
Statements of Negative Stereotypes as percentage of total statements of stereotypes	73%	63%	45.7%

Conclusions

Conflicts, then, underly the dualistic, dichotomised perspectives on society held by Shetlanders. The identities incomer and Shetlander, and the stereotypes associated with them, have become the main language in terms of which conflicts between individuals and groups are discussed, and in terms of which people's behaviour is evaluated. This is simply because these conflicts have emerged in these directions. Like all aspects of culture, the structuring of social perspectives will change with the unfolding of new conflicts of interest or with the development of common interests.

I stress that perceived conflicts of interest exist between individuals and groups who are *attributed* the incomer and Shetlander identities. Here my argument could short-circuit. If one adopted the view that individuals and groups act as representatives of each category, then explanation of events could be phrased as follows: individuals and groups are involved in conflicts because they belong to categories of people with different interests. In other words, belonging to these two categories accounts for people's involvement in the conflicts. Such deterministic theorizing is typical of gossip about individuals and groups (e.g. X does something "because he's an incomer"): gossip phrased in this way is one of the ways in which representational models feature at the level of trans-actions. This, however, would be too deterministic for an analytical model. I argue that the categories incomer and Shetlander should be seen as the idiom in terms of which individual and group conflicts of interest are expressed by Shetlanders. The categories are cultural products of social actions, they are not the determinants of social actions.

Acknowledgements

The data used in this paper were collected in the period May 1978 to January 1979, as part of a broader investigation of the social effects of oil related development. This broader research was financed and sponsored by the Shetland Islands Council, the North Sea Oil Panel of the Social Science Research Council, and the Scottish Development Department. The first of these defined the geographic limits of the study.

Notes

1. People's perspectives on society have been referred to in various ways: as "descriptive representational models" (Caws 1974); as "internal observer's models" (Ward 1965, 1966); as "actor's analytical models" (Lloyd 1974, 1979); and as "actors' descriptive knowledge of social structure" (Stuchlik 1976). Sociologists seem to refer to these as, simply, "images of society" (see, for example, Bulmer 1975; Davis 1979). Whatever we choose to call them, it would seem that such models emphasise generalizations created from the outside (metaphorically speaking): people set themselves apart from their immediate social environment in an intellectual sense, isolate bits and pieces from it and arrange these bits and pieces together somehow. This structuring is relatively fluid, as a result of its continual manipulation in everyday activities like gossip, where the models function as a set of reference categories for explaining, or accounting for, the behaviour of others.

References

Bulmer, M. ed. (1975). *Working Class Images of Society*. London: Routledge and Kegan Paul.

Caws, P. (1974). Operational, representational and explanatory models. *American Anthropologist* **76**, 1-10.

Cohen, A. P. (1978). The same — but different! The allocation of identity in Whalsay, Shetland. *Sociological Review* **26**, 449-69.

Davis, H. H. (1979). *Beyond Class Images: Explorations of Social Consciousness*. London: Croom Helm.

Lloyd, P. C. (1974). *Power and Independence: Urban Africans' Perceptions of Social Inequality*. London: Routledge and Kegan Paul.

Lloyd, P. C. (1979). *Slums of Hope? Shanty Towns of the Third World*. Harmondsworth: Penguin.

McFarlane, G. (1978). *Gossip and Social Relationships in a Northern Irish Village*. Unpub. PhD Thesis, Queen's University of Belfast.

Newby, H. (1977). *The Deferential Worker: A Study of Farm Workers in East Anglia*. London: Allen Lane.

Pahl, R. E. (1968). The rural urban continuum. In *Readings in Urban Sociology*, (R. E. Pahl, ed.). London: Pergamon Press.

Stuchlik, M. (1976). *Life on a Half Share: Mechanisms of Social Recruitment among the Mapuche of Southern Chile*. London: Hurst.

Ward, B. (1965). Varieties of the conscious model: the fishermen of South China. In *The Relevance of Models for Social Anthropology*, (M. Banton, ed.). London: Tavistock.

Ward, B. (1966). Sociological self awareness: some uses of the conscious models. *Man* (N.S.) **1**, 201-15.

ON THE INFERENCE OF FOLK MODELS: DISCUSSION AND DEMONSTRATION

KAY MILTON

Discussion

The question has been raised, in the introductory paper to this volume, of how far the analyst can know that the model he infers corresponds to what the actors hold in their heads (Holy and Stuchlik, this volume: 22). The question of "psychological validity" (cf. Wallace 1965) carries differing implications depending on the type of knowledge being inferred and the type of data being used as the basis for inference. Where the analyst is inferring knowledge only from observable actions and not from verbal statements, then his inferences might be said to be valid once he is able, on their basis, to replicate the actions (cf. Hanson 1975: 61; Holy and Stuchlik, this volume: 24). If the aim of the analysis is simply to describe the use of, say, a set of kin terms, then his ability to replicate this use renders his analysis valid, regardless of how far his understanding of the actors' kin categories corresponds with their own (cf. Burling 1965: 117). If the analyst is concerned only with stating what categories exist in the actors' knowledge and not with inferring the criteria they use to distinguish these categories, then it is irrelevant how far the criteria he uses in his analytical presentation correspond with those employed by the actors (cf. Pospisil 1965: 189), and the question of validity extends only to the inference of the correct categories. Most studies that have investigated folk knowledge have, however, aimed to understand more than this; how folk models are constituted as well as how they are used; not only what categories exist in the actors' knowledge, but also how the actors differentiate these categories, how the criteria for differentiation are chosen, etc. D'Andrade, for example, aims to find out how Americans "go about believing", rather than simply what they believe, with regard to illness (D'Andrade 1976: 155). Sanday is concerned with discovering how people process information on kin categories (Sanday 1968). Since this kind of knowledge can be inferred only from people's verbal statements (Holy and Stuchlik, this volume: 22), which are generally taken to be less ambiguous indications of what they know than are their non-verbal actions, the question of psychological validity might be thought not to arise. I shall argue, however, that certain methods commonly employed in the inference of knowledge have led the analyst to construct models which are not those held and employed by the actors in their every-day life.

The methods that are generally used in this type of analysis are based on two facts, both mentioned by Holy and Stuchlik. Firstly, knowledge, being a mental phenomenon, is not directly observable (*Ibid.:* 3ff.). Secondly, verbal statements are highly indexical; their meaning depends on a large body of knowledge possessed by the actors but not actually stated (*Ibid.:* 23). These two basic facts ensure that, however long an analyst spends observing the everyday life of his informants, he can probably gain only a partial under-standing of their shared body of notions. In view of this, analysts have attempted to devise special tasks for their informants, designed to elicit far fuller accounts of their folk knowledge than would other-wise be obtained. There is a basic problem, however, in the use of such techniques; this problem lies in the relationship between know-ledge and actions.

While pure cognition — knowing — is not a purposeful activity, the invocation of knowledge is (Stuchlik 1977; Holy and Stuchlik, this volume: 18). Since knowledge can only be made available to others through actions (including verbal statements), it is always invoked for a purpose; whenever it is invoked it is being used by people. Given that the type of understanding we are aiming for is "from the actors' point of view", any particular item of knowledge can only be understood in terms of its purposeful invocation. Hence Bourdieu's comment that classificatory systems cannot be adequately under-stood through strictly "internal" (structural, componential) analysis which, " . . . in artificially wrenching them from their conditions of production and use, inevitably fails to understand their social functions" (Bourdieu 1977: 97). The fact that knowledge is always linked, through purpose, to the action of its invocation, has certain implications for the techniques that are normally employed by analysts to get at people's knowledge.

Firstly, since the anlayst is trying to obtain knowledge that would not normally be revealed in everyday life, the tasks he sets his informants are necessarily not those they would normally encounter.

On what basis, then, can it be assumed that the model revealed through the completion of such tasks is the same as that on which the actors base their everyday interaction? In his study of American beliefs about illness, D'Andrade uses a technique common in ethno-science; that of providing the informants with sentence frames, com-piled by him, which they are asked to complete with words selected by them from a list, again compiled by the analyst. In order to ensure that the frames made sense to his informants, he constructed them from statements made by them in a series of informal inter-views. In a similar way, the disease terms used for the completion of frames were also collected during these interviews (D'Andrade 1976: 156). Informants were then asked to consider each frame in relation to each of the disease terms and to complete the frames in such a way that the sentences then made sense in terms of their knowledge. In some cases at least, it seems reasonable to assume that informants were being asked to answer questions that would never otherwise occur to them. While it seems likely, for instance, that the actors quite often consider the fact that measles is catching, it seems unlikely that they consider as frequently the fact that polio is, and the possibility of heart attacks being catching is probably almost never entertained. D'Andrade recognises the difficulty posed by asking informants what are, to them, novel questions, and suggests that their ability to answer them indicates, in their model of illness, a generative capacity, which he incorporates into his analytical description of the model (*Ibid.:* 160-161). Nevertheless, the bias that we would expect a folk model to exhibit, with certain notions being better established than others, can only be obscured by this technique. It might be argued that, if the informants already possess a notion of "polio" and also know that some diseases are catching, then the notion that polio is catching is potentially a part of their knowledge even if they have never before considered the possibility. By the same token it might be argued that anyone whose culture contains a notion of metal and a notion of birds potentially knows about metal birds even before they have seen any aeroplanes. Since we are interested in inferring the knowledge that the actors actually hold and use in their everyday lives, rather than knowledge which they might hold under different circumstances, I would suggest that questions which encourage informants to consider new possibilities are of limited value.

Secondly, although in setting informants such tasks to fulfil the analyst may be divorcing the invocation of knowledge from the social situations in which it is usually done, he is merely replacing these situations with another, that of the inquiry itself. Answering anthropologists' questions, in other words, is as much a purposeful activity as is any activity in which knowledge is revealed, and its purpose is therefore just as much a condition of its understanding. The models revealed through formal methods, therefore, are not models that are free of social considerations, they are models used for the specific purpose of answering the questions posed by the analyst. It could be argued that this does not matter, since the questions have been constructed with the purpose of revealing specific knowledge and the results are, therefore, being understood in terms of the purpose for which the task was performed. This argument assumes, however, that the informant defines the task in the same way as does the analyst. While the analyst might see the informant as setting out to provide him with specific items of knowledge, there is no guarantee that the informant will perceive his own actions in this way. His intention may be simply to get rid of the anthropologist in the shortest time possible. That informants and analysts can hold very different definitions of the task at hand is illustrated by an example from Cancian's study of Zinacanteco norms (Cancian 1975). Two of her informants, when asked to arrange written normative statements into piles on the basis of similarity did so, not on the basis of the similarity of norms, but on the basis of the similarity of the first words of each written statement.

The results of the sorting task performed by these particular informants were, needless to say, omitted from Cancian's analysis. It would appear, therefore, that the analyst has already decided what the model should contain and her results are selected accordingly. Similarly, she rejected all the statements made by only one of her three informants on the grounds that they appeared to represent the idiosyncratic interests of the particular informant (*Ibid.:* 44). If this procedure is considered legitimate then it seems pertinent to ask whose model we end up with, that of the actors or that of the analyst?

My criticisms of formal methods for inferring and describing folk models are perhaps best summarised as an over-authorship on the part of the analyst. It has been pointed out (Holy and Stuchlik, this volume: 22) that folk models are necessarily authored by the anthropologist. Nevertheless, since the object of the analysis is other people's knowledge and not our own, it seems reasonable to demand that the analyst's control over the content and form of the model should be minimal, even if the analytical representation of it is inevitably his.

What, then, can be proposed as a useful alternative approach? D'Andrade has pointed out that:

At present, the most frequently used (and perhaps most effective) technique for the study of cultural belief systems is for the individual ethnographer to immerse himself in the culture as deeply as possible and, by some series of private, unstated, and sometimes unconscious operations, to integrate large amounts of information into an organized and coherent set of propositions. (D'Andrade 1976: 179)

In other words, the anthropologist's understanding of folk models is based largely on the impressions he has formed through living among his informants. The most desirable advance in the scientific study of culture would seem to be, as D'Andrade goes on to suggest, somehow to make this enterprise explicit and replicable. In the remainder of this paper I have tried to do precisely this, or at least to go some way towards it.

Demonstration

On the following pages I shall describe the model held by the Wakasigau of the religious categories into which they divide their social world. A brief outline of the area and the religious developments that have occured there will provide sufficient background knowledge to the description.

Kasigau is a large, isolated hill in the south-western corner of Kenya. Around the base of the hill are five villages, with an average population of around 600. Most of my fieldwork was carried out in two of these villages, with shorter visits to the others. The Wakasigau (people of Kasigau) identify in many ways with the people of the Taita Hills, about thirty miles to the north. They speak a dialect of the Kitaita language and consistently cite "Taita" as their tribal identity. The following account of recent religious developments is derived solely from what my informants told me.

The Wakasigau were first exposed to Christianity at the beginning of this century when missionaries attempted to establish a church in Kasigau. These attempts failed and there was no further intensive contact with Christians until the period 1918-1936. During this time, as a result of events that occurred during the First World War, the Wakasigau were exiled from their home and living on the lower slopes of the Taita Hills. Here, the Anglican Church was well established and many Wakasigau were converted to Christianity. In 1936, they were allowed to return to their homeland on the condition that (among other things) they start building churches there. At the time of my fieldwork the buildings were still far from finished, but Kasigau is now a parish in the Mombasa diocese of the Church Province of Kenya, which is itself a province of the Church of England. The Anglican Church is almost always referred to in Kasigau as CMS (Church Missionary Society), which is the organisation that provided the missionaries in the area. All the Wakasigau I spoke to claimed to be Christians, and most claimed to be CMS.

During the early 1950s, some people within the Anglican Church in Kasigau started claiming that they were "saved". This, I was told, was part of the wider "African Revivalist Movement" that had begun in Ruanda in the 1930s and spread across Uganda into Kenya. Members of this fellowship identify themselves and are identified by others with the label "Tendereza", a Luganda word that occurs in the song sung by members.

In 1957 American missionaries brought the Gospel Church to this part of Kenya and many Wakasigau joined. Some, attracted by the money and free bicycles offered to preachers in the Gospel Church, went on training courses and obtained certificates for preaching. All but one of these local preachers gave up the work when the money ran out, about three years later, but this one carried on and the Gospel Church in Kasigau has retained some popularity in spite of many of the early converts having returned to CMS. Members of the Gospel Church and of the other fellowships that have broken away from it are also regarded, by themselves and others, as "saved".

No further developments took place until 1976 when a nationwide split occured within Tendereza. In Kasigau the split was reflected by four people breaking away from Tendereza and forming their own fellowship, still within CMS. This is referred to by various names, the most common being *"Dini ya Kupaa"* (Swahili, meaning "the religion of going upward", or "ascending").

Also in 1976, a split occured in the Gospel Church in Kasigau. A Gospel member from the Taita Hills came under the influence of a group of Kikuyus who were following items of Christian doctrine which had been previously ignored. The news spread from the Taita Hills to Kasigau, where the majority of Gospel members wanted to introduce the new items. There was some disagreement over this issue with the certified Gospel preacher, and the majority broke away and formed a new fellowship, leaving the preacher with only a few followers. The new fellowship became known as *"Ilago"* or *"Wailago"* (Kitaita, meaning "The Word" or "People of The Word").

In 1978 the Ilago fellowship further split into two, a larger section deciding no longer to follow the Kikuyu movement, leaving a residue of just four or five members who continued to do so. The smaller fellowship I shall refer to as *"Neno"* (Swahili, meaning "The Word").

Towards the end of 1978 and during the early part of 1979 the leaders of the Gospel and Ilago (excluding Neno) fellowship decided to settle their differences, at least to the extent that they started holding joint prayer-meetings and services. Consequently, they are now often referred to, by their own members as well as by outsiders, as a single fellowship, usually under the heading "Gospel".

As a result of these developments the Wakasigau see themselves as being divided on the basis of religious affiliation into a number of categories of varying degrees of inclusiveness. The most inclusive category is "Christian", to which all Wakasigau see themselves as belonging, and the vast majority also claim to be CMS. Of a total adult population of about 1200 there are probably no more than 100 (8.3%) at any one time who consider themselves "saved". Of these, about 40 are within CMS (Tendereza and Dini ya Kupaa), 50 or more are Gospel or Ilago, and only about 5 belong to the Neno fellowship. It is difficult meaningfully to generalise about numbers, however, since membership is always changing. I have used the term "fellowship" here to refer to the least inclusive categories since this is how the actors often describe them.

The Wakasigau conceptualise their religious categories in terms of attributes shared by the members of each category. The problem of the analysis is to describe the categories as they are defined by the Wakasigau, in other words, to infer the criteria used by the actors in distinguishing between categories and to use these criteria to describe the categories. I am therefore doing more than simply stating what categories exist in Kasigau knowledge and in aim my analysis has more in common with those of Cancian (1975) and D'Andrade (1976) than those of, say, Burling (1965) or Pospisil (1965).

During my fieldwork I acquired a model of religious categories in Kasigau which was, to all intents and purposes, "correct". By this I mean that I was able to use this knowledge in ways that were meaningful to my informants. I could accurately predict, on the basis of my knowledge of someone's religious affiliation, what his behaviour would be in particular situations, to the same extent as could the actors themselves. Similarly, I could use people's observed behaviour as indications of their religious affiliation, again with the same degree of accuracy as could my informants. The problem, as D'Andrade suggests, is to make explicit the process through which I acquired this knowledge; to present it as it was presented to me. Since the major source of information on knowledge of this kind lies in people's verbal statements, what follows is essentially an analysis of what was said to me, on the subject of religious categories, throughout my fieldwork.

Information on the actors' conceptualisations of their religious categories was collected mainly in the course of informal conversations, either between myself and an informant, or among a number of actors in my presence. Notions about religious categories were also invoked more formally in the context of sermons and testimonies at services and prayer-meetings. Within the context of informal conversations, no attempt was made to question informants systematically or at great length about religious categories. Questions were asked that were pertinent only to the topic in hand and the subject of religion (introduced more often by one of the actors than by myself) was pursued only as long as the actors were interested in pursuing it. The fact that I am presenting here only what was said on religion does not, of course, imply that this topic was of overriding importance for people in Kasigau. It was talked about quite frequently, but by no means all the time, and no more than several other topics of interest (such as sorcery, illness, local disputes, agricultural matters, etc.). Out of 100 conversations recorded at random during 1979 (all of which took place among two or more of the actors in my presence, and during all of which I avoided exerting any influence over what was said), in only 9 were religious matters the central topic, in 18 religion formed a secondary topic, in 12 it was given a passing reference and in 61 it was not mentioned at all.

The method outlined here of collecting information was used in order to avoid what I regard as the pitfalls of more formal methods of data collection (this chapter: 139ff.). More specifically, since people's knowledge is acquired through everyday social interaction, the model I want to infer is that which is exchanged and invoked in everyday social interaction, and not that which is invoked only for the purpose of answering an anthropologist's questions, however this task might be perceived by the informant. Rather than wanting to eliminate any bias that might be present when an informant, instead of setting out to provide a list of characteristics, is concerned with supporting specific arguments for his own private ends, I treat this bias as a feature of the model exchanged in everyday life and therefore as something that should be revealed in the description of the model. Whatever features of the model are revealed in everyday conversation must be reflected in the actors' knowledge since it is through such conversations that their knowledge is acquired, modified, reinforced.

From the contexts outlined above, informal conversations and more formal sermons and testimonies, specific statements were selected as indicative of how the actors define their religious categories. These statements, those that explicitly make an association between a specific attribute and a particular category, number 358 and were made by a total of 99 informants. The numerical relation of informants to statements is very uneven, one informant having made 37 statements and 36 informants having made only one statement each; 85 of the informants made up to 5 statements each while the remainder (excluding the one who made 37 statements) made between 6 and 15 statements each. These figures cannot be assumed accurately to reflect the variation in individual interest in religious matters, since they apply only to those statements which I have selected as relevant to the description of religious categories.

The statements selected as indicative of how the actors define their religious categories are of the type "Gospel people clap their hands when they sing", or "Saved people don't dance", etc. This information was analysed as follows. All the attributes (total 91) mentioned by informants in relation to religious categories were listed. Each statement was then examined against the list and the particular attribute mentioned and the type of association made were noted. For example, the statement "Saved people don't dance" incorporates a negative association of the attribute "dancing" with the category "Saved". The statement "Unsaved people do dance" incorporates a positive association of the same attribute with the category "Unsaved". The characteristic mentioned plus the type of association made constitute a criterion by which the category is defined. In this way, the full range of criteria revealed by informants as defining each category was established, and the number of times each criterion was mentioned in relation to each category was noted.

The full list of categories mentioned in the 358 statements is shown in Table 1. Most of the category labels are self-explanatory. "Saved" refers to all those who are considered to be saved, whatever fellowship they belong to. "CMS Saved" refers to Tendereza and Dini ya Kupaa together. The lumping together of other fellowships — Ilago + Gospel, Ilago + Neno, Gospel + Ilago + Neno — is a product mainly of the historical development of these fellowships. Before April 1978, Gospel and Ilago were recognised as separate fellowships, but Neno had not yet come into existence. Consequently, many of the statements that lump Ilago and Neno together are those that were made before this time — when they had not yet split up. It is important to realise that in these cases, "Ilago + Neno" is not conceptualised by informants as a compound category, a combination of the two, but as a single undifferentiated category. On the other hand, it was not unusual for informants to lump these categories together even after the split had occurred, in which case what is being invoked can be regarded as a compound category. Similarly, Gospel, Ilago and

TABLE 1

*Showing the categories mentioned by informants and the number of
statements made about each*

Category	No. of statements made
* 1. Saved	123
* 2. Ilago + Neno	58
* 3. Ilago	28
* 4. Tendereza	24
* 5. Gospel	19
* 6. Neno	18
* 7. Gospel + Ilago + Neno	17
8. Christian	17
9. Unsaved	15
*10. Dini ya Kupaa	12
*11. Ilago + Gospel	11
12. CMS	5
13. Good Christians	5
*14. CMS Saved	2
*15. Saved people other than Ilago + Neno	2
16. People other than Ilago + Neno	1
*17. Saved people other than Tendereza	1
	358

*=Saved categories

Neno can all be classed together under one heading: Gospel + Ilago +
Neno. In view of the historical development of these fellowships,
this label hides a number of possible combinations. It could be a
compound category made up of three separate fellowships, or a
combination of Ilago + Gospel and Neno, the former two being
undifferentiated, or a combination of Gospel and Ilago + Neno, the
latter two together being seen as one category. The model I present
here fails to distinguish between these different conceptualisations.
This is mainly because for the purposes of this paper I am not taking
account of changes in the model over time. To reveal the different
conceptualisations hidden in what appear here as compound
categories would require, not only a detailed analysis of the
information on a temporal basis, but also an analysis of other
statements that make explicit the relations among categories, which
is beyond the scope of this paper. The rather complex and somewhat idiosyncratic categories that appear at the end of the list (15,
16 and 17) are the result of particular individuals making statements
that compare their own behaviour with that of other people
generally or that of other saved people; statements such as "We
(Ilago + Neno before the split) do such and such but other saved
people do not."

In presenting the criteria used by informants to define their categories (Table 2) I have omitted all criteria mentioned only once in relation to any particular category. This was done purely for the sake of convenience, to limit the length of the table, and not because I do not regard statements made only once as being part of the actors' model. On the contrary, I would assume that since many of these statements, made in the course of conversations, were meaningful to participants other than myself, they are well-established and agreed upon notions whose relevance to the ongoing social processes at the time I collected the information was simply less than that of statements made more often. Since two of the categories were mentioned only once, they do not appear in Table 2. A further two categories are omitted since, although mentioned more than once, no criterion was mentioned more than once in relation to them.

In interpreting the information contained in Table 2, two things should be borne in mind. Firstly, the statements were made, in most cases, for the purpose of setting one category off against another rather than for the purpose of setting one category off against *all* others. For example, an informant might say that Tendereza do one thing while Gospel do another. The first attribute can be taken as part of that particular informant's concept of the category "Tendereza", and the second as part of his concept of the category "Gospel", but because the statement was made specifically to distinguish between Tendereza and Gospel, there is no necessary implication that the criteria mentioned are exclusive to either of these two categories. That mentioned in connection with Tendereza might also be known to be a characteristic of Dini ya Kupaa, while that attributed to Gospel might also be known to be a characteristic of Ilago. Secondly, the varying degrees of inclusiveness of categories must be taken into account. The category "Christian" includes all others, while the category "CMS" includes both CMS Saved and those unsaved Christians who are also CMS. Since it is impossible to be Tendereza, Dini ya Kupaa, Gospel, Ilago or Neno without being saved, it can be assumed that all the characteristics mentioned in relation to the "Saved" category also pertain to these less inclusive categories. The criteria mentioned in relation to the five fellowships can be expected to be those that set them apart from each other rather than those that set them apart from, say, unsaved people. There were, of course, occasional statements that did not deal with the boundary between, say, Saved and Unsaved, or with boundaries between fellowships, but which instead contrasted directly, say, Unsaved with Ilago. Such statements were usually of the type in

TABLE 2

Showing the criteria used to define each category, the number of times
each criterion was mentioned and the number of informants mentioning each one

Criterion	No. of times mentioned	No. of informants
A. Saved		
Don't use the services of traditional curers	13	11
Confess, repent and repudiate their sins	11	11
Don't dance	10	9
Say that they are saved	7	7
Don't receive/approve of receiving bridewealth	6	6
Don't drink alcohol	5	5
Use the greeting "Bwana okaso" (Praise the Lord)	4	4
Don't practise traditional customs	4	3
Believe Jesus to be their saviour	4	4
Don't practice several days' mourning at the house of a deceased	3	3
Don't practise circumcision of girls	3	3
Don't cry and wail at funerals	3	2
Are not susceptible to sorcery	3	3
Don't smoke	3	3
Don't listen to or perform secular music	3	3
Don't get possessed by spirits	3	3
Experience an inner change (on being saved)	2	2
Sing at funerals	2	2
Don't practise polygyny	2	2
Don't do things with people who are not saved	2	2
Don't wear jewellery	2	2
Don't practise mother-in-law/father-in-law avoidance	2	2
Don't indulge in pre-marital sex or adultery	2	2
B. Ilago + Neno		
Wash each other's feet	14	14
Don't receive medical treatment of any kind	12	12
Hold their own separate meetings	3	3
Don't have or want an organised church	3	3
Hold meetings at night	3	3
Don't listen to or perform secular music	2	2
Live like the early Christians	2	2
Use only their African names (i.e. not Christian names)	2	2
Don't use the services of traditional curers	2	2
Exclude those who are not saved from their meetings	2	2
C. Ilago		
Don't have or want an organised church	5	5
Don't receive medical treatment of any kind	4	4
Wash each other's feet	3	3
Hold their own separate meetings	2	2
Cast out spirits	2	2
Are baptized repeatedly	2	2
Believe that sickness is brought by spirits	2	2

TABLE 2 (Cont.)

D. Tendereza

Choose whom to greet "Bwana okaso" (Praise the Lord)	3	3
Do receive medical treatment (from hospital and dispensary)	2	2
Hold their own separate meetings	2	2
Do have an organised church	2	2

E. Gospel

Don't wash each other's feet	6	5
Don't receive medical treatment of any kind	3	3
Clap their hands when singing	2	2
Hold their own separate meetings	2	2
Are baptized by complete immersion in water	2	2

F. Gospel + Ilago + Neno

Don't receive medical treatment of any kind	4	4
Are baptized by complete immersion in water	2	2
Hold their own separate meetings	2	2

G. Christian

Don't use the services of traditional curers	3	3
Are not susceptible to sorcery	3	3
Have been baptized	3	3
Don't dance	2	2
Don't practise initiation rites	2	2

H. Neno

Don't receive medical treatment of any kind	4	4
Do receive bridewealth	2	2
Don't have or want an organised church	2	2
Wash each other's feet	2	2

I. Unsaved

Do smoke	2	2

J. Dini ya Kupaa

Don't receive/approve of receiving bridewealth	6	5
Don't accept loans	2	2

K. Ilago + Gospel

Don't receive medical treatment of any kind	2	2
Don't have or want an organised church	2	2

L. CMS

Do have an organised church	2	2

M. Good Christians

Don't practise polygyny	2	2

which an informant was comparing his own category with that of another individual about whom he was talking at the time; for instance, "We do this, but he is Ilago so he does such and such a thing".

Some of the criteria mentioned in Table 2 require further comment. It will be noticed that a number of categories have certain criteria in common. Categories B, C, D, E and F are said to "hold their own separate meetings". With regard to Gospel, Ilago and Neno (and permutations of these three) this refers to the fact that these fellowships hold their own services on Sundays, and frequently hold meetings at night which can go on until dawn. When the criterion was mentioned with regard to Tendereza, the intended meaning was "they hold different meetings from us", the speakers being, on one occasion a Gospel member and on the other an Ilago member. The statements refer to the fact that, on Sundays, when there are three or four different kinds of service in progress at once, Tendereza attend the CMS church along with other saved and unsaved CMS members.

It will be noticed from Table 2 that both Christians and saved people are said not to use the services of traditional curers (*waghanga,* sing. *mghanga*) (Table 2, G and A). These services consist of the prescribing and making of herbal mixtures, some of which are taken orally, some of which are rubbed on the body, and the making of charms intended to protect against sorcery or evil spirits or the consequences of one's own misdemeanours. Such medicines are regarded as belonging to the realm of evil and darkness and as being, not only inappropriate to a Christian existence, but also unnecessary since a true faith in God is regarded as sufficient protection against evil. (Hence the statement – Table 2, G – that Christians are not susceptible to attacks by sorcery, while saved people are neither susceptible to sorcery nor get possessed by spirits – Table 2, A). The fact that the category "Christian" and the category "Saved" have attributes in common is an indication of the fact that saved people are regarded as particularly good Christians. What all Christians ought to do, saved people almost invariably do. This is also indicated by the fact that the non-practice of polygyny is thought of as a characteristic both of "Good Christians" and of "Saved". While there are many people who are not saved but are good Christians, all saved people are assumed to be good Christians. The fact that such criteria are mentioned in association with different categories of differing degrees of inclusiveness is a product of two things. Firstly, the common recognition that not all Christians behave in a way that is generally regarded (and preached) to be ideal Christian behaviour. It is common knowledge that many who are Christians in the sense that they have been baptized (Table 2, G) still continue to use traditional medicines and quite openly marry more than one wife.

If they are "good" Christians, however, and more especially if they are saved, they will not do these things. This is especially so in the case of saved people since being saved involves making an open declaration that you are saved (this being, according to some, an essential difference between saved people and good Christians – Table 2, A), and this simply will not be believed unless the individual concerned practises what is generally recognised as good Christian behaviour. On the other hand, being a "Good Christian" depends solely on other people's perceptions of one's own behaviour and does not involve any claim being made on one's own part. Secondly, in view of the way in which the data were collected, statements were often made, in the course of conversations, to explain or justify the actions of specific individuals. In one such case I was told that a woman had objected to her husband bringing a traditional curer to treat their son: the explanation given was, "she is a Christian so she doesn't use that kind of medicine". Had the woman been saved, this would almost certainly have been pointed out instead of the fact that she is a Christian. I treat this statement as evidence of the knowledge outlined above, i.e. that Christian behaviour ought to fulfil certain demands. The fact that it often doesn't and that this is commonly known is indicated by the fact that the same characteristics are attributed to less inclusive categories. The non-use of traditional medicines was also invoked in relation to the category "Ilago + Neno" (Table 2, B). In both cases it was mentioned in relation to particular individuals who were sick and the issue was raised of whether or not the traditional curer would be asked to help.

On the subject of medicine, it will be noted from Table 2 that, while Christians and saved people are seen as not using traditional medicines, Ilago, Neno and Gospel people (Table 2; B, C, E, F, H, K) refuse all medical treatment, including that offered by the hospital and the dispensary. Since all these people are saved it would be superfluous to state that they don't use traditional medicines (except in cases such as the two mentioned above). What sets them apart from other saved people, and from unsaved people, is the fact that they have given up using medicine altogether and spurn even that from the dispensary and the hospital, which the majority of the population now regard as being more effective and generally superior to traditional medicine. This non-use of medicine is regarded as being somewhat peculiar by other members of the community. The recognised rationale behind it is that all diseases are caused by spirits (Table 2, C), and that, although medicines may alleviate the symptoms of an illness, the only effective cure is to cast out the offending spirit (Table 2, C). While most non-Gospel, non-Ilago and non-Neno members of the population accept that some illnesses are caused by spirits, they also feel that in most cases, whatever the cause of the illness, a medical cure is just as effective and often more so than any other, and is always worth a try. In contrast to this, I was told by one prominent member of the Ilago fellowship that, not only is sickness the work of the Devil, but so too is medicine: "That is how he works, through men. Once they wore rags and had long hair and were dirty (reference to diviners and traditional curers), now they are clean and wear nice white coats to make people think they are all right."

The emphasis on particular criteria indicates which boundaries, between what categories, were being stressed at the time. 29 (29%) of the 101 statements about Gospel, Ilago and Neno fellowships included in Table 2 (B, C, E, F, H and K) concern the non-use by members of these categories of Western medicine, the characteristic that sets them off from all other members of the community, saved or unsaved. Similarly, 19 (26%) of the 74 statements about Ilago and Neno categories included in Table 2 (B, C and H) deal with the fact that members of these fellowships wash each other's feet. This is done when they visit each other's houses, and the practice was adopted under the influence of the Kikuyu movement (this chapter: 142). It is a re-enactment of the incident described in John, Chapter 13, in which Christ washes the feet of his disciples. This was the central issue in the split (in 1976) between Gospel and Ilago and knowledge of this is reflected in the fact that informants mentioned 6 times that members of the Gospel fellowship don't wash each other's feet (Table 2, E). Another issue that was introduced under the influence of the Kikuyu movement was that of whether or not true followers of God's Word should have an organised church with an established hierarchy. The distinction between having and not having church organisation is often expressed in terms of the distinction between "religion", meaning all the wordly trappings of Christianity, and "salvation", which is seen as a spiritual rather than a wordly condition. Church organisation was opposed by those who followed the Kikuyu movement and supported by the one remaining Gospel preacher, who was interested in retaining his position of leadership on the basis of his certificate. This is reflected in the fact that not having or wanting an organised church was mentioned most often in relation to the Ilago and Neno fellowhips, considered separately (Table 2, C and H), and not in relation to Gospel considered on its own (Table 2, E). It has since become a bone of contention between Ilago and Neno, members of Neno claiming that Ilago have slipped back into "religion" while they themselves are interested only in pursuing "salvation". The fact that not having/wanting an organised church was mentioned twice in relation to the category "Ilago + Gospel" is a reflection of the fact that these two fellowships started worshipping together early in 1979. Both statements were made after the reunion had occured, one by a member of Gospel who was objecting to their entire worshipping group being referred to as a church, and one by an official of the Anglican Church for the purpose of derogating Gospel and Ilago members in the eyes of other CMS members to whom he was speaking.

Similarly contentious issues, the acceptance or non-acceptance of bridewealth and the borrowing of money, which formed the basis of the split between Tendereza and Dini ya Kupaa, are the subject of all the statements mentioned in Table 2 about the latter category (Table 2, J). The fact that saved people generally and, to a lesser extent, "Good Christians" don't like accepting bridewealth is generally known (Table 2, A and M). What sets Dini ya Kupaa apart from these other categories is that its members absolutely condemn the acceptance of bridewealth rather than reluctantly condoning it.

Although my main concern here is with the criteria that are used to define categories, it is possible, on the basis of the data presented, to make observations on other features of the model, for example on the differing degrees of emphasis given to different categories. There would appear, from the numbers of statements made about each category, to be an overwhelming amount of attention paid to the saved categories. Over one third of the statements were made about the category "Saved" (34.2%), and statements about this and the less inclusive saved categories account for 88% of the total. The amount of attention paid to this area of the model is out of all proportion to the actual membership of saved categories in Kasigau. As mentioned above, saved people account for less than 10% of the adult population. This apparent anomaly, the disproportionately large amount of attention paid, at the notional level, to what constitutes a comparatively small proportion of Kasigau society, can be explained in terms of one aspect of the dialectical relationship that obtains between the level of notions and the level of actions (cf. Keesing 1971); namely, the process through which the actors' notions emerge from the transactions in which they engage (for a detailed discussion of this process see Holy, forthcoming). Given that what the members of a society know is derived from their actions with and towards each other, it is to be expected that there will be a degree of quantitative correspondence between the two levels, in the sense that more will be known about those areas of culture which are most frequently invoked in action. In Kasigau, the saved people are the ones who, so to speak, make the most noise about their religion. While it is possible to share the company of someone who would regard himself as, say, CMS unsaved, probably for several weeks, without him making any comment about his religion or doing anything to indicate what his religious affiliations are, it is difficult to spend even a few minutes in the company of saved people without their saved status being made obvious. Indeed, as is indicated in the discussion of how categories are defined (Table 2, A; this chapter: 151), one of the essential characteristics of saved people is that they tell people they are saved. The very nature of their beliefs means that their faith is bound to play an important part in what they do. Thus the characteristics (behavioural, ideological and so on) of saved people are made obvious to themselves and to others much more frequently and more forcefully than are the characteristics of any of the unsaved categories. It is to be expected, therefore, that the part of the model that derives from the actions of saved people should be more elaborate and more intensively discussed than other parts of the model.

Of the less inclusive saved categories, far more attention is paid to the Gospel-type fellowships (Gospel, Ilago, Neno) in their various combinations (78.6% of all statements made about less inclusive saved categories) than to the CMS saved fellowships (19%). Again it would be true to say that members of the Gospel, Ilago and Neno fellowships tend to draw more attention to their religious activities than do other saved people. The songs are sung so loudly that the entire village cannot help but know when a Gospel meeting is in progress. Also, large numbers of children are attracted to Gospel and Ilago meetings by the songs and lively sermons and prayers, and some go as far as claiming to be saved. The activities of children are a constant talking point both within households and between members of different households.

Further Discussion

Probably the most likely criticism to be levelled at this method of inferring folk knowledge is that the model derived from it is fragmentary. It does not represent, or even attempt to represent, all the actors' knowledge of what defines their religious categories, and therefore does not get at the entire body of knowledge that remains implicit in any social situation; the knowledge that is used by the actors to make sense of what is said and done, but which is not explicitly invoked. I would answer this criticism in two ways. Firstly, in order specifically to get at this knowledge and to build up "complete" models, it has been found necessary to set informants special tasks, the drawbacks of which I have discussed above (pp. 139ff.) I have argued that the assumption that such tasks give us direct access to the knowledge the actors use in everyday life, and therefore to the way they understand their everyday life, is a false one. Instead it gives us access to the knowledge used specifically to cope with the task set by the analyst. Secondly, the body of knowledge which remains implicit in any situation, has, nevertheless, been socially acquired. It has been built up through being invoked in social transactions, though obviously over a much longer period than most anthropologists are able to spend in the field. Although we cannot get at all this knowledge directly, we can acquire some of it through the same process as that through which our informants acquired it, by internalising what they, in the course of their everyday interactions, make socially available. If we want to acquire an understanding of their culture which is in any sense "internal" (cf. Hanson 1975), then I would argue that this is the only satisfactory way of achieving it.

If we base our inferences of people's knowledge solely on what they, in the course of their everyday life, make available to us, then one problem discussed by Cancian is eliminated. I refer to the problem of ensuring that the conceptual domain being studied corresponds with a similar domain in the actors' conceptual world. Cancian chose to study "norms", an analytically defined area of culture. But she is concerned to describe them, classify them, etc., as the actors themselves would do so; i.e. she wants to describe their model of norms. Without the assumption that the actors do have a model of something that might be called norms, this exercise is obviously meaningless. Cancian expresses the problem in the following way:

> When researchers attempt to define a domain from the actor's point of view they are caught in a dilemma. On the one hand, they clearly do not yet know the defining characteristics of the domain, and they are committed to avoiding the imposition of *a priori* definitions in order to discover the native category system. On the other hand, the researchers must have some conception of the domain in order to select a particular procedure as appropriate for defining it. (Cancian 1975: 39)

Cancian concludes that this dilemma cannot be totally resolved. I would argue that the dilemma is a product of the method she uses to get at the actors' knowledge. She has set herself the problem of devising tasks (or, as she puts it, "selecting procedures") that will elicit from the actors the sort of knowledge she wants. She therefore has to decide beforehand what sort of knowledge this is – in this case descriptions of norms. If we treat actors' statements delivered spontaneously by them as the only source of the knowledge we are trying to infer, then we are spared the problem of having to define the domain beforehand. The analyst's definition of the domain, instead of being the basis of the entire study, is relegated to what I would regard as its proper place, that of a device for limiting his study of the actors' culture to what is, at any one time, practically possible. I have referred to the model I have described here as one of religious categories. What this means is that I have based my choice of what to include and what to omit on my own concept of religion. But insofar as this concept only limits the knowledge to be represented, purely for practical purposes, and does not in any way determine what knowledge is revealed to me by informants, then what this concept is, and whether it is theirs as well as mine, does not matter. I am in no way suggesting that the outer boundaries of the model of religious categories presented here, correspond to clearly drawn boundaries in the actors' knowledge. On the contrary, I would assume, again on the basis of what informants told me, that the boundaries are far from clear. For instance, on several occasions I heard comments that defined what I would call residential or geographical categories by the same criteria as what I have called religious categories. I was told, for example, that "People of Makwasinyi (one of the villages) wail at funerals", and that "People of Rukanga don't practise female circumcision". These categories, and all the other categories that the Wakasigau see as being comparable or contrastable with them, I have omitted only to make the body of knowledge I am dealing with a manageable size, and the fact that this is done on the basis of my criteria and not theirs does not in any way alter the fact that what is being described is the actors' knowledge and not my own.

The anthropologist who has most consistently and most successfully used the somewhat impressionistic method described by D'Andrade (this chapter: 141) to understand and interpret other cultures is, perhaps, Geertz. He makes very clear that his aim in the analysis of culture is to understand what things mean "from the native's point of view" (Geertz 1973, 1976). This understanding he distinguishes from the process of socialisation undergone by the analyst in the field, the latter being what gives the analyst the ability to acquire an understanding (Geertz 1976: 236). He does not, however, give any indications of how he thinks this ability should be put into practical use in interpreting cultural phenomena, except in a very negative sense by rejecting certain analytical devices (Geertz 1973: 29). I would argue that unless the process through which we arrive at "the native's point of view" — infer their folk models — is, as D'Andrade suggests, made explicit and replicable, then any claim that we have inferred their knowledge at all cannot be upheld.

Acknowledgements

Fieldwork in Kasigau was carried out for a total of 15 months between July 1977 and September 1979, and was financed by a research project grant from the Social Science Research Council.

References

Bourdieu, P. (1977). *Outline of a Theory of Practice*. Cambridge Studies in Social Anthropology. Cambridge: Cambridge University Press.

Burling, R. (1965). Burmese kinship terminology. In *Formal Semantic Analysis*, (Hammel, ed.). *American Anthropologist* (Special Publication).

Cancian, F. (1975). *What are Norms?* Cambridge: Cambridge University Press.

D'Andrade, R. G. (1976). A propositional analysis of U.S. American beliefs about illness. In *Meaning in Anthropology*, (K. H. Basso and H. A. Selby, eds). Albuquerque: University of New Mexico Press.

Geertz, C. (1973). *The Interpretation of Cultures*. London: Hutchinson.

Geertz, C. (1976). 'From the native's point of view': on the nature of anthropological understanding. In *Meaning in Anthropology*, (K. H. Basso and H. A. Selby, eds). Albuquerque: University of New Mexico Press.

Hanson, F. A. (1975). *Meaning in Culture*. London: Routledge and Kegan Paul.

Holy, L. (forthc.) *Strategies and Norms*. London: Charles Hurst.

Keesing, R. M. (1971). Descent, residence and cultural codes. In *Anthropology in Oceania: Essays presented to Ian Hogbin*, (L. R. Hiatt and C. Jayawardena, eds). Sydney: Argus and Robertson.

Pospisil, L. (1965). A formal analysis of substantive law: Kapauku Papuan laws of land tenure. In *Formal Semantic Analysis*, (E. A. Hammel, ed.). *American Anthropologist* (Special Publication).

Sanday, P. R. (1968). The 'psychological reality' of American-English kinship terms: an information processing approach. *Am. Anthrop.* **70**, 508-23.

Stuchlik, M. (1977). Goals and behaviour. In *Goals and Behaviour*, (M. Stuchlik, ed.). Queen's University Papers in Social Anthropology, Volume 2: 17-47. Queen's University: Belfast.

Wallace, A. F. C. (1965). The problem of the psychological validity of componential analysis. In *Formal Semantic Analysis*, (E.A. Hammel, ed.). *American Anthropologist* (Special Publication).

MODELS, REASONING AND ECONOMIC BEHAVIOUR

SUTTI ORTIZ

Religious beliefs, mythologies, ritual symbols have provided anthropologists of all persuasions with rich material to argue about how such all encompassing constructs emerge, what they in fact represent, and how they affect social behaviour. At one time, beliefs and mythologies were discussed as if they were alienated products with their own logic, their own set of structuring principles, with internally defined modes of transformation and intellectual elaborations. Although the complexity of these constructs warrant their treatment as separate entities, one wonders whether we have not overstated the case of intellectual self-sufficiency. Several questions still remain unanswered: how are abstract descriptions and explanations integrated to form coherent systems; when is it that they can be treated almost as if they have a separate existence from social reality? The danger is that their alienation may be only a consequence of our professional needs to systematize and intellectualize our observations. I fear that sometimes we contrive an objectification in order to simplify the integration of our systems of thought as a datum in our own theories about cause and meaning.

The field of economic behaviour does not often provide us with neat, well integrated constructs characteristic, for example, of ritual or political behaviour. Hence they offer the analyst a salutary contrast to sharpen generalizations about how ideologies emerge, what they represent, how they affect behaviour and when it is that they acquire a self-sustaining life of their own. I hope the information and analysis I present here will be used not only to argue about economic behaviour, but also to shed some light on more general discussions about models and modes of thought.

Paez Conceptualization of their own Economic System[1]

In previous writings I have described the economic system of the Paez but using my words and my constructs. I have used my perception and my model of their reality. The Paez do talk about their reality but not about economic systems.

On the subject of production, productive relations, they are more likely to talk about their own concrete experiences or to describe recent changes in strategies, or in modes of production than to intellectualize about the economic system. Local non-Indian commercial farmers, on the other hand, will readily talk about national and international markets as determinants of coffee prices, about the response of farmers and tight money and interest rates, about the consequences of governmental policies.

The Paez do, however, recognize that prices, outputs, credit, are interrelated in some way; that how these events interrelate and coordinate with land and labour availability determines what each farmer actually plants. But their choice of words is quite different from mine. They will talk about *"las cosas del gobierno"* (the things of the government), *"de los civilizados"* (of civilized men) and contrast it with *"como se acostumbra o acostumbraba a trabajar por aca"* (how one works here or used to work here).

The things of the government or the civilized world are the prices for cash crops, the availability of credit, development institutions, forestry inspectors, banks, people with money. What all these things have in common is that they operate either in mysterious ways or in an unpredictable way. Most Paez know that prices fluctuate with supply and demand, yet they lack the information to predict price swings for cash crops, hence coffee prices are described as things of the government, arbitrarily set by some official in Bogota. The banking sector is another unfathomable institution which seems to them to behave in unpredictable ways. How, they ask, can one explain that some times they charge more for the money they lend than other times; how can one explain that one has to pay the same penalty whether you are a day late or a month late; how come they do not take into account that yesterday roads were muddy, the river overflowed and one could not be expected to arrive on time at the bank. Because the civilized economy (they do not use the word economy) is unfathomable, anything said about it is easily believed. Not surprisingly, information which circulates by word of mouth tends to become transformed in the most fantasmagoric stories: banks will close down, permission will be required for every agricultural activity, punishment will be severe, etc. In other words, what is being lumped together is not just what is different, it is not a definitional referent, it is what is uncertain and incomprehensible, hence, to be distrusted. Mistrust has an historical reality as well. The Whites were the conquerors, they imposed tribute in labour and kind, they invaded their territory, they took land which had been under cultivation. Mistrust has both historical and intellectual roots; the way of the Whites is to be distrusted because it is unfathomable, but also because it was and still is exploitative.

Although not yet fully comprehended, how the White men make money and how they get what they have ultimately will be understood. Those who have been close to that world, those who have gone to work in White man's world, who have traded with him, have had a chance to experience and begin to understand. But experience is not enough for understanding. If the Indian opens himself to the experience and thinks about it (*raciona*) then he can begin to comprehend. If he closes himself to the experience (*se cierra*) he may keep his ways, but he will also be cheated by the Whites. To comprehend the ways — or as the Paez say, to be able to see from the top down — is important. The Indians who open themselves to the experience and *racionan* are not an allegoric illusion to convey that Indian knowledge can be expanded to comprehend other worlds, but a concrete reality. The *indios racionales,* or "progressive" Indians (see Ortiz 1973: 177-78) are identified with personal names.[2] Whereas anthropologists may prefer to characterize these Indians by their comprehension of the other world, their ability to master foreign constructs and to adapt foreign categories to their own system, the Paez identify the *indios racionales* using more concrete criteria. They are characterized by the similarity of their farming strategies to those of the local Whites: their reliance on cash crops (which are things of the Whites), their disdain for traditional labour exchanges, etc. Both characterizations are accurate. However depicted, what is conveyed is that the *indios racionales* are mediators between two economic realities: The way things are done here versus the way of the civilized men; the ordered and known versus the partially known and not yet clearly systematized; the historically bounded social unit versus the unbounded world of the Whites. As mediators they have an ambiguous position, not surprisingly they are regarded with mistrust. Yet because they are interpreters they are also valued: they are a source of information, or protection from the manipulations of the external world. The stories told to back the evaluation of any one of the *indios racionales* are pertinent and accurate. These Indians have reason to challenge the old ways as well as reasons to protect. Reluctantly and unknowingly they serve as interpreters. Although their position is ambiguous and feelings towards them ambivalent, the *indios racionales* are not anomalous.[3] There is no place for anomalies in the Paez conceptualization of the White economic order. The categories are not yet so neatly bounded as to allow a judgement that they belong nowhere. The *indios racionales* are good objects to love and hate, but not yet good subjects for reflection.

It is understandably easier for the Paez to talk about the clearly bounded system of "the way things are done here" than the more uncertain amorphous unbounded way of the *civilizados*. When pressed to clarify about the local order they will talk in terms of their community (*resguardo*), the *cabildo,* the families; in other words, using social categories they will talk about their mode of production: access to land; responsibilities to give food, labour; shared responsibilities to give sustenance. "Land is not only the fruit of our work, the source of our food, but also the core of our social organization" (from Sevilla Casas 1976a: 123, my translation). Only secondarily there may be references to supernatural beings, but not to the supernatural order, which does not mean that when talking about the supernatural order an explanation of the mode of production is not also encompassed in the global model.

The core of their organization is the communal identity with the land assigned to them originally by the Spanish authorities, not the ancestral territory of the Paez people. By royal decree, each population cluster[4] was assigned a territory which was to be shared equally by all residents. Some fields and pasture land were to be worked communally, others assigned to each component family to farm as they wished. No outsider, regardless of ethnic background, had rights to that territory. That was and still remains the legal foundations of Paez identification of community with land. Although no reference is made to the Spaniards and their royal decrees, the Paez talk at great length about their land where their local ancestors (usually a *cacique* known for his or her bravery against the Spaniards) buried their treasure. They talk about the need to defend it from encroachment by outsiders, the responsibility of the *cabildo* (community council) to organize its defense. When someone's field is invaded by a Colombian farmer (a White, an outsider) they will decry the invasion not as a personal loss to the Paez farmer in question, but as a communal loss. Hence the *cabildo,* rather than the family, is expected to organize and pay for the defence.

Communality is not just symbolized by the sharing of a territory which is in fact subdivided into family farms, but by the sharing of a communally held and communally used land. Demographic pressure has altered the ideal order for the *resguardo* of San Andres.

Only the field of the Virgin providing thatching grass for the church remains as a communal holding; the pasture land and corn fields have been distributed long ago. Communality also implies joint responsibilities. Each adult must contribute in the upkeep of roads, bridges, buildings, which are to be used by them all. At the sounding of a horn, men or families come together on Monday morning whenever necessary.

The mode of production cannot be and is not described only in terms of joint rights and sharing of obligations. It is also described in terms of the identity of a family with the land they have tilled. It is only as a married man that a Paez farmer has a right to a share of land which is vested in the family rather than the person. The husband farmer supposedly is only the administrator of the resources to be shared by all.

It is not enough to be married and a member of the community to be recognized as a farmer, the Paez explain. The land has to be transformed from *monte* into *roza*. The transformation can only be achieved with the labour of the family, only occasionally aided by friends and kin. By transforming the land a Paez not only claims the products, but also the right to its continued use. The territory belongs to the community, but the labour to the family (except a limited labour time which may be required by the *cabildo*) and it is labour that makes land into a farm, land into food and cash.

Demographic realities have put a terse note not only on the equation of community and land, but also on the equation of man and family with land. A Paez farmer can no longer count on as much land as his family can till nor can he count on sufficient land to feed his family. He can only count on whatever land he may receive from his father, what he manages to take away from others, what land he may be able to buy outside the *resguardo* boundaries (Ortiz 1973: 86-132). In other words, for the past generation the Paez has had to transgress traditional modes of production, he has had to cheat his own kind. Changes in allocation and transfer of land are ignored in general descriptions though acknowledged in other contexts. Only indirectly do they allude to them when describing the poverty of some of the families – a poverty for which the outside order, the ways of the Whites, is made responsible.[5] Despite demographic realities, the Paez describe their economic order in terms of self-sufficient family units with a diversified farm.

Farming, spinning, weaving, grinding and building bring to the family the satisfaction of eating well, feasting with friends and keeping warm. The head of the household will gain prestige as administrator and man of responsibility if he has managed to claim enough land and grow sufficient food to care for family and friends. It is the quality of his administrative ability or the quality of the labour that brings stature to the person rather than the bulk of commodities he is able to exchange in the market. In fact, a Paez family expresses their pride in their farming accomplishments by showing you the comfort of their house, their generosity with food and the assertion that it was gained by their own effort, that is that they did not have to buy or sell any food. Although the realities are quite different, it is important to the Paez to maintain a belief in self-sufficiency, a belief that the livelihood and status of the family are achieved by using their own effort to transform the communal patrimony.

Self-sufficiency nowadays implies other realities: the need for cash to acquire some of their clothing, kerosene, salt, etc. Hence the maintenance of idealized economic order implies the need to participate in the external order as well. Such a need is conceptually integrated in the generalized description of the way we do things around here as a separate non-competitive activity. Each farmer is supposed to reserve enough land so that, according to a generalized estimate, a family can harvest one or two loads of corn, grow 800 manioc plants, plant a few pounds of beans and have available some plantains. He should use the remainder to plant cash crops. Cash cropping and food production are conceived as separate activities, preferably in perfect balance. Although farmers may complain that they cannot expand their cash crop activities, they attribute their frustration to land shortage, not to the need or obligation to retain some land to produce enough food and sugar cane to feed the family and entertain friends. The types of crops suitable to the area of the San Andres *resguardo* and local managerial and production techniques make it possible to sustain the conceptual dichotomy.[6]

Self-sufficiency is, of course, impossible to maintain even in the production of foodstuff. Some farmers lose their entire harvest or are too sick to till the soil. When in need a family has the right to ask for help. Food thus circulates within the community in response to hunger, etiquette, or fondness (*lleve algo como cariño*). The flow of food is thus explained purely in terms of social obligation — other transactions are denied. Perhaps because of the close and terse relation of San Andres *resguardo* with the civilized economy this was a favourite topic of conversation.[7]

As social identity and prestige are gained by the successful trans-formation of family fields into food and cash, it would be improper to sell family labour directly for cash. At least until the seventies Paez farmers preferred not to talk about their wage labour activities or to discuss the state of the local economy in such terms. Everyone knew that those who could not plant cash crops or had little land for that purpose would be forced to work for wages. Yet they preferred to discount distress and attribute wage labouring activities by some families to their laziness. The Indians supposedly had no business selling most of their labour for cash, regardless of whether they had enough land or not. Poverty is to be solved by making more land available to the community, not by demanding that wages be increased. Working for wages challenges the notion that work transforms virgin soil into food for the family and through this transformation the family can claim a place in the community. At the same time, wage labour does not entirely threaten the basic tenets of Paez economic order. Work creates what a family needs; wages jointly shared, just like commodities produced, allow the family to buy salt, spices and satisfy other needs. Neither has wage labouring threatened family unity. Furthermore, the Paez have always distinguished conceptually between work for wages or in their own fields and time spent helping others or preparing a communal field; in practice as well, wage labour never interferes with *minga* work. Total dependence on wage labour may be an anomalous state of affairs to be condoned and, interestingly enough, to be partly ignored. But, partial dependence is neither anomalous nor does it in practice entirely threaten the status quo; quite to the contrary, it allows for the maintenance of family self-sufficiency when farmers do not have sufficient or adequate land for cash cropping, the favoured alternative.

Thus, when generalizing about the regional economic order, the Paez briefly refer to the uncertainty of the civilized order and then proceed to describe more fully their own economy using the sociopolitical order to describe modes of production. They stress the boundaries of such an order and equate them with the political and social boundaries. They talk about contrasting social categories: communal land, family land, communal obligations, family labour, and the tensions engendered by that conflict of interest between family and community. Relations are the consequence of transformation of labour and land into commodities and food. When discussing economy in such general terms they ignore the points of contact between the two worlds, or refer to them in denigrating terms: "they are too lazy to have their own land," "they laugh at you if you sell food in the market." Only the mediation gained through knowledge is valued although with some feelings of ambivalence. "There is nothing we can do about the ways of the Whites, we have to learn to get along with them." Only vague moral sanctions are verbalized in support of their economic order. Rarely would the loss of an animal be explained by the anger of the guardian spirit or the infertility of the soil be attributed to the anger of the gods. Although the well being of the farmer does in reality depend on the maintenance of the bounded economy, no major intellectual effort is made to insure its preservation. Another important general point is that the civilized economy was loosely described, not yet systematized, thus leaving open the possibility of eventually incorporating some of its aspects into Paez mode of production.

Cognitive Constructs used in Reasoning Strategies

An Indian farmer in San Andres does not explain his farming activities in terms of the state of the world, modes of production, or whether he likens himself to *indios racionales.* Whether he does or does not attempt to borrow capital is, in fact, explained in terms of his belief in the chances of being granted a loan, and his estimate as to his ability to repay the loan. No reference is made to "the world of White men" or its unfathomable aspects, although the existence of such a world is often implied in his judgement that he may or may not get a loan. He is also not likely to explain his farming strategies in detail by referring to population pressure, the behaviour of the *cabildo,* the flow of goods, labour, and obligations or *cariños.* Nevertheless, the likelihood of inheriting more land or gaining the labour cooperation of his sons and neighbours as well as the likelihood of being helped if faced with hunger must enter into his calculations. Even when a farmer describes his farming strategy in very general terms using the customary rule of thumb that about one hectare should be planted with maize, beans, manioc and plantains, the rest with cash crops, and, if possible, some pasture land reserved for cattle, he does not refer to modes of production or the state of the world. He simply says "it is what we need" rather than saying "to be self-sufficient farmers, as is expected, we need so much acreage with food crops."

I admit to no great revelation when I stress that when searching for solutions to concrete problems, farmers reason from lower level constructs rather than from generalized models. Yet, it needs to be reiterated because not all problems are resolved in similar fashion. It remains for us to determine when it is that generalized categories are used and when it is that lower level constructs impinge more directly in the conceptualization and resolution of a problem. The need for a specific answer (farmers need to decide exactly how much maize to plant, how much money and labour to use) limits the value to farmers of generalized statements about the state of the world. Yet, as we shall see later, I do not think that this is the entire story.

It is also of interest to keep in mind that the farmers interviewed, whose activities were recorded fifteen years later, did not summarize, for example, how much labour or seeds they had used nor could they tell me their annual or seasonal income or their total household expenses; farming activities are not seen as a total enterprise, rather, each activity or time related set of activities is discussed independently (Ortiz 1979b). Coffee, for example, is supposed to provide cash for household necessities; a mixed field of beans, maize, etc. is supposed to provide food for the family; sugar cane is to provide cash for luxuries or sap for beer production to host friends; animals are meant as savings for future investment or to cushion disaster. In other words, they conceive of farming as a set of related problems which must, however, be resolved separately though not totally independent of each other. The problems they must resolve, for example, are: how much coffee can they afford to plant to have enough cash to buy the most important items; how much food to grow to feed the family given labour constraints; the adequacy of remaining land for pasturing animals or complementary cash crops; the advisability of buying more cattle either with savings or perhaps on credit. These are, of course, only some of the questions that some of the Paez farmers will ask themselves. In other *resguardos* they will think of wheat, potatoes, or laurel wax instead of coffee and sugar cane (Sevilla Casas 1976b). I illustrate my points with strategies used by farmers which were studied in 1960-61 and again in 1975-76.

In previous publications I have used decision theory to analyze the choices made by farmers and to evaluate the strategies pursued. I chose decision theory not because it exactly portrayed how they reasoned out their strategies, but because it allowed me to link my findings to those of other economists; hence, to generalize about some of the problems faced by the peasants as well as the change of growth of transformation of their economic system. I did adapt the decision model I used so that it would more closely portray the behaviour of the farmers as well as the way they, rather than an economist, processed information. Whatever the utility or validity of that approach, I shall neither discuss it nor rely upon it here. What I am doing now is simply describing the constructs the Indian farmers use when discussing their strategies. In order to avoid any possible confusion, I will not describe, even if appropriate, any of their mental activities as a decision or even as choices. Instead, I elucidate how the information they use is structured, recalled and used; which ones are the rules of thumb or hints used to work out their strategies.

The constructs used to think out and describe their farming strategies are not integrated into a body of knowledge or a neat "folk model". Unlike the descriptions about the state of the world, which are more or less cogently presented, the above constructs are haphazardly outlined. Some are phrased as generalized statements, others as propositions and still others as rules of thumb or judgements based on practical experience. Formal differences are no doubt relevant, but for their analysis I require a detailed record of how constructs were verbalized and how context affected verbalizations; information that I lack.

The constructs elicited can also be characterized according to their mode of derivation. Some of them clearly reflected how the Paez describe the economic order and no doubt were derived from the representations discussed in the previous section. Other constructs, however, are more directly inferred from information that farmers gather in the course of their activities. I will list the constructs according to their mode of derivation.

Although all the following constructs are derived from generalized representations of the economic order they differ in some interesting ways. In some cases the general representations are individuated, in other cases they are given a concrete character. I cannot, however, offer any further insight as to the significance of the difference and must limit myself to alert others to its conjectural relevancy. The elicited constructs that are derived from generalized representations are the following:

1) Land given to a family should be used for its own sustenance. It is the responsibility of the head of the household to make the land yield enough food and cash to feed and clothe his family.

2) A family must demonstrate the need for the land they control or request by maintaining it under cultivation.

3) Produce should be used primarily to feed the family, kin or close friends. Enough food should also be produced to "care" for guests or close friends. One should plant enough seed to harvest two loads of maize, about a hundred stems of manioc, a few pounds of beans and some plantains.

4) Cash cropping should not interfere with food production.

5) The price of commodities in the national market is unpredictable.

6) One cannot expect to get a loan or to be able always to buy on credit.

7) When food is sold to kin or friends the price requested should not be the same as the market price but should be set by custom and not fluctuate from season to season.

The second set of constructs inferred from information gathered in the course of farming are:

1) One cannot afford to continue planting or maintaining a cash crop field when returns fall consistently below the income required to cover costs of production and a fixed share of the family's cash needs. Paez farmers are quite clear as to what family needs are subsidized from each cash crop (see Ortiz 1979b).

2) If the returns from one cash crop are good they should be re-invested in the same activity. By the same token if an animal is sold at a good price, some of the money should be used to buy another younger and cheaper animal.

3) Virgin highland should first be planted with maize and then converted into pastureland.

4) One must get to know the soil by farming it; only then can one decide how long the fallowing period must be, how far to space plants or seeds, how often to weed. This is why one cannot believe what the government advises.

5) Well established commodities (coffee, cattle, potatoes) will always find buyers.

6) The monetary return for labour when sold as a commodity (i.e. wage labour) is lower than when labour is used in commodity production (i.e. for cash crops).

7) Animals are never lost, hence, it is good to invest money left after harvest time in calves for eventual resale (in reality animals are lost but there is a low frequency of loss).

8) Prices of regional food crops (or of major cash crops during harvest season) are high when there is little for sale and drop when food (or cash crop) becomes available during harvest.

All of the second set of constructs are summary arguments derived by associating bits of information gained in the course of farming. In other words, they are in themselves part solutions to farming problems which are verbalized as propositional or normative statements; they are judgements based on practical experience and for this reason these constructs can be identified as rules of thumb. If we want to understand how these rules are derived we have to examine how individuals process information in problem solving exercises.

The information that is processed is, of course, information stored in memory rather than the verbal replication of distinct experiences. Hence, I have to consider, at least briefly, how information is often transformed, what new meaning it may acquire during the retention process. In an earlier publication (1979a) I pointed out that when a yield is noticed, it is immediately associated with other similar prices and yields previously experienced; they are at once coded in the same category. For example, when a farmer hears that coffee is Col $405 he compares this with other prices and if he judges all prices as being equally significant he will not bother to distinguish one from the other.[8] The prices will be subsumed under one category symbolized by one of the numbers recorded. The variations are eventually forgotten and the farmer will eventually say that prices have not changed.[9] The difference is lost because it was not significant for the farmer. Its significance depends on whether or not it affects returns. Information is categorized not just in terms of its relevancy to the farmer's concern (in the afore-mentioned example in terms of how they affect returns) but also because of shared semantic associations, shared spatial and temporal associations or because of frequency of incidence. All of these modes of classifying information may coexist providing a farmer with rich and neatly structured information to think out his problems. The task is further facilitated by the fact that categories are identified with symbols that often imply a judgement and thus automatically link the category to an already established argument. A farmer, for example, is made readily aware, thanks to his mode of classifying information, that good prices are likely to happen with regularity and to associate such prices semantically, historically and spatially with other events leading him to the obvious generalization that prices fluctuate in response to supply, demand and the whims of the government.

It is thus easy to see how, through the association of stored categorized information, arguments do evolve. Restle (1975), in fact, discusses problem solving as a search process, the search being guided by the structure of the information stored. These structures resemble the classificatory systems outlined in the anthropological literature. Unlike anthropologists, Restle would stress that there is a multiplicity of systems of classification operating at one time each one using a separate set of principles. The same information may be integrated into a variety of structures or classificatory systems so that problem solving through scanning can become a complex process.

Whereas psychologists have readily accepted that retention and retrieval of information is very complex they have tended to over-simplify problem solving processes when using simulation models that rely heavily on the logic and use of computers. According to these models when an individual faces a problem he resolves it by scanning for similar solutions stored in memory or by scanning for the identification of an element in the problem with the principle that links it to others and defines its meaning. The difficulty is that the memory scanning models imply a stepwise process that continues until confirmation is attained. Confirmation is reached only with a positive response to a yes/no question. In real life situations yes/no judgements are rarely possible. For example, if we look carefully at the rule that weeding frequency depends on the relevance of weeding for each crop in a specific field, then the judgement problem becomes very difficult. Relevance implies an association of X weedings with high yields. Yet, X is not easily determinable because high yields relate to other factors besides weeding frequency. Paez farmers are well aware that weather, annual changes in soil condition, quality of seeds, are equally relevant. Only if farmers remember long sequences of once and twice a year weedings with corresponding yields are they likely to be able to sort out sufficient numbers of associations to determine the strength of relevance of any association. Given that information is not stored neatly as sequential lists, but rather integrated into more general arguments (see Ortiz 1979a), it is not always possible for a farmer to judge the proposition that two annual weedings will contribute to high yields, whereas one annual weeding will be detrimental. Unless chance provides farmers with a biased sample that allows for clear-cut distinction, they are not likely to be able clearly to confirm a proposition through memory scanning. At best the exercise will allow them to state that it is likely, but not certain, that X number of weedings helps maintain high yields, or as the Paez says "it depends, one never knows."

Even if we accept the simplified memory scanning pattern — verification model of the information processing school of psychology, we still have to determine what is the problem solver scanning for. Greeno (1973) suggests that the search focuses most likely on a significant relation between concepts. It could be the relationship between weeding and yield as discussed above or the relationship between price and related problematic factors. The Paez farmer, when trying to understand why prices fluctuate for any one commodity, will be expected to search for the factor that varies concomitantly. For this particular case he is likely to note that when the local market place is flooded with maize or potatoes the price of each is lower than when supplies are scarce. Such an association is clear and likely to be vividly retained. In fact, the Paez are quite aware of the relationship and state it as one of the guiding rules about the advisability of producing food for local market. It is not, however, so easy for them to check through memory scanning the association of supply to coffee prices. When coding information about coffee prices, farmers fuse that information with information on yield (see page 170 earlier in this paper). Furthermore, they have minimal information on annual regional and national coffee outputs which are as relevant as their own. Consequently, though there is a belief in the association based on the analogue relation between food prices and food supplies, there is no certainty about it. The Paez farmer expresses the uncertainty by saying that "coffee prices are things of the government." Hence, problem solving through scanning is possible only when: information retains its identity after classification; classes are clearly demarcated to allow a judgement of inclusion or exclusion; when relations are simple enough to be able to establish that the association is significant rather than coincidental.

Some of the difficulties faced by the problem solver are eased when the relationship he is trying to determine or confirm is embedded in a propositional rule which offers a network of other possible associations. If the above suggestion, as put forth by Greeno, is correct then we can expect Paez farmers to find it much easier to solve problems which are anchored in propositions about the state of the world than those which do not offer a set of ramifying associations. Generalized models are hence quite useful tools, they provide a network for the generation of rules of thumb.

When the problem cannot be resolved by searching, it may be resolved through metaphorical associations — a process familiar to anthropologists. Whatever the technique or techniques initially used (Anderson 1976) to search for a solution to a problem, the search does not end until a satisfactory solution is found. In some cases, empirical results dramatically signal that the resolution has been achieved: seeds germinate, coffee trees begin to yield heavily and more regularly. However, most intellectual or farming problems are not likely to lend themselves to such neat confirmations. Our trust that a "satisfactory" solution has been found rests either on our belief of their internal consistence, the power of some of the propositions contained in the argument — in fact, the import of rules of thumb may be to give credence to most common solutions — or the familiarity with which the solutions are regarded. Associational reasoning thus is just as likely to lead to syllogistic reasoning as it is to lead to further associational processes. Nor, for that matter, can it be discounted that an argument is reasoned syllogistically or dialectically even at initial formulation. There is one important point to keep in mind — that syllogistic reasoning requires that cognitive structures be discrete entities. Thus, we have to agree with Hallpike when he suggests that "cognitive skill developed in relation to the demands of specific environments, some of which may inhibit the development of formal propositional thinking . . . " (1976: 263).

Although it seems reasonable to assume that the reasoning process used may relate to the nature of the problem and the nature of the cognitive categories, I lack the appropriate data to advance the argument further or even to stress its plausibility. All I can do, in the hope of encouraging others to explore the subject in more detail and with adequate data, is to summarize the most obvious aspect of the derivational processes which are implied in the content of the rules previously listed. Since the rules of thumb are not always expressed formally, it is difficult to analyze their structure and derivation.

Classifying, Learning and Knowing

The primacy of the social in the analysis of myth and ritual has been the guiding theme since Mauss and Durkheim. To question would not only be heretical, but also a wasted effort. Yet, the acceptance and further refinement of their seminal assumptions without reconsidering their initial formulation has narrowed the field of inquiry.

For Durkheim and Mauss the primacy of the social could be discerned in the categorization of the immediate world. Classificatory systems were not considered by them to be either the product of individual activity or of abstract understanding, rather as a social process whereby ideas are arranged for reasons of sentiment. It is because men were grouped that they grouped nature into classes, the classes reflecting social grouping and the relationship between classes reflecting relations between social entities. The genesis and functioning of logical operations could be studied, according to Durkheim and Mauss, only after classificatory systems were understood sociologically (1963: 88).

While scholars still share the interest of Durkheim and Mauss on classifications, they have dropped what Needham has described as the more awkward aspects of the initial argument: sentiment and cognitive process. Eventually a classification came to be regarded as a paradigm of native thought, as a prerequisite for ordering experience. Structuralism further narrowed the field of inquiry by focusing on those cultural themes which reveal most clearly the attributes of the human mind and modes of classifying social and natural reality.

Ritual language offered the richest arena for discussing the impact of classificatory systems on thought and communication. At first the concern was with isolating the categories, but eventually the analysis narrowed to modes for deriving categories. Having disregarded sentiment and cognition, because they encumbered arguments, modes of classification had to be derived from the structure of texts and communications. Hypothetical modes had then to be verified logically rather than empirically. Efficiency, simplicity and consistency became important evaluative criteria. Binary opposition has been elegantly defended by the above criteria as a primary mode of classification. Its relevancy cannot be questioned. Its acceptance and analytical use "has revealed some of the cultural themes expressed in ritual" (La Fontaine 1972: XVIII). Yet, though "The formal simplicity of dichotomous and the continuous partition of all things by two offers the most efficient means . . . for a clear statement of shared premises in social interaction" (Fox 1975: 128) one cannot expect all cultural classifications to conform to the binary format, J. Fox warns us. In fact, to assume otherwise leads us to disregard a large residue of text and mythological information (see Douglas 1967) as well as other parallel mental processes (Leach 1970: 88).

To recapture the social significance of the residue alluded to by Mary Douglas, the analysis of texts and symbols had to be supplemented by the analysis of ritual action; structure had to give way to meaning; the classificatory principles had to acknowledge the import of content. Barth, in his analysis of initiation rituals amongst the Baktaman of New Guinea challenges the significance of binary logic as a primary classificatory system (1975: 180, 185, 212-13). Furthermore, he does not see Baktaman knowledge as a neatly integrated corpus of material: " . . . the nature of this integration is both loose and partial: they (symbols) are not linked to each other in logically necessary patterns, and it would be false to construct a set of premises from which they can be deductively derived." The symbols and the concepts they embody are, according to Barth, cognitively interconnected — even though they are not fully integrated into an argument — through metaphors, the multiplicity of connotation of some symbols, the overarching qualities of others. Thus Barth, by bringing us back to the work of Audrey Richards, Firth and Turner, reminds us that in our efforts to formalize how knowledge evolves more knowledge, we had neglected perhaps a cumbersome but important aspect of the process: communication and sentiment. He thus returns to Durkheim's and Mauss' conjecture "that the scheme of classification is not the spontaneous product of abstract understanding, but results from a process into which all sorts of foreign elements enter" (Durkheim and Mauss 1963: 8).

Dan Sperber reminds us of the other cumbersome concern mentioned by Durkheim and Mauss: the cognitive aspects of classifications and symbolism. Symbolism for him is a cognitive process "which remains throughout life as a learning mechanism" (1975: 89). But unlike his predecessors he insists that we must focus on the individual, as it is within the individual that symbolic data integrate themselves into a single system.

It is now possible to relate the Paez construct and rules to what has been said about ritual, mythological thinking and classificatory systems. Knowledge about the economic order amongst the Paez is only partial. Their immediate world is clearly outlined. But the "not them" (ways of the civilized men) oppositional category is only vaguely differentiated.[10] Furthermore, knowledge about the economic order is only poorly integrated into Paez grand design of the universe. The only reference made to an order beyond economy is to the guardian spirit of animals and the possible anger of the ancestors when one of their resting places is ploughed (resting places are discerned by old pottery or other relics). Magical practices could have provided occasions for examining the symbolic integration of the economic order with Paez grand design of the world. But such practices had lapsed when I was there. In fact, the progressive secularization of the economic order limits our efforts to analyze the significance of its portrayal. It is indeed very tempting to postulate a set of contrasting categories: our land: :the land of the ancestors; known economic relations: :unknown economic relations; them: :us; spirits: :animals. But we have no way of determining whether the list is contrived for the purpose of arriving at the tempting equation of man: :nature. Furthermore, the contrasts become murkier as we use the approach to isolate the themes within the category of Paez economic order: family is not an oppositional contrast to *resguardo*, nor for that matter is work and *minga* (work performed in communal fields or kinsmen when invited). In fact, as Paez economic order is not portrayed in a text or formalized communication, it would be improper to use structure to sort out major themes. Instead, themes had to be selected on the basis of stress (emphasis, distress, repetition) on metaphorical associations of some of the symbols used (e.g. *indios racionales* and *indios cerrados*). Furthermore, as categories are likely to be generated in the process of social intercourse as well as in the process of thinking about the social order (Douglas 1975: 313), knowledge about Paez social dynamics was used to infer some other conceptual categories and conceptual associations, Analyzed in this manner, the generalized models of the economic order reflect descriptions of economic reality as well as solutions to the problems created by the existence of an uncertain unknown world. The solutions offered are: compartmentalize subsistence and cash crop production; protect Paez mode of production by regulating the points of exchange between the known and the unknown; minimize unpalatable consequences by obliterating from accounts threatening developments; stress the social significance of the familiar mode of production. In other words, the solutions generated by the overall constructs or models are not solutions to a number of practical problems, but to the problem engendered by the uncertainty of a world that they have to cope with: Colombia's cash economy. Although the models should, in their content or structure, reveal their intellectual origin and process of integration, it is impossible to elucidate such processes. It is even difficult to construe how the Colombian mode of production will be eventually portrayed. It is unlikely that it will either mirror or contrast the Paez economic order, or it would thus have already been diagrammed. Furthermore, since one of the main themes conveyed in the general model is an outline of solutions to the problem of uncertainty, it is more likely that "the ways the Whites do things" will be resolved by subdividing such a world into a set of discrete problems (very much like their approach to their annual allocations problem): the way the banks do things will be resolved independently of the way the government determines prices.

Paez farmers think out their problems not in terms of generalized models, but in terms of sets of rules and categorized information on relevant ongoing events. The system whereby relevant events are classified and systematized is likely to be quite different from the principle used to class the themes of the general models. Modes of classification reflect intellectual concerns during the cognitive process. The intellectual concerns of a farmer noting price changes in the market for cash crops are quite different from the same farmer in the role of informer on the state of the world.

Even at the level of coding observed data, classificatory principles may differ. For example, we have seen that prices are coded according to their effect on income into "good," "bad," "barely enough," etc. Work was not, however, evaluated in terms of how its intensity or results affected well-being, but in terms of what it engendered. If used to plant food or cash crops in the family field, it was said to be *trabajo* (labour). Wage labour was likewise labeled, as it also engendered something (cash) to be used for family consumption. When performing the same activity in a friend's field they would not say they went to work for him; they would say that they were invited to a *minga.* Work engenders cash and food, *minga* engenders social relations. The activity is classified according to *what* it engenders rather than *how much* it engenders or the quality of life that can be derived from what it engenders (see Ortiz 1979c). The wage received for labour was not always separated from other aspects of the relationship implied when the return was a certain amount of cash and food. In other words, different principles of classification are inconsistently used.

Not surprisingly, the economic experiences of Paez farmers are coded into sets of related classes which are not integrated into a system. Furthermore, the classifying criteria are sometimes complex (all the elements considered when judging prices) and encoding judgements difficult and often inconsistent. The anthropologist finds himself having to analyze a number of sets inconsistently differentiated and often not clearly bounded. A Paez may fit an experience or event in more than one class, may be uncertain where it belongs, or may not be able to classify it at all. Such a complex, not fully integrated and fuzzy system of classifying economic events contrasts sharply with the exemplary systems often described in the literature. It is quite possible that the difference rests on contrasting concerns of a farmer trying to make sense of the ever-changing world which affects his well-being and of a ritual specialist who is concerned in structuring a fluid world to give it a self evident quality. Yet, if we accept Barth's interpretation of Baktaman ritual, the above answer is not adequate and the question which Douglas raised (1975) requires a more profound analysis.

Attention should also be paid to the symbols used to denote the classes. The level of generality varies within the classificatory system even at the same hierarchical level. In some cases the symbols used will encourage metaphorical associations as well as the use of specific rules of verification acceptable to the farmer. Ultimately economic rules, though not generalized constructs, have to survive the test of adequacy. Incongruous rules may survive until perhaps by chance information is collected to demonstrate that they contain false and dangerous propositions. The ritual expert, the participant in a ceremony, does not have to be constantly alert to the consequences. The great concern for adequacy gives poignancy to economic rules, but introduces chaos into modes of derivation.

Postcript

I have avoided using the term model in this paper only because of the myriad of entrenched arguments often implied by its use. Yet, as the term embodies the theme of the conference I cannot totally ignore it. In fact, the word model can be used interchangeably with some of the terms I use here and I have used it when talking about decision making in earlier publications. My decision model was a construct simulating an intellectual process. It was the analyst's model based on what the Paez said and the economists wrote. My task here was to paraphrase as closely as I could what the Paez say. I would not argue that their description of their economic reality or of Colombian economic reality is a folk model.

But I wanted to go beyond arguments as to whose reality we are depicting. Instead I wanted to examine what type of constructs (or models) are used to describe reality, to integrate knowledge, to resolve problems. I hope to have convinced the reader that the constructs used vary in nature; sometimes they are akin to systems of classification, other times the constructs used are akin to so called folk models, and still other times instead of a single construct what is kept in mind is a set of independent judgements. I also hope to have shown that all of the above mentioned types of constructs or sets of constructs are used for similar purposes: to communicate, to think out problems, to confirm solutions, to conclude a search. Our task should now be to examine how each type of construct is derived, how its form and structure affects reasoning and behaviour. I have only barely touched upon the first point. I also believe that we must turn our attention to the relevancy of the use/absence of symbols to identify complex high level constructs or folk models. Although the Paez example is in itself not suitable material for such speculations it may be useful for comparative purposes because of the dearth of symbols used to identify high level constructs. The Mount Hagen concept of *noman,* for example, as a symbolic statement about a variety of constructs represents a different mode of structuring knowledge than the mode characteristic of the Paez.

Notes

1. The data used in this section consist of conversations recorded during my initial field work in 1960-61 and subsequent interviews of the same farmers by Ann Osborn in 1975 and 1976. At this time Miss Osborn was asked to administer an open ended questionnaire intended to elicit how prices, yields were classified and strategies used to think out farming problems. Unlike during my first field work, no attempt was made consistently to examine

whether what they said corresponded to what they did.

2. In our conversations, Indians preferred to be identified as *indios racionales,* perhaps in order to please me. It is quite possible that with the politization of local Indian population, Indians may now prefer to be identified as more traditionally oriented Indians. There certainly has been an increase in the influence of *cabildo* and renewed interests in traditional ways to symbolize historic rights to the region.

3. Strictly speaking, anomaly is "an element which does not fit a given set or series" (Douglas 1966: 50). Ambiguity is an element which can be interpreted in two ways. Ambivalence is an element which belongs to more than one frame of reference.

4. The *resguardos* were assigned to protect Indians from intrusion and confiscation of their lands. An existing population cluster was used as the centre for the *resguardo* and the boundaries were marked as so many leagues from the centre with some adjustment for ecological and demographic realities. *Resguardos* were small and not intended to group a tribe, rather to insure the survival of existing and sometimes mixed populations. No outsider, regardless of ancestry, was permitted to claim membership once the *resguardo* was established.

5. Boundaries, of course, have been moving and territory shrinking illegally. The point here is not to deny the reality of exploitation by Whites, but to illustrate how they conceptualized their world in terms of our land. It is possible that politization has affected their concepts, but as I have no information on the subject, I have to disregard the effect of recent developments. Contrary to the reality of land distribution within the *resguardo* in 1961, Indians talked about equality and self-sufficiency of family units. Poverty, when acknowledged, was explained as the result of White intrusion rather than unequal distribution or exploitative techniques of some Indians (which was readily discussed in other contexts).

6. Dr. Sevilla Casas has resided in San Andres and studied the economic activities of Indians in neighbouring areas. His findings are of interest because they clearly show the effect of ecological and sociological factors on economic performance. The Indians of Tumbichukue were not able to plant coffee and were much more willing to work as wage labourers. It would be of great interest to incorporate his findings with the realities of San Andres in 1961 and by so doing perhaps correct some of my initial assumptions as they are contained in this paper.

7. Sevilla Casas, in several of his publications (1974a and b), points to differences in rules of thumb between San Andres and other *resguardos.* Not only are Indians from other places more willing to work for wages, but they also do not look down contemptuously on those who sell food on the market square. Such differences are relevant and confirm my initial suspicion that the rule emerged as a response to ongoing conditions rather than being rooted in past traditions (Ortiz 1973: 5–7).

8. When farmers were interviewed in 1976 they were asked a number of questions and encouraged to talk about prices and yields in order to determine how the information was classified and organized for retention. The

object of the study was to determine what information was available to farmers when formulating expectations, as well as determine whether farmers could, in fact, evaluate prospects and decide accordingly how much of each crop to plant. The information and its analysis are published in "Expectations and Forecasts in the Face of Uncertainty," *Man* **14**: 64-80, 1979.

9. Colby and Cole (1973) remind us that we need to pay more attention to the effect of clustering and narrative structure in the recall of myth and folk tales. In other words, that certain transformations are the consequence of loss or recall alterations.

10.It is not entirely surprising that the economy of the Whites is only vaguely defined by the Paez. Experiences, thoughts are likely to be highly structured if central or of symbolic significance. Mary Douglas (1975) has outlined many examples where this is so and where secondary processes developed in order to retain and bolster the integrity of relevant constructs. But this particular construct is not central; it is not required to communicate any messages about the linked category of Paez economy, nor does it have any other symbolic significance.

References

Anderson, J. (1976). *Language, Memory and Thought*. New York: John Wiley and Sons.

Barth, F. (1975). *Ritual and Knowledge Among the Baktaman of New Guinea*. New Haven: Yale Univ. Press.

Colby, B. and Cole M. (1973). Culture, memory and narrative. In *Modes of Thought* (R. Horton and R. Finnegan, eds). London: Faber and Faber.

Douglas, M. (1967). The meaning of myth, with special reference to "La Geste d'Asdiwal." In *The Structural Study of Myth and Totemism* (E. Leach, ed.). ASA Monograph 5, London: Tavistock.

Douglas, M. (1975). *Implicit Meanings, Essays in Anthropology*. London: Routledge and Kegan Paul.

Durkheim, E. and Mauss, M. (1963). *Primitive Classification*. Translated with an introduction by Rodney Needham. London: Cohen and West.

Fox, J. J. (1975). On binary categories and primary symbols: some rotinese perspective. In *The Interpretation of Symbolism* (R. Willis, ed.). London: Malaby Press.

Greeno, J. G. (1973). The structure of memory and the process of solving problems. In *Contemporary Issues of Cognitive Psychology,* New York: John Wiley and Sons.

Hallpike, C. R. (1976). Is there a primitive mentality? *Man* (N.S.) **11**, 253-70.

La Fontaine, J. S. (1972). *The Interpretation of Ritual*. London: Tavistock.

Leach, E. (1970). *Levi-Strauss*. London: Fontana.

Ortiz, S. (1967). Colombian rural market organization: an exploratory model. *Man* (N.S.) **2**, 393-415.

Ortiz, S. (1973). *Uncertainties in Peasant Farming: A Colombian Case*. Monographs in Social Anthropology, London School of Economics. London:

Athlone Press.

Ortiz, S. (1979a). Expectations and forecasts in the face of uncertainty. *Man* (N.S.) **14**, 64-80.

Ortiz, S. (1979b). The effect of risk aversion on subsistence and cash crop decisions. In *Risk, Uncertainty and Agricultural Development*, (J. Roumasset, J.M. Boussards and I. Singh, eds). New York: Agricultural Development Council.

Ortiz, S. (1979c). The estimation of work: labour and value among Paez farmers. In *The Social Anthropology of Work*, (S. Wallman, ed.). ASA Monograph 19, London: Academic Press.

Restle, F. (1975). *Learning: Animal Behaviour and Human Cognition*. New York: McGraw-Hill.

Sevilla Casas, E. (1976a). *Atraso y Desarrollo Indiigena en Tierradentro*. (Mimeo) Bogota: Universidad de los Andes.

Sevilla Casas, E. (1979b). *Estudios Antropológicos sobre Tierradentro*. (Mimeo) Cali: Fundación para la Educación Superior.

Sperber, D. (1975). *Rethinking Symbolism*. Cambridge: Cambridge University Press.

MODEL-BUILDING IN ACTION:
GENEALOGICAL CHARTERS IN WHITE SOUTH AFRICA

ELEANOR PRESTON-WHYTE

.... it is generally known that the people we are studying are
not mindless subjects; in model building they are able to hold
their own with any anthropologist.

(Holy and Stuchlik in this volume)

First the idea of a family register came into being, then that
of a family celebration and then the two hand-in-hand. It
was rapidly clear that the two ideas went together well, since
without a genealogy, a celebration would have no binding
force, while a celebration would, in itself, awake interest and
concern in the genealogy.

(*Die Familie Krige* by J.D. Krige)

Introduction

Holy and Stuchlik have drawn attention to the complex relationship
between two levels of reality " . . . the (level of) notions, knowledge,
or models, which . . . constitute the world, and the level of actions
which are continuously reconstituting the world" (this volume: 26).
They argue that the process whereby actions "affect or shape"
models has been somewhat neglected by anthropologists. This paper
attempts to show how action and interaction within a restricted set
of social activities sharpens and even formulates the conceptual
model which some white South Africans hold of their origins, of the
part played by their forbears in the development of South African
society and thus of current social and political relationships for
which the past provides a charter in the Malinowskian sense.

The field of social action to be examined includes three interconnected elements — the frequent gatherings of several hundred
white South Africans of the same surname (Afrikaans — *familiefees*

or *familie saamtrek;* English — family reunion),[1] the formation of surname societies (Afrikaans — *familiebond;* English — family association) and the collection and publication of family histories and genealogies (Afrikaans — *geslagsregister;* English — family tree). The participants in these activities state that they are commemorating the arrival and subsequent exploits of their forbears in South Africa, and they conceive of their actions in purely kinship terms — witness the fact that only the descendants of the particular progenitors concerned (Afrikaans — *stamouers*), are expected to attend surname gatherings. I, however, contend that their actions have wider social implications to the extent that they involve the creation of a number of "myths of origin" which, while clearly celebrating the social achievements of particular families, also reflect and even bolster the wider cognitive model which many white South Africans hold of their society and of their dominant position in social and political life. The examination of the dynamic process by which family histories and genealogies come into being and are disseminated will be used, therefore, to illustrate two interconnected aspects of "model-building in action". The first involves the creation of family legends and the second concerns the interaction between this folk mythology and worldview. I hope to demonstrate also that the models which are constructed are, in Geertz' original sense (1966: 7-8), both models "of" in that they represent what is accepted as past social reality, and models "for" in that at the same time they justify current social and political aspirations and arrangements. Both the representational and generative properties of models will be seen to be present.

Before presenting the evidence and argument of the paper, I must stress that surname gatherings, societies and genealogical research of the type to be described, occur only amongst the white South Africans. Genealogical information is, of course, present and highly valued amongst South Africans of African descent but is a matter of oral tradition rather than archival research. Most of the black genealogies which have been published were collected by white missionaries and academics (Cairns 1978; H.F. Heese 1980). With a few notable exceptions (Buthelezi 1978; Mutwa C. 1966) Africans in South Africa have not yet explored their "roots" as have many Afro-Americans (Hailey 1976). This may be because there is no real question as to where the roots of black South Africans lie.[2]

Ethnographic Background

White edited South African newspapers and magazines frequently publish letters requesting that "all members" of a particular family contact the author who is compiling a "family register". The Genealogical Society of South Africa recently listed some four hundred "families" on which such research is being undertaken by private individuals. Surname gatherings are covered by press, radio and television and it is by no means unusual for individuals either to travel long distances to attend these events, or to belong to surname societies which have formal constitutions, membership fees and which issue regular newsletters. During the last six years I have attended seven Afrikaans and four English surname gatherings held in different parts of the country lasting between one and four days each. I have ample documentation on another seventy-six gatherings, some dating back to 1914 and have investigated ten flourishing surname societies and interviewed over fifty people involved in family research. The case of one predominantly Afrikaans speaking family, to whom I will refer by the pseudonym Krumm, illustrates some of the cognitive and social elements involving the development of sentiments of family pride and corporate action which for many white South Africans results from the sharing of a surname. Associated with a common name is the belief in descent from a putative ancestor who emigrated to South Africa from Europe.

The Krumms held their first national *familiefees* in 1973 in the small town where the first man in South Africa to bear the name Krumm is believed to have settled, married and established a family after he came to the Cape from Germany in the mid-eighteenth century. The *fees* lasted for three days and was attended by two hundred and fifty Whites, most of them South Africans who have been born Krumms, had married a Krumm, or who could trace descent or affinity with South African Krumms. The majority had not met each other before and, although most lived locally, one hundred and fifteen spent some nights away from home during the gathering, thirty-six having travelled over 1,000 km to be present. Three of the *feesgangers* (participants) were from England. The *fees* was the brainchild of J.D. Krumm who had spent two years previous to the *fees* researching the origin and spread of the family both in South Africa and in Europe. Apart from extensive archival work, he contacted the heads of all Krumm nuclear families known to him and to his close kin. He wrote to all Krumms listed in the telephone directories of major urban centres and personally visited as many of these families as possible, often undertaking long and expensive journeys to meet those who did not respond to letters. His findings appear in the form of a family history and family register published to coincide with the *fees*. Before consulting this source, most Krumms held fragmentary and conflicting ideas about the "origin of the family" and knew only a few of the total genealogical relationships between living and dead Krumms. However, a six foot wide genealogy incorporating J.D. Krumm's genealogical researches was displayed at the *fees* and was the centre of tremendous interest and lively debate involving a number of corrections and additions in response to new information produced by those present.

Planning for the *fees* began a year in advance. An action committee sent out invitations to all known Krumm families, to female Krumms and to their children and spouses. Press releases advertising the event were sent to both English and Afrikaans newspapers and, although the genealogy included only persons born with the Krumm name and their spouses, anyone who could trace a cognatic or affinal link to a Krumm was encouraged to attend the gathering. Cyclostyled letters kept family members informed of arrangements and called for information on family history, jokes about family heroes, for assistance with catering at the *fees,* and for volunteers to perform in a family concert. J.D. Krumm compiled a commemorative brochure which included a eulogy on family achievements written by a Krumm who is also a wellknown South African author. This booklet was illustrated by another family member who is a celebrated artist, and it included as well as a programme of events, information on the origin of the family and on its major branches in South Africa. At the *fees* lectures were given on family history and also on heraldry, a possible coat-of-arms for the family, and on the importance of establishing a family archive. Bus trips were organised to local farms and houses associated with Krumm ancestors and the family concert was preceeded by a cheese and wine party at which a "family toast" was drunk and stories told "about the old days" and about revered and loved forebears. Traditional Afrikaner hospitality was provided in the form of a *braaivleis* (barbecue) and each formal event was opened with a prayer and appropriate scripture reading. The *fees* ended with communal attendance at a Sunday Service. A full tape and photographic record was made of events and each *feesganger* signed an attendance register which is to be kept "for posterity".

The formal events of the *fees* were interspersed with periods during which participants interacted informally. Those who knew each other caught up on family news, while those who had not met previously made efforts to trace genealogical links with each other. The general expectation was one of a kinship relationship and the opening gambit "and how are you related" was constantly to be heard. In my field notes I wrote "Though many people had not met before, there were no strangers – only *familie* (family)". Sentiments of family pride were continuously voiced both in the formal speeches and in private conversations and found expression in suggestions that a family fund be started to defray the costs of the *fees* and to found a family archive, and that a family association be established. By the end of the *fees* over £750 had been collected and some years later the *Krumm-bond* (Krumm surname society) came into being. In its constitution the aims of this society are stated as furthering family cohesion (*samehorigheid*) and sentiment (*sentimente*) and initiating and maintaining social and cultural contacts for family members. These are to be achieved through the holding of regular gatherings, the registration of a coat-of-arms, the circulation of a regular newsletter and the establishment of a family archive. To date three local Krumm gatherings have been held in South Africa and one in Australia, the registration of the coat-of-arms is in progress and the archive grows apace. The newsletter is now in its twelfth edition. J.D. Krumm has visited Germany and contacted members of what he believes to be the original Krumm family in Europe. His interest in family history has continued and one of the characteristics of the newsletter is its regular articles on newly discovered information about the family both in this country and abroad. Other members of the family have contributed enthusiastic articles on their own family research and upon visits to the *Heimat* (home of origin in Germany). J.D. Krumm and the committee of the *bond* scour the national newspapers for mention of Krumm achievements and regular mention is made in the newsletter of sporting, cultural and academic successes. Information is also given in each issue of recent births, marriages and deaths and every effort is being made to keep the *geslagsregister* up to date.

In interviews J. D. Krumm admitted that continued family research and the editing of the newsletter are extremely time consuming. However, he regards these tasks in the light of a family obligation. In a newsletter published in 1976 he explored the issue of the value of genealogical work. Under the heading "South Africa in Difficult Times" we read

> In these times of economic, political and social stress, is it not foolish to fritter away one's time with such things as family registers and newsletters? Does it not take time and money which might be put to better use? Should we not rather give attention to the present and the future and leave the consideration of the past to more tranquil times?

> But then I realise anew that we are rooted in the past – what binds a

person more to where he belongs than the history of his progenitors? If I know that eight generations of my ancestors helped to build this land, then I will think eight times before packing up and emigrating. Our ancestors did not always have an easy life, but once they had surmounted their problems they forged forward with twice as much perseverance. Within our family we have a wide spectrum in regard to language, religion and class. There is, however, a powerful bond of kinship that binds us all, and this gives us courage for the future.

. . . We (as a nation) are working towards military, religious and spiritual preparedness. Knowledge of one's family history and of the unity of kinsmen is surely one of the Keystones of Spiritual and Mental Preparedness. Therefore it is essential that we invest in family registers and newsletters — to be sure they represent money well spent."

(My translation)

The wide range of activities shown by the Krumms is typical mainly of Afrikaans-speaking families. In some cases, particularly in English families, gatherings last only one day, are far less organized and formal, and no surname society is formed. The interest in family history and genealogy is, however, as great and "family trees" and heraldry are researched and circulated within the family. The analysis which follows is based largely on the full complex of activities shown by families like the Krumms.

Analysis

Interest in genealogy and family history are not limited to white South Africans (Hailey 1978) and surname gatherings and societies flourish elsewhere (Ayoub 1966; Mitchell 1961, 1967, 1978). Cross-cultural comparison, however, falls outside the scope of this paper, in which I limit my discussion to the South African situation. I begin with an analysis of how model-building occurs in the creation and spread of what I call family myths of origin. This is followed by a consideration of how these myths reflect and even contribute in some measure to a number of wider social values and assumptions held by white South Africans. Implicit in my analysis is the assumption made by interpretative social scientists that perception of the world is subjective and that individuals actively reconstitute the cognitive model which they hold of the social world around them and of their place in it.

The Process of Model-building

My interest in the application of the concept "model" to this material developed out of attempts to explain the social actions involved in surname gatherings such as the *Krummfees,* which bring together hundreds of people most of whom have not met before and who have no connection other than a common surname, as well as the wider complex of family research, publication and the formation of surname societies. When first attending surname gatherings I was fascinated to observe *feesgangers* learning the family history, expressing and internalising sentiments of family pride and, in many cases, actively adding to the picture of the past by contributing either anecdotes or genealogical information to an accumulating pool of *familiegeskiedenis* (family history). This process entailed a general deepening of respect for the past, and a growing conviction on the part of many *feesgangers* that the past has relevance for the present in that not only physical features but also the character of forbears is transmitted "through the blood" and may, therefore, influence contemporary life and experience.

The events which occur at surname gatherings do not merely foster spontaneous enthusiasm; as the second quotation at the head of this essay suggests, they may be calculated to generate such feeling. Although by no means all those who organise gatherings conceptualize their actions so clearly as this writer, the generally offered explanations of items on the programme as "appropriate" or "fitting" suggests a similar, if unconscious motive[3]. Some speeches appear calculated to encourage family sentiment as part of wider national pride. For example, the du Toit *fees* was held to coincide with the opening of a national monument to the Afrikaans language to which their ancestor, S. J. du Toit, popularly known as Totius, contributed so much with his translation of the Bible. The speech of welcome included the following words:

> The Biblical words remind us that a (good) name is to be treasured far above riches. Once again our nation is gripped by the power of a wonder. Our founding was a wonder. Our struggle was a wonder, the wonder of the spoken word, our own language, the wonder of Afrikaans . . . And out of a whole nation God chose a few apt representatives (ripe seeds) with the name du Toit and planted them here in our beloved South Africa to grow and flourish. And without the wonder of Afrikaans in the development of which our family had and still has so great a share, our churches would close, our Bibles be silent, our prayers go unheard and our souls become estranged from God. Therefore we honour our family name, the name that we treasure above riches, the name that helped to develop the wonder of Afrikaans . . .

Similarly, in 1951, only three years after the National Party had come to power under D. F. Malan, the Malan family held three local *feeste* in different parts of the country, all stressing pride in the achievements of the family in public life.

The date of many surname gatherings is chosen to coincide with the anniversary of an important event in family history which may be that of the arrival of the progenitor in South Africa or the birth or death of notable family members. Both organisers and participants feel that it is appropriate for these events to be marked by large gatherings of family members. The direct association between the present and the past which the choice of these anniversaries makes explicit helps to foster emotions of pride and the feeling that, as one woman put it,

> We belong to an important family which has made its mark in this country — we have never been "nobodies" and many of our men have been leaders of their communities in times of crisis. I think that these leadership qualities are still with us — look how many of us are in politics and also education . . .

In many and varied ways, therefore, the holding of surname gatherings and the events and ceremonies which occur at them serve to develop and deepen family sentiment and a reverence for the past. The speakers who extol the contribution of forbears to South African society are often themselves well known South Africans and their very presence adds to family pride and gives the gathering the stamp of authority and public approval. Photographs in the press and radio or television coverage further underline the importance of the gathering. This, indeed, is myth making in action — the creation and consolidation of family legend. Many of the people who attend surname gatherings for the first time arrive with only a vague idea of who their ancestors were and what they achieved. They leave with not only a body of clearcut knowledge about the history of their family but also with a picture which glorifies the past and centres on the achievements of "great men and women" with whom they are proud to identify as kinsmen (*stamgenote* or *bloedgenote*).

The sentiments of family pride which are created and expressed at gatherings are, however, nebulous and often highly symbolic and need to take tangible form if they are to last beyond the few days of the *fees* or reunion itself. If, furthermore, they are to feed into a wider model that white South Africans hold of the past in relation to the present, they must be kept alive. This, I suggest, is achieved first by the ongoing activities of surname societies and, second, by the research and publication of family histories and genealogies. *Surname societies* The *Krumm-bond* is typical of white South African surname societies. To its holding of local gatherings, registration of a coat-of-arms and circulation of a newsletter may be added features such as raising money for a bursary fund, the erection of a monument to the *stamouers,* or even the organisation of a group expedition to visit the *Heimat* in Europe. Membership of one of these societies acts as a continual reminder of family sentiment and its very existence suggests to members that the family is a corporate unit. Many people who might hesitate to travel long distances to attend a gathering, still receive the newsletter and are informed of what occurred at the *fees* and of the achievements of other family members. Interviews with members show that they read with growing interest the instalments of family history and the progress of family research. A number of people have been encouraged by newsletters to do research of their own or to value old letters and family relics once considered "so much junk". These formal associations create, then, an ongoing emotional climate in which the family and family history are cherished and valued. Each time a newsletter arrives it is read with interest and pride, particularly if some notable family achievement is mentioned and, when registered, the coat-of-arms is often used on personal stationery and even in interior decoration. The newsletters also keep members who have met but who live far apart "in touch" with each other; they also publicise family publications when these appear.

Membership of surname societies is by virtue of birth or marriage. They are, therefore, closed societies or corporations. In the constitution of at least one *bond,* membership is even restricted to the white descendants of a particular progenitor. In this sense surname societies may be viewed as elitist associations and, indeed, some of the members of surname societies see them in this light. The organiser of one *bond* said to me "It is only the really big and important families that have societies — what would small families have to say about themselves?" There is definitely a good deal of prestige to be gained from belonging to a surname society which includes a number of well known South Africans and which continually stresses family achievements in all walks of life. On the other hand, it is true that by no means all the people who are eligible to join a particular *bond* do so, and organisers often bemoan "apathy", particularly about the paying of membership fees. Still, hundreds of white South Africans do participate actively in these societies and no fewer than four new *bonde* have come into being over the last two years. For the anthropologist their existence provides evidence of corporate activity initially based on the sharing of a name. They may, however, have other implications.

The constitutions of all surname societies enshrine reverence for the family but some go further and explicitly link commitment to the family with wider spiritual and even political values. The constitution of the *Le Roux familiebond* reminds family members not only to honour the family name but also the Protestant faith which their Huguenot forbears suffered so greatly to protect and propagate. It also admonishes them to use their gifts, talents and strength to the benefit of nation and fatherland. Similarly one of the goals of the *du Preez-bond* is to encourage family members to make useful contributions to their local communities and to be faithful and true citizens of "our land, South Africa" (du Preez 1961: 191). Thus while surname societies aim, first and foremost, to keep family sentiment alive, some emphasise more general values held dear in sections of white South African society. In this manner family sentiment is directly linked with a wider cognitive field involving moral and socio-political values which go far beyond the domain of the family.

Family histories and genealogies Published and manuscript works on white South African family history and genealogy stretch from the purely anecdotal which are derived largely from romantic family oral tradition to the consciously "scientific" based on archival material and private papers. The latter adopt quite stringent criteria of historically admissible evidence. Some are published with the financial help of the Genealogical Unit recently set up by the Human Sciences Research Council which is the major governmental body sponsoring social research in South Africa (Lombard 1977). These works carry with them the weight and stature of "science" as well as of tradition though privately printed family histories are often acknowledged as the "more readable". Works which are purely genealogical tend to be used largely for reference — that is, for identifying descent and mapping current agnatic and affinal relationships. Family histories contain skeletal genealogical information together with fuller information and anecdotes about certain forbears and eulogies over the past and present acheivements of many of those listed in the book. Both aspects may be combined into one book (Krige 1973; Van de Bijl 1968) and in at least one case a family genealogist has produced two publications, the one a popularly written *gedenkboek* (commemorative or remembrance book) and the other a more formal *geslagsregister* which was financed by the H.S.R.C.

(Viljoen *et al.* 1977; Viljoen 1978). Other families have also produced *gedenboeke* to honour their forbears or to commemorate large *feeste* (Smit 1949; du Preez 1962). These are often financed by pre-publication orders from family members. In addition to formal works are a myriad of typed and cyclostyled lectures, essays and transcripts of talks given by family historians. To this category may be added surname society newsletters and written speeches prepared for surname gatherings.

A feature common to all these works is that they have been written by enthusiasts and usually by members of the families concerned. However "scientific" the approach, they stem from family pride and are aimed at informing their readers about the family, its history and achievements. I have already argued that general family sentiment and legend are fostered during both the formal and informal events which occur at gatherings, but there is a more specific sense in which family mythology in the form of genealogy and history are created at these events.

Time is invariably set aside at gatherings for "telling stories about the old days", repeating family jokes and, most importantly, drawing up or correcting a genealogy. Though some family histories and genealogies are compiled without the holding of a gathering, family historians recognise these occasions as an ideal opportunity to collect outstanding information. The following incident occurred at the *fees* of a family for whom no published history or genealogy as yet exists. The family historian who I will call Pieter de Wit, had, however, done extensive archival research and had already mapped out the history of the family, but gaps in the genealogical data were holding up completion of the manuscript. As *feesgangers* arrived they were asked to "report" to Pieter in order to check details of parentage, marriages, births and deaths against his records. These had been compiled largely from the replies to a genealogical questionnaire which he had some years before sent out to the heads of most nuclear families with whom he was in contact. Only about a quarter of these forms had been returned fully completed and some of the information did not tally with other records. Pieter looked upon the *fees,* at which some 400 people were expected, as providing an ideal opportunity to rectify some of the omissions and confusions in his data. During their interview with him, *feesgangers* gave information not only on their own nuclear families and immediate relatives, but also filled in details on other people from memory. At one point a woman of about 35 came in with her husband and three children. She had been born into the family but did not have any idea of how she fitted into the *geslagsregister.*

She could name her father and mother but knew nothing of her paternal grandparents beyond their names. Unfortunately her father did not seem to have had contact with any brothers and the trail seemed cold. Pieter de Wit asked, "But what are your Christian names?"[4] When it turned out that she had the names given to girls born into a particular branch of the family, he said, "Oh you must be descended from Christoffel Henry who married Wilhemina Aura van der Walt and the girls still keep the names . . . . tell me . . . . did your grandfather ever live in the Marico district?" There was a long pause before the woman answered. " . . . .yes, I think, maybe . . . . my father said they had left the Northern Transvaal when he was very young . . . . but now you mention it . . . . I think that was the area they came from . . . . So do you think that could be the case?" "Yes . . . . possibly . . . . your age and your father's age seem to be right . . . . there was another son here . . . . I didn't know what happened to him . . . . " The woman looked amazed but gratified. I overheard an onlooker saying, "Well . . . . she must be a de Wit, look at her son . . . . he has the hammerhead (*hamerkop*)."

So the genealogical record is built up. Genealogists strive to get their facts accurate but there are cases where records and memory fail and the indirect evidence of names, apparently similar physical features, places of origin and the genealogist's intuition must come into play. This type of "guesswork" is roundly condemned by professional genealogists but there is always the strong and almost overwhelming desire to complete the genealogy and "tie up all the loose ends". Towards the end of the de Wit *fees* an appeal was made over the public address system for *feesgangers* with information and experience of particular "branches" which were still not fully documented, to call at the registration desk "to see if they can help".

Once it is published, a genealogy or *geslagsregister* stands almost as a "Bible of descent" as it was once described to me. People often cavil at details such as dates and the spelling of names, but the overall record is accepted as "the truth". The result of family research and publications have indeed come to produce documents which are accepted and read as "history". Unlike genealogies in non-literate societies, publication fixes for all time both the "genealogical charter" and some of the sentiments aroused and expressed during surname gatherings. In a literate and scientifically oriented society family histories and genealogies come to be *the* tangible proof of the achievements of the past. Each time they are read the deeds and also those responsible for them live on in the present. This is surely myth-making in action.

Another significant point is that the deeds and their perpetrators are all white, indeed whiteness is often explicitly mentioned in these documents as a virtue. In the newsletter of one surname society we read that "In 1797, a century after the birth of (the *stamvader*), all 32 of his grandchildren were pure white . . ." Genealogies are not only "Bibles of descent", they are also Bibles of white descent in a country where the vast majority of people are black, and many who are classified "non-white" bear the same surnames as Whites. In this, they reflect the reality of South African everyday life in which Blacks are excluded from normal interactions with Whites and, in particular, from marriage with them. For the genealogist, marriage is the basic building block of the past as it is in the present, and white family trees and *geslagregisters* tell the story of 300 years of supposed *"apartheid"*. *Feeste* and reunions are similarly microcosms of the total society. They are never multi-racial; one family have recently refused to admit a coloured man of the same name as themselves to their *fees*. Blacks are present, it is true, but in their capacities as servants to cook the meals and care for the children. This point was highlighted by a passing joke by a *feesganger* who said, as she pointed to a coloured nursemaid caring for her grandchildren, "She is probably also a Krumm!" White South Africans are all too aware that marriages have occurred in the past between Whites and Blacks and that sexual unions continue despite the Mixed Marriages Act. In the rituals of surname gatherings and in many of the publications on family and genealogy this fact is ignored. Instead, the myth of white purity is celebrated and validated by the strict genealogical tally of white marriages and births down the generations in South Africa.

The Content of Family Myths of Origin

It is not only whiteness which is enshrined in family publications. As a *genre,* these works show a number of other recurrent themes; a stress on the European origin and settler status of the first man or conjugal pair to bear the family name in South Africa, evidence of their high moral and religious fibre and as full as possible picture of the reason for emigration and the early years of settlement and expansion in this country. This includes express mention of all famous men and women and of their contributions to South African society. Implied in these themes is invariably a claim by the descendants of the settlers to the land which their forbears developed and "civilised". Taken together these features constitute, I suggest, a mythological charter much in the sense in which Malinowski originally used the term (1948). For South African Whites the past is peopled, if not by gods, at least by upright and godfearing *white* men and women who, having of their own free will left either Europe or the Cape, often in response to religious or political persecution, ventured into the African unknown to forge a free, safe and glorious heritage which cannot now be denied to their descendants.Excerpts from published *geslagsregisters* and family histories, from the speeches made at gatherings and from surname society newsletters may be used to document my claim.

Settlers of European origin

In 1671 Francois Villion of Clermont, France, came as a young man to the Cape of Good Hope and settled as a Free Burgher in Capetown. He was the first French speaker, the first French Protestant and the first Huguenot to arrive at the Cape – a good seventeen years before the organized mass emigration of Huguenots took place. On 17/5/1676 he was married in Capetown to Cornelia Campenaar, a young girl of Middelburg, Holland. Their union was blessed with six children, of whom two sons and three daughters later married. Six years after their marriage the couple settled on the farm Idasvalley, just outside Stellenbosch after Governor Simon van der Stel laid out eight new farms just outside the town (which now bears his name) and allocated them to Free Burghers. Here the *stamvader* died in 1689 – just after his countrymen arrived at the Cape as part of the great Huguenot emigration. (Translated from Viljoen 1978: 5)

About 50km. southwest of Lingen, lie the villages Lengerich, Lienen, Ladbergen and Brochterbeck, all approximately 10km. apart. All four of these villages lie in the County of Lingen and therefore experienced the some bloody history. Here the early history of the Krige family was played out . . .
In 1721 the Dutch vessel *Het Vaderland Getrou* casts anchor in Table Bay. Amongst the soldiers on board is a certain Willem Adolph Krige who ends his journey from Europe here and goes ashore. He apparently intends to settle here, for when his ship continues its voyage to the East, he remains behind and exchanges his soldier's uniform for the humble garb of a groom in the service of the Dutch East India Company. In this unpretentious fashion, the founder of the Kriges becomes a South African. (Translated from Krige 1973: 1, 7)

The style used, particularly in the second excerpt, compounds historical fact and romanticism, but what is important is that the European origin of the *stamvader* (progenitor) is carefully documented. Details, where known, are always given of the date of the *stamvader's* arrival, name of the ship he sailed on and nature of his passage. Mention is usually made of his parents and, where possible, information on grand- and great-grandparents is given and illustrated by photographs of portraits and reproductions of the handwriting or baptismal certificates of either the *stamvader* or of his forbears. Details are usually included of the social standing of the family and of the occupations and achievements of the European forbears. Though in a few cases these are aristocratic, mostly they are fairly humble. The country of origin is often described and details given of the town and village thought or known to have been the birthplace of the *stamvader*. A good deal of information on local European history is also often given, and the inability to document these basic facts is a source of distress. In the case of the Viljoens, because there are a number of villages of the same name, it is not absolutely certain which is the village of Clermont from which Francois Villion came (Viljoen *et al.* 1977: 11-12) but research on this score has been underway for some time. Investigation of this nature may involve personal visits to Europe.

Pride is often expressed in the nation and language of forbears. Flattering stereotypes of the national character abound and the progenitor is said to have shared these to the full — traits such as doggedness, refusal to give up in the face of hardships and setbacks, love of freedom and a refusal to accept political or religious domination. Works on the descendants of French Huguenots often contain descriptions of the persecutions experienced by Protestants for their faith and suggest either implicitly or explicitly that it was the search for religious, political or personal freedom which motivated the emigration of the forbears to a new and unknown land.

These sentiments, if in a light-hearted vein, appear in the foreword to the Van der Bijl genealogy:

We can also claim to be a typical South African family with mainly Dutch, French and English blood flowing in our veins. The Dutch have the reputation of being an adventurous, stubborn nation. Those who arrived here shortly after van Riebeeck (not necessarily civil servants but under their own steam as *Vry Burghers)* were probably dissatisfied with the economic, social and other conditions in Holland and possibly were an intransigent section of a stubborn people. After the revocation of the Edict of Nantes, Frenchmen, tired of being persecuted because of their beliefs, decided to emigrate to a wild distant country rather than bend the knee. Members of some of the most distinguished families came; again a headstrong section of an unyielding nation. Then the 1820 Settlers, possibly disgruntled with economic conditions in Britain, were another

> obdurate and inflexible section of a resolute and dogged nation. So
> this fusion of bloody-minded sections, steeped in the teachings, traditions
> and outlook of the Old Testament, of three resolute nations, renowned
> for their determination and will to hold on, became the amalgam which
> was the basic material forming the new South African nation. (van der
> Bijl 1968)

A religious vocation is often given as the main reason for emigrating
from Europe. A fair number of the progenitors of both English and
Afrikaans families came to South Africa in the early to middle nineteenth century as missionaries and they are represented as being
committed to bringing the Word of God to the "dark continent".
The official programme issued for the family gathering of the
descendents of the Reverend Charles Scott and his family held in
Natal in 1975 ends with the words:

> Thus did our forbears decide to pull up their roots and to start a
> new life in an unknown and uncivilized country despite all the hardships and
> difficulties to be faced and overcome. Indeed their faith in God is our
> example for us to follow.

In similar vein we read how the Eastern Cape missionary, John
Brownlee "was to live and toil among the wild tribes of South-east
Africa for fifty-four years, till he laid down his life at the age of
eighty, never having seen his native land again." (Holt 1976: 7-8).
Even in cases where forbears came to South Africa for reasons
quite unconnected with religion, their adherence to the Protestant
faith in particular, is emphasised either directly or indirectly.
Indeed migration to South Africa is usually seen as the will of God.
To quote the Mentz *Gedenboek:*

> Whatever the considerations that moved him, one thing is clear to those
> who believe in God's guidance: it was preordained by God that Joachim
> Frederik Mentz should come to South Africa and here become the
> patriarch of a new generation of Afrikaners who would play their part
> in the development of this country and in the building up of our Church
> and nation. (Translated Smit 1949: 1)

Accompanying genealogical research is an interest in heraldry (J.A.
Heese 1975; Pama 1959, 1965, 1972). As in the case of the Krumm
family, many white South African families and surname societies
are seeking to have a coat-of-arms registered with the South African
Bureau of Heraldry. The costs of research, drawing up and the
registration of crests may amount to over £500, yet this money is

considered well spent. Once it is registered and family members use the crest on stationery, jewellery and for wall decorations, the device comes to be a symbol of family corporation, identity and achievement. Apart from these more obvious functions, the proud possession of a coat-of-arms may be interpreted as yet another move to emphasise links with Europe. It manifests, too, a desire to establish and verify a non-African past and heritage which is distinct from the African experience of Whites today. The helms and swords, the mediaeval symbols and devices, are both exotic and non-African and the Latin inscriptions speak of antiquity and permanence rooted in the age-old experience of Western society and not of the relatively "recent" history of Africa as it is conceptualised by most white South Africans.

Crests and coats-of-arms are usually thought to be associated with a gentle, noble or even royal lineage. Though there may well be strong elements of this type of status seeking involved, the nature and meaning of the heraldry complex of many families is established in family histories as not aristocratic and indeed quite ordinary. For modern white South Africans the virtue of a coat-of-arms may, therefore, reside in its use as a subtle but *public* statement in a new country that a family has a past — has "roots" elsewhere and the stability which comes from a long European history. Most Whites do not regard Africa as having experienced history in the "cultural" or "civilised" sense before the arrival of their ancestors up to 300 years ago. It is therefore important to link themselves with a European past in order to be associated with "culture" and "civilisation" as they understand these concepts. The fact that European forbears were not noble, while possibly disappointing to some, is not the major issue. What is critical is establishing links with "history" itself. By no means all white South African families can do this and the members of those who can are proud of this fact.

Family histories and a distinctive coat-of-arms come to symbolise not only the identity and antiquity of the family concerned in relation to other white families, but by establishing a direct link with Europe they emphasise also that many Whites, though born, reared and intending to stay in South Africa, are not "of Africa" in the same sense as are most indigenous Blacks. Instead, by having "come from Europe" Whites are born different to and also superior to the indigenous "races" of Africa whose forbears the white settlers found living here. Blacks, as we will see, are always portrayed as being completely different from the settlers in that they had not received the gift of Christian awareness — a gift which many of the progenitors and *stamouers* of today's Whites are revered for having planted in the African Soil. In the colour conscious milieu of South Africa today it is race which makes the significant difference between South Africans: in the past it was religion, settler status and the access to power and wealth which these factors conferred. Family histories make this point and by linking white South Africans with "the outside" bolster their belief in their innate difference from Blacks and their right to social and political dominance. Even greater authority is given to a social system in which Whites rule Blacks by the implication that it was God's will and His design which brought Whites to South Africa and which led to the founding of the white South African nation out of so many strong and vibrant European strains.

The spread of white settlement The European origins of progenitors having been established, most family histories and genealogies proceed to chronicle the process by which their descendants settled in the new land and helped to develop "civilised" society there. The contrast between the settlers and the indigenous population is made clear by means of anecdotes detailing the hardships and privations suffered in the course of establishing farms or mission stations and in problematic and dangerous interactions with *non-Whites*. I use the term non-White advisedly because it reflects how the authors of these works view the people concerned. Into this category fall not only members of the indigenous populations, the Khoi, San and Bantu-speaking people, but also slaves and their descendants. All are portrayed in the most negative terms – the slaves being seen as lacking in moral fibre and the indigenous Blacks as savage, unpredictable and dangerous. For instance, in a newsletter of one surname society we read how the *stamvader* arrived in the country as a

> fatherless child who, poor and illiterate, found refuge in the new port of Cape Town where he had to make a living. Despite the many temptations of dissolute slaves and racial mixing, he did not falter, and eventually raised a large and healthy family . . .

The chronicling of the early years of settlement usually involves mention of well known places and landmarks and many publications are illustrated with plates taken from old drawings which show dramatically how change and progress has occurred, and how the cultural landscape has been altered by the efforts of family members. For the members of the family often the most attractive aspect of a family history is the pen pictures of famous people – the Kriges, the Viljoens or the du Toits, who have actually contributed to the building up of the country in some concrete or dramatic way, or who are, today, in the public eye. The frontispiece of the Swart family book (de Villiers 1977) shows the first State President and his wife, and in the introduction we read "and the first State President was also a Swart — don't think that the Swarts forget this for a moment." The Viljoen *Gedenboek* contains articles on numerous famous white Viljoens, one of which is entitled "Five Generals" and gives photographs and descriptions of the military achievements of these men which span 75 years of South African history. The history of the Great Trek (the movement of Afrikaners from the Cape into the interior) is represented in family history as spreading over the whole of South Africa a fine network of white influence and achievement. The histories of Trekker descendants focus on the men who lead Trek parties and repeatedly mention well known places and battles (e.g. Retief n.d.; Uys 1974). In so doing these histories cover the indigenous landscape with the veneer of white culture and control. At one *fees* held by a family of Voortrekker origin, the major speech chronicled the migration of their forbears from the Cape to their present "home" in the Eastern Transvaal and linked the family with 200 years of Afrikaner expansion and achievement. It was significant that although the European *stamvader* was honoured, the major focus of attention was upon one of his sons who left the Cape with one of the best known trekker parties. It was his life and that of his two wives and 17 children which was recounted and glorified, when gravestones were unveiled on his grave and that of his second wife. It is again these trekkers who are to be given greatest attention in the forthcoming family history.

Despite the fact that such publications are based on historical fact, the choice and use of material is essentially romantic and celebratory. The exploits of forbears are put in the most favourable light possible and their achievements are stressed far more than their failures. It is true that factual material is present; indeed, many of these works are the result of years of careful research, but the end result is an exploration and glorification of achievement and success. Some researchers maintain that they are interested in the "bad as well as the good", but in the final publication it is the good and heroic which predominates. The very fact that the concern for history develops from an interest in particular people — that is those of the family concerned — influences the assessment of the overall historical situation and makes complete historical objectivity unlikely if not impossible. These publications are truly myths which resemble the tales told in most societies about the great and glorious exploits of the heroes of the past and for this reason I would describe them as a folk mythology. Despite the fact that they are Western in origin and written down rather than handed down in an oral form, they operate in much the same way as do myths in other societies to validate social relations and explain the world — in this case the social and cultural past. Various writers have shown how flexible and changing myths and, in particular, genealogies are in other African societies. Bohannan (1952) and Comaroff (1974) have, indeed, demonstrated that many major genealogical features are open to constant negotiation. A similar dynamic process of genealogical and historical construction is, I suggest, observable in the creation of white South African "myths of origin".

The hard won right to remain   From the expression of such admiring sentiments about ancestors it takes no great imaginative leap to suggest that the hardships endured and the contributions made by settlers have earned for their descendants the right to live in and enjoy the fruits of the adoptive land. The programme of the Scott gathering quotes a text apparently often used by the Reverend Charles Scott, "We went through fire and water; but Thou broughtest us into a wealthy land". It is not, however, only the right to exploit what South Africa has to offer which is emphasised, but the determination of white South Africans to continue to live in South Africa whatever the cost. This intention may be couched in religious terms with the suggestion that a sacrifice will be required to bring it about.

> We believe the Heavenly Father brought us here for a purpose — yes, it was part of His Great Plan that we might propagate the Christian belief and live here as Christians to the benefit of all the other peoples who share our land — and we are all determined to continue this trust . . . In order to fulfil this trust we will continue to look to God above for guidance and strength and in the words (spirit) of our National Anthem — "We will offer what you ask, We are for you, South Africa". (Translated from Viljoen *et al.* 1977: 10)

Apparent, too, may be the suggestion that both this and future generations of white South Africans will have to guard their inheritance, as did their forbears, by force. These sentiments are expressed clearly in the following words which ended a speech made at a *fees* held in 1975 —

> Dear kinsmen, today we live in a world of confusion . . . Every day we read of the powers of evil, of communism, of bloodshed and such like

things. We, in South Africa, are constantly being threatened by these powers — especially, as I see it, by Russia and Communism. Should it become necessary to take up arms in the defence of our Republic, we must not rest upon the laurels of the past generations, but we must walk along their Pilgrims' Trail and share in their endeavours.

Other *feeste* held recently have shown an increased emphasis upon the need to be strong and to withstand onslaughts from outside the country. In those held by families of Voortrekker descent the emphasis on willingness to fight as did their forbears for the father-land and for cherished values has been clear. At a *fees* held in the Transvaal in 1976, a direct comparison was drawn between the periods of the Great Trek and the Anglo-Boer War, when mothers willingly sent their sons to fight and die, and the near future when members of the family will again have to make this sacrifice with a smile on their lips. One can, of course, search in vain for these sentiments in the publications of some families (particularly English-speaking opponents of the ruling Nationalist Government) and also in those publications produced before about the mid-seventies. I see the trend to emphasise military preparedness as a response to the growing insecurity of many white South Africans and Afrikaners in particular.

In another, but related context, where it is accommodation, rather than resistance, which is stressed, we can still see how sensitive family mythologies are to changing circumstances:

Our first Viljoen festival is held three hundred years after our ancestors, Francois and Cornelia, settled in this country. It coincides also with the end of an era in the history of the white man here in South Africa. Where the white man previously governed those people of this country who are of a different colour to him, and acted as their guardian, a situation has now arisen where we find that these "foster" children want to reject this guardianship, and wish either to share in the government of this land, or to be independent of the white man. In the same way that our ancestors were faced with challenges three hundred years ago, so the future also challenges us today. Drastic changes can be expected — changes that will demand of us the highest degree of tact, good strategy, understanding, sacrifice and adaptation. I do believe, however, that Viljoens, whose forbears played so crucial a role in the history of the Old Cape and later also in all the Provinces of the present Republic, will accept the challenges of our times, and will help to build a secure future in this country for, amongst others, the descendants of today's Viljoens. (translated from Viljoen 1977: 7)

These words reflect an awareness of the inevitability of change, but they may also be interpreted as an attempt on the part of the speaker to *prepare* his listeners for the social and cultural accommodations which he regards necessary to ensure their survival both as a family and as leaders in South African society.

The seven years during which I have attended surname gatherings have coincided with the appearance of overwhelming evidence of radical and previously unimagined social and political change in neighbouring African States. White South Africa has been experiencing what could be referred to as an organization change during which it may be possible to monitor the dynamics of model change. It is, I feel, significant that during the earlier Krumm *fees* of 1973, little of either the mood of preparedness for armed conflict or radical social change was apparent. In the newsletter of some three years later (this chapter: 187-8) however, these senti-ments were not only expressed but a direct link was made between the encouragement of family sentiment and national loyalty. After 1975, similar emphases became increasingly evident in speeches at a wide range of gatherings and in their associated publications. It is also worth noting that the Viljoen family at whose *fees* such an eloquent plea was made for social accommodation rather than military resistance is one from which a number of today's political, military and administrative leaders have been drawn. There is a joke current in white South African circles to the effect that "The country may be ruled by Bothas, but it is run by Viljoens".

It is true that neither a single speech — however prominent the speaker — nor a series of speeches at many *feeste* can alone alter the model which white South Africans have of social reality. My argument is, however, that there are many occasions, some social, some political, some religious, some reaching many people and others only a few, in which models of social life are defined or created as a result of interactions and transactions between individuals. From the point of view of this paper, it is significant that "family" gatherings and their associated publications are deemed appropriate arenas in which to make statements which go beyond what the outsider might see as the restricted field of kinship activity. Though the people concerned conceptualise their actions as having to do with family affairs (*familiesake*) only, yet the implications of what is being said and written go far beyond the family domain and stress wider social values such as whiteness, the love of God, good citizenship and loyalty to the State. The folk mythology of the family reaches out to reflect and reiterate the world view of wider society and there is a continual interaction between two levels of cognitive activity.

Conclusion

I believe that two types of model-building are occurring in the activities which I have described. The first involves the creation of a number of separate yet similar family myths. These are compounded of pride in the achievements of forbears and mean that descendants share vicariously in the greatness of the past and claim prestige in current society by association with the past, particularly a past which goes back to Europe and Western civilisation. Hence, not only the writing of glorious family histories but also the use of coats-of-arms as a symbol of the past. The second type of model-building is far broader in scope and major elements of the model are whiteness and white achievements in a country where Whites are in the minority and jealously guard the right to rule. In this case the model provides a charter for white social and political dominance which is reiterated at each gathering and each time a family history or genealogy is read, remembered and repeated. The men and women who attend gatherings and who publish family books are, indeed, building up step by step and, as it were, relationship by relationship, the model of the social world which they cherish and which reflects what is from their point of view, social reality. Their model is for them an eminently satisfactory one in that it explains how their forbears came to South Africa, settled the land and achieved social prominence and distinction there. It also justifies white rule and provides a programme by which a secure future for Whites in South Africa may be achieved; in many cases this survival appears to be through the use of force although in one case, as we have seen, compromise is recommended. The model is thus a dynamic and changing one which alters and accommodates to organisational and social change and provides encouragement to future action.

My analysis raises the problem of how conscious an activity model-building is. I introduced the paper with a quotation which suggests a conscious motive for holding a *fees*. The writer's words, indeed, read rather like an orthodox structural-functional analysis of ceremonial and it is of interest that he is himself a university graduate and that his wife has a postgraduate training in cultural anthropology. Even in the case of individuals who have no similar social science background there is, however, a consciousness that it is "good" to get as many members as possible of a family together and that holding a *fees* fosters sentiments of family pride and loyalty. Those who organise surname gatherings and run surname societies are, I think, to various degrees consciously model-building in the sense that they aim to instil sentiments of family pride and loyalty in the minds of people who share their surname.

The extent to which they are aware that they are creating what I have called a "folk mythology" is problematic. Those who take a consciously "scientific" approach are concerned over the pitfalls of "glorifying" the family and try to guard against them. I have argued, however, that the very nature of their endeavour which stems from family pride rather than the disinterested assessment of "pure" history, makes complete objectivity extremely difficult if not impossible. The writers of family histories and genealogies believe, however, that they are genuinely recreating the past and are certainly not aware of the wider social and political implications which I have suggested that their "models" contain. How then do these wider social ramifications occur?

In writing family histories and in planning the programmes of surname gatherings the organisers are faced with a wide range of historical data and with various alternative modes of action. Their final choice reflects both what they deem to be important and what they know will be attractive to their readers and audience. For this reason their decisions are determined to a large extent by wider social preoccupations. It is, therefore, not surprising to find typical white South African values stressed such as social and political achievement, religious fervour and a determination to retain what is held valuable — that is the right to live in South Africa and to continue to lead the country. All model-building is, as I see it, a *social* activity done by individuals in relation to their social environment and must be sensitive to some extent to wider social reality as they see it and to the responses of fellow men. Indeed, individuals create the social world around them and, as such, give life and substance to it in their models. The myths of white South African family histories are the results of *action;* they are made together and derive from corporate activity, but they are also worked out by the individuals within a social environment, and, therefore, they observe its limits and simultaneously strengthen its foundations. It is the human mind, however, that is the active mover in the process and it is the individuals who make up and spread myths and models. Their consciousness of what they are doing at one level need not extend to other levels of cognitive activity.

Complex social events often demand several theoretical approaches to interpret them satisfactorily. In keeping with the theme of this volume I have explored only one aspect of the set of activities described above — that of the nature and sociopolitical implications of the concept or "model" of the past which I believe is developed and disseminated at White South African surname gatherings and in family research and publication. To some extent this analysis does violence to the data for model-building is by no means the only (and it may not even be the major) element involved in their actions. The analysis goes beyond what the actors themselves say that they are doing and on this score may be open to some of the criticisms raised by the editors of this volume in their introduction. On the other hand, in suggesting that white South Africans are drawing up genealogical charters which have current social and political relevance in that they both explain the social world and justify its existence, I am following in well-worn anthropological footpaths, many of which were explored in earlier A.S.A. Monographs (Banton 1965; Geertz 1966). Perhaps the most interesting aspect of my data is that it has allowed for the documentation of model-building in action and has demonstrated that mythological and genealogical model-building is not limited to Black Africa, but is part also of white South African social interactions.

Acknowledgements

I gratefully acknowledge the financial assistance received from the Human Sciences Research Council of South Africa and from the University of Natal which made it possible for me to attend the 1980 A.S.A. Conference.

Notes

1. These Afrikaans words are used to some extent interchangeably for surname gatherings. There is a slight tendency to use *saamtrek* (come together) in the case of smaller and regular meetings and to reserve *fees* (festival) for larger and irregular meetings such as the Krumm-*fees* (Kapp 1975).
2. I am indebted to Professor Raymond Firth for drawing my attention to this point, and to Professors John Argyle, Basil Sansom and Bill Epstein for their insistence on the fact that what I describe has many elements of status-seeking in it. The wider study of white South Africans of which my research forms a part, was initiated by Professor John Argyle of the University of Natal, Durban, South Africa, and I wish to express my gratitude to him for his continuing interest and encouragement in my research.
3. At some gatherings teeshirts, ties, mugs and plaques with the coat-of-arms emblazoned on them are for sale and at one *fees* a record made by the family choir was available and a family song had been composed for the occasion. Visits to places of interest connected with forbears and to their graves are a common feature of gatherings as are communal meals, a family concert and communal worship. These events all seem to emphasise family pride and corporation.
4. Traditional Afrikaner naming patterns were, and in some cases still are, strict. Thus the same names may appear down the generations.

References

Ayoub, M. (1966). The family reunion. *Ethnology* 5, 415-33.
Banton, M. ed. (1965). *The Relevance of Models for Social Anthropology*. ASA Mon. No. 1. London: Tavistock.
Bohannan, L. (1952). A genealogical charter. *Africa* 22, 301-15
Buthelezi, M. G. (1978). Early history of the Buthelezi Clan. In *Social System*

and Tradition, (J.W. Argyle and E.M. Preston-Whyte, eds). Cape Town: Oxford University Press.

Cairns, M. (1978). Genealogy of a Cape muslim family. In *The Early Cape Muslims*, (F.R. Bradlow and M. Cairns, eds). Cape Town: Balkema.

Comaroff, J. L. (1974). Chiefship in a South African homeland. *J. South Afr. Studies* 1, 16-51.

De Villiers, C.G.S. (1977). *Geslagsregister van die Familie Swart*. Pretoria: H.S.R.C.

Du Preez, J. W. (1962). *Du Preez Gedenkboek*. Johannesburg: Private Printing.

Geertz, C. (1966). Religion as a cultural system. In *Anthropological Approaches to the Study of Religion*. (M. Banton ed.). ASA Mon. No. 3. London: Tavistock.

Hailey, A. (1978). *Roots*. London: Pan Books.

Heese, J. A., Nienaber, G. S. and Pama, C. (1975). *Families, Familiename en Familiewapens*. Cape Town: Tafelberg.

Heese, H. F. (1980). Familiegeskiedenis van 'n Paarlse Familie. *Kronos* 2, 11-16.

Holt, B. (1976). *Greatheart of the Border: A life of John Brownlee Pioneer Missionary in South Africa*. Lovedale: Lovedale Press.

Kapp, P.H. (1975). *Ons Volksfeeste*. Cape Town: Tafelberg.

Krige, J. D. (1973). *Die Familie KRIGE - Herkoms en Genealogie*. Pretoria: Craft Pers.

Lombard, R. T. J. (1977). *Handbook for Genealogical Research*. Pretoria: H.S.R.C.

Malinowski, B. (1948). *Magic, Science and Religion*. New York: Doubleday and Co.

Mitchell, W. E. (1961). Descent groups among New York City Jews. *The Jewish Journal of Sociology* 3, 121-28.

Mitchell, W. E. (1967). Kin groups and assemblages. In *Kinship and Casework*, (H.J. Leichter and W.R. Mitchell, eds). New York: Russel Sage Foundation.

Mitchell, W. E. (1978). *Organized Mushpokeh: The Jewish Clubs of New York City*. The Hague: Mouton.

Mutwa, C. (n.d.) *Indaba, my Children*. Johannesburg: Blue Crane Books.

Mutwa, C. (1966). *Africa is my Witness*. Pietermaritzburg: The Natal Witness.

Pama, C. (1959). *Die Wapens van die ou Afrikaanse Families*. Cape Town: Balkema.

Pama, C. (1965). *Lions and Virgins: Heraldic State Symbols, Coats-of-Arms, Flags, Seals and other Symbols of Authority in South Africa. 1487-1962*. Cape Town: Human and Rousseau.

Pama, C. (1972). *Heraldry of South African Families/Coats-of-Arms, Crests, Ancestry*. Cape Town: Balkema.

Retief, P. J. (n.d.) *Die Retief-familie in Suid Afrika*. Private Printing.

Smit, A. P. (1949). *Gedenk-Album van die Mentz-Geslag 1749-1949*. Stellenbosch: Pro Ecclesia Drukkery.

Uys, I.S. (1974). *Die Uys Geskiedenis 1704-1974*. Kaapstad: Kaap and Transvaal Drukkery Bpk.

Van de Bijl, J. (1968). *Van Der Bijl 1667-1967 Geslagsregister/Genealogie*. Cape Town: Balkema.

Viljoen, H. C. (1978). *Die Viljoen – Familieregister*. Pretoria: H.S.R.C.

Viljoen, H. *et al.* (1977). *Viljoen-Gedenkboek, Uitgegee deur die Viljoen – Familiebond*. Stellenbosch.

THE OBLIGATION TO GIVE – AN INTERACTIONAL SKETCH

DAVID RICHES

Instead of reducing the relationship between notions and actions, or postulating it as a nonproblematic one, this relationship should be the main subject of analysis (Holy and Stuchlik, this volume)

Anthropological studies which have explicitly employed the analytical distinction between notions and actions have so far been mainly concerned with the processes whereby the notions, or folk models, affect or shape the transactions of people. The other side of the equation, processes whereby concrete actions affect or shape folk models, has been considerably neglected (*Ibid.*)

Introduction

One broad folk idea, probably common to all societies, is the expectation that, between people in certain social categories, goods and services[1] should be rendered without explicit consideration of return, and that identity in such social categories rests importantly in relations of kinship. In accord with the quotations cited above, the concern in this paper is with the activities – again probably common to all societies – in terms of which this folk idea is "shaped". In so far as social notions exist only because they are invoked in everyday social interaction (see later), I shall be asking: to what circumstances of everyday life may the invocation of the folk idea be plausibly regarded as a rational response (cf. Riches 1977: 131-2)?

In social anthropological analysis there is a tendency to conflate notions and actions (cf. Holy and Stuchlik, this volume); it is therefore important to stipulate precisely what the subject of enquiry is.[2] In so far as the interest here is with notions, the focus in this paper is on certain obligations and/or entitlements as these are expressed as ideals. As far as the obligations/entitlements are concerned, these refer to the rendering of goods or services in a particular transaction. In this respect, a defining feature of the obligations/ entitlements is that they embody altruistic connotations. Both the range of situations when it is expected such obligations, etc., will be discharged and the types of goods or services which it is expected will be rendered, vary from society to society; but in the terms in which the obligations are expressed the rendering of resources is not contingent on a specific return within a specific time.[3] The *obligation to give* resources under these terms, and/or the obverse, *the entitlement to receive* such resources, is the subject of the enquiry. Thus when one of my Eskimo friends complained about a particular hunter who had returned from the country laden with meat, but had failed to distribute it, the ideal he cited elaborated a good deal on the hunter's duty to share and on his own entitlement to a portion — it said nothing about the meat that he would be sending in return at some later date when he himself had had a successful hunt.

At a different level of social reality are people's actions and interests relating to such obligations. While certain of these actions and interests may well be germane to explaining the existence of the obligations, these are not the subject of enquiry, nor do they affect the definition of the subject. At this different level of reality, we may cite the varying interactional styles and motives in terms of which the obligation to give/entitlement to receive is invoked. People may give disinterestedly (altruistically) or for calculating long-term material benefits; they may give grudgingly or willingly (or refuse to give); the recipient may initiate the transaction (by requesting resources) or the donor may initiate it (by proferring resources). Some of these styles and motives are evident in the Eskimo material I present later. The point to be made here is that in all such instances the obligation to give, etc., may be legitimately invoked: the varying styles and motives therefore do not affect or invalidate the definition of the obligation, the existence of which we are attempting to explain. To return to my Eskimo friend, as regards his problem with the stingy hunter it could be observed that in the past he had given meat to this man and therefore might now expect to receive something in return. Obviously my friend knows this, but this fact is not incorporated in the way he expressed his entitlement; in no manner does it qualify the existence of the entitlement as he expressed it.[4] In identifying both obligations and interests as being pertinent to gift-giving obviously I am in company with Mauss (1954). But Mauss did not stress that obligations and interests constitute two levels of reality: people give because of their interests and justify giving by invoking their obligations. My concern in this paper is with explaining these latter (the obligations) in terms of some of the former (the interests).

Let me turn now briefly to the theme of kinship. In a manner similar to a number of important anthropological studies which have investigated the connection between kinship, social obligation and social activity (especially Sahlins 1965; Fortes 1969), I intend in the first instance to elaborate propositions about the "obligation to give" as this is instituted in dyadic relationships in societies in which all social interaction proceeds on a face-to-face basis. Following a number of writers who offer a clear distinction between kinship and descent (e.g. Scheffler 1974; Keesing 1975), my concern then is with kinship proper rather than with relationships based on descent, i.e. my concern is with genealogical ties defined with reference to a living individual or pair of individuals. It is obvious that the obligation to give is invoked in a number of contexts outside that of the dyadic kinship relationship, for example in the context of membership in a corporate descent group or in the rendering of tribute or tax. To the extent that such contexts are in evidence in a particular society, the social and spatial distribution relating to the exercise of the obligation will clearly be markedly influenced. But in my view, these contexts presuppose the existence of the obligation to give as this is instituted in kinship. So far as descent group corporations are concerned, it is in the invocation of the kinship idiom in the descent construct (referring to the relationship between the member and the ancestor) that the member's acquiescence in the obligation to give is in part sustained (cf. Riches 1979a: 154). And in more complex societies the rendering of tribute and tax is justified through quasi-kinship and citizenship idioms which again probably rest in some manner on the existence of kinship itself (cf. my discussion later in this paper on the Eskimo "neighbour" idiom). It is on the fundamental setting of the dyadic kinship relationship that this study concentrates.

Assumptions

In Fortes' classic exposition of the relationship between kinship and social activity, kinship is seen as having structural autonomy *sui generis,* an embodiment of a morality that has strongly altruistic connotations, and a powerful determinant of social transactions in which an expectation of return, at least in the short term, is not engendered (e.g. Fortes 1969: 110, 229). In view of the epistemological assumptions incorporated in this study it is held here, in contrast, that the notions associated with kinship have an interactional basis. Sahlins, noting that just as kinship may be treated as constraining social activity of a certain type, the performance of certain types of activity may be regarded as sustaining the existence of the kinship relation, has gone some way in this direction (Sahlins 1965: 139-140). He puts the issue in the following general fashion:

> A specific social relation may constrain a given movement of goods, but a specific transaction — "by the same token" — suggests a particular social relation. (*Ibid.:* 139)

In general terms, this statement is obviously true; but unless we enquire into how, exactly, such a "suggestion" is made, as it stands it entertains more than a hint of circularity. In this paper I offer a two-stage argument which in effect reverses the commonly held connections between kinship, the obligation to give and social activity. First I enquire into the rationale of the obligation to give and conclude that its existence rests in a particular constellation of social activities; then I consider the rationale of kinship and suggest that it is sustained in the fact that it is the appropriate idiom in which the category of people subscribing to the obligation to give may be described.

As might be expected in a topic of such wide generality, the knowledge in terms of which the notions of the "obligation to give" and "kinship" are sustained is incorporated directly in a number of basic assumptions which we may make about the nature of human social activity and the demographic conditions of preliterate society. There are five basic assumptions:

1) In human existence in preliterate societies the bulk of social activity is carried out between people living near at hand; this is a statistical fact. Moreover, the nearer at hand people are, the greater the range of social activity carried out between them. The limited facility for wide-ranging movement and distant communication in such societies accounts for this. From an evolutionary standpoint these facts may be appreciated in terms of the relatively simple technology available in such societies, and, in the case of band (nomadic hunter-gatherer) societies, in terms of relatively low population densities.

2) Concerning the presence of notions in human society, the interactional approach incorporated here holds that this derives from the notions' invocation in social activity (cf. Stuchlik 1977). Therefore,

so far as explaining notions is concerned the analyst may cite the constraints on individuals engaging in goal-oriented activity. By definition, a constraint is a factor an individual takes into account as a benefit or liability accruing in the performance of some specific activity.

3) In social activity, people act rationally and maximise value.The philosophical basis to this assumption has been elaborated elsewhere. I do not propose to repeat it here (cf. Stuchlik 1976; 1977; see also my remarks on transactionalism, below). If we hold that we may discern the purpose of a social activity by examining the range of circumstances in which the actor is involved and considering to which of them the activity may be plausibly regarded as a rational response (cf. Riches 1977: 132), then this assumption is necessarily incorporated.

4) This assumption refers to the immediate gains and losses accruing in single transactions in human social interaction. As regards the various single transactions in which he is engaged with various other individuals, it is held that the actor has the facility to form an impression of comparison as between the gains and losses in the respective transactions. It is not supposed that such comparison is made in any detailed or quantitative fashion.

5) This assumption refers to the long term gains and losses accruing in a sequence of transactions in human social interaction. As regards a series of transactions in which he is engaged with a specific other individual, it is held that the actor has the facility to form an impression of summation as to the immediate gains and losses accruing in each of the transactions. Again, it is not supposed that such summation is made in any detailed or quantitative manner.

Analysis

The following account of the notion of the obligation to give and the idiom of kinship as it relates to this notion may be construed in two ways. First, in so far as the presence of a notion rests on the basis for its invocation in some prevailing situation, the analysis offers insights into these ideas as they currently exist in pre-literate societies. Second, the analysis is arranged in a manner such that an insight into the process by which the ideas emerged in human society may be appreciated. The evolutionary implications of the analysis are discussed in a later section.

The clue to the identification of a social situation in relation to which the obligation to give is sustained is based in Gluckman's important presentation of the idea of the multiplex relationship (Gluckman 1955). A multiplex relationship is one in which a number of purposive activities are instituted. Multiplex relationships prevail particularly in band and tribal societies — especially they are exemplified in the kinship relationships which are pervasive in these types of society — and in Gluckman's work it is the connection between the particular character of such relationships and the procedures of law in such societies that is of interest. Specifically, Gluckman's argument is that the emphasis (evident in Lozi court hearings) on not breaking relationships, on conciliation, and on taking into account the total personalities of the disputants, relates to the multiple interests embodied in the bonds between most disputants, the bulk of whom are linked by some sort of kinship or local tie. A particular dispute may hinge on just one interest; but it must not be allowed to jeopardise the several other interests in which the disputants are mutually involved.

Importantly, Gluckman associates multiplex relationships with the "face-to-face relations [which] dominate Lozi life" (1955: 21). It is this fact of tribal life that is basically expressed in my first assumption (above), *viz.*, that in preliterate society the bulk of social activity is carried on between people who live near at hand. But while Gluckman (of course working with epistemological assumptions different from those embraced in this paper) sees multiplex connections as an entailment of a specific type of social structure, I shall be arguing the other way around, namely that a specific type of social structure, characterised by the notion of the obligation to give and the idiom of kinship is an entailment of multiplex connections. It is through my first assumption that it is possible to argue in this way. If the bulk of social activity in preliterate society is carried on between people who live near at hand, then the existence of multiplex connections among such people inevitably follows — in short, through the first assumption the existence of multiplex connections is derived without reference to ideas of social structure. It may be added at this point: the closer at hand people are, the greater the multiplicity of interests which may be expected to prevail among them. In the family of procreation, where a good many of these interests are biologically based, multiplicity will tend to be at its highest level.

Now let us turn to my argument that it is to the existence of multiplex connections that sustaining the "obligation to give" may be regarded plausibly as a rational response. The argument relates to the pursuance of private interests under conditions of multiplicity.

Compared with the situation where connections are single-stranded, the pursuance of private interests under conditions of multiplicity means that in a given transaction a person is able to exercise a relatively high demand on the resources of *alter*. In spirit, Gluckman's analysis indicates why this is so; it is because people will not be prepared to jeopardise the existence of a connection in which many other vital interests are subsumed. Thus high demands may be made because *alter* may be expected not to refuse them. This contrasts with single-stranded connections; here, if the same demand were made, *alter* may be expected to break off all dealings. In short, among people with multiplex connections, the successful realisation of private interests amounts, *par excellence*, to getting "something for nothing with impunity" – this, paradoxically, being how Sahlins (1965: 148) characterises what he calls "negative reciprocity", a form of transaction analysts normally consider as being most typical among people who have rather little to do with one another.

It is my contention that it is in respect of people's perceptions of the multiplex connection that the notion of an obligation to give is sustained. Specifically, it is held that the obligation to give relates to people's evaluation of the circumstances of a single transaction in the context of multiplicity. The nature of this evaluation I call the "multiplex predicament".

Let us look at the circumstances of the single transaction; here we cite assumption 4 (see above). Supposing people have the facility to compare the gains and losses accruing in various single transactions, then, if the comparison is between single-stranded and multiplex connections, in multiplex connections one may have to give up more than one would like, or accept less than one would wish. Now, let us examine the basis for the way this state of affairs is evaluated; here we cite assumption 5, and consider a sequence of transactions with a given other. Supposing people have the ability to sum the short-term gains and losses accruing in such a sequence of transactions, then in a multiplex connection one knows that, even though one may be yielding to high demands at some particular time, one will be able to exact high demands in return on some later occasion.

The obligation to give refers to the rendering of resources in a single transaction. It is my suggestion that because of the probable long-term benefits accruing, the probable immediate liabilities of the multiplex predicament may be evaluated in positive terms, and in so far as such liabilities are so evaluated, the obligation to give exists. Thus, when in a single transaction resources in quantity greater than one would wish *have* to be surrendered, it may be represented as a duty: *as an ideal* one must regard it as one's obligation and as the recipient's entitlement.

In effect, I have been arguing this far that, in the notion of the obligation to give the liabilities often accruing in the multiplex predicament are misrepresented: surrendering substantial resources in a transaction is conceived of as desirable. But it follows that if this misrepresentation is to be sustained, it must also be concealed: it must in some manner be expressed as being a natural and positive state of affairs. It may be suggested therefore that a decision to misrepresent the multiplex predicament necessarily embodies a decision to engage in some behaviour in terms of which this misrepresentation may be obscured.

It is my thesis that the misrepresentation relating to the obligation to give is achieved through entertaining obligations of "redundant social transactions". In general terms, "redundancy" in social transactions refers to the rendering of goods and services which the recipient has both the ability and the entitlement to secure through his own immediate efforts. In the notion of redundant transaction there is an implied contrast with the idea of the obligation to give. In behaviour to which the obligation to give relates, the demands to which one responds normally refer to *alter's* inability or lack of entitlement to secure certain goods or perform certain services by his own efforts. But at the same time redundant transactions appropriately express the representation of the multiplex predicament as being a natural state of affairs: such transactions aptly capture the altruistic connotations embodied in the idea of the obligation to give — they explicitly mimic the obligation.

The similarity between redundant transactions and the obligation to give which they express is important. In so far as a decision to misrepresent the multiplex predicament *necessarily* embodies a decision to conceive of behaviour which expresses this misrepresentation in positive fashion, then, necessarily, it must be possible to conceive of the obligation to give and the idea of redundant transaction as parts of a single notional package. In fact, in the folk model, redundant transactions are conceived of as being assimilated to the obligation to give: in the folk notion, the idea of the obligation to give incorporates situations where *alter* is unable to secure resources through his own efforts, and situations where *alter* is so able. Unless specifically mentioned, succeeding discussion on the "obligation to give" assumes the incorporation into this notion of the obligation to render redundant transactions.

If the obligation to give is an expression of the multiplex predicament, what is its relationship with the kinship idiom? In social anthropology, some treatments of the relationship between the kinship relationship and the obligation to give treat the obligation to give as an entailment of kinship. I shall argue the other way around, namely that people sustain notions of kinship in order that social connections which are multiplex and hence incorporate recognition of the obligation to give may be denotated.

Let me outline the basis for this argument. I suggest that embodied in the obligation to give is the notion that people should share information about the exigencies of the social and ecological environment. Consequently, people may be expected to identify and label that part of the social environment within which multiplex connections prevail. I propose that the kinship idiom may have its basis in the fulfilment of this task.

Why should this be so? Notwithstanding the considerable literature on the existential status of kinship (which is well beyond the scope of this paper to discuss), I believe an answer is offered if one incorporates the view, put by a number of writers, that the kinship idiom is in some way modelled on the "natural" relations of the family of procreation (cf. Keesing 1975: 13). Most writers who have oriented their discussion in terms of the natural basis[5] of the statuses and activities in the procreative family have come to see the problem of kinship notions from the point of view of ontological *differences* between the natural relations of the family and the social relations of kinship outside the family. They ask: how do kinship statuses which are not directly concerned with matters of procreation, etc., come to be constructed out of naturally-grounded family statuses? Or: how do activities which are not naturally grounded come to be instituted in the naturally-grounded family (and, by extension, kinship) statuses? (cf. Barth 1973; Scheffler 1974). My feeling, however, is that if we are interested in the basis of kinship, we might do better to pose such questions in terms of asking what is *in common* between the realm of the family of procreation and the realm of kinship outside the family. I would suggest that what is crucially in common is that in both these realms multiplex connections prevail. In this respect, the significant fact about the family of procreation is that it is, *par excellence,* the location of multiplex connection, many of them biologically based; also, the family of procreation incorporates the full range of physical strengths and levels of experience which the various tasks of everyday life outside the family imply. It is on this basis that the denotation of multiplex relations outside the family of procreation incorporates an idiom – an idiom of natural relations – which is founded in the family. Specifically, it is on this basis that the social recognition of consanguineal connections outside the family for the description of certain social categories is *legitimised.* This social recognition of consanguineal connections is basically what we know as kinship.

Dynamic Implications

A test of plausible analysis is if it can suggest ways of handling social change. Moreover, a test of this particular analysis is if it can handle the emergence of obligations to give which are not instituted in relations of kinship. It is my contention that change in the extent to which the "obligation to give" prevails in respect of a given relationship, or variation in the extent of the obligation to give as between different relationships, is expressed in terms of change or variation in the character and content of redundant transactions. I shall refer to two case studies to exemplify this. But first, let me emphasise the importance of redundant transactions in expressing the existence of the obligation to give. Reference is made here to Bloch's study on the morality of kinship, specifically to the greater emphasis in the morality (the obligation to give) in what we may gloss as "close" kinship and the lesser emphasis in "distant" kinship (Bloch 1973).

Bloch reviews the composition of agricultural work teams in three societies and interestingly discovers that they contain a much higher proportion of distant kinsmen than might be expected. He argues that such is the strength in the morality in close kinship that people do not continually have to reiterate the importance of the social connection through actual interaction (by joining a work team) if this connection is to be maintained. By contrast, with distant kinship the morality is weaker, and if the social connection is to be maintained frequent social interaction must be entertained – hence the composition of the work teams. The approach to this issue offered in this study is that the morality in close kinship, strong though it may be represented as being, does not have an intrinsic strength; just like the morality in distant kinship its existence is sustained through continual social interactions – interactions which I have called redundant transactions. But precisely in the fact that among close kinsmen there is a greater multiplicity of interests (which Bloch, concentrating on just one type of interest, does not mention), it may be expected that the redundant transactions relevant to this relationship proceed in realms of life other than agricultural work cooperation – for example, in the performance of various chores relating to mundane everyday existence. Among distant kinsmen, by contrast, the multiplicity of interests is far less, and so also is the scope for the entertaining of redundant transactions. It may well be that, for these people the exchange of labour in work teams, which incorporates a measure of redundancy, constitutes the sole opportunity for the exercise of such transactions.

Let me turn now to my first case study. Here I wish to consider the fact that, in the manipulability of obligations of redundant transactions, different emphases in the obligation to give, pertaining to different social relationships, may be connoted. Here I draw on material on food sharing from my fieldwork in a modern Canadian Eskimo settlement.

Port Burwell, in the Northwest Territories of Canada, is a small isolated village on an island just off the northern tip of the Labrador coast. Its Eskimo population numbers around 150 people, and there are also around a half dozen permanently-resident Euro-Canadians, employed by the Canadian federal government to advise on, and participate in, the development of economic, local government, and education and health facilities. Thanks to government loans, the Eskimos' engagement in the local productive economy, which is built mainly on various fishing, sealing and caribou hunting enterprises, utilizes substantial amounts of sophisticated technology, including several types of net traps and longliner fishing boats. This economy is organised under the auspices of the Eskimo-owned (though, in effect, Euro-Canadian-run) cooperative, which also operates a small retail shop. Together with improved opportunities for wage labour and increased social welfare inputs, the Eskimo per capita monetary income is now more than four times its value in the late 1950's, in the period prior to modern development when a largely traditional nomadic hunting and trapping economy was practised. Today, over three-quarters of the Eskimo population in Port Burwell are of immigrant background, having journeyed to the settlement from a number of neighbouring communities in the early 1960's, when the special economic opportunities due to the exceptional natural resources in the area were first appreciated. Thus, although everyone in Port Burwell recognises everyone else as a "neighbour", a relationship in which a number of important obligations are instituted, the predominant theme in Port Burwell Eskimo social structure is that it consists of a number of kinship factions. Each faction corresponds to an immigrant group originating from a particular source community and reflects the fact that the members of each group are closely related through ties of kinship; at the same time kin connections between the kinship factions are relatively few in number.

The Eskimos are emphatic that in both the kinship and neighbour relationships, the notion of an obligation to give is implied; from kin and neighbours, a measure of succour and assistance, especially in respect of securing food, may be expected. But they are emphatic also that kinship connotes a greater emphasis in respect of this obligation than does neighbourhood[6]. In this connection they cite the fact that, in adoption, a child may be given to people who are kinsmen (preferably close kinsmen), but not to people who are just neighbours; only kinsmen are sufficiently trusted to treat the child properly. Concerning how the greater emphasis in the obligation to give in kinship is expressed in everyday interaction, we may look to certain contrasts in food sharing patterns in the Eskimo community. In the data that follow certain obligations in food sharing are illustrated.

In any instance of food sharing a donor household is at the centre of a number of recipient households.[7] Using network terminology we may say that, in different situations, different "sets" of households emerge as recipients of food (Mayer 1966: 99). In general terms, three important constraints inform the composition of household-centred sets of distribution in Port Burwell. First, there is the extent to which the household giving away food is doing so at the same time as other households. Second, there is the extent to which food sharing is initiated by the donor or by the recipients of food. Third, there is the extent to which food sharing is an auspicious occasion, in which, for example, a delicacy or some rare type of food is being given away. These constraints mean that sets of distribution would tend to be larger, firstly when the household giving away the food was the only household in the settlement giving away this type of food; secondly, when the household giving away the food had initiated the distribution— here the onus was on its members to aspire to the Eskimo ideal that everyone in the settlement should receive a share; and thirdly when the distribution constituted an auspicious occasion. At the other end of the scale, sets of distribution would tend to be small when food sharing took place after hunters had returned from mundane "everyday" expeditions. Indeed, on these occasions, hunters would often strip the animal of its skin, and leave the carcase to be scavenged by dogs and gulls, and to rot.

A consideration of all instances in the sharing of locally-produced food would indicate that situations in which meat was neither particularly scarce nor a delicacy were by far the most common events of distribution. They usually involve households living fairly close by one another, and might be described as "convenience sharing". These events contrast with the much more hectic and extensive sharing which would occur when some auspicious meat was landed in the settlement, or when fresh food was generally in rather short supply.

Observation of everyday, mundane sharing indicates that each household is surrounded by a "set of convenience", several households upon which it can rely for the occasional provision of its daily food supply. The size of a household's set of convenience (normally between three and five other households) reflects primarily the probability that the members of the set will between them effectively satisfy its demands for food. The composition of a set of convenience in the main reflects certain physical constraints. First, a household tends to depend on neighbouring households which are in sight and whose activities (such as bringing home meat) it can easily observe – here we note that various large government buildings and topographical undulations in the settlement area constitute the main barriers to sight. Second, it tends to depend on households which may be reached without having to climb long, steep, rocky hillsides. The collection of meat from neighbouring houses is mainly the task of women. Many have to carry children on their backs; several are afflicted with respiratory complaints.

Let us now relate these patterns in the distribution of meat to the distinction between kinship and neighbour relationships. Before we do this, it may be indicated that the various kinship factions do not live in "quarters" of the village; members of the various factions are displayed throughout the settlement. In the main this relates to the fact that the prefabricated houses in modern Port Burwell are of extremely varying size and quality, and people's residence in a particular house reflects, among other things, the size of their family, their desire to live in the more modern, roomy houses, or their concern to live by the waterfront.

In the following discussion I use the term "close neighbour" to describe members of a household's set of convenience who are not kinsmen. Other non-kinsmen in the settlement I call its "distant neighbours". The average household recognises just under a quarter of the twenty-seven households as kin-related.

Because of the physical constraints to the composition of sets of convenience, a number of proximate households would tend to share virtually the same set of convenience. Such shared sets may be labelled "community sectors". There are no Eskimo terms for "close neighbour", "distant neighbour" or "community sector".

However, I contend that these social categories are a part of Eskimo knowledge. They reflect certain preferences in the allocation of certain types of food in certain types of situation, and these preferences are explicitly stated.

Through the notions of community sector and convenience sharing certain differences in kinship, as opposed to neighbour, relationships may be made evident. Community sectors are not corporate groups. Their boundaries are imprecise and fluid. Certainly, in so far as the dictates of convenience encouraged every-day sharing across sector boundaries, then such sharing would occur. However, these various generalisations that I have offered about everyday distribution of local food do not hold in all instances of sharing. In sharing with kinsmen, Port Burwell Eskimos often *inconvenience* themselves. Commonly hunters would set aside portions of meat for the households of parents and siblings, even though these people lived on the other side of the settlement and there was nothing particularly special about the animal that had just been butchered. Such an emphasis on sharing food with kinsmen was also evident on more auspicious occasions of distribution. On these occasions sharing is not always a settlement-wide affair. However, *all* kinsmen - however far they lived from the distributing household — would normally claim a share.

In the totality of food sharing transactions among Port Burwell Eskimos it appears that there is what we may call a greater "intensity" in kinship relationship. Neighbours are obligated to one another in food sharing; but people who are also kinsmen are obligated even more. When they share with kinsmen people are in some way more conscientious than when they share with neighbours. And what is particularly interesting here is that this greater intensity in kinship is in fact manifest rather clearly in transactions which do not reflect the rendering of the obligation to give in the strict sense. Rather, it is manifest in a greater quantity of *redundant* food sharing transactions.

In general terms, a good deal of Port Burwell Eskimo food sharing is redundant. Particularly on auspicious occasions people would commonly share out and claim meat for purposes other than the rendering or securing of immediate (short-term) sustenance. For example, a household would send a representative to close neighbours to claim shares of caribou meat when its own head, on the very same morning, had returned with several carcases of the same animal. The Eskimos themselves acknowledge that such transactions are not entertained for narrow economic ends - that they in some way constitute special gifts. As I have indicated, redundancy in food sharing is even more evident in the case of kin-based sharing. A hunter would take to kinsmen on the far side of the settlement meat which he knew perfectly well these people could secure from the household next door.

Now we may return to the suggestion that in the manipulability of redundant transactions differing emphases in the obligation to give may be connoted. In the Eskimo material, the contrast between kinship and neighbour relationships is pertinent here. Specifically this is the case concerning the question of the emergence of neighbourhood as a relationship in which specific social obligations were instituted. In the traditional period, in the era before modern development, such a notion did not exist in Eskimo society.

We may appeal to the circumstances in which Port Burwell was established as a modern settlement to account for the emergence of the neighbourhood relationship. Before the modern period just twenty-five people lived in the Port Burwell area, one hundred and fifty miles from the nearest trading post. These Port Burwell "natives" remained in the area because of the excellent hunting and fishing it afforded, but reluctantly they were considering having to abandon it because of the difficulties in travelling for trade. Particularly for the natives of the area, then, the inception of the modern settlement signified that the chronic conditions of the 1950's would be alleviated, and the arrival of the immigrants indicated that Eskimo life in the Port Burwell area would continue. In the instigation of the scheme of social and economic development, the native ideal of remaining in the place that they "loved" was facilitated. Thus the decision by the immigrants to come to Port Burwell to participate in the scheme was construed as an act of generosity. We may propose that the emergence of (redundant) obligations in food sharing among the native group and the various immigrant groups has its origins in the signalling of a recognition of this generosity. During the period of field work this recognition was indeed still being made explicit. At a community meeting in 1970, an elderly man stood up and congratulated the immigrants for moving to Port Burwell, and urged that still more might like to come.

How did Port Burwell Eskimos know that redundant food sharing was the appropriate means to signal appreciation of the arrival of the immigrants? The answer is straightforward. In the traditional period, the obligation to give in social relationships (specifically kinship relationships) was mainly asserted in redundant food sharing. Indeed, degrees of closeness in kinship might be signalled in terms of the character and content of such redundant transactions. Among non-kin in modern Port Burwell the fact that generosity was being extended might appropriately also be expressed in food sharing. In food sharing trust among non-kin might be asserted; yet, in the occasions and content of redundant transactions the greater emphasis on the obligation to give in kinship might be maintained. As we have seen, among kinsmen, redundant sharing occurs much more frequently, and on more mundane occasions, than among neighbours.

The second case study concerning the manipulability of redundant transactions refers to matters of change in the degree of emphasis in the obligation to give within a specific relationship. Specifically, I am concerned with the contention that, whether or not there is the facility to engage in redundant transactions may determine whether or not a relationship in which the obligation to give is embodied can continue to exist. I refer to the well-known state of affairs that at a certain critical level of crisis, the obligation to give, particularly as it pertains among distant kinsmen, may de discontinued (cf. Sahlins 1965: 158). Laughlin's study of the So of Uganda provides the case material (Laughlin 1974).

Laughlin is basically concerned with the application of Sahlins' scheme of reciprocities (Sahlins 1965) to diachronic study. Specifically, he is interested in demonstrating the existence of shifts in the morality of exchange pertaining to given social relationships as a result of extrinsic ecological change. In this he maintains that there is no necessary connection between a particular type of exchange morality, for example generalised reciprocity (the obligation to give), and a particular type of social relationship — in this case, the kinship relationship. Thus there may be circumstances where particular kin, who once invoked the obligation to give when exchanging, now do not do so and transact on a completely *ad hoc* basis. Comparing data collected among the So in times of economic plenty with data collected in times of severe economic shortage, and considering the social change that would occur if the former situation were replaced by the latter, Laughlin indicates that as conditions deteriorate there is indeed the likelihood of a diminution in the genealogical range of kinship within which an obligation to give continues to prevail.

Laughlin argues that such a diminution under harsh circumstances is adaptive to these circumstances, and this may well be so. But one would wish to know on what basis the So themselves construct the diminution. A possible suggestion here is that, as economic conditions deteriorate, the scope for the exercise of redundant transactions among more distantly related individuals is severely restricted, if not removed. In so far as this is the case then the obligation to give in their relationship is no longer expressed; henceforth, all their interaction must proceed on an *ad hoc* contractual basis. That the scope for the exercise of redundant transactions among distantly related individuals *is* severely restricted in time of food crisis rests in the fact that, among people who are distantly related — and particularly if they do not live in the same household — redundant *food sharing* constitutes probably the main type of redundant transaction in which they are engaged; in times of food crisis, when everyone's economic predicament is dire, obligations in respect of *redundant* transactions are likely to be set aside. By contrast, people who are closely related — particularly those who live in the same household — are engaged in a plethora of other types of redundant transaction, those concerning the performance of routine everyday chores, for example. In so far as these redundant transactions are unaffected by the level of the food supply, the obligation to give in close kinship relations continues to be asserted, and close kin continue to offer one another succour.

Evolutionary Implications — From Contract to Status

An analysis which purports to outline the factors in terms of which some important and probably universal folk model is sustained inevitably invites speculation as to the process by which such a model emerged. It is obvious that such speculation is a difficult and risky enterprise (cf. Riches 1977: 142-3). But if we may be offered insights into the evolution of a fundamental social idea in a first human society, I believe the enterprise is worth contemplating. As an initial "rule of thumb" it may be supposed that an analysis has evolutionary implications if two basic conditions are met. First, the circumstances in terms of which the folk idea is sustained must plausibly have prevailed at the time when the idea supposedly emerged. Second, if the folk idea consists of a complex of notions — as in this case — the relations between the notions which the analysis posits must be of a linear kind; in this way, to the extent that a specific notion presupposes a specific other, we are offered an insight into a chronological sequence. In the case of the folk idea studied here, both these conditions would seem to be met. We may reasonably speculate that multiplex social connections, underlain by limited technologies and sparse populations, prevailed in the earliest human society. And in so far as the kinship idiom presupposes the obligation to give, and the obligation to engage in redundant transactions presupposes the obligation to engage in non-redundant transactions, we may again reasonably speculate that in the connections posited among these notions in this study we are offered an insight into the creation of these notions. I conclude, then, that the analysis offered in this study may well have evolutionary implications.

Supposing that this supposition is acceptable we may highlight certain particular dimensions in the evolutionary sequence. The first dimension refers to the problem relating to the analytical conceptualisation of the emergence of social notions. The issue here relates to Evens' recent important critique of anthropological interactionism (Evens 1977). This critique is directed specifically at Barth's transactionalism (Barth 1966; see below). Emphasising the "transpersonal" nature of social notions, Evens demonstrates that Barth's attempt to formulate a model of how, purely on the basis of individual motives, social notions may be created, is flawed. The issue here is especially with social notions in which expectations of performance of some piece of social behaviour are embodied. Evens holds that in Barth's model it may be possible to demonstrate how patterns of social activity arise, positing a number of individuals in similar situations engaging in parallel in similar social strategies. But, Evens insists, with Barth's tools, expectations that particular behaviour should be performed, and the couching of these expectations as obligations, cannot be explained. The conclusion is that in the transactional model it must be acknowledged that the emergence of new notions (and, most particularly, new expectations of behaviour) is critically mediated through the existence of other, "overarching" (or, more generalised) notions.[8] If these strictures are accepted it follows that there are certain overarching notions — notions of "highest order" — which cannot be reduced to notions of a more generalised nature; these notions are presumably not amenable to an interactional account. From the way in which notions relating to the obligation to give and the idiom of kinship have been treated in studies which purport to embrace the interactional position, one may suppose that these are examples of such notions of highest order. In the explanation of social activity, kinship and the obligations with which this idiom is associated are commonly cited as constraints which the actor importantly takes into account in decision making. But the constraints in terms of which these notions themselves are sustained are seldom considered.

In view of Evens' strictures, a possible importance of this study is the suggestion that the obligation to give, its basis in the multiplex predicament, is sustained fundamentally as a *self-imposed* obligation. Evens' critique is particularly telling as regards expectations concerning the allocation of resources. In the higher order notions which his discussion posits, expectations that resources be allocated to some specific individuals (and not to others) are legitimised. However, in so far as the existence of the obligation to give rests on the expectation that one should be denied resources by others, rather than that one should deny resources of others, this legitimisation is not needed. In the obligation to give, then, it may well be that a transpersonal social notion exists independently at least of higher order notions referring to *expectations* in inter-personal activity. In my view, if the analysis in this study has an evolutionary dimension this is of critical importance.

Another important evolutionary implication of this study - which again refers to Barth's transactionalism − concerns the relationship between altruistic and self-interested *strategy* in social activity. To introduce this concern we may briefly consider the central assumption of transactional theory, together with its explanatory implications − the tautology that, in social activity, people maximise value. In my view, the notion of transaction, as elaborated by Barth (1966), is a representation of this assumption. However, the explanatory pertinence of the assumption has, I think, been widely misinterpreted. Thus, a common criticism of transactionalism is that to cite maximisation of value (or satisfaction) to explain social activity is obviously true, and therefore trivial. Proponents of this view commonly advocate that "transaction" should be restricted to certain types of strategy, specifically to profit (or utility) maximising strategy. Such a strategy, it is suggested, should be counterposed against other types of strategy, among them strategy which embodies altruistic intention. Indeed, as is by now well-known, Barth, himself, at one stage proposed that this should be done when he contrasted the idea of transaction with the notion of incorporation.

But in fact it seems plain that in the notion of transaction Barth was attempting to elaborate an assumption about the nature of *all* social processes, specifically that social activity may be regarded as reciprocal prestations in which the actors involved maximise value. Thus, properly, profit maximisation and altruism have to be subsumed within a general notion of maximisation. Indeed, as Evens points out (1977: 588), Barth clearly subscribed to this view too; in the bulk of Barth's exposition, incorporation is in fact treated as a sub-type of transaction. Clearly, then, it was not intended that social activity should be explained directly in terms of value maximisation. Rather, explanation consists in isolating the benefits and liabilities accruing in the performance of social activity; since maximisation is assumed, the explanation states that, given the actor's situation, the extent to which the listed benefits outweigh the listed liabilities is greater than the extent to which supposed benefits outweigh supposed liabilities in any other possible course of action.[9]

It is evident, then, that altruistic strategy and utility maximisation strategy may be treated as possible courses of action for securing benefit; in one situation, altruistic strategy may be expected, in another situation, utility maximisation strategy may be expected. It is also implied that strategies of altruism and profit maximisation are contrasting and mutually exclusive. However, the argument in this paper goes one stage further. If one extends the idea of utility maximisation to incorporate all strategy in which the goal is the pursuance of immediate personal advantage – earlier we called this strategy "private strategy" – it may be argued that the existence of altruistic strategy *presupposes* the existence of private strategy. The thesis in this paper, that sustaining the obligation to give has its basis in the facts of immediate private bargaining, accounts for this: the obligation to give embodies the notion of altruism as a prescriptive ideal. But the existence of altruism as an ideal does not necessarily *directly* imply the existence of altruism as a motive and a strategy – it is a fundamental assumption of this study that actions do not directly derive from notions. My suggestion is that the derivation of altruism as a motive from altruism as an ideal is mediated through the notion of prestige. Again, I believe this mediation has evolutionary implications.

There is a good deal of discussion in the anthropological literature on the relation between the securing of prestige and the rendering of goods and services in social activity. Some writers argue that the existence of prestige relates to the uneven distribution of competence in human society. Because of this uneven distribution there tends to be imbalance in transactions – specifically in food sharing transactions – over time. The prestige which accrues to the more able people in society exists in order that these people should remain in the community for which they provide a disproportionate quantity of resources. This is not the place to detail a criticism of this and related views (cf. Pryor 1977 for one attempt at such a criticism). It is in relation to people's interdependence in a range of purposive activities that in my view the imbalance in respect of one type of activity should be construed. In this interdependence unequal food sharing accounts may be readily subsumed. On the question of prestige, the suggestion offered here is that this notion has its basis not in a determinant of the flow of goods and services in respect of one type of activity, but rather as an expression of recognition that such a flow has occurred; in prestige, someone's disproportionate contribution in some activity whose successful performance everybody values is acknowledged. If this is correct, it has significant implications: it means that the *activity,* giving goods and services, is afforded value. In so far as this is the case, altruism as a motive exists.

Conclusion

The challenge in this paper has been to apply a certain set of epistemological assumptions (those outlined by Holy and Stuchlik earlier in this volume) to a well-known folk model — the notion that, among kinsmen, support, protection, assistance and presents (redundant transactions) will be rendered. In accord with these assumptions it is held that this notion, which people in probably all societies manipulate in the course of personal advancement, exists in that it is sustained in a body of largely taken-for-granted (and hence mostly unspoken) knowledge. It is this knowledge and the social interactions to which it refers that I have sought to uncover. Very many of the issues that I have touched upon are extremely important and should be properly discussed at far greater length; for this reason, this account is best regarded as sketch.

Notes

1. By "service", I mean any activity from which *alter* derives value.
2. Compare the recent work of Pryor (1977), in part devoted to an evaluation of the work of Sahlins, Mauss and Leach on kin-based transactions. His main analytical thrust refers to a distinction with respect to distributions between two people as regards whether the account is balanced (exchange) or unbalanced (transfer). Objective observations and statistical analysis *and* actor's evaluations decide whether a specific set of transactions should be regarded as a net exchange or a net transfer. As I shall make clear, the concern in this study is with the actors' statement of the ideal as regards the rendering of a single transaction, from A to B.
3. Clearly I am close here to Sahlins' notion of "generalised reciprocity" (Sahlins 1965) and Fortes' notion of "amity" (Fortes 1969).
4. Cf. Pryor (1977: 29) for a similar set of points relating to his analytical distinction of different patterns of economic transactions.
5. As regards "natural basis", I am of course concerned with the actors' conceptions of physical connections. For the difficult case of the Trobriand father, see Sider (1967).
6. "Neighbourhood" is used here as the abstract mode of "neighbour", in the

same sense that "kinship" is the abstract mode of "kinsman".

7. In the main, Port Burwell Eskimo households are nuclear family households.

8. A study with which Evens would find favour is Holy's recent account of change in norms of inheritance among the Toka of Zambia (Holy 1979). Holy shows that a change from matrilineal to patrilineal norms may be interpreted in terms of change in individual preferences in production, but that this interpretation makes sense *only* in the context of more generalised (and unchanging) Toka notions, which state that people who pool their labour in production are entitled to share in the rewards.

9. Here it may be added that, obviously, this sort of explanation is effective only if, first, the existence of the benefits and liabilities cited in explanation has been established independently of the activities being explained, and second, the notion of explanation does not imply prediction. These matters have been discussed elsewhere (Holy 1976; Riches 1979b).

References

Barth, F. (1966). *Models of Social Organisation*. London: Royal Anthropological Institute.

Barth, F. (1973). Descent and marriage reconsidered. In *The Character of Kinship*, (J. Goody, ed.). Cambridge: Cambridge University Press.

Bloch, M. (1973). The long term and the short term: the economic and political significance of the morality of kinship. In *The Character of Kinship*, (J. Goody, ed.). Cambridge: Cambridge University Press.

Evens, T. (1977). The predication of the individual in interactionism. *American Anthropologist* **79**, 579-98.

Fortes, M. (1969). *Kinship and the Social Order*. Chicago: Aldine.

Gluckman, M. (1955). *The Judicial Process among the Barotse*. Manchester: Manchester University Press.

Holy, L. (1976). Knowledge and behaviour. In *Knowledge and Behaviour* (L. Holy, ed.), Queen's University Papers in Social Anthropology Vol. 1. Belfast: Queen's University.

Holy, L. (1979). Changing norms in matrilineal societies: the case of Toka inheritance. In *The Conceptualisation and Explanation of Processes of Social Change*, (D. Riches, ed.), Queen's University Papers in Social Anthropology 3. Belfast: Queen's University.

Keesing, R. (1975). *Kin Groups and Social Structure*. London: Holt, Rinehart and Winston.

Laughlin, C. (1974). Deprivation and reciprocity. *Man* **9**, 380-96.

Mayer, A. (1966). The significance of quasi-groups in the study of complex societies. In *The Social Anthropology of Complex Societies*, (M. Banton, ed.), ASA monograph 4. London: Tavistock.

Pryor, F. (1977). *The Origins of the Economy*. New York: Academic Press.

Riches, D. (1977). Discerning the goal. In *Goals and Behaviour*, (M. Stuchlik, ed.), Queen's University Papers in Social Anthropology Vol. 2. Belfast: Queen's University.

Riches, D. (1979a). Ecological variations on the Northwest Coast: models for the generation of cognatic and matrilineal descent. In *Social and Ecological Systems* (R. Ellen and P. Burnham, eds), ASA monograph in social anthropology 18. London: Academic Press.

Riches D. (1979b). Introduction. In *The Conceptualisation and Explanation of Processes of Social Change,* (D. Riches, ed.), Queen's University Papers in Social Anthropology, Vol 3. Belfast: Queen's University.

Sahlins, M. (1965). On the sociology of primitive exchange. In *The Relevance of Models in Social Anthropology,* (M. Banton, ed.), ASA monograph in social anthropology. London: Tavistock.

Scheffler, H. (1974). Kinship, descent and alliance. In *Handbook of Social and Cultural Anthropology,* (J. Honigmann, ed.). New York: Rand McNally.

Sider, K. B. (1967). Affinity and role of the father in the Trobriands. *Southwestern Journal of Anthropology* **23**, 90-109.

Stuchlik, M. (1976). Whose knowledge? In *Knowledge and Behaviour,* (L. Holy, ed.), Queen's University Papers in Social Anthropology Vol.1. Belfast: Queen's University.

Stuchlik, M. (1977). Goals and behaviour. In *Goals and Behaviour,* M. Stuchlik, ed.), Queen's University Papers in Social Anthropology, Vol. 2. Belfast: Queen's University.

CULTURE AS ENHABILMENTIS

PHILIP CARL SALZMAN

Traditional Hindu society was firmly hierarchical. But consensus upon the nature of that hierarchy was far from firm. Indeed, it is misleading to refer to "that hierarchy", for this phrase implies a unity, a consistency, an agreement, that did not exist. For whatever the particular complex pattern of overt social relations at a given moment, however actual behaviour manifested hierarchy at a particular time, there were present and available, as Burghart (1978) has demonstrated, several distinct models of hierarchy portraying and advocating divergent patterns of social, political, and ritual relations. These contrary models provided the ideological basis for alternative hierarchical structures in Hindu society.

The three contrary models identified by Burghart in 18th and 19th century documents from the northeastern region of the subcontinent are each associated with one of the major social categories, the Brahmans, the ascetics, and the king.

> . . . (I)n the traditional Hindu social system the Brahmans, ascetics, and the king each claimed their superiority in the particular world in which they lived and . . . each person based his claim in terms of a particular hierarchy which was the exclusive and exhaustive order of social relations in Hindu society. The Brahman claimed his superiority according to the hierarchy of the sacrificial body of Brahma; the ascetic claimed his superiority according to the hierarchy of the cycle of confused wandering; and the Hindu king claimed his superiority in terms of a tenurial hierarchy which was derived from his lordship over the land. (Burghart 1978: 520-521)

These three models, although similar in being hierarchical, are not congruent in structural form nor in the social world defined

(Burghart 1978: 523). The Brahman model, reflecting the sacrificial body of Brahma, is based upon the relative purity of functionally differentiated parts, that is, the Brahmans, warriors, tillers and herders, and servants who together make up an organic social whole. In the cycle of confused wandering embodied souls, upon which the ascetic model is based, the separate, isolated souls are defined in a temporal world by that which embodies them at the moment of transmigration, with those of the world's myriad souls enmeshed in desire trailing behind those closer to the path of desirelessness. The territorially differentiated but functionally undifferentiated terrestrial world of the king, with all people differentiated by their rights and duties in relation to the kingdom, make up the king's model. Thus, while all three models are hierarchical — the king at the head of his territorial administration, the Brahman embodying the purest of the various functions, and the ascetic the most advanced along the path of desirelessness — there are distinct structural forms which can be likened to a pyramid for the kingdom, an organism for the world of differentiated functions, and a continuum for wandering souls.

Given these three substantially different, partially contradictory models, how did kings, Brahmans, and ascetics manage to deal with each other in a common social setting? What impact did these divergent models have upon action, interaction, and social relations in an environment defined by the very multiplicity of their mutual presence? The evidence available suggests that the various actors with their different models of society and precedence negotiated patterns of interaction and deference for particular social events (Burghart 1978: 533). There was no simple division of authority into temporal and spiritual realms; rather, the transactions between the actors generated complex relationships in which the powers and claims of the others were taken into account and honoured through mutual respect, deference, and avoidance (Burghart 1978: 531). Action patterns and structural relations thus seem to have been based upon a process of negotiation and compromise, with the reference positions of the actors defined by the three models.

The general implication of this analysis is that unity in regard to the correct image of society, consensus among the participants on the appropriate model, is not something that can be assumed. Rather, it is an empirical question to what degree unity, agreement, consensus exist in a given society (Burghart 1978: 533). In this ethnographic case, society is seen to be not of a piece, but of several divergent, contradictory elements; it is thus less a seamless, unified whole, than an uneasy truce, a delicate balance, generated by transaction and negotiation and manifested in ambiguity, avoidance, and equivocation. Traditional Hindu society might be in this respect unique; the multiplicity of established societal models is, perhaps, not found elsewhere. These possibilities must be considered, and ultimately the question must be decided on empirical grounds, on the evidence. However, one purpose of this essay is to suggest that the multiplicity evident in traditional Hindu society is by no means unusual, that multiplicity in models of society is widespread and is only one of a number of forms of multiplicity found generally.

But there is more to this question than multiplicity in models and compromise in interaction. Burghart points out that:

> The Hindu social system, as we know it today, is the product of four millennia of interaction between aboriginal populations and various alien peoples who invaded the subcontinent from the west. It is doubtful that there ever was an original historical period during which existed a "pure" Hindu social system. (1978: 534-35, note 1)

During this long period there were undoubtedly substantial changes in social and political conditions and circumstances: some periods characterized by political independence, others by dependence; some periods characterized by peace and stability, others by disruption; some periods characterized by cultural continuity, others by confrontation and admixture. The question that must be raised here is whether, in these changes of circumstance, one or another of the Hindu models of society might not have come to the fore and significantly if not entirely dominated social patterns. For example, in conditions of disruption, central control would be difficult and decentralized organization more effective. Would one of the models be more opportune under these circumstances? It has been argued (Leach 1959) that the caste system, based upon the Brahman model of society, is especially suited to decentralized control of a complex, differentiated system. Perhaps, then, it might be suggested that the multiplicity of models is not only a set of disparate elements in need of practical reconciliation, but is also a set of alternatives, any one of which can be emphasized or deemphasized, taken up or set aside, put into practice or allowed to remain a possibility.[1] Each model provides a set of directives for the organization of society, and thus presents a basis for organization in circumstances which favour it or disfavour the forms of organization conceptualized by the other models. The other models, and the alternative forms of organization they represent, do not disappear when the models are in eclipse and the forms of organization are not being put into practice; in one way or another — through close identification with a particular category of individuals, or through some continued but minimal operation, or through ongoing lip-service, or by means of various other mechanisms — the multiplicity is maintained, the alternatives preserved, and the potential is guaranteed for the future.[2] Thus, these alternatives can be said to be institutionalized in society, existing in or available to the minds of individuals because they are embedded in the fabric of social life.

In the case of traditional Hindu society, the alternative models are all hierarchical, each defining a category of individuals whose primacy is tied to the model, and whose interest lies in advocating the model. Whether such a category of individuals can implement the model in a particular present or finds it impossible to do so, the model will be retained, maintained and prescribed, both for the limited benefit which will accrue in that particular present and the possibilities of enhanced benefit in the future. Should circumstances become opportune in the future, the advocates of a model will be prepared to implement it. In the meantime, at the very least, some skeletal framework — groupings without resources, relationships without content, names without referents, norms without sanctions — is maintained as a "shadow" form of organization, seemingly illusory, but with a potential for activation. Caste categories, sub-caste group identities, territorial distinctions, discriminations of purity, notions of functional differentiation, ideas of political obligation, ideals of repudiation of the senses, all can be maintained at low levels of prominence and minimal levels of implementation. Whichever of these are recessive at a particular time, they remain in the repertoire of the society, and thus are available as alternatives to those currently dominant in practice.

General Remarks about Institutionalized Alternatives

Although the particular set of alternative models found in traditional Hindu society may not be found in other societies, the multiplicity and multiformity manifested in the three contradictory models are far from unique or even unusual. Indeed, this characteristic, generally unobserved or ignored, is very likely widespread, and might perhaps be considered a pervasive feature of society. It is, however, likely to be more prominent in some societies than in others. For example, societies continually subject to repetitive alternations in conditions with decisive impact upon social, economic and political life, will incorporate alternative patterns of social life able to alternate in response to the changing conditions (Salzman 1978b). To the extent that all societies face such changes in circumstance, this pattern will be general. Non-repetitive changes in circumstance also provide occasion for selection among available alternative patterns (Salzman 1980). Institutionalized alternatives thus provide a flexibility and adaptability in society appropriate to the non-static nature of physio-biotic and (both intra- and extra-societal) socio-cultural processes.

Alternative modes of orientation and organization are institutionalized in society through a number of quite different means, sometimes working singly, sometimes in tandem. In the case of Hindu society as described by Burghart, "literary validation", the enshrinement of alternative models in texts having a sacred or otherwise authoritative character, played an important maintenance role. A second mechanism is "ritual enactment", the representation in formal ritual of modes of interaction and bases of association which are not put into practice outside of the ritual context. Thus, the ritual acts as a symbolic charter not for an extant, ongoing institution but for an alternative possibility, for a social structure in reserve.[3] It seems likely that ritual enactment operated in tandem with literary validation in the case of traditional Hindu society (Burghart 1978: 528-532). A third means of maintenance is the "deviant minority", a particular sub-group which carries on a way of life quite distinct from that of society at large and thus preserves orientations and patterns of organization different from those general in the society. A nativistic or millenarian cult group would be an example of such a deviant minority (for a case of the former, see Bourdillon 1977 on the cult of Yahweh in ancient Israel, discussed in Salzman 1978a). A fourth mechanism is "operational generalization", the existence in general practice of a range of variations, of a variety of activities, none of which is dominant but any of which could provide a pattern for broader or even exclusive usage. An economy based upon the exploitation of a variety of resources, and upon a variety of mixes in productive patterns at the local level, provides a diversity from which any particular configuration could be selected and put into more general practice. An example would be "multi-resource", mixed economies and the multiple forms of division of labour associated with them (Salzman 1971a; Bujra 1973). A fifth means of maintenance is "asserted ideology", the repeated verbal expression among the populace at large that a particular social pattern is in general practice in the society, although in fact practice differs markedly from the expressed pattern. For example, tribesmen may eloquently and vehemently assert that they ally with close relatives against distant, while observation indicates that alliances are based upon entirely other considerations and manifest a quite different pattern (Salzman 1978a, 1978b).

Of the five "maintenance mechanisms" identified, three are directly centered upon models of social life, upon plans, templates, blueprints for particular patterns of organization and interaction: "literary validation" is the recording of these models in written form. "Asserted ideology" is the continual enunciation of models by members of the society at large in the course of daily social life. The "deviant minority" mechanism is the advocacy of particular models by non-representative sub-groups in society. In all three of these maintenance mechanisms, what is sustained, preserved, and advocated is a particular model distinct from the actual patterns in general practice in the society and from the models which underly the *modus operandi*. The two other maintenance mechanisms uphold models by somewhat more indirect means: "ritual enactment" symbolically represents certain patterns of interaction and organization without necessarily asserting the model explicitly. "Operational generalization" maintains a variety of patterns in practice, any one of which could provide a model for more general usage. In both of these cases, models may be more implicit than explicit, maintenance being effected by a partial practice, either ritual or operational.

The nature of society suggested by these observations on multiplicity, multiformity and variability, on institutionalized alternatives, on social structures in reserve, is not that of high integration, of overwhelming systemization with each part overdetermined by all of the others or of varieties of epiphenomena determined by an infrastructure or of a multitude of actions and formulations all generated from an underlying structure or a core culture pattern. On the contrary, the nature of society suggested by these observations is that of fluidity, adaptability and variety, of loose integration, of redundancy, and flexibility. People are often shifting between activities, altering patterns of interactions and association, and revising orientations and perspectives. Rather than argue that these shifts, alterations and revisions are in some fashion extra-societal, rooted in psychology or individual interest or the dialectical breakdown of the social order, it is more reasonable to argue, at least tentatively, that these processes are encompassed by society, that they are supported by society, and that to a significant degree they are channeled and structured by society. From this perspective, it is not very fruitful to characterize a society, whether in terms of underlying structures, core culture patterns, or determining infrastructures, as one particular thing, as exemplifying a specificity, pure and singular. No, plurality and multiplicity, fluidity and adaptability, must be at the center of our attempt to understand society.

This is not to say that every society encompasses an infinite degree of variety or flexibility. The possibilities are limited, and the degree to which they are limited and the reasons for the limitation are important parameters to be understood. Society is permissive in that alternatives are encompassed, institutionalized; possibilities are incorporated and sustained, made available for activation. But at the same time, society is restrictive, making available only a limited range of possibilities through institutionalization; people are constrained, significantly although not entirely, by the institutionalized resources readily available to them and the absence of others.

This conception of society leads to a view of change as integral to society rather than extraneous to it (Salzman 1980). Whether the change is repetitive or new, the response to circumstances of which it consists is usually based upon the set of alternative patterns available in the society. Consequently, socio-cultural change is almost always characterized by substantial continuity, in both "dominant" and "recessive" patterns; usually change results from a shift between societal elements, a de-emphasis of certain patterns and an activation of others, or the elaboration of particular parts. Change is less often a new society replacing the old, than it is elements of the society being shuffled into a different overall pattern with a different weighting of priorities; repetitive change takes this form, as does each step between phases of cumulative change (Salzman 1980).

Two Further Ethnographic Exemplifications

The Sinai desert is an international crossroads and has been throughout history. The Bedouin who make the Sinai their homeland have been subject to the flow of peoples through the area and to conditions imposed by the succeeding regimes which have been able to a greater or lesser degree to control the area. This has meant that the Sinai Bedouin have been required to cope with fluctuations in the circumstances under which they live: there have been continual alternations in political stability/instability, and in economic opportunity and prosperity/absence of opportunity and lack of prosperity. More specifically, there have been times of social order imposed by external regimes, and times of insecurity and disorder when control rested entirely with the Bedouin themselves; there have been times when economic production and trade in the larger region flourished, and times of economic stagnation during which livelihood had to be drawn through local subsistence production.

The Bedouin of the Sinai (Marx 1977; discussed in Salzman 1979) alternated their own stance according to the prevailing circumstances. During times of regional economic prosperity, the Sinai Bedouin took advantage of the opportunities and ranged far and wide in their engagement with the larger economic system, working in the caravan trade during earlier times and participating in the labour market during more recent times. For these purposes, far-flung networks evolved and contractual relationships were established. During times of economic stagnation, the Bedouin fell back upon subsistence pastoralism and cultivation in their home territory. Rights of access were guaranteed through tribal affiliation. Lineage and tribal association also provided a basis for social order during times of upheaval. Thus, the Bedouin shifted over both short and long time spans between far-flung network and contractual relations and local collective tribal association, and between engagement with supra-local economic institutions and concentration upon local productive activities.

How were the alternative patterns of orientation and organization maintained when they were not practiced, when they had little relationship to current realities? Three of the maintenance mechanisms described above were at work in Bedouin society. Operational generalization can be seen in the continued maintenance of rudimentary pastoralism and horticulture, run at an economic loss, during periods when the men were primarily engaged in trade and migrant labour which was providing the household income. During periods when the larger economic system stagnated and the externally-based income dried up, the limited pastoral and horticultural resources which had been maintained provided the basis for a local subsistence economy.

Asserted ideology aids in the preservation of local bases of association, the tribe and the lineage, and the tribally-anchored rights of access to collective resources such as land and of political support such as vengeance, during periods when tribesmen and lineage mates are not much interacting with each other in these capacities but are primarily operating through networks and contracts involving non-tribesmen or tribesmen in other capacities. In spite of an extra-tribal social reality, during a particular period, Bedouin would continually express sentiments and expectations asserting the primacy of lineage and tribal associations, ultimate commitment to the homeland, and unalterable ties to "traditional" Bedouin institutions. Furthermore, they would systematically interpret interactions and activities in terms of these groupings and institutions, in spite of the fact that any behavioural analysis indicates a substantial disjunction between the expressed categories and the actual pattern of association or activity.

Ritual enactment of social ties and group membership, buttressing frameworks of association no matter how vacuous the actual content of relationships at a particular time, takes place regularly and repeatedly through informal visits, formal gatherings called by tribal elders, and collective pilgrimages to shrines. Rights and relationships are validated and reinforced through exchanges of food and gossip, and through symbolic expression of membership, as in the calling out of each man's name during formal collective feasts.

Operational generalization, asserted ideology, and ritual enactment thus contribute to the maintenance of "traditional" Bedouin institutions and associated functional capacities, so that even during times of inactivity the institutions are kept readily available, prepared for activation. When the larger regional economic system and Bedouin income from it declines, or when imposed political stability breaks down, the Bedouin can fall back upon their local institutions by putting them fully into practice.

The Yarahmadzai Baluch of southeastern Iran manifest multiformity in a number of key spheres, among the most important of which are their multi-resource economy and their political structure. Operational generalization is the dominant means by which this is accomplished.

The Yarahmadzai economy (Salzman 1971a, 1975) rests upon the exploitation of a variety of resources: prior to "pacification" by the Iranian government in 1935, small stock pastoralism, date palm cultivation and predatory raiding were the main sources of income, supplemented by limited grain cultivation and hunting and gathering; in the recent period, pastoralism and date palm cultivation have continued, with migrant labour and smuggling taking the place of raiding, with irrigation agriculture expanding, and hunting and gathering playing a much reduced role. Within the broad range of productive activities making up the economy, different families and camping groups exhibit somewhat different patterns, both in degree of emphasis upon particular resources and in division of labour and organization for handling the multitude of tasks involved. Some concentrate more on pastoralism, some more on cultivation, some more on migrant labour and smuggling. To some extent this is a function of the development of the family cycle, but preference and the opportunities presented by access to resources also play a significant part. Some individuals shift between the various activities, others specialize to a greater degree and coordinate with others who do the same. The net effect is that there is a variety of activity patterns and of resource usages, each of which is accessible as a model to all tribesmen and which could be taken as a basis for practice. Thus, each variation provides an alternative pattern for those tribesmen engaged in one of the others.

The Yarahmadzai political structure (Salzman 1971b, 1979) combines a segmentary lineage system with a formal chiefship. The segmentary lineage system, based upon unity of collectivities and complementary opposition, is generated by and conducive to decentralization and egalitarianism. The chiefship, based upon a formal authority hierarchy, is generated by and conducive to centralization and differentiation. The segmentary lineage system is invested with the responsibilities for social welfare, security, and intratribal conflict. The chiefship is invested with responsibilities for intratribal conflict resolution and for external relations. Both the lineages and chief are responsible for social order within the tribe, but the lineages represent the interests of their own members and the chief represents the tribe as a whole. Rights and sanctions are invested in the lineages; the chief leads primarily through influence.

The lineage system rests upon the principle of descent with a corollary of political solidarity and collective responsibility. The chiefship rests upon the principle of political seniority. Both of these principles run throughout the entire social fabric, from the smallest to the largest groupings, from casual encounters to formal engagements. Neither structure is a restricted element or a grafted addition.

There is a tension between the two systems resulting from the divergent tendencies — centralization/decentralization, hierarchy/equality — which are inherent to them. This tension is partially controlled through division of rights, responsibilities, and spheres of action. Nonetheless, there are conflicting claims, demands, and assertions, and a certain amount of confusion and conflict generated by tribesmen acting in terms of the two divergent frameworks.

The segmentary lineage system is associated with the requirements of nomadism in a highly unpredictable environment and with the sparsity and undependability of productive resources. The chiefship is associated with engagement between the tribe and external powers, both regional and national. This is reflected in the division of action spheres. Consequently, which of the two structures comes to the fore depends upon the particular circumstances facing the tribesmen at a given time. When, over a particular period, challenges and opportunities arise, more appropriately dealt with by one or the other structure, that structure is emphasized, reinforced, and even elaborated. This was the case with the chiefship during the period following the "pacification" of the tribe by the Iranian government, and during the subsequent period of encapsulation. Thus, the lineage system and the chiefship provide alternative structures each of which can be emphasized and developed as is opportune in changing circumstances.

The Upshot: A Particular Understanding of Culture

Following from the preceding discussion is a particular understanding of culture. By culture is meant models, templates, plans and symbol systems which are institutionalized, established, customary, recognised and expected in society. Included are models of and models for, models descriptive and prescriptive, models general and specific.

The particular understanding of culture arising from the considerations presented in previous sections of this essay stresses the "pragmatics" of culture, the effects of culture, what culture "does" in the world. This is the view of culture as enhabilmentis,[4] as equipment which *enables* various forms of orientation, organization and action. Models are thus likened to tools, and the collection of models in a society to a tool kit. Some models, like tools, may be in use and others in storage but available if required. Or, to characterize the general by a particular, models in society are like enabling legislation, which makes readily available the necessary means for action should that action prove desirable. Thus institutionalized models, if not currently practiced, manifested in action, are maintained and secured, available for activation; they can be put to work, can be applied in practice, at some later point.

This view of culture as enhabilmentis emphasizes the independent nature of culture and the reciprocal interaction between culture and the conditions and circumstances of the world. Culture is independent, a force in its own right, because models cannot be conjured up or established at will; for this reason it is a presence that has a determining impact, if a partial one, upon human action. At the same time, culture is flexible and responsive, providing a variety of models which can be drawn upon as required. This multiplicity of culture further illustrates independence, for the range of culture with its divergent and contradictory alternative models is far greater than the action patterns in practice or the conditions and circumstances present at any given time. But it is in relation to these conditions and circumstances that certain models are emphasized or deemphasized, activated or set aside, and thus it is here that the reciprocal interaction between culture and the world is evident.

The notion of culture as enhabilmentis, as an enabling equipment, is, in its general tenor, hardly new or original. The view of culture as a tool kit, as an adaptive mechanism, has been a strain in anthropological thought since the earliest times. But it is, at the present time, what can be called a recessive strain. The currently dominant views of culture might perhaps be grouped in two great schools, the semiotic and the materialist. The semiotic approach, whether of formalist or phenomenological leaning, concentrates upon culture as a system of meaning, and exhibits a tendency to think of culture as self-contained and self-sustaining. The materialist approach, whether dialectical or anti-dialectical, regards culture as more or less a reflection of non-symbolic forces, regards culture as derivative and dependent. Neither of these approaches is very compatible with the view that "the relationship between notions and action . . . should be the main subject of our analysis" (Holy and Stuchlik, earlier in this volume: 26) an opinion of considerable merit. But the difficulties of the semiotic and materialist approaches to culture go beyond matters of focus and emphasis; to put it baldly, these approaches are ineffective in accounting for what people do, how people act in the world: the semiotic approach interprets through explication of meaning and significance, but does not even begin to attack the problem of explanation, of accounting for why people act the way they do. The materialist approach attacks the problem of explanation directly and vigorously, but inevitably fails because it restricts its consideration to part of the human reality, and is able to approach success only to the degree that its premises are compromised. Consequently, in order to overcome the deficiencies of the semiotic and materialist approaches, it is necessary to activate the recessive strain in culture theory and reinstitute in current anthropological practice the approach to culture as enhabilmentis.

The strengths of the perspective proposed here are that

1) the relations between ideas and actions receive close attention,

2) meaning is seen in its worldly context,

3) there is no exaggeration of either the constraints or the permissiveness of circumstances and conditions in the world, and there is no

exaggeration of either the constraints or the permissiveness of cultural resources, and

4) recognition of the reciprocal interaction between culture and the forces of circumstance provides a basis for explanation and thus corrects the deficiency of the semiotic approach without falling victim to the simplistic reductionism of the materialist approach (or the disingenuous dissimulation of pseudo-materialism).

Other Approaches to Culture and Their Problems

"You have no position, you are always in between," I said. "Between," he replied, "is the only honest place to be." Richard Sennett, *On Lionel Trilling.*

The weaknesses of these other approaches to culture deserve closer scrutiny and more explicit documentation, although full explication and demonstration are obviously beyond the scope of this paper. But it is possible, at least, to specify more precisely objections to these approaches and thus to delineate more clearly the deficiencies which the proposed perspective purports to correct.

Culture as a system of meaning, as a framework for understanding and action, as guiding principles and commitments, is the emphasis found in the semiotic approach. There is, of course, a wide range of positions which can be labelled "semiotic", and great variation can be found in the degree of emphasis on formal as opposed to substantive analysis, and in the degree to which symbol systems, meaning systems, are understood in their own terms rather than in an action context. In spite of these not insignificant differences in emphasis, semiotic approaches to culture share two fundamental biases: One is the unity of culture. Whether the focus of attention is the underlying structure or the core symbols, culture is treated rather like a deductive system, characterized by integration, self-containment and self-sustainment. Partly, this bias is an artifact of methods of analysis, but it leaks damagingly into substantive understanding. Variety, divergence, and alternatives in meaning are not – in spite of some recent discussion of multivocality – seen as a central feature of culture (cf. Feinberg 1979). The other bias is the primacy of culture. In spite of occasional disclaimers, semiotic theorists stress the logical and causal primacy of meaning systems in human life. The core of the argument is that culture provides the basis for orientation, that people act according to their orientation, and consequently action and its consequences can only be understood and explained in terms of culture. Neither the alternatives built into culture, nor the impact of non-cultural factors, is adequately taken into account in this formulation.

An instructive and provocative theoretical formulation of the semiotic approach is Sahlins' recent *Culture and Practical Reason* (1976). Here Sahlins argues that one cannot account for human actions and institutions in terms of practical problems and their solutions, for what counts as a practical problem is a function of the cultural framework, as are the solutions to the problems. Thus, practical problems, with all of their "material" aspects, do not exist on their own, do not "confront" people in some independent and objective fashion; rather, practical problems and their solutions are "selected"from the objective world by the system of meaning, of orientation, of understanding, of commitment. From this point of view, culture must be prior, for there is no experience except through culture, and so no action except in cultural terms. Explanation of action patterns and institutions must, therefore, be in terms of culture and its selective and directive functions; conversely, any attempt at explanation in terms of "objective" conditions is futile.

The difficulties in the semiotic approach as represented by Sahlins' position are several, but they feed into one another: First, the cultural framework can only determine results in so far as it is monolithic; to the degree that culture is plural in nature, harbouring various alternatives, then some selection comes through the individual choice of actors and not exclusively through the cultural framework. What is the basis of individual choice here? Not the culture, for it is among the elements of the culture that the choice is being made. The second difficulty is that there are many objective conditions which impinge upon the individual whatever his attitude toward them. The obvious limiting case is death, which has a fairly decisive effect upon any individual whatever his prior opinion about the matter. Many conditions and circumstances, from natural environmental processes, to demographic patterns, to politico-military instrusions, impinge upon peoples and have substantial impact upon them; these impacts cannot be avoided or controlled through cultural "selection". The fact is that the consequences of these processes for the people involved are a product of the mutual interaction between the cultural framework and the objective impingements. And dare we think, as Sahlins seems to do, that such interactions have no significant impact upon the cultural frameworks themselves? But there is more to say here, for objective conditions do not exist only through external or non-social forces; the exigencies of social life itself place constraints upon actors individually and collectively, as manifested in the fact that, for good or ill, one is accountable to one's fellows, whatever meaning one gives to his own actions, and is affected by the response of his fellows, however much he may be able to "select". Here too, actions and their consequences are the result of a mutual interaction between a framework of meaning and an objective social environment. The third difficulty is that ultimately only explication is possible, explanation is not. For in this perspective, culture lies at the back of action and its consequences, but cannot itself be explained or accounted for in any fashion. Culture is taken as given, as if it were the result of spontaneous generation. Only vague references to "history" seem to promise any accounting, and this promise goes unfulfilled . But how could it not go unfulfilled, for, if culture can encompass current objective conditions, why should it not have equally done so in the past? In this view, culture cannot come to be, it simply is. This position is not satisfying, nor does it seem to correspond to the facts about culture and its changes through time.

In sum, the semiotic approach correctly points out that culture does constitute reality by direction and selection and that the interaction between the individual and the world is mediated by cultural frameworks. However, it overemphasizes the monolithic nature of culture and thus underemphasizes the degree of permissiveness and underdetermination; it disregards the powerful impact of objective forces and conditions; and it abdicates responsibility for explanation of culture in general and culture change in particular.

The materialist approach to culture is relatively simple in principle. Culture is seen to be derivative and dependent, reflecting the material forces at work, without force and dynamic of its own. Nothing is caused, initiated, or constrained by culture, which is no more than the expression of other forces. This "reflectionist" view of culture is presented here in its extreme form; it exists, in fact, in every degree of graduation to the point where culture is hardly less efficacious than material forces, a point where some might say that materialism becomes pseudo-materialism. The continuum moves from the point where material factors are in every instance determinant, to a point where culture has some mild influence as long as it is in tune with the material forces, to a point where it is an independent force but weaker than material forces, to a point where material forces determine "in the last analysis" and "in the long run", rather like God in Western culture, growing more and more distant as the centuries pass, until His presence is so little discernible as to be virtually absent. But it is not the purpose of this discussion to delve into the multitude of sectarian variations on this theme, nor to examine the myriad of lively discussions that has flowed from it. Rather, it is most useful for our purposes to examine the position in its general thrust, and to ascertain difficulties which are found in the various versions to one or another degree.

The central difficulty with the materialist approach is that, although various sets of objective conditions can be identified, it is not possible to infer from these what action patterns and institutions will be. Different peoples respond to objective conditions in their own peculiar ways, selecting particular objective conditions to stress and paying less attention to others, and construing those objective conditions according to their own lights. The significance of this for the reflectionist view of culture is obvious, for the phrases "their own peculiar ways" and "their own lights" are no more than other ways of referring to cultural orientations. It is simply not the case that culture reflects objective conditions in any simple, direct, dependent fashion. Recognition of this fact has resulted in notions such as "false consciousness', which are a straightforward admission that culture does not reflect objective conditions and that explanation of action patterns and institutions in terms of objective conditions alone is impossible.

It is not difficult to illustrate these points in the anthropological literature. Harris (1974) describes the rebellions of the Jews against the Romans, and finds roots for the rebellion in exploitation and oppression. And perhaps these "objective" conditions did play a crucial part in the events described. But what about other objective conditions, such as that the Romans were much more powerful militarily, were likely to crush the rebellions, and did so repeatedly? Why was one set of objective conditions decisive, and others not so? On what basis was the selection made? Harris answers:

> Classes, races, and nations usually accept the challenge of such odds not because they are duped by irrational ideologies, but because the alternatives are abhorrent enough to make even great risks worth-while (1974: 174).

And where would the bases of judgements about which "alternatives are abhorrent enough" and which "great risks worth-while" come from if not the cultural framework? And how else can we account for the fact that among peoples in similar objective situations some rebel and some do not?

Asad's critique (1972) of Barth's *Political Leadership Among the Swat Pathan* provides another instructive illustration. Asad challenges Barth's account of the "objective conditions" among the Swat Pathan, arguing, for example, that an historical perspective would show that there has been increasing accumulation of agricultural land in the hands of a small number of large holders, and that small holders were losing their property and becoming dependents. Thus the social system in the Swat valley is not, as Barth would have it, based upon a multitude of competing factions, the net effect being short term circulation of power and resources and long term balance and equilibrium. On the contrary, the class system, according to Asad, is the dominant feature of the society, and this is demonstrated by the historical changes.

Now Asad's critique is carefully developed and suggestive, and if correct, would provide a better understanding of certain aspects of the system, particularly developmental dynamics. However, even on the basis of his analysis, Asad cannot explain why the Swat Pathans and other members of the society act the way they do, that is, as if their society was based upon a multitude of competing factions, and so on. Asad can identify the "objective conditions," and perhaps he believes he can point out people's "real interests," but he cannot on the basis of these account for the way people actually act. To his credit, Asad acknowledges this, saying that ideological factors are the missing term in the equation, the element that must be taken into account if explanation is to be possible (1972: 93). This is quite correct, but it is an admission that actions and institutions cannot be explained by objective conditions alone, and that ideology (read "culture") is to some substantial degree an independent, efficacious force in human life.

In sum, the materialist approach correctly points to the forces both internal and external to society which impinge upon people and with which people must cope whatever their cultural framework. However, it overemphasizes the independence and decisiveness of these forces, because it does not adequately take into account the extent to which the impact of these forces is determined by culture, the ways in which different cultures provide different ways of coping with these forces. Furthermore, the materialist approach does not acknowledge the extent to which "interests" are culturally defined, and thus lends itself more easily to advocating what people "should" do than to explaining what people do in fact do.

Another theoretical approach of some currency is transactionalism, which, while substantially different from traditional forms of materialism, tends strongly toward reflectionism in its treatment of culture. As represented by Barth's *Models of Social Organization*, transactionalism emphasizes the way in which forms of social organization are generated by the decisions of aggregates of individuals and the way in which norms are generated through transactions. Now to a significant extent, transactionalism simply emphasizes a different level of analysis, that of the individual and individual choices, and thus is complementary to other approaches. But it is more ambitious than this, and makes the substantive argument that people do not do what they do because they are conforming to norms, but rather choose what to do on the basis of interests. And, as mentioned above, norms are the result of transactions, of people bargaining on the basis of their interests.

While there could be no objection to transactionalism as a focus upon a complementary level of analysis, and while the emphasis upon the processes of decision-making and the formulation of norms is constructive, there are serious difficulties with the modes of explanation and with the implied understanding of causal efficacy in society. Most important for our purposes, is that the "interest" of the decision-making individual is not taken to be problematical for analysis, but is rather assumed to be individualistic in focus and probably material in nature. Thus the extent to which individual "interest" is formed and guided by culture is not examined. Consequently, it is not possible, as Paine (1974) points out, to explain why some people are individual-oriented and others group-oriented, why the interests of some poeple are informed by certain considerations and those of others by other considerations. Nor is the problem solved by Barth's statement that there are certain environmental and cultural constraints within which decision-making and transactions take place, for this merely takes as "given" many important factors which need to be explained and encourages investment in the processes examined of an independence and causal efficacy that they cannot have.

In contrast to the semiotic, materialist, and transactionalist approaches, the examination of culture as enhabilmentis stresses the reciprocal interaction between culture and the conditions and circumstances of the world, and acknowledges the independent impact of culture upon human action without disregarding the extra-cultural constraints and influences. The general thrust of this approach is not unrepresented in current anthropological thinking, although it might be more prevalent in case analysis and "middle range" formulations than in general theoretical debate.

Fellow Travellers and Their Enemies

One statement with the same general orientation of the position proposed here can be found in Cohen's *Two Dimensional Man.*

> ... the central theoretical problem in social anthropology has been the analysis of the dialectical relations between two major variables: symbolic action and power relationships. (1974: 13)
>
> Both culture and power relations are seen as independent, efficacious forces. Symbolic formations thus have an existence of their own, in their own right, and can affect power relations in a variety of ways. Similarly, power relations have a reality of their own and can in no way be said to be determined by symbolic categories. (*Ibid.:* 36)
>
> Thus, an ideology ... is not just a reflection of the various elements involved in the organization of the group, but is itself a significant variable in its own right, contributing further to the development and functioning of the group. Once developed, it becomes an autonomous factor which can motivate people and impel them to action in its own right. (*Ibid.:* 81)

Culture, here, is not taken to be monolithic and static.

> The first point that stands out immediately is the general flexibility of symbolic forms. One of the major characteristics of symbolic formations is their multiplicity of meaning. (*Ibid.:* 36)

This multiplicity in culture plays an important part in societal adaptability.

> Indeed it is this very flexibility that ensures a measure of continuity of social organization. (*Ibid.:* 39)

Culture can thus be a "maintenance mechanism", keeping a form of organization "in reserve" until it is required.

> By objectifying roles and relations, symbolism achieves a measure of stability and continuity without which social life cannot exist. Power is an erratic process. A vengeance group such as a lineage in some societies may have to wait for years before it finds itself involved in a case of homicide that will require action on the part of all of its members. But it must be ready for action all the time; for such an event can occur at any moment. Its members cannot afford to disband in the meantime, but must keep their grouping alive. This continuity of the group can be achieved mainly through group symbolism, not through the irregular exercise of power by the whole group. (*Ibid.:* 31)

Thus, reflecting the autonomy and interdependence of symbolism and of power, "socio-cultural causation operates dialectically, not mechanically" (*Ibid.:* 36)

The position that causality in social life is a dialectic of symbolic action and power relations, in Cohen's words, or a reciprocal inter-action between culture and the conditions of the world, in the words of this author, has not gone unchallenged. Sahlins (1976) has argued that there are only two possible positions on the question of socio-cultural causality, that of practical reason, in which human action can be understood in terms of response to and solution of practical problems, and that of cultural reason, in which human action can be understood in terms of commitment to and orientation through a symbolic framework.

> The difference is not trivial, nor will it be resolved by the happy academic conclusion that the answer lies somewhere in between, or even on both sides (i.e. dialectically). For there is never a true dialogue between silence and discourse; on one side the natural laws and forces "independent of man's will" and on the other the sense that groups of men variously give to themselves and their world. The opposition cannot be compromised; ... the relation can only be an encompassment. (Sahlins 1976: 55)

Now, while it would be a mistake to underestimate the poetic power of such a phrase as "never a true dialogue between silence and discourse", it is not obvious to this reader that a sound, logical argument lives within it. Nor are the uncompromisable opposition and the necessity of encompassment anything but asserted. Surely some more persuasive demonstration is required before the interactional or dialectical approach is abandoned.

In the absence of any such refutation, the position taken here is, using Sahlin's terminology, that practical logic and cultural logic must be combined to provide an adequate picture of the forces at work in shaping human life. Both practical considerations and cultural emphases have powers of determination and the actual situations that men find themselves in are the result of combinations of the two. Practical circumstances, themselves partially determined by cultural considerations, influence ideas and values which in turn influence practical circumstances and material conditions in succeeding phases. Thus, societal configurations and processes have been generated by the ongoing interaction of practical exigencies and cultural emphases, by the continuing mutual influence of material forces and symbolic foci. The synthetic cultural/practical view espoused here is not as neat or elegant as the single determinant formulations which have the appeal of *a priori* truths, but what reason have we to expect the complexity of human life to be amenable to neat and elegant universal solutions?

A second formulation in the spirit advocated here is that of Gellner (1978) in his recent discussion of ideology. Gellner points out that it is critical to address "two distinct, though interrelated questions . . . : (a) the social construction *of* reality; (b) the role of ideology *within* reality" (1978: 76, emphasis in original). Taking up one of these questions while neglecting the other, he argues, results in a misleading picture of human conduct and thus in an inability to provide explanatory precision. To avoid this, the only sound theoretical starting point is the recognition that

> In the world of conduct, the conventional and the technical *compete* with each other. Means-ends (technical) effectiveness makes itself felt, whether or not it conforms to the conventions ("grammar") of the culture . . . . Actual conduct, unlike speech, is a by-product of two quite different sets of factors — the cultural conventions within which the conduct takes place, and the real-world causal connections which are quite independent of those conventions. (1978: 78-79, emphasis in original)

Neither Cohen nor Gellner bases his general conclusions on the considerations set out in the earlier parts of this essay. They have not developed certain arguments presented here, such as those about institutionalized alternatives and mechanisms of maintenance, and they might not find themselves in complete agreement with these arguments. But the positions of Cohen and of Gellner reflect an awareness of the subtle interaction of the various and partly autonomous elements in human life, and they reflect a slight impatience with powerful but simplistic visions which seem to dominate anthropological inquiry at the present time. In these respects, their positions and the approach to culture as enhabilmentis are consistent and express a common viewpoint.

Coda

The arguments set out here — ethnographic, "middle range," and heuristic — developed out of a struggle with ethnographic "fact," not from first principles. Their value must be tested in the same context. They must be evaluated empirically, that is, they are accountable to "data," to inquiry structured to challenge them. In this sense, the perspective set out here is a "research strategy", as any heuristic formulation must be. No clear and simple answer is provided by this perspective, but having been born of the "facts," it might serve to illuminate them.

An indication of this is, perhaps, the parallel between the place of ideas in anthropology and other fields of inquiry and the place of ideas in human life at large. The approach to culture as enhabilmentis stresses the use of culture in the world, the multiplicity of culture, the ability of culture to preserve and maintain alternatives, and the partially autonomous impact of culture. Are these features not also characteristic of the culture of anthropology: do we not continually draw upon our culture in coping with academic and career problems and circumstances; are not "literary validation", "asserted ideology" and "deviant minorities" ways in which alternative models are maintained in anthropology; is not a multiplicity of alternatives characteristic of our academic culture; are we not convinced that our culture is, at least partially, autonomous in its impact upon our cognition and perception, our imagination and response? If this is granted, if thinking of our anthropological culture as enhabilmentis does seem justified, then perhaps there is some basis for expecting such an approach to be applicable to the wider social world, of which we are an integral, if peculiar, part.

Acknowledgements

I have benefited greatly from the comments and suggestions of colleagues. Changes have been made in the text in response to some criticisms; other arguments it has not been possible to answer here, but much valuable food for thought has been provided and will greatly assist in further formulation and reformulation. I gratefully thank Jon W. Anderson, Dan R. Aronson, Talal Asad, Donald Attwood, Abner Cohen, Ronald Cohen, A. L. Epstein, Sir Raymond Firth, John G. Galaty, Michael Herzfeld, Jerry Hyman, Emanuel Marx, Michael E. Meeker, Robert P. B. Paine, Harold K. Schneider, and Bruce G. Trigger.

Notes

1. Holy and Stuchlik (this volume: 18) point out the existence in society of "a variety of folk models". They emphasize as the cause of this variety the differentiated position and participation of individual members, and certainly this is an important factor. But one must not overlook what for this essay is equally important, that many people, in spite of their differentiated positions, have access to alternative models, either by carrying multiple models themselves or by being able to draw upon models held by others. This is more evident in the case studies which follow; in the Indian case described

here, the shifts between alternatives are at a societal level rather than an individual or group level. There is a shift in dominance between groups and models rather than a shift of individuals and groups from one model to another.

2. As Holy and Stuchlik put it, "The existence of these plans [for action in society] is perduring: people have and share them even when the action is not performed" (*Ibid.:* 3). What is stressed in the present essay is that this can be true for the long run as well as for the short.

3. The notion of "ritual enactment" as a mechanism for the maintenance of organizational alternatives, of a "social structure in reserve", entails a challenge to Bloch's argument (1977: 287) that ritual expresses "an invisible system" which we call social structure, is culturally specific, has little relevance for practical affairs, and which is contrasted with the infrastructure, a more or less universal mode of organization required for practical activities. This rather mechanical dualism of Bloch, not much mitigated by reference to the two systems as "moments in a long conversation", neither allows for a significant impact of culture nor considers the way in which alternatives are institutionalized in society.

Furthermore, while stressing "ritual enactment" as a way of institutionalizing alternative modes of organization, it is not my intention to suggest that ritual always or even usually does this; rather, I argue only that "ritual enactment" is frequent and significant. At the same time, I would by no means rule out, as Bloch seems to, the expression and reinforcement in ritual of current social arrangements and practical affairs.

4. Enhabilmentis: "Enablement . . . The action or means of enabling. . . . 3. An equipment, implement . . . 1495 *Act* II *Hen.* VII, c. 64 Armours Defensives, as . . .Crosbowes and other *enhabilmentis* of Werres" (Oxford English Dictionary, Vol. III, pp. 138-139, emphasis added).

References

Asad, T. (1972). Market model, class structure and consent: a reconsideration of Swat political organization. *Man* 7, 74-94.

Barth, F. (1967). *Models of Social Organization.* Occasional Paper No. 23. London: Royal Anthropological Institute.

Bloch, M. (1977). The past and the present in the present. *Man* 12, 278-92.

Bourdillon, M. F. C. (1977). Oracles and politics in ancient Israel. *Man* 12, 124-40.

Bujra, A. S. (1973). The social implications of developmental policies: a case study from Egypt. In *The Desert and the Sown: Nomads in the Wider Society,* (C. Nelson, ed.). Research Series No. 21. Berkeley: Institute of International Studies, University of California.

Burghart, R. (1978). Hierarchical models of the Hindu social system. *Man* 13, 519-36.

Cohen, A. (1974). *Two-dimensional Man: An Essay on the Anthropology of Power and Symbolism in Complex Society.* Berkeley: University of California Press.

Feinberg, R. (1979). Schneider's symbolic culture theory: an appraisal. *Current Anthropology* **20**, 541-60.

Gellner, E. (1978). Notes towards a theory of ideology. *l'Homme* **18**, 69-82.

Harris, M. (1974). *Cows, Pigs, Wars and Witches: the Riddles of Culture.* New York: Random House.

Leach, E. (1959). Hydraulic society in Ceylon. *Past and Present* **15**, 2-26.

Marx, E. (1977). Communal and individual pilgrimage: the region of Saints' Tombs in South Sinai. In *Regional Cults,* (R.P. Werbner, ed.), A.S.A. Monograph No. 16. London: Academic Press.

Paine, R. (1974). *Second Thoughts about Barth's Models.* Occasional Paper No. 32. London: Royal Anthropological Institute.

Sahlins, M. (1976). *Culture and Practical Reason.* Chicago: The University of Chicago Press.

Salzman, P. C. (1971a). Movement and resource extraction among pastoral nomads: the case of the Shah Nawazi Baluch. *Anthropological Quarterly* **44**, 185-97.

Salzman, P. C. (1971b). Adaptation and political organization in Iranian Baluchistan. *Ethnology* **10**, 433-44.

Salzman, P. C. (1975). *Kin and Contract in Baluchi Herding Camps.* Unpublished manuscript, 134 pp.

Salzman, P. C. (1978a). Ideology and change in Middle Eastern tribal society. *Man* **13**, 618-37.

Salzman, P. C. (1978b). Does complementary opposition exist? *American Anthropologist* **80**, 53-70.

Salzman, P. C. (1979). *Why tribes have chiefs: a case from Baluchistan.* Presented to the Conference on Tribe and State in Iran and Afghanistan since 1800, London. To be published in Conference Proceedings.

Salzman, P. C. (1980). Introduction: processes of sedentarization as adaptation and response. In *When Nomads Settle: Processes of Sedentarization as Adaptation and Response,* (P.C. Salzman, ed.). New York: Praeger/Bergin.

Sennett, R. (1979). On Lionel Trilling. *The New Yorker,* 5 November 1979.

PROCESSURAL MODELLING AND AGGREGATE GROUPINGS IN NORTHERN AUSTRALIA[1]

BASIL SANSOM

One of the fundamental theoretical problems of sociology is that of the nature of social continuity. Continuity in forms of social life depends on structural continuity, that is, some sort of continuity in the arrangement of persons in relation to one another. (A.R. Radcliffe-Brown 1952: 10)

The orderliness of any social system will be characterized by the measure of self-liquidation it allows or promotes. (S.F. Nadel 1957: 130)

In the things they say and do, Aborigines in the Australian North give the lie to Radcliffe-Brown's assertion that social continuity "depends on structural continuity, that is, some sort of continuity in the arrangement of persons in relation to one another." Northern Aborigines

1) are people of labile social groupings who

2) enter into intermittent rather than lasting association with those who (for the nonce) they make their relevant others and

3) defy the very notion of status by entering into and then yielding up positions that (in a phrase of Nadel's) are "self-liquidating" and not fixed.

Unsurprisingly, Aboriginal social discourse is conducted in a mode that does not admit the local unreality of perduring groups. In constructing the reality they experience and know, Northern Aborigines treat groupings as the product of process and recognize an achieved grouping for what it is — a realization of the here and now.

My last assertion can be expressed anew in local terms. Aborigines of Darwin and the city's hinterland say that they "run with mobs". In the camps that they frequent, people can be rallied to agree that there is no "picture for" a mob, no possible model for and of a mob considered as a typical entity that people in thought and action will reproduce through time. On the other hand, those in the know can craft a "picture for" any extant and created mob in which a set of people are currently conjoined to run together. Although there is no "picture for" a mob abstractly conceived as a type of grouping, there are words and strings of words in standard use to tell one how to put a mob together, how to manage it and how to strive to keep its members in active association. The breakdown of a mob — its dissolution — can also be systematically described. People tell how you "gotta organize" to get a mob going and to keep it going. Failure to sustain a mob is treated by them as we would treat the bankruptcy of a firm. A mob that becomes defunct is a failed venture, whose members "didn bin get all that business straight". And in this vein, the camp of a long-lived mob is a place where "always something happening". The rise and fall of mobs is thus referred to the conduct of significant social action. Drawing on a lexicon of culturally provided words and notions, I shall deal with processural modelling in Northern Australia to show how, in that region, social continuity vests in cultural forms rather than in structural arrangements.

Though in this essay a general argument will be advanced, I deal with the social discourse that belongs to a particular population of Aboriginal Australians. They are, in the first instance, people who have translated their own culture into the language of their colonial power. Most of the time, they speak not English but Aboriginal English, a developed language that evolved out of a halting and limited pidgin to be fluently established as a comprehensive creole tongue. And Aboriginal English is held to its own forms and to its peculiar lexicon precisely because this language exists to serve as a medium for the presentation and representation of the elements of a style of life that is itself distinctive. Aboriginal English is a product of the disassociation of Aboriginal culture in Australia and supplies the means for the perpetuation of a style for the ordering of social relationships. Aborigines of Northern Australia will assimilate their English to standard English only when and if they themselves assimilate to the mainstream way of life. Nor am I crystal-gazing, for the test of this proposition is to be found in contemporary linguistic usage. Many of the Aborigines of the population of which I write can, as they say, "talk high" or "speak properly English" — enter into the colloquial speech that is not so much "standard Australian

English" as the standard outback English of white Australian country folk. My point is this: to discuss Aboriginal business, speakers go into what they call "that pidgin". Furthermore, they speak pidgin that is "really rough" where rough talking means talking in English that is not "high". My first two propositions are then these:

1) Aboriginal English is distinctive and its distinctiveness is maintained because the language itself contains the modalities and terms for social discourse about distinctively Aboriginal styles for the ordering of social relationships.

2) In consequence, the departures of Aboriginal English from standard Australian English are not to be read as imperfect translation and deficient speech. Rather, the lexical selections of Aboriginal English have precise referents in cultural and social forms that are platitudes of Aboriginal social organization, but are in no way reproduced when the representatives of mainstream Australian culture go about their business. Aboriginal English is, in sum, an argot for and of Aboriginal forms for social action.

Countrymen and Country

As I shall show, the composition and recomposition of any single mob in the region around Darwin in the Northern Territory is an aspect of a wider set of social processes in terms of which members of a determinate population of Aborigines are distributed and redistributed among the mobs and camping sites of a particular hinterland. Members of this population call one another Countrymen and, in a population thus made up of people who have an appellation for one another, the criterion for membership in the population is mutual recognition of Countryman relationship between persons and sets of persons. The Countrymen belong to a range or stamping ground and, within it, individual Countrymen have their own beats, well-travelled routes that, for individuals, are the tracks and roads between those camp sites that they most assiduously frequent. The Countrymen call this range their country and they "read country" to tell of the attributes of land and the social use of land. Country is not only country for use, but sites on the country have religious and mystical significance, for country was created by the numenal figures of the period of creation, the Aboriginal Dreamtime. These figures made and marked the land and the exploits of creator-beings are recounted in song cycles and celebrated in esoteric cults into which adults, as they mature, are initiated. To comprehend country wholly is to be able to read it in two ways. One reads country to map people onto it as habituees of country, which means that the use to which habituees put country must be detailed. One reads country again to account for the forms of the landscape which was shaped during the period when creator-beings were active in the work of memorializing their experience in created dreaming sites. To comprehend country thus is to possess it, to enter claim to title for it. People who can read a country thus say that they have "got" it. The Countrymen with whom I moved in the Darwin region had, in this sense, "got" a country of some thousands of square miles. It included cattle stations back of Darwin, land on fractions of three Aboriginal reserves and camping sites on the fringes of Darwin and on the outskirts of three small country towns. Ask a Countryman what country he has "got" with fellow Countrymen and the answer will be a listing of place names and, in particular, the names of places for camping. The listing of place names is matched to a second listing — the tally of Countrymen and women and sets of Countrymen and women who, like the speaker, have "got" that whole country or some part of it. Knowledge of country and, hence, title to it comes only of experience. One learns to read country by moving over it with people who can instruct one in its use and in the stories and songs that imbue land with meaning. Habituation and shared experience and sharing in sacred knowledge thus generate association between persons and between people and the land.

During the time of my fieldwork, the population of Countrymen who had "got that country" back of Darwin numbered some 500 souls. They were people who treated urban fringe camps as places "for holiday" and for living independently of master-servant relationships between black and white. They provided a work force on the cattle stations of the Darwin hinterland and these are small-scale enterprises of fluctuating fortunes that offer only seasonal and sporadic employment opportunities. On settlements on Aboriginal reserves, Countrymen enter into the regimes of total institutions to participate in the economic and political arrangements of protected, artificially isolated and economically subsidised communities. For Countrymen there are then three major options: time can be spent on the settlements, in town or while working on a cattle station. These options are generally taken up in turn in the course of individual lives. In a region of movement, patterns of movement themselves provide grounds for the stratification of the population. Countrymen and women of standing tend to be more settled, more wedded to particular places in which they exercise control over people and resources. The footloose male and female mover, whose stories of each year's experience are tales of shifts between camp after camp, are people not "settled down" but "running round". Social command and stabilized occupancy of place are things that tend to come with age and so the division between the settled down and those running round is generally a divide in which age and youth, economic security and economic insecurity, command and lack of command, are compounded contrasts. To say that someone is "settled down" is thus, in context, no comment about mere residential stability. It is an implicit allocation of social status.

I have so far given country as an emergent range taken into possession by the set of people who have the established ability to read country because they have both experience of the land and the competence to repeat relevant, land-linked myths. Countrymen as a category share readings of country and so are united in one sort of understanding. Sharing in understandings, they are, in their own terms, made "all same". The population of Countrymen is an emergent categorical grouping. It is made up of people who have, through time, established themselves as relevant others for one another. They are people who know one another and know the same country. In Northern Australia, social identity is established with reference to the distribution of knowledge among persons and groups of persons. And people come to know one another as they come to know country, by moving in company in the groupings that they call mobs and then by moving between one mob and another. Folk modelling in this region has always to do with the comprehension of emergent social states and forms — with an emergent and changing pattern of land occupancy and use, with an emergent population made up of Countrymen who are currently but not permanently counted as such, with mobs or local groupings that are neither fixed in composition nor in membership nor location. The folk modelling of such emergent states is governed by three principles:

1) Social relationships and social groupings are referred to knowledge and to the distribution of knowledge that underwrites their constitution.

2) Knowledge itself is the product of shared experience and, therefore, the field of social knowledge will be differentiated because people are told apart from one another as, on the basis of experience shared and unshared, they have more or less in common with one another.

3) Shared understandings are contained in ways of speaking — in particular languages, in linguistic codes and in particular linguistic styles and competence in and command of a language, code or style is the precondition for gaining access to the knowledge that the particular modality contains. (To "read" the country back of

Darwin, you have first to get the "pidgin" of the region "straight". Competence in the highly localised argot becomes a social diacritic in a region where linguistic styles proliferate and where each style captures the people who "go into" it, so: "We got same lingo, same style: wefella all Countrymen". There are always recognized linguistic differences to set different sets of Countrymen apart.)

The consistent and general application of these principles to the modelling of social forms requires a complex and well-articulated set of rules to govern both the containment and the provision of knowledge.

For the rest of this essay, I shall be concerned with two things. First, there are rules governing and enjoining the type and quality of information to be provided and withheld. Second, I deal with conceptual processes for the treatment, production and interpretation of knowledge that serves the definition of emergent social states which are to be explained by modelling their coming into being. I have chosen to deal first with the nature of a formally recognized speech act, the performance of which is an essential if Countrymen hungry for knowledge are to be given necessary daily rations of information in order to update their appreciation of the emergent state of regional affairs.

Giving Words

In Aboriginal English the speech act I describe is called "giving the word" or, sometimes, "giving that story".

When a speaker announces that he has a word to give, that speaker commands the floor — is given immediate and unstinted attention by an audience. And those who give the word hold the floor for as long as they have proper words to give. To be true to form, the act of giving words must continue to be confined to the communication of messages of a particular type. Only a special ratified class of statements can be "given". Other statements are not "given": they are simply said.

In this context, the "word" to be given stands for a particular kind of statement. Words are formulated, in the first instance, consensually by the members of a particular mob. The statements issued by mobs as collectivities are of three sorts. Given words:

  a) specify the grounds for relationships between mob members;

  b) define the state of relationships between mob members and relevant outsiders,

  c) indicate degrees of worth or blame that mob members currently attach to persons singled out by them for attention.

The attentive receptivity with which auditors greet acts of giving the word is easily explained. The messages contained in given words supply information that is socially enabling. Not to accept a gift of such words is foolishly to sustain a social loss. Not in command of current given words, one is not *au courant*. And this in a region of movement and of changing mob allegiances where it behoves all social actors to keep track of their mobile fellows and to know as well about the current standing accorded to all Countrymen. A typical occasion for the giving and attentive receiving of words is when a visitor "comes up" to spend time as a guest in camp. The guest's first duty is to give words - to supply avid auditors with the sum of his knowledge of official pronouncements issued recently by mobs of his acquaintance which, further, are communiqués of which his auditors may well not yet be aware. It is, in sum, incumbent on each person to give words to those he meets, to share official knowledge with them and to receive previously unheard official knowledge in exchange.

The significance and importance of such communications is, perhaps, best conveyed by considering a second activity – the act of "putting" an erstwhile absentee "back in" a mob.

Putting a Fella Back In

When I now return to visit Darwin to enter again into a fringe-camp, it takes about three days for my social arrival to be accomplished. For a period of some fifty waking hours I am conscientiously given words and required to respond appropriately to the messages I receive. Even though I know how Aborigines do business, how they talk about and conduct their affairs, this knowledge of a culture remains knowledge of forms without content until I have been wholly and completely put back in. While I know how things work in the Darwin region, I, the returning absentee, am wholly unaware of current states of regional and mob affairs, and not cognizant of verdicts that have recently been brought down on persons. Among other things, this means that I know neither what style to adopt when greeting friends and acquaintances nor how to ground everyday relationships of debt with others. The returning absentee is socially incapacitated until the business of putting him back in has been completed. Once put back in, the returner is capacitated, in possession of essential warranted knowledge, command of which is the precondition for social intercourse. Short visits to Darwin from a place outside the normal ambit of the Countryman are nugatory. Spend but two days in town and you leave before you have made your arrival.

The returner has to catch up on a deal of information. For the period of the returner's absence, members of various mobs have from day to day issued the headline statements or determinations that register current states of mob affairs. Those who have remained true Countrymen for the relevant period have collected the communiques of regional importance day by day. The returner has to be made *au courant*. For this to be achieved, the returner must be given the sum of determinations that still have currency within the population of Countrymen. There will be:

a1) Statements that register either the addition of persons to formal membership in some mob or the loss of any person or persons to a mob of the returner's erstwhile acquaintance. (This includes news of births, deaths, defections and additions.)

a2) Other words discriminate between moves of people "for holiday" and moves that are "going over other side" — i.e. formally changing both residential association and primary mob allegiance. There are thus two sorts of moves: those that leave allegiance intact and those that signal new affiliations. The grounds for a person's presence in a place are thus announced to endow the person with the status of mob-member or guest in camp.

a3) Statements are issued to register the grounds of and for attachment of mob members to one another. These include: (i) Announcements of shifts within a camp and mob. Mobs often have two, three or four leading men within them and such leaders control their own sections of a camp. Internal alignments and realignments are noted and bruited abroad. (ii) The grounds for attachment of females to mobs and to particular males within mobs are also registered and re-registered in a region where marital relationships are fragile. There is a merry-go-round of marriage, non-marriage, remarriage and resumption of marriage on the part of both men and women and so, again, these are issues of status to be registered (cf. Sansom 1979).

b) Debts between mobs are registered as "blame" and, the facts of blame noted, alliances between mobs are remarked with reference to each instance of blame. Members of one mob "blame" another mob as a collectivity for injury done to their own accredited mob members. Such injury includes attack by sorcery, the putting of a person into trouble (especially police trouble), the blame that attaches to a mob when one of its members has snatched a woman to wife from another mob against the will of the woman's guardian or former husband. In Aboriginal English, formal charges of blame are not only given words about a matter. It is said as well that: "The Blue Grass Station mob got *warrant*. Themfella blaming that Petey bla that Darwin mob for grabbing young girl". For as long as a warrant is out and the charge of blame alive, there is a "trouble". When troubles are noted, further words are in order. Separate mobs either enter statements of alliance with protagonists or note their disinterest. "Wefella helping that Blue Grass mob" is the announcement that the Darwin mob that harbours Petey the wife snatcher and his snatched wife faces an alliance made up of the deprived Blue Grass mob together with its supporters.

c) The given words that relate to the social worth of individual persons are words in which heavy debts, under which individuals labour, are all registered and publicised. And these are both economic debts and charges of wrongs. Notice that in the example given above the stances of mobs are noted, but young Petey is named as the person for whom there is a warrant. In the conduct of inter-mob politics, Petey could lose his supporters and trouble-helpers. The warrant for Petey would then remain and a further fact of status would be noted: "That Petey walking lonely. Nobody gonna helping him for woman trouble.". In a region where people "run with mobs", "walking lonely" stands for the dereliction of the socially isolated person who has been extruded from mob membership, who can rally no supporters, but must face the world on his own cognizances. And when a warrant is coupled with the declaration of a person's loneliness, you are being told that if you take young Petey to your bosom, you accept his trouble too and enter into alliance with him in opposition to the injured Blue Grass Station mob.

Given words, in sum, deal with political demography. Taken together, they specify the size, strength, composition and – by inferences drawn from them – indicate the power of different mobs. Given words are supplied on the basis of an assessment of any auditor's prior knowledge and a teller of given words can find his utterances cut short if auditors remark: "Yes, we already got the word for that business".

For the returner who has not got the clutch of words that recent businesses have produced, putting back in proceeds in stages. There are two hierarchies to order the procedure – one relates to the content of messages, the other to the closeness of persons to determine their order of speaking. "Heavy" words are given in the first rounds of putting a person back in; then come lighter words which are made lighter either because they concern more socially distant people or concern things that in themselves as categories of blame or information have a lighter weight of import. Thus the people deemed close-up to the returner speak first and speak of heavy things. Then they yield to less close-up people, who impart their grave stores of news. And implicitly in this order for telling, which tellers establish by negotiation among themselves, the returner is told who of those present are persons entering claims to be close-up at the time of his re-entry. As for content, news of deaths comes first. Then comes news of the jailings that have removed people from the scene. Then there is news of the truly sick — sufferers whose lives are in danger. Then come statements about the warrants issued to pin blame on persons who are endangered pending settlement of troubles. Giving words to the returner puts him back in, allows him to greet mourners properly and mourn briefly with them. When the heavy news is all given, the volunteering of words by putters in who vie for first informer status, yields to the previously silent returner's enquiries. Once broadly put in the picture, the returner will ask for further information to fill in any blanks that he discerns, asking for words about people who so far have been left unmentioned. Too early and too avid a search for information about any absent others is tantamount to an allocation of value — present company are less important, less close-up in the returner's regard than those after whom he is enquiring. Clearly, "thatfella only got time for that other mob". When putting in is completed, the returner is said to be "really Countryman agin".

While the returner is given words that are important headline statements about current dispositions, he is not vouchsafed "details". And "details" here refer to the particularities of happenings that are the very events that led to the formulation of the "words" that register outcomes of happenings and verdicts on them. While it is obligatory to give the word to anyone judged a Countryman, details belong to people of an experience — to those who "went through" a business together. Having dealt with obligation to impart information, I now turn to the duty to withhold it.

The Telling Details Rule

The telling details rule is in two parts and can be formally stated thus:

a)   Do not tell details about current business within a mob that you have joined either as mob-member or visitor: tell outsiders, or non-witnesses of happenings only the word about happenings that are in train.

b)   Do not tell details about a completed business that has now been brought to its resolution in the word. Thus, were the troubles of young Petey, the wife-snatcher, to be resolved by arranging some sort of pay-off with the blaming mob, young Petey's marriage would no longer be jeopardised. The word on Petey and his wife would then be: "Them twofella marrit, we got witness for that". There is no mention of antecedent dispute, no telling of the fractious beginnings of wedded association, for now the trouble is over and what is left is the relevant outcome — two people living legitimately in recognised marital association. In the following passage, Stanner notes the retrospective operation of the telling details rule. He writes that:

> An attitude of "assent" shows out in the astonishing extent to which the Aborigines appear to forgive and forget *after* the juridical system has worked. Continuous reproach or obloquy are quite uncharacteristic. (Stanner 1966: 58)

A Question of Value: Going Through Together With

The telling details rule defines a spatio-temporal jurisdiction. Details belong to the time of and for their consideration and they belong as well to a relevant set of people either clustered round a trouble or joined together in an enterprise. Details are neither vouchsafed to outsiders nor discussable in public after the completion of business or the resolution of trouble. There is no need for detail once a trouble or business is finished up — words express the outcome and these words are official comuniqués, in which the people of a trouble or a business have assented to agree. Locally, words are attested: "We all witness for that word". So when business is completed the word supervenes and to repeat detail is in fact to contest the word, to treat a finished up business as if it were still irresolute, a matter open to further negotiation. The telling details rule puts a period either to business or to trouble, leaving the warranted outcomes of completed events intact. In this respect, people who try to tell details wilfully endeavour to reverse time — to turn back the clock by denying the determinations that with consensual backing authoritatively define current states of affairs.

While business is in train, the telling details rule forbids the incorporation of outsiders. Locally, it is said that to "have the details" of a business is to "have that business" itself. Knowledge of business detail is treated as title to a share in a business and all businesses are owned — the property of those made party to ventures or to troubles. In this regard, to break the telling details rule is to give away not information but a business. So the rule protects proprietary rights in happenings that interested parties stage. But there is more. The telling details rule points to the source of social value in the world of Countrymen. Their yardstick for value is the co-participation of persons in happenings, and their social reality is constructed with constant reference to the significance of such shared experience.

On the basis of experience shared and unshared, people can be told apart. Darwin Aborigines talk of "going through something together with" — that is, being parties to a business or dealing in partnership with a trouble. Through sharing in events, people establish their indebtedness to one another and, over time, discriminate between those whom happenstance has distinguished as their close-up Countrymen. People not close-up, but "jus Countrymen", are either active enemies or irrelevant others. In this vein, to "miss a happening" is to lose out on an opportunity for co-experience. And the misser of happenings has established no new grounds for others to estimate his worth, neither owes debts to those others of the happenings, nor is owed anything by them. The perpetual misser retreats from those whose business he leaves alone — becomes "jus Countryman" and not a close-up other. Those categorized as "jus Countrymen" are not close-up. They are potential consociates for those who thus label them. But they are not actual consociates — valued fellows who, in the recent past, have joined with a speaker to further aims jointly entertained.

I have now brought my description to a point where I can deal with the constitution of a mob. So far four things have been established:

1) Given words express the outcomes of finished business and such statements about outcomes live on serving to project the past into the present. A given word is a two-part determination that (a) indicates what happened and (b) defines the official social consequences of a happening. The second part of a determination is thus a particularistically derived prescription for the here and now. Cryptically, it specifies the only official relevance accorded to a finished happening.

2) Given words that mobs produce are essential determinations that, taken together, define the state of political demography within a region — the location of persons and the social grounds for their dispositions.

3) The telling details rule suppresses the resurrection of past social irresolution — the uncompleted venture and the unresolved trouble yield to "finished up business".

Mobs in Darwin and the hinterland are constituted with reference to the existence of given words and the telling details rule. They are formed as spatio-temporal jurisdictions that contain businesses (mob members are exclusive owners of the events of a business) and pronounce verdicts on the social outcome of happenings. A mob with these capacities is constituted to form what I call a jurisdiction of the word.

The Organization of Companies into Mobs

In the world of Countrymen, social continuity is processurally achieved by organizing "companies for business" into whole mobs and drawing on whole mobs to recruit their members to form "companies for business". The "company for business" of Aboriginal English corresponds with Mayer's (1966) action set. It is a grouping recruited to a purpose and will disband as soon as its declared purpose is fulfilled. The action set can, of course, also dissolve because business purpose is never achieved. Such a company becomes the company of a "try" that failed.

In the English of the Darwin hinterland, short-lived companies for business are distinguished from groupings which, potentially, have a greater capacity to endure. These are called "whole-mobs" and, technically, a whole mob almost corresponds with Mayer's (1966) notion of the quasi-group. It is a set of people who are often drawn together as parties to business, who frequently conjoin in shared ventures. However, a whole mob is made up of people who do not form a grouping with a single main purpose — an interest group. Rather, members of whole mobs engage and re-engage with one another to forward a clutch of business purposes. Potentially, all whole mob members can share in all troubles and enterprises to which any of their number may become party.

A company for business is recruited to an order of business and many such orders are distinguished. There is police business, ceremony business, cattle station business, motor car business, money business, woman business and so on. Nor does business stand merely for a business aim. Police business stands for an order of procedures, a mode for the management of a category of affairs. Business modes are called "styles": so there is a style for police business, for ceremony business, etc. Locally evolved styles characterize the region of the Darwin hinterland where people are said to be "all same" and "Countrymen" when they have the same styles — when they know how, in their world, different businesses are forwarded. And there is only one way to learn a local business style — by going through that order of business together with other locals who form a company for that business. As a person's life unfolds, his competence in business styles is intensified while his repertoire of knowledge of business styles of different orders is expanded. Older people have "got" more businesses — they normally have been through the experience of a greater variety of business types than have youngsters. Mastery of business styles (which comes of experience in which others share) again provides grounds for discriminating between persons. People "count up" or "reckon up" their business competencies, for being versed in a business style is a talent. Recruited to a business of a known order, the person who has "got" that business is a master and not an apprentice. Leading men in the camps are known as Masterful Men and in this appellation the two dimensions of their command are noted and conflated — Masterful Men command both a clutch of business styles and the set of persons brought to the business they promote.

Competence of the members recruited to a company for business must be an organizer's immediate concern. Organizers, however, are also conscious of the longer term effects of staged participation. Participation with others in a venture becomes a fact of achieved experience that can be recognized, endowed with value in a determination or "word", and then carried forward by business partners into ranges of future action.

Two principles of recruitment lead to the emergence and maintenance of whole mobs. Organizers tend to favour:

1) the bringing of selected members of their own mobs to their ventures, and

2) the recruitment of those of their Countrymen who, while not mob-fellows, have histories of consociate experience with persons and subsets of persons who belong to the mob of the organizer's current allegiance.

The process of organizing whole mobs into companies and companies into mobs can be represented in a diagram.

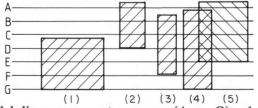

The parallel lines represent persons (A — G) who belong to a whole mob. G is a person who takes the initiative in bringing companies together. In one instance (1), he recruits DEF to a business; in another (4), his business company is expanded to include all but one member, A, of the whole mob. Further, in a fifth instance, E has recruited a company and, for a time, is party to two businesses (4 + 5).

Mobs last and remain viable and whole for as long as their members are caught up in repetitive rounds of recruitment, for as long as mob-members join and re-join in aggregation and re-aggregation. And, over time in the region, mobs are radically re-composed. Some become defunct and some are established as new creations. For the survival of a mob there is a local prescription: "Always gotta be something happening". A mob without business is an impossibility and the dissolution of mobs is put down to a single main cause — it was a grouping in which there was no action. Whole mobs are to be found where the action is and are seen as both product of and pre-formed contexts for future action. Mobs last for as long as they hold this promise.

Constitutionally, a mob is to be defined as the sum of the current and unsuperseded determinations or words that its membership has produced. The total set of words that currently define a mob are that mob's articles of and for association. They define a realized social formation for the time being. At the conclusion of to-morrow's business, when all is reckoned up, there may well be new words to tell how the mob's collective destiny has been disastrously altered, how the finishing up of business has finished up the mob itself. With such disbandment, there is neither mob nor mob words for a period has been put to the existence of a spatio-temporal jurisdiction. When a mob dissolves, erstwhile members go their separate ways to negotiate into membership of other spatio-temporal jurisdictions. Whatever pretensions to status they may claim will have to be registered in the mob of their new affiliation and then broadcast as official "words" that will be issued from the mob of the mover's new allegiance.

Of Mobs and Time

Among Aborigines back of Darwin there are two solutions to the problem of social continuity and time. In the first instance, people work to distribute and redistribute knowledge to define current states. There is:

1) a state of country in which a range is contracted, expanded or internally modified through patterns of more and less intensive use of places and the routes between them. A "reading" of country provides a commentary on the current definition of the range.

2) A state of each mob within a region — announced in the sum of current determinations or "words" about the mob in question.

3) A regional state of inter-mob relationships, defined with reference to given words of Class b above.

State of country, of mobs and of inter-mob relationships are synchronic realizations and susceptible to change. It requires a societal running commentary — the continuing exchange of given words about territory, mobs, and social relationships to define these states. Definitions of ranges of mobs, and of inter-mob politics, are characterized by both particularity and synchrony. The provided time-bound definitions do not picture standard perduring patterns of either the "ownership" of sites and country or the shape of social groupings. There is, however, another culturally provided way for viewing and explaining social developments within the social field constituted by Countrymen in association with a range.

People invoke a principle that is expressed as "running together for years and years". The phrase is applied to distinguish associates of long standing from Countrymen of whom one has more casual and fleeting knowledge. However, a second criterion is also brought to bear. Persons currently at odds with one another seldom voice the "running together" phrase to describe their relationship, even if they have indeed previously been either friends or rivals over time. "Running together with" is usually reserved for positive purpose — to identify others who are both:

a) one's associates of long standing, and

b) people with whom one is not outrightly at enmity.

The "running together" notion invokes time and a history of consociate movement. Personal histories, however, are compromised by present dispositions, as living enmities put one-time associates out of court.

The social construction implicit in the conceptions that are elaborated with reference to "running together with" are, again, best represented in a diagram:

This depiction of an individual's interrupted experience of others shows A spending time with B, C and D. These others come into and fall out of the picture as they "run together with" him and then go their different ways. Note that the diagram is not meant to represent hand-in-hand companionship. Being "with" stands for being joined with others on the socially recognized basis that makes people one another's "company". Being company in this way means working together in declared association and this is the relevant sort of social bonding that Aboriginal speakers talk about, measure and put into "given words".

In the first instance, Countrymen are constituted as an ego-centred set. They are somebody's relevant others. However, all sets of those who are relevant others for the individual members of a grouping of people can be taken together and counted as the Countrymen of a mob. When this is done, a composite structural form is yielded. The composite form is aggregated into existence, for it is based on the maintenance of the original definition of "Countrymen" that I have already given. Countrymen are the persons whom an individual claims to have "run with" over the years: the Countrymen of a mob are the sum of the Countrymen of all mob members.

When I enter a mob to join it, my Countrymen have access to my mob through me. I am thus positioned to mediate relationships between my fellow-members of my mob and those outsiders whom I acknowledge as my own consociates. Because mobs are internally differentiated and in them leaders are to be distinguished from the led, I must, in my mediation of relationships between insider and outsider, always take the division of authority into account. Subordinates within a camp give their own Countrymen access to the section of the camp and mob that a particular leading man controls. A leading man's own Countrymen and those of his respective followers are thus sectionally added to the mob to be made the Countrymen of a collectivity. The resulting structure looks like this:

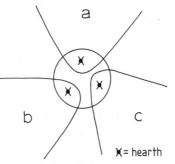

The particular tripartite structure I have sketched mirrors the shape of the camp at Wallaby Cross which, for the period of my fieldwork, was dominated by three leading men. The camp was divided into three sections, each centred on the hearth of a leader's wife. Visiting Countrymen entered the camp as guests of a leading host and were required to acknowledge a sectional affiliation by camping or finding accommodation in that leader's section of the camp. In general, a visitor is thus placed under tutelage as a chosen leading man assumes responsibility for the visitor for as long as he or she remains a guest.

The structure produced by bringing Countrymen to a camp is, however, more complicated. Many called "Countrymen" do not only have links with individuals, but are consociates held in common by members of a mob. Thus, if we are fellow-members of a mob, my own set of Countrymen may closely resemble yours. The result for the structuring of relationships is given in this sketch.

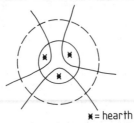

x = hearth

To the drawing of a sectional camp with three hearth-centres and three separate sets of Countrymen who are aggregated to each section, I have added a circle inscribed as a broken line. This is to distinguish between two sorts of Countrymen: those known to all or most mob members and those who can relate to the mob only through particular social ties. There is in the diagram an inner ring that encircles the close-up Countrymen of a mob — people linked to the mob by a web of multiple ties. To such Countrymen, each member of a mob has individual right of access. They are "Countrymen bla wefella" and are distinguished from people who are merely "Countrymen bla Tommy Atkins" or "bla ol Luke". People of the latter sort, who have only particular access to a mob, constitute a category; they are the "not close-up Countrymen" of the mob considered as a collectivity. The close-up Countrymen of a mob are people who have shared past time with the range of people who make up the mob's current membership. In company with mob members, they will all have "run together for years and years".

As I have drawn it, a mob consists of a circle of consociates haloed by rings of close-up and more distant Countrymen. I have thus provided labels for three sorts of identity that people can assume in relation to one another. And, over time, people pass through the structure I have drawn, changing one identity for another. A distant

Countryman can be brought into the inner ring and made close-up; a close-up Countryman may be relegated and become distant. With fluctuations in mob size and with changes in the composition of a mob, there is an exchange of personnel between the ringed categories of the diagram – one Countryman may be newly recruited to a mob while, after a period of absence, another may return to join a mob once more. Given all this, the sociology of such labile groupings must be the sociology of shifting identities and of the processes by which always potentially alterable identities are endowed and re-endowed in rounds of allocation. Groupings are realized to be re-composed and personal identities endowed to be transformed.

Dialectic

Because each Countryman of the Darwin hinterland has more to do with Aboriginal others than with Australian whites, relationships between Countrymen can be treated in analysis as events within a segregated social field, in which social processes are determined by an internal dialectic. The contents of this social field are constituents that relate to one another as parts of a system of internal relationships. My present task is to define, as Meillassoux (1973: 188) would put it, "the contradictory process through which the system changes to perpetuate itself" and which, hence, perpetuates the repetitive realization of aggregate groupings that are structured in conformity with the principles set forth above.

As they live out their lives, Countrymen continually experience and have to deal with the consequences of an essential contradiction that is the result of a continuing necessity to derive social identity in two distinct and competing modes. In the first place, one is a Countrymen – that is, an acknowledged member of a population of Aborigines who are all associated with a general range or territory over which they are distributed and, more particularly, in which they are represented in concentrations that belong to particular places which have been appropriated as scenes for Aboriginal exploitation. These are camps for mobs. To emphasize one's identity as a Countryman is to lay stress on one's general access to all others who are Countrymen and to stress, as well, one's potential access to all members of a total population and to all the scenes that represent the sum of one's chances for entering into significant relationships with others in the exploitation of discrete sets of local resources. Further, one's identity as a Countryman must be prime in all thinking in which longer-term prospects and possibilities are entertained. Considered over years, the progress of each and every member of the population of Countrymen is to be detailed as a history of two sorts of movement. There is the movement between places in company with so-called mobs and the sort of movement that is marked by a person's shift between one mob and another. I say the movement of mobs so-called, because any account of a shift as mob-movement is likely to be a compromised description. Did all the accredited members of a mob pack their swags and move together to a new site? Were no persons either added or lost to membership in the shift?

As I have been at pains to show, all descriptions of the continuity of mobs in time must be fictive. Such fictions are won only by glossing over and ignoring the countervailing evidence of arrivals and departures to make them incidental and so not worth mentioning. But, in general, personal chances and individual futures are determined by participation in a total social field of relevant relationships and it would be foolhardy to construe them otherwise. This is to relate personal destinies to long-term social participation within a system: let me now do the same for the destinies of mobs.

Members of mobs, in their domination of scenes, protest exclusive possession and hold potential usurpers off. But recognizable mobs do not historically belong to scenes at all. Rather, a set of scenes belongs to the wider population of Countrymen taken entire. Only the collectivity of all Countrymen can claim that there was continuous representation of their number on the historical scenes they claim. Thus, in a court hearing in Darwin where supplication was made to gain tenured right to land for fringe dwellers, I could argue in evidence that Aboriginal Countrymen of the hinterland had maintained a representative presence on the urban fringes for at least forty years — the period for which I could elicit reliable memories of Darwin experiences from the people I questioned. Seen as Countrymen, a grouping of people has been represented on the city fringes for as long as its members can credibly remember. But this sort of continuity cannot be ascribed to a mob presence. The large mob at the fringe camp I call Wallaby Cross is not credibly that mob which occupied the site now called "That Warehouse Camping" and which, when Darwin was a smaller place, was the major site exploited by fringe dwellers. Ol Frank, who spends about half of his time out of town, alleges that his present mob was once *the* mob of the Warehouse Camping site: at the centre of the Wallaby Cross mob, a leader called Tommy Atkins claims that the Warehouse mob of times past is the Wallaby Cross mob in its previous location.

Nor are these expressions of views contentious. Both Tommy Atkins and Ol Frank are right. Stretch time into the past and most, if not all, scenes have demonstrably belonged to most Countrymen. Project time and, on the basis of past experience, the scenes and sites of the Darwin hinterland belong not to particular aggregations which, in any case, belong to their own brief periods of realization, but to the general category of those who share generally in time with one another. Think in terms of scale and this treatment of the association between people and place makes further sense: today the Countrymen number about 500 and the sites they claim within their territory are many and well distributed. The capacity to hold such a range of places in more than notional possession belongs to 500 and not to a mob even when, as at Wallaby Cross, it can boast above 80 members.

Given words for the presentation and representation of events construct realities in mob-prejudiced perspective. The subsuming mob-reality is created by demanding personal subscription of mob-members to a set of overriding definitions — the stock of the mob's given words that define the status and worth of persons; that specify stances in the conduct of inter-mob affairs and which also detail the standardized prescriptions that tell one how to do things properly in locally established style. Time and again, mob-approved assertions are structured over and against a competing reality. And the major alternative definitions are structured in the terms that I have just used in order to note the continuing and long-term relevance of deriving one's identity from membership in the category of Country-men.

In mobs there is both studied over-communication of current relevancies and overweening emphasis on the significance of mob-derived identity. Underlying contradiction that gives a system its dynamic is evident in the way in which a mob-reality is only made subsuming by denying its competitor, the recognition that each person has his own consociate set, his own consociate identity that does not correspond with the mob-reality, especially with regard to discrimination between distant and close-up Countrymen. Contradiction in a system produces its dynamic and to define the nature of systemic contradiction is thus to account for the perpetu-ation of a social form. The nature of the system is, however, further determined by derivations of value. I have posited that the Country-men derive value from the events of participation from sharing in experience and assigning worth to time spent with consociates in co-experience. Further, I argue that, given this mode for deriving value, the attested determination produced by a collectivity serves as the essential instrument for carrying the relevancies of past experience over into futures. Among Countrymen, the personal time of biography allows individuals to project long-term plans. However, individual plans in the long term do not belong to the public realm, in which given words are given freely. Thoughts and statements about long-term plans and extra-mob associations belong to private communication between intimates. One cannot, in public in a mob, reminisce about good times past spent in other, rival company. To do so would invite the challenge: "which way you wanna go?" If other people are so "good", why not go and join them?

Conclusion

Peoples of labile groupings, fleeting associations and self-liquidating social position and identity have been a bane of Anthropology. It is easy to say why. In and through their activities such peoples all defy standard prefigured solutions germane to conventional analyses of continuity in social life. With reference to such people, the sociology of the corporation, the study of hierarchies of office, the ethnography of propertied family lines must all be put aside. And the sociology of familial continuities, of estates, corporations and offices is sociology of entities that perdure. Corporation, lineage, office are words employed to describe contexts for one or other "sort of continuity in the arrangement of persons in relation to one another" (Radcliffe-Brown 1952: 10).

In the Darwin hinterland, "continuity in the arrangement of persons in relation to one another" is uncharacteristic and the search for this order of continuity is pointless and unreal. Anthropologists who go out to find corporations and the like among peoples of labile groupings, fleeting associations and self-liquidating statuses, roles or identities have, through their use of terminology, continued to bemoan the absence of the perduring entity. For certain parts of New Guinea, one anthropological verdict is that people of labile groupings oxymoronically have "loose structure". More generally in anthropological and sociological writings, there are two sorts of prejudiced responses to problems of institutionalized labilities. One trend is a negativism that makes people of labile social groupings sociological have-nots. The second trend is relegation: people of fleeting association and self-liquidating statuses are made the deviants of comparative sociology. As Meillassoux (1973) and Wilson (1973) both remark, there is a lexicon of have-not appellations and a clutch of labels for relegation. Start with

Tribes without Rulers (Middleton and Tait 1958) and proceed through pre-capitalist economies to arrive at structures, statuses and roles that are "informal, parallel, supplementary, interstitial, secondary, subordinate, loose, flexible, or even quasi" (Wilson 1973: 5). And, as Wilson notes, such negativism and relegation originate with the anthropologist who "simply feels constrained to assimilate other social systems to his own" (Wilson 1973: 5).

To comprehend discontinuities and continuities of social life in a part of Aboriginal Australia, I have turned away from many provided terms and concepts of anthropology to report folk words that comprehend a social order in which groupings are labile, in which association is short-lived and in which the very idea of status has to yield to a conception of social worth. And, in general, the sociology of labile groupings will advance only when investigators give ear to the ways in which people of ephemeral groupings, *pro-tem* relationships and short-lived entitlement model their own social arrangements.

For Aborigines of the Australian North, social continuity does not vest in "the arrangement of persons in relation to one another". It vests instead in a conceptual order, in the repetitive invocation and employment of styles for doing business and rules for the provision, control and management of warranted social knowledge over time. Continuity in Northern Australia is in the perdurance of cultural forms of and for action. And these forms belong to populations whose members by command of them are made "all same". The sociology of office demands that office and incumbent be thought apart. To understand continuities in the Darwin hinterland, forms for action and social action must be separated, for social continuity in this region is founded in the perpetuation of the shared formal understandings that are brought to the organization of the activities out of which social groupings are produced.

Note

1. Fieldwork in Darwin was conducted during the author's tenure of a Research Fellowship at the Australian Institute of Aboriginal Studies. This essay summarizes trends of social action that are more fully reported elsewhere (Sansom 1980).

References

Mayer, A. C. (1966). The significance of quasi-groupings in the study of complex societies. In *The Social Anthropology of Complex Societies,* (M. Banton, ed.).

ASA Monograph No. 4. London: Tavistock.

Meillassoux, C. (1973). On the mode of production of the hunting band. In *French Perspective in African Studies,* (P. Alexandre, ed.). London: O.U.P. for International African Institute.

Middleton, J. and Tait, D. eds (1958). *Tribes Without Rulers.* London: Routledge and Kegan Paul.

Nadel, S. F. (1957). *The Theory of Social Structure.* London: Cohen and West.

Radcliffe-Brown, A. R. (1952). *Structure and Function in Primitive Society.* London: Cohen and West.

Sansom, B. (1978). Sex, age and social control in mobs of the Darwin hinterland. In *Sex and Age as Principles of Social Differentiation,* (J.S. La Fontaine, ed.), ASA Monograph No. 17. London: Academic Press.

Sansom, B. (1980). *The Camp at Wallaby Cross.* Canberra: Australian Institute of Aboriginal Studies.

Stanner, W. E. H. (1966). *On Aboriginal Religion.* Sydney: Sydney University Press.

Wilson, P J. (1973). *Crab Antics.* New Haven & London: Yale University Press.

"NOMAN" : REPRESENTATIONS OF IDENTITY IN MOUNT HAGEN[1]

ANDREW STRATHERN

Anthropological theory is fundamentally concerned with the relationship between individual action and the constraints of social structure. Since this is also a practical problem which is experienced in every society, we are likely to find that people themselves have developed concepts of action which reflect and bear on the question of social conduct within their own milieu. Concepts of this sort may be treated in some anthropological theories chiefly as ideologies, but to do so from the beginning is tendentious, if not itself ideological. Difficulties of analysis are shown in the distinctions which have been made between "models of" and "models for" the world, by Clifford Geertz (1966: 7-8), and between "operational" and "representational" models by Peter Caws (1974). Like all dichotomies, these two sets of distinctions have the merit, as well as the drawback, of sharpening up differences which may in practice be not very easy to illustrate; hence a temptation to shift such binary sets into continua, giving the analyst room to place empirical cases along it, like birds in a row. A move from dichotomy to continuum is not my aim here, but I do want to suggest that if we agree that dichotomies refer to ideal forms then particular stretches of what we call "data" obtained from the informants will reflect aspects of either form. Analytically, we may mine this open-face for the layer that is ideological; descriptively, it will contain much more.

The term *noman*, as used by Melpa-speakers in the Mount Hagen area of Papua New Guinea, engages us in all the problems implied by these opening remarks. There is a trend in anthropology today to talk extensively about "the individual," "the person", and "the self", and the significance these terms have is one of ideological liberation: if roles and status, those twin agents of structural-functionalism (a hybrid creature invented by mythologists such as I. C. Jarvie), can be stripped off, then the true individuals with their own identities will emerge. There is no doubt that Fredrik Barth, Jarvie and others correctly led the way to a proper reconsideration of the individual, and therefore of choice, in social analysis. Their brand of methodological individualism, however, leaves structure still rather mysterious, hence there is room instead for macro-theory to identify the explanatory causes of things — a point which Jarvie glancingly notes at the end of his book, *The revolution in anthropology* (1964: 222-24). It is a pity, however, before we pigeon-hole transactionalism in this way, not to stand back again and see that in itself also it needs to be complemented by, set along-side, indigenous theories of action. We may expect that in a society within which individual choice, uncertainty, and strategy are overtly recognised as important, and in which an important part of social relationships consists of networks of individually created and maintained exchange ties, the idea of individually chosen action will itself be strongly conceptualised, and is therefore worthy of close analytical attention. This is so with *noman.*

Like those powerful symbols which Victor Turner has discussed in his various treatments of Ndembu religion (e.g. 1962: 173; 1967: 50-51), the idea of *noman* is condensed and multivocal. The basic point to grasp about it, however, is that it mediates, and therefore answers, that problem of the relationship between individual and society which I remarked on initially. In different contexts *noman* translates as individual capacity, will, intention, desire, motivation, understanding, social consciousness, and human sociality. The fact that its various translations move right across the board from individuality to society suggests further that the basic message is that an important feature of human beings is that they can span these different spheres of consciousness while remaining themselves. If so, *noman* is indeed a representation of identity. Another way to approach its translation is to say that it itself identifies the realm of mind and thought, and that for Melpa-speakers this also picks out the sphere of what is especially human[2].

Formulations of this kind begin to ring a little suspiciously when stated so abstractly. What evidence have I? Why do I wish to present the Melpa as philosophers? As to the latter, I do so only in order that we can locate the concept in a general way, and also to acknowledge at once its power as an idea, for I will insist that its social mediation is not simply ideological. The evidence, of course, is contained in linguistic categories and contexts, which have to be inspected now more closely.

My first acquaintance with the word *noman* came as a result of difficulty with asking "why" questions in Melpa. There are several ways to do this, with differing force, but whichever way one puts it the answer is likely to seem both tautologous and unsatisfying on first inspection. "He/she/they did it thinking in the *noman*"[3]. An important part of the reply is indeed tautologous in Melpa: the individual action is intended, in the sense that a psychological agent, the *noman,* does intend it. The individual is in this way constituted. While the answer to probing queries by a fieldworker may also signify that the decision was private and inscrutable and so questioning should stop, this is not its only or final feature. Rather, one is also invited to consider that it is a state of the *noman* which has produced the course of action, and the state of the *noman* is susceptible to comparison and evaluation.

The most extreme, and again striking, idea about conditions of the *noman* is that it may experience *popokl,* a serious kind of anger (see M. Strathern 1968, and A. J. Strathern 1968 for parallel discussions of this idea). *Popokl* forms within the *noman,* and thus guides action, and it does so always in reciprocity with the actions of others, chiefly their denial of proper reciprocity itself. Anger of this kind may lead to revengeful action or to sickness; if the second, it is sent by ghostly relatives, who perceive the persons' distress and make them sick to draw the attention of their kinsfolk; or else sickness is a punishment for the person's own wrong doing, similarly effected by the ghosts, who perceive that the person's *noman* has led him or her into mischief.

This link, via *popokl,* between *noman* and the ghosts, is vital, because it is one of the bridges between *noman* as individual will and *noman* as social consciousness. If a person's *noman* has veered too far into self-will at the expense of others, the ghosts, acting on the *noman,* can bring sickness. If others have denied their social relationships, the ghosts see the *noman* of the agrieved persons and allow them to communicate their anger by an external sign also. In each case the movement is towards social communication and away from an initial isolation and denial. Here the message, therefore, is that a proper *noman* is one which is oriented towards maintaining relationships with others. The hidden, invisible action of the ghosts on the inner person is like the person's own private motivation, which, proverbially, cannot be clearly discerned[4]: but its result is movement outwards towards correction, through mobilising others who must support the victim or extract a confession from the guilty. At a deeper level, again, *popokl* within the group will destroy it: people will die unless it is brought into the open[5]. Life and growth   themselves depend on a good *noman.* Children, for example, will remain stunted if a brother commits adultery with his brother's wife or if a mother's kin wanted some bridewealth and were wilfully denied it.

This point meshes interestingly with what may be called the most encompassing meaning of *noman,* that it defines the sphere of humanity. "We have different bodies (skins), but we have the same *noman*"[6], my fieldwork hosts generously say in accepting my guests whom I occasionally bring to stay. Underlying this dictum is the notion not only of common humanity but that *noman* is a creation of social life itself. It is here that we find the first contradictions, also, in usage, which suggest that there are tensions involved. Different informants solve these in different ways. In particular, I will compare the views of Wömndi, a man of early middle-age and moderate status, and Ongka, an established virtuoso big-man in his sixties. In April 1979 I talked separately with both men about *noman,* and asked them some overlapping questions.

At the broadest level, a proper or "straight" *noman* is what should characterise adult human beings in society. Both principal informants agreed on this. Two points follow, tested in my questions: "wild" things, which are seen as outside of society and its planned purposes, do not have *noman* (in this sense); nor do children. The next question was: "are, then, children wild?" and this was designed to test Melpa ideas of socialization. Again, both men agreed: children are definitely not "wild", because they are, instead, *mbo,* "planted" or "cultivated" things. It is the realm of the cultivated, which is produced only by the actions of people, that is here contrasted with the wild, and the children pre-eminently belong to the "cultivated", being produced directly by their parents[7]. *Mbo* is one of the general terms signifying consanguineal or affinally mediated connections between persons. And here the inclusion of strangers within "humanity" is seen as the generous act it is, for they are not *mbo* by birth. In fact, it is only by operating with *noman* in its most general sense that they can be defined as human at all. Children of the group, unlike strangers, are *mbo,* but they do not have *noman,* it has to develop within them. How, then, does it do this?

My next question was: "do people teach *noman* to their children?" The term for "teach" also contains the word *mbo,* and translates as "to strike a *mbo* in someone". Both men resisted this particular formulation. *Noman* is not a *mbo* which can be implanted exactly in this way by unilateral transfer. In other words, it is not knowledge, but understanding, the capacity to grasp meaning and translate it into action. Yet both also insisted that education is essential; and also that when the *noman* is formed it is in fact a *mbo,* for *noman mbo* is contrasted again with that which is wild, *römi*[8]. Here is Wömndi:

> When children are newly born they have no *noman,* none, you know, their mothers simply keep them at the breast and they drink there, they stay that way till they are some two years old, and then too their *noman* is not really straight. Such children are attracted by anything that sways about or is brightly coloured, they have no true *noman,* that comes a little later . . . they have no *min* (life-soul) either[9], when they are really young. Only when fire burns them and they feel pain and exclaim or when they stub their toes as they run around and they call out do they show they have a soul *(min)* . . . Parents tell them, when they search for rubbish or stones on the ground "Hey, don't touch that, it is dirty!" or "Don't go there, you'll fall down the slope, come back!" We tell them this again and again and again, we look after them with our hands and eyes until at last they are big and they have a *min* and a *noman.*

Ongka's account is parallel:

> A child does not know that it will be hungry, that it gets wet in the rain, that it should eat food, it is just "crazy" and walks around without any intentions, and so it continues on and on until gradually it grows, it gets its teeth, it learns to speak, its fontanelle closes, and it thinks "If I go there I will get hurt, I will get sick." Before that it knows to cry only when it is hungry and receives food brought to it, a small child has no *noman* that is straight. We watch the place on its fontanelle where it throbs up and down, when the throbbing stops, that is when the *noman* is truly there, until then the wind as it blows can blow right into their heads . . . But the *noman* is there by itself (when they grow up), no one can implant it. It is not working, simply, and so adults show children what to do. A child has its *noman* for some while and then the mother, if it is a girl, shows her a netbag and tells her to help with digging up the crops; the father, if it is a boy, fashions a bow and arrows for him, or gives him a small axe to help with the garden work, and tells him "Let me show you how to chip, cut deep, and cut through the wood." The daughter, when she grows up, thinks how her mother showed her the way of making netbags or using a full size digging stick and so she takes on this work. It is things that they show their children, they do not show them any *noman,* the *noman* is there, and then they show things. The father schools his son, the mother her daughter, and so they learn."

The role of parents is clearly seen as crucial, for if they did not "show" children how to do things, the children would not "know" (i.e. acquire culture as knowledge). But children must have the aptitude, and this is shown by the autonomous development of their own *noman*. Till then, parents must act to warn children of the consequences of action, for children at first have no sense.

Of the two men it was Ongka who most insisted that the *noman* itself develops, and unlike Wömndi he had a definite theory of why people's *noman* may differ, in particular why the sons of a father who is a big-man may not grow up to emulate him. Ongka himself had lost an eldest son who, he thought, had good capabilities. His other two grown-up sons do not measure up to his standards. Hence he has some need of a rationalisation on this point, whereas Wömndi's sons are all too young for this point to worry him. But in general in this society there is a lack of any rule that a particular, or any, son should or can succeed his father (see A.J. Strathern 1971: 208 ff.); there is knowledge that where a son does become a big-man, the father may not have been one; or, if he was, then any one of his sons may "get" or "find" his *noman*, since it is the *noman*, as we could predict, which is taken to be the vital factor in explaining success. It is here that the notion of *noman* both organises experience and gives it an ideological twist: big-men see themselves as having a *noman rondokl*, a strong *noman* which enables them to become prominent. While the stereotype is primarily a mental one, it spills over, in a secondary fashion, into the physical, such that unsuccessful men are symbolised as short, unfavoured in appearance, and mentally dull[10]. Social and economic factors, which actually contribute to the incidence of such "rubbish-men" and help to hold them in their dominated position in the society, tend to be discounted. Since, according to Ongka's theory, *noman* cannot be totally or directly implanted by social teaching, if a person does not succeed this must be due to the initial lack of a sufficiently strong *noman*. *Noman* thus takes on the mantle of "intelligence" in this representation. Wömndi, questioned on this point, showed interest, but had no pat answers. His own father was quite overshadowed within his small   local group by Ndamba, a major living big-man (who is also father-in-law to Ongka). Wömndi is in some respects in competition now with Ndamba's sons. His comments on this family were, however (to my mind), extremely accurate: no one son has "found" Ndamba's *noman* in all its respects. The eldest son was scarcely mentioned; the middle had his father's good sociability and concern for visitors; the youngest had the father's capacity for work, something which the second conspicuously lacked. So

Ndamba had in a sense "divided" out his talents, but all would be needed if a son was to succeed to his status. Wömndi had no particular theory as to how this was so. Ongka, however, had, and that a biological one:

> As to this topic, if a man understands truly his father's *noman,* well, you know that the father marries a woman of a different group, and if he has his father's strong, true mind then he perhaps also has the "crazy" *noman* of his mother, or maybe it is the other way around. You see that a good-looking woman may still be suffering from gonorrhea, or have an unpleasant disease like leprosy. Well, if a married pair are joined together, man and woman, they exchange their "grease" (*kopong*), their grease is mixed together, perhaps the man's is good and the woman's bad, or the reverse, but one *kopong* makes a *mbo* in the other, and a wise man's son may turn out foolish. If one married into one's own family this might not happen, but we marry out, husband and wife are from different places and their grease is mixed together and produces children, one or other parent may have a *noman* that is not straight, it is *klawa,* "wrong", and this informs the other and so the child turns out that way.

It is clear that Ongka has invented here the beginnings of a deterministic "genetic" theory, as we might say, and that he begins by imagining that the mother's contribution could be faulty. He quickly redresses that point, but remains with his deterministic view. While Wömndi's account is innocent of such a turn in the theory, a part of his own description could in fact fit with Ongka's stereotype. This is where he discusses grease, *kopong,* in the form of sperm, a substance which is central to Ongka's own presentation. He was harried by my own persistent questions here, but eventually fitted the pieces together. "Where does *kopong* come from?" I asked. He answered that it was from the fluid in the spinal cord (*mbukltiköm*) which ends at the genitals, and connects at the top with the head, where it becomes the brains, *peng koya.* Since in Wömndi's scheme the *peng koya* is also important as the means whereby the *noman* is made straight, and correct action is selected from possibilities presented by the joint innovation of the *noman* and the heart (*muntmong*), it follows that, in a sense, brains are directly injected along with semen. This, however, is not Wömndi's conclusion, but mine, and it smacks of artificiality. We can recognise, though, that the potential for such a piece of ideology is there[11].

One stereotype which both men avoided was a simple pejorative view of women's *noman.* In public debate, during court cases, men do sometimes contrast the single-minded character of men (*rondokl,* strength) with the multiple and changing desires of women (fickleness, weakness). But this view belongs precisely to public rhetoric, enunciated when a definite conflict is on hand: a wife who wishes to leave her husband, or an accusation that a wife has spread tittle-tattle about other women, for example. The interview situation, in which I and the informants participated, perhaps falls between the public and the private. At any rate, both men gave elaborate analyses of men's and women's actions, indicating, in their view, that both sexes were inconsistent in action and fell short of the ideal, a strong and single *noman*. I directly invited them to produce stereotypes by my question: "Do men and women have a single *noman* or do they have *noman* that are different (*elpa-elpa*)?" In this question I meant to elicit a "cosmological" elaboration on the theme of male/female contrasts and the one and the many [12]. Instead, I was given two varieties of social elaboration. Both took the question as referring to the social relations between the sexes, and their basic interpretation is very significant: *noman* is a concept which operates socially rather than cosmologically. It is worth recalling here the response of another informant (Ru), much earlier, who when asked if one could see the *noman* if one cut open dead bodies, replied: "Don't be silly, the term is just a metaphor". Ongka and Wömndi understood me to mean "Do the sexes act in unity and do they have firm intentions?" Their answers were both strongly in the "operational" vein, that is, their own observations of people's actual practices were drawn on[13].Wömndi told me:

> Only a few people think properly. In a few cases a husband and wife have a *noman* that goes straight, they work at cash crops together, they look after the house and children; but only a very few of us do that. Men are badly behaved. Men neglect their wives, they do not share with them the money from selling coffee beans. They tell the wives who have harvested and dried the coffee, "What? Did your father plant this coffee and give it to you? Why, it is in my garden that you have harvested it, coffee which I planted!" The men then take the best dried beans and sell it to the visiting buyers, and they go off and buy beer to drink, play cards, chase prostitute girls and give them money in return for pleasure, while they give drudgery to their wives at home. Such men do not have a *noman* that is straight. Just a few men, though, are different. They say to their wives: "We have harvested the coffee beans together and got money for them, now you have this pound and I will take this one and I can pay back some debts or buy some food for ourselves and the children to eat together." But there are many, many men who follow the other pattern. Now we have stopped the easy sale of beer, before that many men just took the coffee their women had worked hard to prepare and used the money from it at once for beer — these men definitely do not have straight *noman*, no, they do not! Their women then say "Oh, that is what you did, all right!

I won't pick your coffee, I won't look after your house, I won't harvest the sweet-potato for you to eat." They go off somewhere else. Their husbands say "What do you think you are, a European woman?" The pair are at odds. Men do not have a single *noman* as they walk around, nor do women. Their *noman* lie in different directions (*elpa elpa petem*). A man thinks, "Ah, I'd like to leave this wife of mine and marry two or three new ones. But I don't have enough wealth, women are not something wild in the bush that you can go up to and take for nothing, they have their guardians, who will ask me to supply gifts before I can take away their daughter." So the man goes home and wonders how he can raise enough wealth. Gradually he raises it, and at length he marries the new wife. We men have many *noman,* not just one. We don't want to live and die with just one woman. Only the rare man whose *noman* and heart (*mutmong*) "die" completely on a woman, thinks that he would like to stay with one wife for ever. Women's *noman* works in the same way. A few women think, "Let me stay with this man and look after his children, my mother and father chose him for me, so let me stay with him." To the contrary, many think "Why should I? This man makes me *popokl*, is he God or what, I want to go off and marry a new husband!" And so they are at odds. Really, only a few people have a single *noman,* both men and women usually have many different *noman.*

Wömndi's use of *noman* here shows the context for a further gloss, at the "individual" end of the spectrum: *noman* as wish or desire, shown in the standard phrases for "liking" something: "to make *noman* to be", "to make *noman* to lie there", or "it makes *noman*"[14]. The many *noman* of men and women are in their many desires. Such *noman* are not single but multiple, and lead in different directions, so by definition they are not straight, *kwun*. In his picture, men and women are in practice both wayward. Ongka adds another dimension again: men and women are deceitful.

Ongka made his exposition, on the different *noman* of people, by giving four examples of trickery, two by men and two by women. The arrangement is characteristic of Ongka's logical and neat discussions. The topic also reflects his concern with individual manipulation and the role of big-man in penetrating through trickery in order to settle disputes. I will summarise the hypothetical, but realistic cases he cited.

1) A big-man has many wives. One of them wishes to get rid of the others. She takes pig-fat out of her gourd container and smears it on her lips and hands and tells a co-wife that she has just eaten a leg of pork, brought secretly to her in her garden by the husband. The other wife is angry because she has been evidently left out of the distribution: "What? We are all equally his wives; is he trying to treat you like his mother or sister?" She takes a stick and they fight.

The husband and other men break up the battle and ask what is going on. The angered co-wife says "You gave her pork and not me, that is what is going on!" He says "I did not! What is this?" "She told me so." "I did not, you are lying," replies the first. "What? You showed me the grease on your lips and hands." "So!" says the husband to the first. "You are playing tricks, and next thing you'll poison me!" and she gets into trouble. That is one kind of *noman*. We scare her by talking about her ways and the woman desists.

2) A truthful man makes proper exchanges, returning wealth for wealth. But a rubbish-man thinks "I have nothing. I don't work and I don't rear pigs. What shall I do?" He goes on a visit and pretends he has a huge pig or cassowary at home and receives pigs in expectation of these in return. He uses the pigs to pay his existing debts, and when the partner calls on him denies that he ever promised returns or went begging and says that he has nothing just now, so his partner goes without. Men look the same, they have the same bodies, but their *noman* are different, *elpa-elpa,* and this man is a liar, like the woman first cited. A truthful man, however, realizes that if he behaves like this he will be made ashamed, and so he makes proper returns for goods received, and people say he has a true *noman* and keep giving to him.

3) A thief will offer to look after property, and while doing so will steal it himself. Then he exclaims: "Who has taken it?" He will swear the most powerful oaths and offer to undertake ordeals, and people are puzzled. But he is a liar and a troublemaker.

4) A good wife looks after her husband, makes gardens, rears pigs and thinks how to provide food for her family and the herd. But a lying woman may observe her one day in innocence asking a man for a light or a cigarette and politely smiling or conversing with him. Then the liar rushes off and says "I saw those two canoodling together, the woman is going to commit adultery, she was startled when I saw them at it!" The first woman's husband is angry and they beat her till she protests that the witness is lying. This kind of lying testimony we call "chipping" talk, it can cause severe trouble. We listen to their conflicting accounts and then a big-man whose *noman* is strong says "This is something like a matter I once heard before." He listens again and then says "You, you are lying!" He says this to the witness, because he has watched her mouth and the tip of her nose carefully and he knows. This, then, is another example of lying. I have described two kinds of male *noman* and two of female *noman* which do not go straight.

Ongka's bad characters are not just fickle and selfish, then, as are Wömndi's. They are jealous, covetous, and deceitful, and strive to increase their material gains or status directly at the expense of others, whom they attempt to trick. Big-men are presented in a benign and virtuous light as the ones whose intellect, experience, and judgement enable them to see through these unpleasant strategies and reward those who are quiet, truthful, and hard-working. His presentation of big-men is thus partly ideological, and there is little doubt that for him morality is pivoted around this image of big-manship, such as Wömndi's centres on the husband-wife partnership as such. *Noman* in these tales appears in both of its guises: as individual will and as socially correct understanding. As the former, it may be "wrong", *klawa;* the latter is *kwun*, straight, an image both men employ. It is not, then, that men and women have *noman* that are constructed differently, they are not psychologically differentiated as in some western versions of gender stereotypes. It is just that they cannot often be in harmony with each other's wishes or in correct alignment with society's rules.

As might be guessed from Ongka's disquisition, he is also powerfully aware of the disruptive consequences of the *noman* lying in different directions. First, this may inhibit action altogether. There is another Melpa tag which I asked him to expound: "above there are many *noman,* below there is one". "Yes," he said, "this refers to a time when we can't make up our minds. The *noman* on top says that it wants to take something, but the one down below says no, don't do so, or vice-versa, and the *noman* on top strikes the *noman* below and makes it shake (as in an earthquake), it presses it down and we are not clear what to do." Another phrase for this situation is "the matter is cutting me in two." [15] On another occasion Ongka described how in one's throat there may be two desires, or *kum* (representing the entirely amoral, selfish, and appetitive aspect of *noman* itself)[16] : these are *namb* and *pilamb,* "let-me-eat" and "let-me-think-about-it", and they can pull a person in opposite directions, just as the upper and lower *noman* do in Ongka's present image. For Wömndi such matters have to be resolved by the brain, *peng koya.* The seat of motivation is the heart (*muntmong*) which thinks it would like to get or do something. This it communicates to the *noman,* which communicates with the *peng koya.* The *peng koya* deliberates in concert with the *noman,* and action is then taken. One can see here how the heart is seen as the instigator, plausibly enough as the seat of motivation or wishes/emotions. *Noman* and *peng koya* monitor the *muntmong.* Although such a distinction is not elaborately maintained, repeated records of Ndamba's practical utterances on *noman* and *muntmong* in an earlier field session in 1978 had led me to the same conclusion [17] . The all-important matters for the Melpa, however, are alignment, (the *noman* must be straight) and unity (the *noman* must be single). If it is not, *popokl* may result. Or if *popokl* over certain issues is present in a sub-clan, then the men's *noman,* again, will lie *elpa-elpa,* and they will not come together for collective action. This was the situation among Ndamba's sub-clansmen during August-September 1979 when they should have been holding an exchange ceremony, and people themselves commented how their *noman* lay in different directions and wondered how many grievances or contradictory desires underlay these circumstances. If there are indeed grievances, the ghosts will bring them out by sickness and misfortune, so the situation worries people in general as well as big-men, who depend significantly on psychological unity for the success of their leadership. Finally, good social relations should be maintained. The person who is overtly rude and abrupt may cause fisticuffs or stick-fighting to break out. Such a person is said to have a *noman* which *peta rop petem,* lies askew, the direct opposite of *kwun,* straight, so that he or she becomes a symbol for the refusal of social communication which is at the back of *noman* growing different, *elpa-elpa.* Each person then pursues his or her private goals, does not tell the others, who cannot see into one another's *noman,* and the community fragments, always a possible outcome in a society based on exchange networks. Wömndi said:

> This can apply to either a man or a woman. Someone comes to them and says "I've come to look for something", or "I've come to suggest we go somewhere together." The thoughtful person answers quietly "Oh, so you have come for that," or "So you would like to go there with me." We ask them quietly. In this way we show that we have a *noman* which is straight. But the man whose *noman* is askew says "What? Why? What have you come for? Go back and carry on along the path to your own house!"

Ongka's picture is in parallel:

> That is what we call a man who is abrupt and aggressive. Such men listen to what one says but do not take it in, they race out with the ends of their noses up in the air and start punching or fighting people with sticks. "Wait," we say, "we haven't sorted out the talk yet and you're already fighting. You must be a man whose *noman* is askew." Now the man whose *noman* is straight thinks "I won't fight just yet, I'll try to understand properly what is being said before I do that."

Here Ongka uses a contrast between *ment,* "downwards", and *woint,* "upwards", terms primarily used for "downhill" and "uphill". The image is relevant to the general working of *noman.* "Taking words in" is taking them "downwards", and downwards is from the ears, where they enter, to the *noman,* located in the centre of the chest beside the heart and above the liver and stomach. So taking words in depends on the channel of communication with the *noman* lying straight. If it is askew, of course, the words cannot be taken in, and so they cannot be measured. (In the *peng koya* imagery they could be, but the point is that communication always has to circulate through the *noman,* as blood through the heart). Hence the idea of the *noman* askew is exactly an image of blocked communication. [18]

From the examples I have given it may be concluded that social communication is a dominant value for the Melpa, and this is true. Also that the "individual" or "wilful" aspect of the *noman* is denigrated. The latter conclusion is only partially correct, however. In fact there is strong approbation for individual creativity and achievement in Melpa thought. Even the simple assertion that explanation of action begins from recognising individual intention indicates that the individual person, both male and female, is strongly conceptualised, and the integrity of individual decision-making is supported. When people's *noman* "lie *elpa-elpa*", they may all be pursuing perfectly legitimate aims in terms of their private concerns. Since people are all born predisposed to having different *noman* (Womndi was emphatic that even twins do not have the same *noman*), "lying *elpa-elpa*" is, as it were, the expected and ordinary state of affairs, and unity is something to be worked for and achieved only occasionally or by a few. Further, individual ability is praised both in the idea of the big-man and in the notion of the artist, who makes a new design or a song and wears a new decoration by virtue of his *noman.* In this case no-one has even to "show" the creator how to do it, as Ongka instanced parents showing tasks to their children. Instead, the creator shows his or her *noman* by the act of creation. The same is basically true of all dancers when decorated: their decorations are their creations and as such are products of *noman,* and this *noman* has then to be communicated to the spectators who will judge the good luck, unity, and relationship to the ghosts of the dancing group through inspection of the ornaments worn (see M. Strathern 1979: 250). Individual creativity is thus converted into social communication again.

Individual capacity is exemplified further by the abilities of big-men to innovate and of ritual experts to communicate with the ghosts. Ongka's own life-story shows at several points how he sees himself as an innovator, and the theme is strong in the speeches of many a younger big-man nowadays. "Let us seize the new" is their motto. Ongka buried his first wife, whom he loved and admired, in a new way to show his concern for her. He prides himself on being one of the earliest to go in for purchasing vehicles, and on having been an adjutant of the first Australian patrol officers, as well as on adopting the anthropologist into his community when older big-men warned him that I was a dangerous cannibal spirit who would soon eat him up. The introduction of new goods into the great *moka* exchange festivals is another innovation with which Ongka credits himself (i.e. that the Kawelka gave a car to their main partner, the local M.P., just as a generation earlier they had given his mother in *moka* to his father, a pre-eminent big-man and peace-maker). The only innovation he refused was the cargo-cult, on the grounds that it was simply an unscrupulous trick and an attempt to get something for nothing. (see A.J. Strathern 1979: 39, 85 ff., 97-101, 122, 126, 133-5. We may compare his stories of tricking as instances of bad *noman*).

With the ability of ritual experts we encounter another, and final, aspect of *noman: noman* operates to extend human ability to communicate. Ghosts cannot properly be seen or touched; although folk-tales suggest they appear to people, usually this is in dreams. In conscious waking life they can be apprehended only in the *noman;* whereas in dreams it is the person's *min,* the sleeping double, as it were, of *noman,* which slips out of the body and directly, in classical fashion, consorts with other *min.* The *noman* proper does not operate in dreams, nor does it survive death as the *min* does. Quintessentially, it depends on, is an expression of, everyday living consciousness. But the ritual expert's *noman* is such that ghosts can enter it, and he or she can report the ghosts' messages by first whistling in the throat and then translating this into ordinary comprehensible language (*mbo ik,* "planted talk"). The *noman* of a sacrificiant expert or big-man must be in harmony with the ghosts when pigs are killed, in order for him to transmit and receive messages accurately. And there is always room for some uncertainty. People say: "I do not see truly with my eyes, I think with my *noman* only."

My chief descriptive point throughout this examination has been to stress that *noman* serves as a marker of humanity by bridging in various ways the gap between persons within society. Several conclusions emerge, which can now be recapitulated:

1) The concept of *noman* is multivalent, enabling its users to distinguish good and bad forms of individual action (wilfulness vs. creativity, adulthood vs. childhood, the "straight" vs. the "askew", unity vs. fragmentation).

2) Such a multivalent idea is well suited to Melpa society, in which much stress is placed on individually-chosen exchanges, yet it is also important to co-operate for group occasions.

3) Particular aspects of informants' wisdom about *noman* can be identified as ideological, e.g. as buttressing the position of ·men in general or of the big-men who are dominant. But it would be wrong to interpret all, or even the bulk, of their statements in this way.

4) Similarly, it would be wrong to categorise statements about *noman* as purely "representational models" or "operational models." Nor are the statements themselves so highly elaborated as to make it entirely justifiable to abstract logically tight versions of such models from what people say. What can be done is to see the significance of the distinction between "one *noman*" and "different *noman*" as applied to the recurrent problem of co-operation within groups.

5) This in turn indicates that the Melpa are mostly interested in "models for", i.e. varieties of the operational model as they see them. In a society in which political and ritual action takes precedence over myth and local political processes are matters of intense concern, such a concentration is not surprising. It helps to explain why my questions about the "physiological mechanics", as it were, of *noman* were usually turned into social moralising by both principal informants.

6) Where *noman* does work as a kind of "model of" is at the boundary between people and those things which are *römi,* wild. Such wild things do not have ordered intentions (in this representation – in other contexts they are presented as having a kind of society); they search "aimlessly" for food; they do not recognise relationship.[19] It is important for the Melpa to except children from this category, because even though wild things can be tamed by giving them *mbo* food, which is domesticated, their *noman* can never become properly straight, as people's should. In another sense, then, (that of "basic character") wild creatures do have a *noman,* but it is one which is *römi.* Children are not romi, even though they lack a *noman* at birth, because (a) their *noman* is latently present; (b) as they grow up they recognise relationship; and (c) they are in any case produced and nurtured by ordered intentions within the realm of kinship (hence, they are *mbo*). The master or overarching opposition is thus that between the *mbo* and the *römi,* an opposition which we should not equate

with our own distinction between culture and nature, but which operates analogously to define the conceptual area of what is properly human and is therefore characterised by the presence or potentiality of a straight *noman*. That area, as I have noted, is also marked out by the idea of kinship. One of Wömndi's examples makes the point well:

> A pig or a dog will not develop a *noman* which is straight. Look, you can feed a pig from your garden, but the pig will not think of its "father", it will break into your garden and steal from you. A dog, too, will take food from you, but it will go into your house, and not think of its "mother and father" and will thieve food which is left there."

It may be in order now to step back a little further from the specific points I have made about Melpa ideas and explain the convictions which underlie my approach to the question of "folk models" and their "structure".

The notion of "folk model" is an anthropologist's construct. It implies both that the people we study make and use models in a way that is analogous to the way in which anthropologists make them, and at the same time that "their" models are somewhat different from "ours": often anthropologists claim that they are making explanatory models, whereas the people's are devised simply to justify their practical social action, or even to conceal some aspects of their practice. There are two stages to the problems of validity raised by this scheme of folk *versus* analytical models: first, on what evidence do we say that people construct "models"? Do these folk models differ from other categories, such as "norm", "ideal", "picture", "myth"? Second, how is the claim to greater explanatory power to be confirmed?

Clearly, whether we think that people do make models or not depends on how tightly we define the concept of model itself. For my purpose and interest here it is sufficient to say that the term must imply at least a degree of systematic construction of ideas, in such a way that these then provide an important overall set of guidelines for action, or at any rate a framework of assumptions within which action either takes place, or is evaluated, or both. This raises a further difficulty, for the question of what qualifies as "systematic construction" is not easy to settle. As I have hinted, folk models, qua models, are often just as much the anthropologist's invention as our analytical models. In a sense, it cannot be otherwise when both kinds are, in immediate empirical terms, authored by the anthropologist as products of his or her pen. Nevertheless there is certainly a difference between attempting, at least, to delineate, albeit by pulling together into a set of connected statements what as data in one's notebooks appears in a scattered and *unsystematised* form, the coherence of a people's own viewpoint, and *per contra* examining that viewpoint further with the aim of developing an explanation of it in the terms of one's own discipline and its concerns.

What I have tried to write about in the paper has been a concept for action and the interpretation of action, as seen by people in Melpa society. The generality and salience of this concept of *noman* is such that I see it as properly comparable to the categories which anthropologists themselves use in explaining society. To write about *noman* in this way is thus also to argue that in the particular instance Melpa ideas do form a model, and simultaneously that this folk model is as useful and worthwhile for explaining aspects of Melpa social action as other concepts I may care to bring into play: in other words I am saying that the pejorative connotation of "folk" in "folk model" is here inappropriate. In studying usage of the term, as an observer, however, I have succeeded in noting that the wide range of applications which the term has both gives fertile opportunities for manipulation and provides a key to the way in which the Melpa conceptualise the relations between "the individual" and "society".

It is precisely here that the greatest care is needed. Anthropologists from western societies bring to the field a good deal of intellectual baggage about "the individual" and "society". One point is that the whole idea of setting up these two categories as somehow opposed is one which is heavily influenced by centuries of experience of state structures that dispose of coercive sanctions. Where such sanctions are lacking, and other sanctions underpin social relations, we should surely expect that the underlying model of individual/group relations will differ from our own, and therefore the idea of the social person will also differ. If this is correct, and ideas such as *noman* are fundamental representations of identity, society, the person, and so on, by what superior etic means are we to cut through these constructs to some further reality beyond them? I am not here attempting to exclude the application of further ideas, but I am raising the problem of privilege and relativism in a way which strongly echoes the viewpoints of the working paper for the conference prepared jointly by Stuchlik and Holy.

In this regard, the enormously important influences stemming from the writings of Levi-Strauss and Marx have perhaps been deleterious. Levi-Strauss privileges the observer *vis-à-vis* the observed, forgetting perhaps that people in society are also, indeed must be, observers. In the marxist tradition, the idea of "false consciousness" plays a similar role: mystified by ideology, people cannot see the real forces which control them. Perhaps; but this again is likely to be most generally true in societies with marked forms of exploitation, and even then we cannot categorically assume either that people are incapable of seeing their own predicament or that our perception of these predicaments   is necessarily privileged and "correct".

I argue, then, that it is only through detailed ethnographic studies that we can come properly to grips with questions such as "the structure of folk models" and "the dialectical interplay between ideology and action".[20] Further, we have to recognise that the oppositions which are sometimes made between the folk and the analytical and between ideology and action are themselves false, or at least inadequate, being insufficiently theorised. An equation between "folk", "ideological", and "representational", on the one hand, and "analytical", "action", and "operational", on the other, could be just another example of the arrangement of binary oppositions in a cosmological schema. Breaking out of this binary straitjacket, we need to be alive to the possibility that people can explain their own ideas adequately and that understanding this requires the observer simultaneously to make the effort of understanding, in comparison, his or her "folk" presuppositions even while struggling to grasp those of others.

Since *noman,* as a concept, is precisely about understanding the actions of others, this paper can be seen both as a presentation of a particular model and a comment on why models are needed, whether by "actors" or "observers": in other words, I would stress the overlap, rather than the discrepancies, between the supposedly "folk" and the supposedly "analytical".

Acknowledgements

Fieldwork in Mount Hagen, originally begun in 1964-5 and continued since then, was supported in 1978-9 by the Social Science Research Council and University College London. I am grateful to both of these institutions, and also to the Institute of Papua New Guinea Studies in Port Moresby for an Honorary Research Fellowship by means of which research access to the field was facilitated. My debts to Wömndi and Ongka will be made obvious in the paper.

Notes

1. I have reverted in this paper to some orthographic usages characteristic of the German ethnographies on the Melpa, e.g. by employing ö as a symbol rather than φ, and by writing *muntmong* rather than *mundmong*.
2. "Talk" itself does not distinguish humans in this way, according to Melpa ideas, because, for example, birds, which are wild things, have their own "talk" which they use to communicate with one another.
3. *Elim-nga-noman-nt pilipa em, tin nambaetep könimon?* (He/she did it thinking in the *noman*, how can we see?)
4. *Wamb-mbö-nga noman e rukrung petem, nambaetikin könin?* (People's *noman* lies inside them, how can you see it?) The axiom is often cited in quarrels and disputes, as a means of reminding people to be circumspect about one another, since you never know what the other person may actually be thinking or planning.
5. See A. J. Strathern 1975: 352. The association between *noman* and the body was brought home to me when a friend, considering that I looked quite well, asked me "What thoughts are you having these days?" (*nim namba noman mat pin nda?*)
6. *Tininga king e elpa-elpa morom, noman tenda petem.* The opposite is also sometimes said, that people look alike but think differently.
7. See M. Strathern forthcoming. The idea of planned intentions is significant here. Wild things, which are not subject to human care and thought, of course have "intentions", in the sense that they search for food and rear young. But these activities are still described as *roltinga*, activities "at large", without conscious co-ordination. Children similarly lack this kind of co-ordination. *Noman* as "plan" is exemplified in the phrase *noman-nt nomb pora ndumun*, of pork-distribution, "in our *noman* we have already eaten the pork", i.e. we have already decided how to divide it up (and there is none spare), a phrase I heard in a debate between different sets of men in a sub-clan group in April 1979. Another expression is *noman oronga wantpint etep mor* (I have made a sling [of your words] in my mind), indicating that one has adopted a proposed plan.
8. It can be seen that *mbo* refers here to what we could call the cultural aspect of what is biological. For the Melpa, however, the distinction is not between "culture" and "biology" but between what is *mbo* and what is *römi* (cf. note 7).
9. Given the way in which Wömndi here handles the idea of *min*, its translation as "life-soul" is akward. Nevertheless, Wömndi accepts that it is the *min* which is supposed to survive after death and which slips out of the body in dreams. The relationship between *min* and *noman* is a little obscure in his exposition. *Min* appears to correspond to the child's recognition of its own life and possible dangers to that life. The fact that it is *min* and not *noman* which is held to survive death and become a ghost (*kor, tipu*) might suggest that the ghosts lack *noman*. But such a piece of "theological" probing is inappropriate, for the Melpa do not think this of ghosts, nor that they become *rakra*, since they remain relatives, *mbo*, of

the living. According to the Daribi, whose other ideas on the "mind" are close to Melpa categories, *noma'* are "souls, animate, spontaneous and sentient spirit-beings which move around independently . . . they perceive, think, feel and act of themselves, and comprise each a complete personality and will" (Wagner 1967: 42). A young child does not have a *noma'*, it develops within him when his skull hardens on top and teeth appear . . . . The *noma'* is responsible for the operation of breath, centred in the heart, and is also responsible for understanding or thought processes, linked with the liver (*ibid.*: 43). With minor differences, these Daribi views can be found also in the expositions which Wömndi and Ongka gave me of Melpa ideas. The significant point is that the age at which *noman* develops is also the age when speech is just beginning *in fact* and hence communication between the child and its world is expanding fast. Further parts of Wagner's discussion indicate that the Daribi *noma'* is equivalent to the Melpa *noman* and *min* together. Cf. also Rappaport and Buchbinder 1976: 28, 34, on Maring ideas, and Gilbert Lewis on the Gnau idea of *wuna'at* as "vital centre" (Lewis 1975: 208-14).

10. Cf. Reay (1976: 13-14) on Kuma stereotypes of big-men/rubbish-men. R. Brown (n.d.), in an unpublished reanalysis of the Melpa materials, also makes the observation, which I here underpin with points about *noman,* that physiognomic stereotypes reflect social categories of dominance and deprivation. I do not accept, though, that such evidence amounts to the delineation of a system of social classes in Melpa society. This is a problem which clearly requires more scholarly attention than I can give it here (cf. an earlier discussion in A.J. Strathern 1971: 204-8).

11. The Etoro, who practise homosexual insemination of youths by older men as an intrinsic part of the process of physical maturation of males, appear to have developed an analogous viewpoint, since they consider that " a predisposition toward development of the desirable characteristics of one's inseminator is also transmitted in the semen itself rather than by the tutelage" (Kelly 1976: 53, note 7).

12. I already knew from common Melpa usage the point about the upper and lower *noman* which I cite later. It was reported also in the first Melpa ethnography by G. Vicedom (1943-8: vol. 2). M. Strathern discusses the ideological use of the image by men (1972: 160-3).

13. These could also be described as "internal observers' models" (Ward 1965: 124). I do not mean to deny that such models also depend partly on certain ideological assumptions. I am grateful to Dr. Judith Okely for pointing this out to me.

14. Strong desire is expressed by reference to the heart: *na munt nonom,* (it is eating my heart); *mundi kong ronom,* (it strikes the heart).

15. *Ike e na rongenem.* It is this trope on upper and lower *noman* which M. Strathern reports on (1972: 161), in its use as a piece of male ideology.

16. On *kum* see A. J. and M. Strathern 1968, Reay 1976 (for the neighbouring Waghi Valley people's ideas). Not surprisingly, *kum* is synonymous with witchcraft. In Ongka's description *namb* is really the "witchcraft" force in the person; *pilamb* corresponds to the *noman.*

17. Ndamba, like most big-men, refers constantly to *noman* in his conversations. Big-men have few sanctions to hand, other than shame and pride, and it is understandable, therefore, that they should stress so much the need for proper individual thinking. One of his phrases which he used to me when I was put out by someone's actions was *Wamb-nga muntmong unt etim*, (People's hearts act first), i.e. people act on impulse and do not consider things first, as they should, in their *noman*. In this respect, *kitim*, the stomach, stands for "emotions" in a more definite way than *muntmong*, which is partially identified with *noman* itself. (*Muntmong* has the special function, according to Wömndi, of being linked with "breath", *muklnga*, a source of life indicative of the presence of *min*, the life-soul; *muklnga* is also supposed by Christian converts to come from the deity, but this idea has been grafted on to the indigenous concepts — Wömndi's ideas in general show a tincture of Christian influence at several points). *Kaemb*, the liver, is not a seat of thought or of speech, as it is for the Daribi, but of sympathy. It thus stands as an emotional counterpart to *noman* in the same way as *kitim* stands to *muntmong*. In Ndamba's usage, reliance on emotional attitudes is deplored and he praises those whose *noman e weng ndorom* (their thoughts are patient). So careful is his own monitoring of emotions that on one occasion, when our clan had just experienced the sudden and dramatic death of one of its younger men while attending a funeral held by a neighbouring group, with clansmen gathered in a state of shock by night in a men's house, Ndamba announced that he was unable even to cry, because *na noman ti pili na pint* (I cannot think any thoughts). He meant that even grief has to be an ordered reaction, in concert with a general knowledge of how to interpret a death and what to do about it, and at the time he was so taken aback that he did not possess this knowledge and so tears would not come.

18. Exchange relations in general depend on the *noman* of the partners. In purchasing foodstuffs I frequently found that requests for advice on what to pay were met, by the seller and bystanders alike, with *niminga noman-nt pilipa iti-o* (do as your *noman* tells you to), for the exchange was an evaluation by the persons of each other and not just a commercial trans-action with generalised rates. This dependence on the will of the partner goes with the degree of flexibility and volatility in exchange. Exactly the same is true in the usage of the Wiru people of Pangia, Southern Highlands Province, whose term *wene* partially corresponds to *noman*, although for the Wiru *wene* is more diffused through the person and is less a controlling and reflecting agency than is *noman*. In some ways the Wiru notion of *wene* operates even more strongly, however, than does *noman*, for a person may say that he does not "know" another at all until they have exchanged gifts (*wene toamuku*, "I do not make *wene*"). The idea of knowledge as dependent on exchange and communication is thus forcibly expressed. The same is true of the Kewa (Leroy 1979: 198), for whom the term *kone* is clearly analogous to the Wiru *wene*. Since relation-ships depend in this way on feelings, and feelings may change, it is clear that partners must work carefully at maintaining good feelings, and all

partnerships are in a sense uncertain, for how can one be sure of the other's feelings? The point is further alluded to by Sillitoe in his extensive analysis of Wola exchanges (1979: 165-9). Throughout his account Sillitoe stresses the importance of individual actions and networks rather than of groups or leaders of groups. The Wola language is closely cognate with that of the Kewa, their easterly neighbours, and the term for "thought" in Wola, *konay,* is clearly synonymous with the Kewa *kone.* Sillitoe reports that Wola men perform rituals to secure success in exchanges (similar to the Melpa idea of *kil kä*), and that the help of ghosts (*towmow*) is needed for this: if a *towmow* speaks to a man in a dream, he is offering to help the man "by entering the chests of men he deals with . . . and influencing their (*konay*) . . . so they give many valuables to him . . . Thus men try to gain some control over the uncontrollable aspect of an exchange" (Sillitoe 1979: 168). The theme of uncertainty, linked to variable fortune, appears strongly here. Finally, in the urban contemporary context, since many younger Melpa men have migrated to the towns, the concept of *noman* takes on a further twist. Such young men, who are partially cut off from both political and family ties, have tended to develop an "ideology of autonomy", which emphasises their essential independence in the face of urban pressures to work for employers or otherwise conform with the introduced rules of the state. Since *noman* begins "at home" and is expressed pre-eminently, for men, in political affairs, these young men are very close to being characterised as without *noman* at all. Indeed, big-men at home often describe them as being *romi* or *rakra,* a synonymous term: an exaggeration, but one which points to the ideal equation between "humanity", *noman,* and being within the scope of society (cf. M. Strathern 1975).

19. When men compare their dances to those of the birds of paradise, they invest the latter with social characteristics. My term "aimlessly" here is a gloss on the Melpa *roltinga,* which means properly "without ordered intentions". In Wiru usage birds may even be described as Leau, "mad", a term similar in force to the Melpa *kupörl,* which is applied to children and may be translated as "crazy" or "foolish". Ongka, when asked if children were *römi,* answered that they were not, but that they were *kupörl.* In a further application of ideas, a state of *kupörl* in adults may be attributed to the temporary invasion of their *noman* by a wild spirit, *tipu römi.*

20. For one such study, done in convincing depth, cf. Rosaldo 1980.

References

Brown, R. (n.d.) *Production, Appropriation and Ideology: the Case of the Mt. Hagen Social Formation.* Unpublished MA thesis, Univ. of Connecticut.

Caws, P. (1974). Operational, representational and explanatory models. *Am. Anthrop.* 76, 1-10.

Geertz, C. (1966). Religion as a cultural system. In *Anthropological Approaches to the Study of Religion,* (M. Banton, ed.), ASA Monograph 3. London: Tavistock.

Jarvie, I. C. (1964). *The Revolution in Anthropology*. London: Routledge and Kegan Paul.

Kelly, R. (1976). Witchcraft and sexual relations: an exploration in the social and semantic implications of the structure of belief. In *Man and Woman in the New Guinea Highlands*. (P. Brown and G. Buchbinder, eds). Amer. Anthrop. Assoc. Spec. Publ. 8.

LeRoy, J. (1979). The ceremonial pig-kill of the Southern Kewa. *Oceania* 49, 179-209.

Lewis, G. (1975). *Knowledge of Illness in a Sepik Society*. London: Athlone Press.

Rappaport, R. and Buchbinder, G. (1976). Fertility and death among the Maring. In *Man and Woman in the New Guinea Highlands*. (P. Brown and G. Buchbinder, eds). Amer. Anthrop. Assoc. Spec. Publ. 8.

Reay, M. (1976). The politics of a witch-killing. *Oceania* 47, 1-20.

Rosaldo, M. Z. (1980). *Knowledge and Passion: Ilongot Notions of Self and Social Life*. Cambridge University Press.

Sillitoe, P, (1979). *Give and Take. Exchange in Wola Society*. Canberra: A.N.U. Press.

Strathern, A. J. (1968). Sickness and frustration. *Mankind* 6, 545-52.

Strathern, A. J. (1971). *The Rope of Moka*. Cambridge University Press.

Strathern, A. J. (1975). Why is shame on the skin? *Ethnology* 14, 347-56.

Strathern, A. J. (1979). *Ongka. A Self-account by a New Guinea Big-man*. London: Gerald Duckworth.

Strathern, M. (1968). Popokl: the question of morality. *Mankind* 6, 553-62.

Strathern, M. (1979). The self in self-decoration. *Oceania* 49, 241-57.

Strathern, M. (n.d.) No nature, no culture: the Hagen case. In *Nature, Culture and Gender*, (C. MacCormack and M. Strathern, eds). (In press).

Strathern, M. (1975). *No Money on Our Skins*. Port Moresby: New Guinea Res. Unit Bull. Vol. 61.

Strathern, A. J. and Strathern, A. M. (1968). Marsupials and magic. In *Dialectic in Practical Religion*. (E. R. Leach, ed.). Cambridge University Press.

Turner, V. W. (1962). Three symbols of passage in Ndembu circumcision ritual. In *Essays on the Ritual of Social Relations*, (M. Gluckman, ed.). Manchester University Press.

Turner, V. W. (1967). *The Forest of Symbols: Aspects of Ndembu Ritual*. Ithaca: Cornell University Press.

Vicedom, G. F. and Tischner, H. (1943-48). *Die Mbowamb*. Hamburg: Friederichsen, de Gruyter & Co.

Wagner, R. (1967). *The Curse of Souw*. Chicago University Press.

Ward, B. (1965). Varieties of the conscious model. In *The Relevance of Models for Social Anthropology*. (M. Banton, ed.), ASA Monograph 1. London: Tavistock.

MODEL AND IDEOLOGY:
DIMENSIONS OF BEING CIVILISED IN LIBERIA

ELIZABETH TONKIN

My history is of the words "civilised" and "kui" in Liberia, West Africa. These are part of a cluster including "Christianising", "native", "tribe", "country", which have been heard there at least since the 1820s, when agents of the American Colonization Society began to purchase land on the Grain Coast, and to settle on them free or freed emigrants "of color" from the United States. They have to do with the relations between these "colonists" or "settlers" and the "aborigines" of the lands they occupied; with the assertion of control and the legitimation of authority; and finally with aspiration and social mobility. All of them therefore operate contrastively and make or imply division and choice. While I point out some of these oppositions, space forbids full contextualisation: the history of *tribe* and *tribal,* for instance, could fill a separate paper.

Every commentator on Liberia this century has mentioned these words and thought them salient.

> Of course the issues could not all be understood simply by analysis of the words. On the contrary, most of the real issues remained . . . But most of them, I found, could not really be thought through, and some of them, I believe, cannot even be focussed unless we are conscious of the words as elements of the problems. (Williams 1976: 13-14)

I had to be extremely selective in source, period and place and I concentrate on three topics:

1) the models available of the "natives" to the "settlers" in the colonial and commonwealth periods, i.e. before Liberia was made independent in 1847;

2) the rise of the "civilised natives" and

3) the uses of the word "kui".

Quite apart from the broader theoretical lessons which can be drawn, every sentiment quoted has been expressed elsewhere in Africa, and indeed with some updating can be recognised in this country today. The case also shows that one must not make *a priori* distinctions between "folk model" and written law, or "ethnic" and "Western" concepts. And if you replace "native"/ "primitive" by "ethnic"/"folk" and "civilised" by "Western"/ "written" or "developed" you will see that such distinctions have a long and dubious history.

A Civilising Mission? The Aims, Ideology and Models of the American Colonization Society

Through the American colonisation movements (see Staudenraus 1961 for a succinct account) some 14,000 emigrants were sent to Liberia in the 19th century.[1] There were always links between its supporters and the founders of Freetown, although distrust by the former colonies of Britain was marked. The American Colonization Society (hereafter ACS) made its first expeditions to Sherbro, where their settlers reenacted all the disasters of the original ventures to Sierra Leone. They finally purchased land at Cape Mesurado in December 1821 for less than $300, by "the judicious mixture of flattery and a little welltimed threat" of Lt. Stockton, USN, who levelled his pistols at the head of King Peter, the natives' leading representative.[2]

The aims of the Colonization Society were reiterated in its magazine, *The African Repository and Colonial Journal,* (hereafter *AR*), which was also read in the Liberian colonies. Thus in 1827 it is stated that their "specific object" was

> to transfer with their own consent, the free people of colour of the United States to the coast of Africa, and assist them there in founding the institutions of a free, civilised and Christian people.

Thereby "a great evil" would be removed, and Africa introduced to "knowledge, industry and religion". The movement would contribute to the suppression of the slave trade. (Sec. of ACS in *AR* III 1828: 10).

Another example gives more away:

> to found in Africa an empire of *Christians* and *republicans;* to reconduct

the blacks to their native land, without the disturbing the order of society, the laws of property, or the wishes of individuals; rapidly, but legally, silently, gradually, to drain them off; these are the noble ends of the colonization scheme. (*AR* II, 1826: 375)

AR also printed many projections of future black population increase in the US and pieces like the First Annual Report of the Prison Discipline Society, which begins:

the first cause, existing in society, of the frequency and increase of crime, is the degraded character of the colored population. (*AR* II, 1826: 152)

Colonizers thus claimed, in familiar 19th century terminology, that their project would simultaneously "civilise and Christianise" "benighted and barbarous Africa", and that it would give freedom and independence to the "degraded" negroes in their midst. Indeed it is many times clear that these *degraded* American Africans are to *civilise* the *degraded* native Africans themselves. That this was not felt to be an obvious contradiction in terms suggests that deeper, practical contradictions lay behind the "noble ends", and this indeed was so. It has been obvious to most commentators that the colonisationists formed an uneasy coalition ranging from Yankee philanthropists to southern slaveocrats. Their reasons for objecting to the circumstances of freedmen and women could be quite contrary, so they attempted a common platform which omitted acute points of difference.

That they equally had suppressed or unspoken motives in common was brutally made clear by William Lloyd Garrison, who in the 1830s successfully made the ACS a prime target of the Abolitionists. Stripped of his rhetoric, Garrison's accusations were that

the society recognised slaves as property, shielded slavery from direct attack, raised the value of slaves by removing the free Negroes, exploited racial prejudices, slandered and terrorised free blacks, obstructed Negro advancement, and blinded citizens to the impracticability of removing the entire Negro population. (Staudenraus 1961: 199).

"Civilising" and "christianising" were accepted approval words, just as "degraded" was denigratory but could mean either depressed by unfortunate circumstances or degenerated from primitive nobility. All the terms, that is, operated within a blurred model of melioration and progress which has, historically, close ties with an opposed model of decline from Eden or an original classical perfection. The enormously ramified richness of the words "civilised" and "civilisation" cannot, obviously, be gone into here (for a programmatic outline see Williams 1976: 48-50). Even now, phrases like "civilised standards of behaviour" may suggest inchoate resentment at the loss of their former power — compare "patriotism" for the National Front.

The ACS representatives were publicly fair and supportive to their colonists but profoundly patronising. And what in fact could be the good things they were to bring to Africa? What could be the real consequences of enlightening the benighted? The more they particularised "civilisation" the more was left out. The ACS's first Agent was instructed to

> aid the natives in procuring instruction in the elements of knowledge, in agriculture and the arts of civilised life and in the doctrines of our Holy Religion. (Huberich 1947: 49)

Other versions even distinguished the arts and sciences from civilisation, leaving weak aims like decently clothing the savages and changing their housing. Missionary calls to change barbarian practices were avoided, but there are only occasional mentions, by the Pennsylavania and Maryland Colonization Societies, of possible future native-Afro-American assimilation.

Before turning to the ACS native policy in action, there is one previous model to mention. For Americans, civilising and Christianising were part of their responses to American Indians. Indeed demands for black emigration coincided with that of the Indians. Berkhofer describes (1972: 101 ff) the early projects which were overwhelmed in the far bigger enterprise of Indian Removal, whereby throughout the 1820s and 1830s the Five Civilised Tribes were driven steadily westwards, by vicious chicanery culminating in the "Trail of Tears" to Oklahoma (Foreman 1972; Debo 1972).

Although missionaries protested, Berkhofer notes that on the whole they did not object to removal on principle. Such was their dislike of civilisation-in-reality that they supported sending the Indians "to the wilderness to train them in good civilisation" (1972: 100). White Americans later disposed of the savage by their sentimental pictures of the hunter, doomed to the assimilating extinction of modern life (Pearce: 1967). But it was a blind to focus on the hunter savage in the first place. As the fate of the Civilised Tribes makes clear, the real threat to white interests was not the Wild West Indian but those who actually did as they were told and became civilised. For the Cherokee Nation for instance, acquiescence in "Agriculture" was against them, their schools, churches, constitutions and indeed slave-holding did not make them into acceptable Americans.

The ACS divided Africans into three groups: the native Africans, the recaptured Africans and the free people of colour.[3] The colonies owed their existence to the second category. Claims for Federal support for colonization were unsuccessful, but President Monroe was persuaded to stretch the provisions of the Slave Trade Act of 1819 to include the financing of the *Elizabeth* expedition, officially sent to build a reception centre for "repatriated" Africans off captured slavers, but really an ACS project, which went as I have said to Sierra Leone. On paper, the two Agencies were distinguished, but by 1829 $264,710 of government money had been spent ostensibly on 260 recaptives (Huberich 1947: 619-29). Following domestic and Sierra Leonean practices, these worked their way up by undergoing 1-3 years' servitude as house and farm servants of the colonists.[4]

The ACS set out remarkably few rules but these show their perceived interests.

> The colony was founded with the intention of establishing an independent community of small peasant farmers owning in fee simple a tract of land sufficient to enable them to support themselves and their families by their own labours, allotted out of the public domain without payment. (Huberich 1947: 415)

Only the ACS could purchase land; there was to be no individual land dealing with natives. This was at first the only, and remained the principal reference to the natives and their rights *vis-à-vis* the colony. References in *AR* alongside questions of selling liquor suggest avoidance of what were seen as white misdeeds to Indians.

Such plans for a property owning band of agriculturalists reveal the projection of an American dream onto the colonists, a blend of the individualist and the utopian, which was of course to lead to conservatism, not communalism. The stress on agriculture also included teaching it to the natives, a bizarre idea in view of the African reality, but one again standard in America, where the settlement of the hunter was always a prerequisite of missionary endeavour (cf. Berkhofen 1973: 70-1). Outsiders have of course generally criticised African agriculture by reference to their own (ideal) models, expressed through demands for technology. The Liberian coat of arms still displays a plough which notoriously was never in use; development agencies could similarly invent their own banner, with a tractor rampant.

Agriculture was never the main activity of the colonists, who very soon became engrossed in trade. The same phenomenon was already clear in Sierra Leone, but the colonisationists persisted in their beliefs. The separatist Maryland C.S. set up its own colony at Cape Palmas in 1835 with conscious attempts to learn from previous mistakes. These included the failure of agriculture — so Maryland in Africa would be truly agricultural. These plans also failed.

All commentators have observed that trading was highly profitable and some have argued that ex-slaves wanted above all to escape from field work. Such observations are not wrong but they are insufficient. It was evidently necessary for the colonisation societies to believe in the virtues of agriculture, and their refusal to face the facts equally suggests that they had no model or paradigm with which to understand what was really happening. Settler-centred analyses also have ignored the evidence "that Africans . . . occupied a central place in the history of their own continent(s)" (Hopkins 1973: 1). If one looks at the colonies from the native point of view one sees that the colonists were immediately sucked into an active economy in which they were only minor partners. The colonists themselves realised this soon enough.

Cape Mesurado had long been the haunt of traders; at the beginning of the settlement key figures were less the local rulers of official Liberian folklore than J.S. Mills, a mulatto trader who acted as the first Colonial Secretary, and the McKinzie and Hayes families.[5] The first Africans with whom settlers came in contact, in Sierra Leone, were future Liberians — kroomen, who mono-polised the boatwork, and so for many years transported the colonists, and who acted as intermediaries and interpreters in all the first treaties. There were many other coastal speakers of English — with literate secretaries — who wished to increase trade, have European goods and especially schools, which were a usual condition of treaties, though one not often fulfilled.

In the United States, literacy and competence in English were requisite for civilisation. Civilisation then, got to Liberia before the Liberians. The ACS response was instead that it was evidence of the "degrading" effects of the slave trade (see e.g. *AR* IV 1828: 49), whose abolition was a necessary obsession since it was the rationale of a beautiful economy, the redemption of Africa by its own sons, and justified the expiation of American sin on the cheap. The colonists never actually accepted the view that they were to redeem the sins of their white fathers.[6] They did work, and sometimes fight against the slave trade, but this was in fact inextricably linked to the legitimate trade.

It is clear from *AR* that natives straight away sought out colonists to exchange food and produce for goods, and also that they were eager for their children to be fostered, so that in a short time almost every settler household had one or two such servant-wards, a pattern which has persisted ever since. The colonists found they must be both pedlar and buyer for a wholesale trader (Huberich 1947: 418). Soon their interest was to become middlemen, and most of their laws were to this end. The legislators were the few wealthy men (Syfert 1975, 1977). Later one can see that Liberian government policy was based on the effective trade dominance of Europe and the need to manipulate its traders in their own interests so far as possible.

Taken literally, the colonisationists' agricultural aims were self-contradictory — for how could the urbane arts of civilisation develop out of rustic self-subsistence — and disingenuous, for as in Britain, trade and civilisation went together. The ACS was to be the main economic controller and beneficiary, while the Maryland C.S. leaders intended themselves and their own business connections to take advantage of the settlements, port and facilities (Martin 1968: 58-59; Stuadenraus 1961: 161 and Ch. 12). These facts caused colonist disaffection. Meanwhile, interior wars could disrupt the carriage of produce and in turn the fragile economy of the settlements, so that they reverted to agriculture. As among the Africans, trade and farming could be combined, and colonists followed the local model of agriculture partly because they could get cheap labour. Besides "apprentices" and Recaptives, natives were often anxious to work for hire; most building and laying out of new settlements was done by them. As Massing shows (1977: 153) the ACS agents rejoiced in the low rates they need pay natives compared with colonists, and in the massive markups possible.

The colonies' "Upper Settlements" were primarily agricultural, the seaside ones trading points. This has been the indigenous pattern further east, where there is a consistent symbiosis between interior food and labour producers and beach trade and labour processors (see e.g. Tonkin 1979 and forthc.). The settlers, whether consciously or not, fitted into a local pattern of economic diversification.[7] In native-colonist relations economic calculations became, and remained, crucial. Liberian political action depends on what economic needs are at stake, and, with very limited resources, conflicts and competition occurred not only between settler and native, but between settlers, settlements and native groups.

Agent after Agent begged for legal guidance, while the colonists were "unruly" — in early days were in armed rebellion — partly because they wanted self-government and not dictatorial white rule. The MSCS recognised the co-presence of native towns, but these existed in ACS territories too. The ACS accepted treaties in which resident natives were to be subject to settlement laws, but did not clarify what rights they could also enjoy.

From the beginning natives were severely punished. In 1824 "the Court of Sessions . . . sentenced one Krooman of some distinction, to two dozen stripes and two weeks' . . . hard labor, for stealing" (Huberich 1947, 1: 321). In the Census of 1843 the cumulative total of crimes was 373. The colonist J. J. Roberts (last Governor and first President of the Republic from 1847) himself listed 646 and claimed "two thirds of these were committed by natives in the vicinity of the settlements" (Huberich 1947: 770).

The Board were most concerned with "lewdness", profanity and Sabbath-breaking. Sabbatarianism was strong until very recently; the settlers like their senders were principally evangelical Protestants. A law is not necessarily enforced, and one of the longest-running Liberian examples has been educational provision (the ACS while recommending schools did not fund them). Another, in the early years, was for supervision and proper training of native "apprentices". The vision of sober burghers training up their households was largely a fantasy one. But for all the neglect and severity which critical observers continued to report, a very large number of wards were "civilised" in the colonists' own terms, and have been till today.

Governor Buchanan apparently did not object to Monrovia's first Municipality Laws of 1835, which for instance resolved that native Africans should do "fatigue duty" as assigned, while Kroomen and Fishermen should also report their arrival within five days and get a residence certificate, price $1.50. (*Colonization Herald* 6.8.1836, also in *AR*). Similar labour laws later were said not to have been passed (Martin 1968: 310); the effectiveness of the Monrovia rules is not recorded. The colonies already provided that debt was extinguishable by public labour at a rate which was twice as long for natives; their wages were also much lower. The attempts to control and derive revenue from the nomadic Kru are a reminder that the Monrovia Krutown existed before Monrovia and soon became more populous and largely self-governing.

Citizenship from the start was for individual property owners. Property qualifications for elected representatives entrenched wealth/class differentials among colonists even before the creation of the Republic. Voters had to be male lot-owners. Women had been allowed some land from the beginning of the colony, but, like natives, were not enfranchised until Tubman's administration, c. 1946. Though ACS regulations can be construed as giving citizenship to all of negro descent born within their territories, this was not I think their intention and it certainly did not work out so in practice. Instead, provision was made, at least in theory, for citizenship to be won as a reward — for being civilised.

Civilised Natives

In 1839 the Governor and Council enacted that no native Africans except Recaptives could vote before three years' attested residence and "uniform course of civilised life", having "abandoned all the forms, customs and superstitions of heathenism" (Huberich 1947: 1432). There is no reference to these or any other provisions for enfranchising natives in the 1847 Constitution. How the law operated in fact I do not know. A visitor in 1858 counted 17 (cited in Massing 1977: 157). The best source on the processes of civilising and its effects is Martin's thesis on the Cape Palmas colony (1968). The Maryland State Colony Society (MSCS) chose Cape Palmas as a port for American merchantmen. It did indeed come to do more trade than Monrovia, tapping a prolific hinterland, including what is now Ivory Coast and becoming a major collection and disembarkation point for kroomen (for their work see e.g. Brooks 1972; Behrens 1974; Martin 1978). A sympathetic Grebo emissary made treaty negotiations possible (Campbell 1971: 75), the purchase was unexpectedly cheap and to a later Liberian "would stagger one's sense of justice and fair play" (Eastman 1956: 42). The MSCS also encouraged missions, temperance and agriculture. The three native kings "reserved government over their own people", but these were "members of the colony" for defence purposes (Eastman 1956: 42).

Despite early attempts at settling differences, colonists and natives frequently clashed and their good feeling quickly deteriorated. In 1857 the fighting was such that Liberian help was necessary, so that Maryland had to join the Republic. Further "rebellions" occurred in 1875 and 1910. The natives lost their rights and much of the territory secured to them by treaty, but the MSCS had effectively repudiated these obligations long before (Martin 1968: 111). As elsewhere on the Liberian coast (see e.g. Sullivan 1978), native polities were small and divided, but continually "ethnicising" through the politico-economic conflicts in which they participated. The colonists have been rightly accused of divide and rule policies but they also were being manipulated (Tonkin forthc., for a general overview, Davis 1975). In Maryland, native "combination", an ever-present colonist fear, was briefly achieved in the Gedebo Reunited Kingdom, modelled on the Fanti Confederation of the

Gold Coast (Martin 1968: 259ff).

The Grebo leading this movement were part of the African coastal intelligentsia. They observed the white colonial world and were partial participators in the civilised ways of its African subjects. They received mission education there, and in Maryland. Two Grebo wars were even known as "P.E. Wars", from the Protestant Episcopal missioners' involvement. Missionaries brought their suspicion of other models, which here were exslaves, and

> several of the missionaries were slaveholders who made arrangements to bring some of their slaves to Liberia so that they could begin a new life under mission guidance. (Martin 1968: 126)

All the missionaries in Liberia have preferred a virgin field while at the same time clinging to areas where they could get Western supplies and armed protection, either Liberian, or in the case of whites, from white sea captains. This meant their entry into the interior, and consequently their schools, came very late.

A few leading converts endeavoured to work with the colonists, to treat the law on becoming a citizen at its face value. Settlers objected:

> Natives are beginning to be admitted into church and say that they are civilised. We expect nothing else but soon there will be applications made for citizenship . . . We born in a civilised country, instructed by our superiors, yet we have to submit to be brought down with Heathens, their oaths taken with ours what would not be done in America under our masters. (Martin 1968: 108)

"We are like the bats, neither beasts nor birds" said the "Civilised Gedeboes of Cavalla," in 1885, echoing a local proverb (*ibid.:* 209).

Many of the Cape Palmas conflicts which seemed to be over ethnic politics or laager superiority had an economic base, chiefly to do with control of trade and labour but also including land. The native demand for "civilisation" included its wealth, comforts, ability to control others. Americo-Liberians were consistently said to be uninterested in education, perhaps because these features seemed a birth-right part of the settler patrimony — which again determined them in holding on to their self-defined privileges.

Even a few well-educated natives seemed threatening[8] when by 1841, much the largest settlement was Monrovia with 870, and three had less than 100 people, (Huberich 1947: 625). Shick, who computed mortality figures from the Emigrant Roll of 1844, concluded they were "appalling", and due to disease, especially malaria, not military action. The population only grew because of constant immigration (1971: 54). The charter myth of being "pioneers" was actually first propagated by the colonisationists, who again and again claimed that mortality was less than in 17th Century America and told the emigrants to emulate the Pilgrim Fathers.

Thus, faced as they really were with death, seen especially (if not in reality) as from hostile natives, it is not surprising that the Colonists felt they were in the midst of "savages", a word which the missionaries themselves used often enough. Comparison with an experience of American "savages" is also a striking possibility.[9] The emigrants came from all over the United States, but largely of course from the southeast. Here Willis shows that by the mid 18th century "a frightened and dominant white minority faced two exploited colored majorities" (1963: 160) and fear of their combination led to divide and rule. McLoughlin (1974) charts the slaveholding interests of the Cherokees and their anti-black legislation. Colonists could know of a past when half-assimilated "Settlement Indians" were well rewarded for catching fugitive slaves alive or dead, and Indians generally helped to crush slave insurrections. Savages, especially civilised ones, could torture, betray and dominate.

Native hostility was exacerbated by the colonists' fearful chicanery. But often direct contact between them was minimal and mediated by civilised natives, because they spoke English and knew both sets of mores. For an example I summarise my research on a Kru polity, Sasstown (Tonkin forthc.).

"Sasstown" was the name of the Jlao Kru trading point. Settlers or any agents of the Liberian government were rarely seen before the Port of Entry in 1909. Very few settlers have ever resided there. The government tried to restrict trade to Ports of Entry and the extension of such rights to Sasstown and nearby Grand Cess was due mainly to their considerable role as kroomen centres. Treaties purchasing the area were apparently made in 1846 (*AR* XII, 1846: 277) but, like most of the coast except for the colonists' own environs it was not effectively under their control.

The Port of Entry accelerated *indigenous* changes which already included reformist movements, and a Christian element converted in Lagos. Mission schools resulted. Many were determined to open themselves to the outside world; this was as firmly disputed by others. Both sides knew they had to decide on their relationship with the Republic. However, the old game of using the settlers in playing off one internal faction or local rival against another was lost. The Kru "rebellions" were many, but in 1916-7 the settlers, with American aid, conquered the coast.

In all this an increasingly ambivalent role was played by leading civilised Sasstonians, who were traders too and tended to support the Government; with bitter reservations on both sides they eventually became its agents. Yet they were only a little differentiated, largely by the scale of their education and commercial success, from many humbler innovators whose horizons had been broadened by their migration experiences, limited and harsh though these really were.

For many Liberians then, the model of civilisation was not the Americo-Liberian at all, and resulted from the huge social and economic changes in West Africa at this time. In Sasstown political events forced people *in certain aspects only* to repudiate Jlao loyalties. In the dual administrative system (cf Fraenkel 1966, on Grand Cess) which developed, and is now widespread, surveyed areas form Townships, Municipalities and Cities (Sasstown is now a city). These are "civilised", and taxed and administered within the constitution. The rest is Tribal, separately taxed and administered by a hierarchy of chiefs under the effective control of the County Superintendent, but managed through the Department of the Interior, later the Ministry of Local Government and Urban Reconstruction.[10] Membership of these areas is now blurred, but political differences remain.

Liberian politicians always used, even incorporated, non-citizens, or lower class ones, in political conflicts. Natives *did* get voting powers by the granting of "Aboriginal Deeds" so as to support a candidate in return for a financial or other aid. Both chiefs and civilised were involved.[11] Political infighting between settlers was always intense, and politicians were usually merchants or had trading interests that could be fostered or bypassed by political representation. Fair treatment of the natives remained an acceptable sentiment, and the claims in official documents protesting one's own virtue, or denigrating cruel treatment by others, were normally counters advancing one's own or undermining others' political pretensions. Similarly dismissal from office for corruption has often been a symptom of political ineffectiveness.

Settler and native interests were often deeply entwined as well as in conflict, while the still existent stereotypes of "native" and "Americo-Liberian" are clearly not accurate today. The appearance of two rigidly bounded groups is not the starting datum of analysis but its problem. For all the segregation and siege mentality which has contributed to a "settler" identity, settlers never have formed a genetically or socially closed society.

Some "settlers" turned into "natives".[1][2] The 1843 Census showed native connections: of 2390 inhabitants (excluding Recaptured Africans and Natives)

> 587 were born in the Colony of Liberian parents, 12 of Liberian and native parents, and 46 were born of native parents, and adopted in the family of the settlers. (Huberich 1947: 767)

Settler men and women married Recaptives early on and Recaptives took native wives. Settler provenance varied. Transfer from Sierra Leone has always existed − it was a two way traffic and of many types. Probably the largest movement was of Kru, who are still in Freetown (Banton 1957). Many Sierra Leonians came to Liberia as agents for European trading houses; often they settled and became identified with the colonists. Liberia's intellectual, E.W. Blyden, was as much associated with Sierra Leone, and one of his protegés, C.T.O. King, became a leading Liberian and founder of a dynasty which produced a President (Lynch 1967: 167). Blyden encouraged a shipment of 346 Barbadians in 1865 which has provided an outstanding number of national leaders (Holder 1970-1: 21-30).

Wardship was a major method of recruiting natives and transmuting them into settlers. It could also set up alliances that were prized on both sides for different political reasons. One result was the "urban family" acutely described by Hlophe (1974). Survival of an *apparently* pure settler community was largely achieved through this syncretic Liberian creation, by which members, including non-settlers, have been socialised, the small numbers of "Americo-Liberians" increased, and their politico-economic influence maximised. As Hlophe says, this system is relatively open, and is the base for an individual's success in the national political arena. Urban Liberians know exactly such a person's provenance and connections; so often do rural indigenous Liberians. There are links into "urban families" and purely indigenous households of standing in Monrovia, through common membership of lineages etc., so the chain of information and patronage that can be joined is ramified and effective. Thus many central political arguments and decisions are quickly known − the foreign planners' model of ignorant "tribes" is quite wrong (cf. e.g. Metcalf 1974, Clower *et al.* 1966). However, in Liberia politico-economic access is very unequal and Hlophe may underplay ranking within the family. It is clear that the "urban family" form is a testimony of involvement with native Africans and assimilation of many of their practices.

Incorporation has depended on loyalty, which demanded a change of name and that one forewent any solidarity with one's group of origin if, as so often happened, there was a conflict of interest. The degree of assimilation varied, however, and loyalty could be demanded, or given, on separate occasions as well as continuously; congruence need not be total. Thus there has always been a continuum of life-style between "colonist" and "native"; what mattered was particular acts of commitment. That is why "civilised natives" could be as "loyal" as family members and yet deeply involved with "tribal" affairs.

Being Kui

Since both "civilisation" and long experience of white traders preceded the colonists, there must have been words to describe them in indigenous languages. Without past accounts of these languages which include such terms, one has to look at both indirect evidence, and usage today. The colonists were surprised to be called "white men" by the natives, who, suggested one visitor, "appear to think that the word denotes intelligence" (*AR* XVI, 1840: 291). On the West Coast people were labelled by their life-style and occupation. The category "white men" is like the (black) "Portuguese" (Tonkin 1971: 135 and n. 11). White men produced goods in return for people or produce; they established factories and leased land for them. In these respects the colonists were familiar and could be understood with the familiar label which, whatever its vernacular name, was also translated as *civilised.* In the colony's *Liberia Herald,* November 6, 1835, is "A Bassa man's traditional account of the present condition of the civilised man, Krooman and Bassa man 'who were in the beginning created equal' ". It tells how God, deciding that man was getting idle, set him to work clearing a farm, meanwhile preparing dinner. The Bassa man ate his food with his hands, on the floor. The civilised man took a chair, sat down at the table "and commenced eating in a very fastidious and polished manner". Last the Kroo man simply constituted himself "steward or waiter". God therefore "bid the civilised man to go no more in the field but walk about and enjoy himself at his leisure . . . . attended by the Krooman who is at his biding (sic) . . . While the Bassa man is to continue to work in the fields and make palm oil – in a word do anything – and strive to make all the money he can for the civilised or white man as he is termed by them – be his complexion what it may – and in any way be conducive to his interest and happiness and he – the Bassa man – is to be remunerated with a small pittance for his trouble".

The natives could of course perfectly well distinguish complexion, and nationality. The Kru and Grebo have special names for the British, with whom they were especially familiar and whom they at different times petitioned for support against the Liberians. They also have words meaning civilised/modern/Western/white/; in Kru this is *kui*. I was told the meaning derived from *kui* (pl) *ku* (sing) which also has a complex of uses ranging from "the dead" to "oracle". *Ku/kui* is certainly a key word which occurs widely in the Kru group languages, including Grebo (Innes 1967, Schwartz 1975: 75, 113). Several of their member units also have a *kui* "society" a secret organisation primarily against witchcraft (Massing 1977: 86-93).

In a report of 1892 (*Liberia Bulletin* 1: 21): *quedeas* is said to be the native term for the civilised people (presumably settlers). Today the term is widely used in Liberia and occurs in non-Kru languages, although I think it is reasonable to suppose that it is a loan word from the coast. (And coast: country: urbane: rustic: settler: tribal). Like "civilised", "kui"came to stand for a way of life often epitomised by but not confined to the settler.

Liberia's weakness was paradoxically useful, for it could only make gradual and piecemeal attempts to enforce a control whose cumulative effectiveness was often not realised until too late. D'Azevedo shows that to the Gola this realisation came in the 1930s when after action in the League of Nations domestic slavery was forbidden and the Vai and Gola economies disrupted. To his older informants (speaking in 1956-7 and 1966-7) "kwi" are the (Americo) Liberians, their policies and ways "kwi business". But D'Azevedo himself outlines the importance of " 'educated' and 'civilised countrymen' " (D'Azevedo 1969-70, Pt 3: 111) whose role was very like their counterparts' among the Kru.

> Here it was not uncommon for . . . a leading man to be known as an active deacon of a Christian church, a devout Mohammedan, and a high ranking member of Poro or other tribal society . . . By appeal to the various resources of kinship affiliations and complex cultural background, he might declare himself to be a Kpele, a Gola, a Mandingo or an Americo-Liberian in order to reinforce alliances or pursue an advantage. (*Ibid.*: 112)

Missions were important too. In Liberia, entry into national churches has been entry into a traditionally politicised Christianity. Membership of the ministry has been a step on the politician's road, while church membership was necessary for government office of any kind.

Anyone who knows Monrovia well must be impressed by the wealth and astuteness of Fraenkel's observations of Civilised and Tribal in 1958-9 and also by the extent of change in less than twenty years, giddily swift even in comparison with other parts of the Third World, because "development" has been crowded into fewer years. Post-war iron-ore mining and all the commercial consequences of the Open Door policy have led to the freeing of *internal* movement, sometimes officially constrained before, to the usual magnet effect of the capital, and to the complete shift of economic interest otherwise away from the coast. In Monrovia, where once natives tried to "pass" into the small settler-monopolized bureaucracy, events willy-nilly enlarged it, increased schools, and opened up a demand for clerical and managerial skills in a great variety of largely expatriate commercial enterprises. Now there are men and women of openly native origin to be found at every level except for the few key posts at the top. While the rich get richer the poor are getting poorer, but for a very large number of people there was in recent years a transformation of conditions and expectations. The obvious question for observers – let alone participators – is how far this mobility and expansion, which is now being combined with budget deficits and inflation, can be contained within the carefully limited political freedom of a one-party state. Serious riots in Easter 1979 occurred over the price of rice – as an explicit cause – and much of the capital's commercial section was smashed and looted. The HQ of the True Whig Party was among the targets. Although current socio-economic conditions are new for Liberians, an extremely familiar pattern has been coalescing of economic stringency, active political opposition, including the formation of a new political party, and much more widespread unrest. In the past this has escalated to native-settler warfare and claimed assassination attempts.

For many of the capital's inhabitants earlier criteria of kuiness and indeed of 19th century "civilisation" are now the norm. Many of the youthful population are in school, wearing Western clothes, speaking Liberian English increasingly not just as a lingua franca but as an equal or even a first language. Kru, at any rate, use church membership as part of social mobility: here English-speaking is a dynamic element in asserting one's kuiness, and has been analysed by Breitborde (1977). In my terms, kuiness is also redefined, and there is no attempt by the young bureaucrats and technocrats in question to "pass" out of the Kru community or work their way up in some settler-based congregation. Nor are these the crucial institutions they were once, for the descendants of freed slaves who had been only permitted to combine or lead in their churches. The legal distinctions between "Civilised" and "Tribal" seem to have lessened in Monrovia, but "kui" remains a key concept for aspirants, not achievers, who need not measure themselves in such terms.

In Sasstown Territory, by contrast, with fewer than 10,000 people in over 400 sq miles (1974 Census) and − after a past of commercial and migration-centred "civilisation" an economy of agriculture plus government and church mission salaries alone − variations in lifestyle are few. A salary makes you kui and kuiness is necessary for a salary − that is, some command of spoken and written English, a civilised name form (Tonkin 1980), indicative also of christian allegiance as it includes a baptismal name, and for better posts membership of the party and of the United Brothers of Friendship.[13] Contenders for the Superintendency or the Legislature will also acquire a single kui wife, but there are kui in reasonably important posts whose wives have had little formal education and while at least nominal church membership is common in Jlao, church marriage is very rare indeed.

But even in Sasstown the simple dichotomy dissolves on closer inspection. With increased schooling, literacy is less definitive. There are men living in the tribal sections who also own lots. But while there is a dual administration and this is a means of allotting scarce resources, there will be competing interests conducted partly through kui/non-kui grouping. Thus it was suggested to me that the kui opposed the nomination of a Paramount Chief who was literate and fluent in English because they feared he would know too much − and could check on any sharp practices by literates, not be imposed on in the matter of Tribal Certificates, by which agricultural land can be acquired by individuals, and so on.

From the perspective of an old Jlao farmer, anyone who works on a concession or in Monrovia is likely to be kui. But s/he is also likely to have visited outside Jlao, and heads of 40 households composing a "town" 14 miles inland had without exception close relatives in Monrovia, Firestone Cavalla Plantation etc. Being kui therefore was a matter of choice as well as opportunity.

In accounts of the rural interior the aspirant appears with the sometimes cynically or fearfully regarded local "big shot" who legitimates his/her superiority by civilised attributes. Some commentators, like the psychologists and their associates who have focussed on Kpelle practices, do not make this clear. Their approach is seen at its extreme in an ethnographic novel (Gay 1973) which describes Kpelle life through the divergent histories of two brothers, one of who takes the "tribal", the other the "kwi" way. Two equivalent divisions are very useful for experimenters who want to contrast "traditional" and "modern", and this to me makes them prima facie suspect, since these terms belong to Euramerican stereotyping, whose tenacity and force stems from Euramerican concerns. Bellman (1975) described a Kpelle group's own usage. Speakers placed experiences into different orders of reality by categorizing them as distinct *meni* ("business", matter). *Kwii meni* is usually opposed to *Zo meni* ("society business") as a pair of mutually exclusive terms. But this is to clarify, it is a means of counterpointing experiences which in reality can be shared by the same person. One of Bellman's informants explained how he claimed kwii rights to get a case adjudicated at District level and having succeeded, argued in court for special consideration as an especially "country" or non-kwii man (1975: 26-35).

The academic binarists therefore echo an indigenous usage but incorrectly reify it. Most terms opposed to *kwi* are not neutral but denigratory. Kwi and Zo are not really binary oppositions, but identify different domains of knowledge, power and expertise. A common oppositional term, used mainly but not exclusively in English, is "country", which was probably already in use before the colony started.[14]

The three top grades of the Sasstown Government Junior High School wrote me 49 essays about "kui". Overwhelmingly they stressed its positive character. It was identified with the ways of whites, the use of machines, with hygienic habits and rejection of superstition, and above all with wisdom and knowledge, more skilled and intelligent behaviour. Although most counted themselves as kui, 11 said they were aspirants while "attending" (school), 8 that they were both kui and country and 5 that they were country and did not want to be kui. None of the writers have electricity or piped water – hardly any have latrines, and in my experience *everyone* believes in "witch" and "medicine" (super-stition). But many comments were thoughtful, and showed ambition for a better rather than a richer way. Hardly anyone mentioned the legal and economic inequalities between kui and country.

Earlier my assistant taped interviews in Kru, to elicit meanings of *kui*. The response was limited for various reasons,[15] but the 14 respondents (7 women) spoke freely and thoughtfully. They included uneducated women living in a civilised area with educated husbands, and a farmer living with his father who is an early kui leader. Most articulate was a self-defined non-kui from a Jlao interior town. All but one of the respondents defined kuiness especially in terms of cleanliness and proper behaviour. Kui is as kui does, self-respect and not "knowing book" is truly kui action (cf. Lancy 1974: 330). For all the apparent displacement of status evaluation into moral terms, the "interior" man speaks with the confidence of one at ease in his own world, gaining respect and self-respect by his character and "name". He also points out that in the country world of farming, kui people have to obey the country law, i.e. their "superior" rights and powers are in abeyance in this fundamental domain. To him, kui ways are not refinements but pragmatic choices. His words are an important reminder that there are still other voices than the kui.

Conclusion

Despite semantic extension, conceptual re-assignment and a continually changing field of reference, civilised/kui remained key terms which have never lost their first components. I do not want to deny the positive and exciting aspects of "civilisation": if we omit the idealism, enthusiasm and passion which it really evoked for many, we cannot explain its effects. The hard conditions in which they were, literally, placed meant that civilisation did not liberate the colonists as intended, but helped to turn them inwards in parochial, obsessive superiority. But even here, one should not miss the sense of passing on a hard-won gift and the conscious pride in an English-speaking culture (cf. Singler 1976) – which of course changed and "Africanised" as it was practised. People aspire to civilisation because it is attractive. It attracts my readers. None of us wants to spend our lives in hard manual labour for subsistence, however much we respect the intelligence, courage and creativity of many who do. The same duality of feeling is clear in the Kru essay writers. I may myself have wrongly criticised the ideals purveyed to West Africa, in that housing and clothing are a medium of social life and its divisions all over the world. Those who define *kui* as cleanliness do I think transpose social inequality into moral worth – kind hearts can be had without coronets – but cleanly comfort is also a moral pleasure, which for those without the simplest of material goods is expressible in very limited ways.

An historical account also shows that it was the colonisationists who first provided models of disproportion and fantasy, in which the colonists had to concur, and into which they were therefore educated. Not only were vital differences hidden to support colonisation, even the most liberal refused to foresee its implications. Like others they claimed to be preparing blacks for self-government without allowing such a prospect really to enter their imaginations. Only one early ACS board member visited Liberia — for a week. The colonisation journals make eerie reading to anyone who has experienced life on a tropical coast with 200" annual rainfall. But as the gap between ACS dream and the reality widened, so did the colonists learn (if indeed as ex slaves they did not know already) that support from their masters depended on evincing high-mindedness. Several commentators have noted an unusually wide gap in Liberia between style and performance, law and practice. Such "formalism" has a long history, and these discrepancies were first *demanded,* so that the senders' consciences could be protected from reality.

The survival and propagation of the myth of a pure settler caste is more puzzling. In Liberia's conditions an emphasis on unity would seem obviously more useful, especially as the rulers cannot cast themselves as the heroic overthrowers of colonial power. Yet appeals for unity have still been accompanied by statements of difference. Despite open criticism and attack, most of the settler-defined national symbols remain — Pioneers Day, the Declaration of Independence, the coat of arms with its motto "The Love of Liberty Brought Us Here". The pioneer vs. the savage theme is obligatory in education and certainly suppresses alternative versions, even if it does not convince the learners.[16]

I conclude that this case-study is a demonstration model of models. To spell that out would not however explain their content or use. The word model is valuable (cf. Needham 1963: xlii-xliv) but anthropologists do not passively record folk (or other) models and to think so is inverted positivism. They are not cognitively unique: they model, focus, monitor, image and compare as do their subjects. Modelling is a procedure of interest, but we should separate, analytically, the study of mental operation and its content.

In Liberia's history we can see besides blocking and patterning — which alike can be *enacted* — prescriptions which are self-contradictory and labels that encapsulate contradiction. This should lead to further questions. The terms civilised and kui focus attention on a cluster of behaviours which are both uplifting and divisive, have been used by people with opposed ends, and cannot have been defined only by a dominant class. The dichotomising I describe simplifies and allows one to transmute asymmetry into symmetry — or to create straw concepts. So lack of kuiness is called "tribal", which becomes quaint and inferior thereby. "Civilised"/"kui" have repeatedly justified exclusion and inclusion,[18] so dichotomising may correctly represent inequality. Civilisation like "development" is the stuff of unequal social relations, since command over resources, including technology, brings wealth, and wealth enables you to enjoy civilisation's fruits. One can also see the truth of Levi-Strauss's observation that literacy is a means of dominance which alienates before it fulfils.

In this (anthropological) model, a dichotomising (folk) model truly locates polarities even while it may hide the user's condition from himself. To talk of "kui ways", for instance, reveals and hides the fact of an (indigenous) kui leadership and its exploitations of others (who may also call themselves kui). Allied to this use is the assertion I have sometimes heard that the "Americans" (Americo-Liberians) are to blame for some misdeed which was actually done by "our own sons and daughters", who are just as much the holders of power positions which they can abuse. A more penetrating view was expressed by a man who had just returned to Liberia after many years abroad. "They have made us like them", he said.

The significance I have ascribed to *choice* and *assent* demands their place in any theoretical account, following (or perhaps twisting?) an argument made by Dumont. Criticising Bailey's view that "tribe" and "caste" were two ends of a continuum, Dumont claimed that "a tribe . . . becomes a caste when it acknowledges the values of the caste system" (1962: 122). In my terms, the continuum is a model of events (either folk or anthropological); "acknowledgement" is a form of choice, and choice the main form of social action. A choice has to be represented as a dichotomy which may also mediate (represent, distort. . .) events for others. The word ideology has many meanings (Larrain 1979) but the relations between knowledge and the social are, rightly, very old anthropological concerns. I suggest that ideologising (cf. Asad, 1979) must increasingly be our study.

Acknowledgements

This is a summary version of the paper presented just before the Liberian coup of 12 April 1980.

I acknowledge the financial support of the University of Birmingham, The Nuffield Foundation and the Social Science Research Council for my research in and on Liberia.

Notes

1. By the 1962 Census, the population of Liberia was 1,016,433 (nearly 1½

million by 1974) and Clapham calculates that Americo-Liberians formed 0.6% of this — 6,452 people who defined themselves as not members of tribes and not alien (Clapham 1976: 130-1).

2. Report of Eli Ayres, the ACS representative (in Huberich 1947: 190). I do not enter here into controversies about the legality of Liberian treaties. Natives continued to conclude them, with loss of sovereignty and "extinction of native title" — an American/Indian usage — through the 1840s in Liberia, usually without coercion.

3. Colonists included an illegitimate son of an ambassador who was also a leading colonisationist (Brooks 1968: 57 and fn. 35). An early party division in Liberia was between mulattoes and blacks, the former first gaining power, less for their whiteness than for the capital and education it often conferred.

4. The history of the Recaptured Africans is like that of women in Liberia. It deserves a separate account but would run parallel with this one. Recaptives were few compared with Sierra Leone (Hargreaves 1962). The largest number arrived 1855 and 1860-1 (Huberich 1947: 631) and were enfranchised by 1873 through True Whig Party efforts, as a successful support against the mulatto Republican Party (Hlophe 1977: 5).

5. See e.g. *AR* I, 1825: 238-45; Huberich 1947: 203. Hannah Hayes was mistress of Governor McCarthy and Sierra Leone merchants (Brooks 1968: 69, n. 41).

6. The settlers took on very early the rhetoric of raising the heathen especially by labour. Their view of redemption is expressed through the Liberian Humane Order of African Redemption, estbd. 1879, viz "The glory of God in the civilization of the African tribes" (Huberich 1947: 891).

7. The steep rocky capes selected for their defence value were also unsuitable for cultivation, as is much of the "coastal forest savanna mosaic", immediately behind the beach (Schulze 1973).

8. A leading emigrant wrote in 1840 for a teacher, else "the natives would become our equals, and even surpass our youth in literary requirements and as I am one of those who look upon the civilisation of the heathen as a matter of secondary importance to the advancement of the country . . . I am inclined to the opinions of the residents of the Southern states in relation to their blacks — 'they had better remain in a happy state of ignorance' " (in Martin 1968: 154).

9. Martin (1968: 303) notes parallels between US legislation on Indians and the Republic's on natives *after* 1868, but could not discover if this was intentional.

10. Thus Hinterland regulations and Republic law have both operated in the 40 mile county strip, though people often write as if the County areas were totally "civilised" and different from the Provinces inland of them. In 1964 the whole country was reorganised into Counties.

11. See Martin 1969: 20 for group incorporation. *Liberia Bulletin,* 19. 1901:69 (LB succeeded AR) refers to 2 classes of vote. Manipulation of votes 1900-1930 is several times referred to in archival correspondence and informants have explained it.

12. 1839 saw an act against "the custom prevailing of vagrancy to and from the settlements of the natives, throwing off their clothes to the great shame of our citizens and adopting their habits and manners, and in some instances disparagement of our civilised institutions" (Huberich 1947: 506, 1406 and cf. Bridge 1968: 56ff).

13. This is a para-Masonic organisation confined to men of black descent, and to their wives in the auxiliary wing, the Sisters of the Mysterious Ten. The UBF is rarely noticed by commentators but I think mediates between the civilised natives and the Freemason settler leaders. The politically ambitious kui of Sasstown bought and brought the UBF from Sinoe in 1972. Since Sasstown Territory is a partly autonomous sector of Sinoe County, "The Sinoe leaders" are necessary supporters when sueing for office.

14. There are early references for Sierra Leone and for Liberia (e.g. *AR* II, 1827: 379). A Nigerian hearing me on this topic protested that Nigerians had never thought in such a way about "our unenlightened brethren" — a phrase also heard in Liberia (cf. Peel 1978).

15. A war against the Government 1931-7 followed by military control to 1944 means a particular sensitivity to enquiry. However, the exercise shows that i) standard elicitation techniques will not necessarily recover key concepts (as they have sometimes been claimed to do) and ii) the information they give is only informative if it can be rounded out with other sorts of data, including documentary and oral history and in-depth interviews; viz. any "empirical" model has to be constructed from different types of anthropological *and* informant modelling.

16. A single textbook example is *Grade 7 Liberian Literature* (1963, bought 1972). The Introduction says "the pioneers' strong determination to build a nation called forth patriotic expressions. Their concern for the civilization of tribes caused preachers and other orators to urge upon citizens the importance of tolerance and brotherly love for those who were in darkness . . . " After a large section on folk lore, and before a little modern verse, is a section which includes a long hymn written for December 1st 1836 by Hilary Teage, celebrating God's aid when "We were by those beset around,/Who craved to drink our blood,/Whose malice, hatred knew no bound,/Whose hearts of love were void" (etc.). There is also an excerpt from Teage's Funeral Oration for Governor Buchanan, 1841, which stresses his influence over "the natives, our savage restless neighbours . . . (now) freed from the restraint in which fear enchained them" "we . . . possess in ourselves the ability to assert our right, at any time to teach these savages the folly of the enroachment".

17. Blamo (1971-2) views the terms mentioned in this paper, along with many others, as "significant symbols", which have by their use defined and redefined social boundaries. I agree with this, but believe with Williams that "the area of signification is not confined to the system itself, but in one dimension necessarily extends to the users of language, and to the objects and relationships about which language speaks" (1976: 20).

References

Asad, T. (1979). Anthropology and the analysis of ideology. *Man* **14**, 607-27.

Banton, M. (1957). *West African City*. London: Oxford University Press for International African Institute.

Bellman, B.L. (1975). *Village of Curers and Assassins: On the Production of Fala Kpelle cosmological Categories*. The Hague, Paris: Mouton.

Behrens, C. (1974). *Les Kroumen de la Cote Occidentale d'Afrique*. Travaux et Documents de Géographie tropicale. No. 18. Centre d'Etudes de Géographie Tropicale. Bordeaux: CNRS.

Berkhofer, R. F. Jr. (1972). *Salvation and the Savage. An Analysis of Protestant Missions and American Indian Response, 1789-1862*. New York: Atheneum. (1st edn 1965).

Blamo, J. B. (1971-72). Nation-building in Liberia: the uses of symbols in national integration. *Liberian Studies Journal* **4**, (1) 21-30.

Breitborde, L. B. (1977). *The Social Structural Basis of Linguistic Variation in an Urban African Neighbourhood*. PhD Thesis, University of Rochester, New York.

Bridge, H. (1968). *Journal of an African Cruiser (1845)*. Repr. with Introduction by D.H. Simpson. London: Dawsons of Pall Mall.

Brooks, G.E. Jr. (1968). A.A. Adee's journal of a visit to Liberia in 1827. *Liberian Studies Journal* **1**, 56-74.

Brooks, G.E. Jr. (1972). *The Kru Mariner in the Nineteenth Century: An Historical Compendium*. Lib. Stud. Monog. 1. Lib. Stud. Association in America Inc. Newark Delaware.

Campbell, P. (1971). *Maryland in Africa: The Maryland State Colonization Society 1831-1857*. Urbana, Chicago, London: University of Illinois Press.

Clapham, C. (1976). *Liberia and Sierra Leone: An Essay in Comparative Politics*. Cambridge University Press.

Clower, R. W. *et al.* (1966). *Growth without Development: An Economic Survey of Liberia*. Evanston: Northwestern University Press.

Davis, R.W. (1975). The Liberian struggle for authority on the Kru coast. *International Journal of African Historical Studies* **8**, (2), 222-65.

d'Azevedo, W. L. (1969-71). A tribal reaction to nationalism. *Liberian Studies Journal* (1969) **1**, (2) 1-21; (1969) **2**, (1) 43-63; (1970) **2**, (2) 99-115; (1970-71) **3**, (1) 1-19.

Debo, A. (1972). *And Still the Waters Run: The Betrayal of the Five Civilized Tribes*. Princeton University Press (1st edn 1940).

Department of Education (1963). *Grade 7 Liberian Literature*. Division of Higher Education and Textbook Research. Monrovia: Liberian Information Centre.

Dumont, L. (1962). "Tribe" and "Caste" in India. *Contributions to Indian Sociology* **6**, 120-2.

Eastman, E. (1956). *A History of the State of Maryland in Liberia*. Monrovia: Bureau of Information, Department of State.

Foreman, G. (1972). *Indian Removal: The Emigration of the Five Civilized Tribes of Indians*. Norman: University of Oklahoma Press. (1st edn 1932; 2nd edn with foreword by A. Debo 1953).

Fraenkel, M. (1964). *Tribe and Class in Monrovia.* London: Oxford University Press for International African Institute.

Fraenkel, M. (1966). Social change on the Kru coast of Liberia. *Africa* 36, 154-72.

Gay, J. (1973). *Red Dust on the Green Leaves.* Connecticut: Interculture Associates Inc.

Hargreaves, J. D. (1962). African colonization in 19th century Sierra Leone and Liberia. *Sierra Leone Studies (NS)* 16, 189-203.

Hlophe, S. S. (1974). *The Role of the Urban Family in the Emergence of the Modern Political Class Structure of Liberia.* Paper: 6th Annual Liberian Studies Conference, Madison Wisconsin.

Hlophe, S. S. (1977). *A Class Analysis of the Politics of Ethnicity of the Tubman and the Tolbert Administrations in Liberia.* Paper: 9th Annual Liberian Studies Conference, Macomb Illinois.

Holder, B. (1970-71). A history of Crozierville. *Liberian Studies Journal* 2 (1) 21-30.

Hopkins, A. G. (1973). *An Economic History of West Africa.* London: Longmans.

Huberich, C. H. (1947). *The Political and Legislative History of Liberia . . . . with Appendices Containing the Laws of the Colony of Liberia 1820-1839, and the Acts of the Governor and Council 1839-1847.* 2 Vols. New York: Central Book Company Inc.

Innes, G. (1967). *A Grebo-English Dictionary.* West African Language Monographs 6. Cambridge University Press.

Lancy, D. F. (1974). *Work, Play and Learning in a Kpelle Town.* University of Pittsburgh PhD. Thesis. Ann Arbor: University Microfilms.

Larrain, J. (1979). *The Concept of Ideology.* London: Hutchinson University Library.

Lynch, H. R. (1967). *Edward Wilmot Blyden: Pan-Negro Patriot 1832-1912.* London: Oxford University Press.

Martin, J. J. (1968). *The Dual Legacy: Government Authority and Mission Influence among the Glebo of Eastern Liberia 1834-1910.* Boston University PhD. Thesis.

Martin, J. J. (1969). How to build a nation: Liberian ideas about national integration in the later nineteenth century. *Liberian Studies Journal* 2, 15-42.

Martin, J. J. (1978). *Kru down the Coast: A Working Paper.* University of Calabar.

Massing, A. (1977). *Economic Developments in the Kru Culture Area.* Indiana University PhD. Thesis. Ann Arbor: University Microfilms.

Metcalf, J. F. (1974). From economic growth to total development: a strategy for Liberia. *International Labour Review* 109 (2) 119-35.

McLoughlin, W. G. (1974). Red Indians, black slavery and white racism: America's slaveholding Indians. *American Quarterly* 48, 367-85.

Needham, R. (1963). Introduction to: Durkheim, E. and Mauss, M., *Primitive Classification.* (1st edn 1903, trans. R. Needham). London: Cohen and West.

Pearce, R. H. (1967). *Savagism and Civilisation.* Baltimore: Johns Hopkins (2nd edn 1953).

Peel, J. D. Y. (1978). Olaju: a Yoruba concept of development. *Journal of Development Studies* **14** (2) 139-65.

Schwartz, A. (1975). *La Vie Quotidienne dans un Village Guéré*. Abidjan: Inades.

Schulze, W. (1973). *A New Geography of Liberia*. London: Longmans.

Shick, T. W. (1971). A quantitative analysis of Liberian colonization from 1820 to 1843 with special reference to mortality. *Journal of African History* **12** (1) 45-59;

Singler, J. V. (1976). *Language and the Liberian Government: Philosophy, Policy and Practice*. University of London (SOAS) M.A. Diss.

Smith, R.A. (1964). *The emancipation of the hinterland*. Monrovia: The Star Magazine and Advertising Services.

Staudenraus, P. J. (1961). *The African Colonization Movement 1816-1865*. New York: Colombia University Press.

Sullivan, J. M. (1978). *Settlers in Sinoe County, Liberia, and their Relations with the Kru 1835-1920*. University of Boston PhD. Thesis.

Syfert, D. N. (1975). The origins of privilege: Liberian mechants 1822-1847. *Liberian Studies Journal* **4** (2) 109-28.

Syfert, D. N. (1977). The Liberian coasting trade 1822-1900. *Journal of African History* **18** (2) 217-35.

Tonkin, E. (1971). Some coastal pidgins of West Africa. In *Social Anthropology and Language*, (E. Ardener, ed.), ASA Monographs 10. London: Tavistock.

Tonkin, E. (1979). *An Anthropological Study of a Kru Community* (SE. Liberia). Final Report Presented to the S.S.R.C. on grant HR3343/2.

Tonkin, E. (forthc.). Sasstown's transformation: the Jlao Kru c. 1888-1918. *Liberian Studies Journal*.

Tonkin, E. (1980). Jealousy names, civilized names . . . anthropology of the Jlao Kru of Liberia. *Man* **15**.

Williams, R. (1976). *Keywords: a Vocabulary of Culture and Society*. London: Collins Fontana.

Willis, W. S. (1963). Divide and rule: red, white and black in the southeast. *Journal of Negro History* **48**, 157-76.

African Repository and Colonial Journal, Liberia Bulletin. Washington DC.
Colonization Herald, Philadelphia.
Liberia Herald. Monrovia.
Maryland Colonization Journal. Baltimore.

MODELS OF GOOD GOVERNMENT

ROBERT TURNER

Introduction

In 1973 the Local Government (Scotland) Act 1973 became law, and during the next two years a system of local government, gradually developed over the previous century, was comprehensively dismantled. The new system promised a greater degree of public participation, removal of corruption, and economies of scale. What this paper will examine are some of the ways in which this enactment was put into effect and interpreted by the inhabitants of a small Lowland burgh, "Easthaven", not far from Edinburgh. By the attempt to apply them, it is hoped to ascertain the usefulness of certain notions regarding the structure of folk models in the formulation of an anthropological interpretation of the events. This is a straightforward test case; the politically dominant model is made explicit in the terms of the Act and need not be painfully elicited, as in many ethnographic contexts, through extensive interviews with "gifted native informants". In actual practice this model is metamorphosed and reinterpreted in various ways at different levels of the political hierarchy, being coloured by pre-existing folk models of what constitutes good government. The models maintained by actors at each level are by no means fixed; detailed participant observation reveals episodes of transformation, primarily during crises.

Much anthropological analysis is directed towards the formulation of satisfactory explanatory models. The philosopher Max Black provides an uncontentious definition of such a model as: "some material object, system or process designed to reproduce as faithfully as possible in some new medium the structure or web of relationships in an original . . . a symbolic representation of some real or imaginary original, subject to rules of interpretation for making

accurate inferences from the relevant features of the model."
(Black 1962: 222) Explanatory models are useful insofar as they
provide a *simplified* representation of the original, permitting
perception of all the important relationships at once, and permitting
logical inferences regarding those relationships. In order to simplify,
it is necessary to make ontological assumptions, to decide what
constitute objects important enough to be represented in the model.
Whether or not these objects have a real existence independent of
the mind of the model builder is irrelevant to this discussion; they
may be no more than labels for social institutions, say — but they
should be completely defined by specification of their relationships
with the other objects in the model. It should be regarded as
improper to appeal to a hitherto unrevealed property of an element
of a model to clinch an argument, like a *deus ex machina*. I feel that
experience in the real world has properly been explained only when
the model is complete prior to the explanation, not invented in an
ad hoc way as the explanation proceeds. In possession of such a
model we can, at best, predict future experience in the relevant
context; or at any rate have a ready-made interpretation for it. I
should state explicitly at this point that I will use the term "folk
model" to denote any model shared by the members of the
institutions or social collectivities described here, including
Parliament and the Wheatley Commission. In this usage, "folk
model" contrasts with "anthropologist's model"; varieties of folk
model will be handled using adjectival discriminating terms, such as
"operational", "ethical" and so forth.

Not all useful models are explanatory; they may have other
purposes. It is perhaps this question of use which distinguishes most
clearly the anthropologist's model from many folk models. By and
large, the anthropologist has little better to do with his models than
to earn the approval of his peers for their ingenuity, while such folk
models as the political models shortly to be described are specifically
designed to constrain or alter people's lives, to transform the rules
of the game of power. A political model may have no explanatory
content whatever; its force in establishing a state of affairs might be
vitiated if it did, implying its discursive questionability.

However, the anthropologist is not prevented from using such a
model as an explanatory model, or at least as part of his explanatory
model. There may even be an advantage in doing so; because it
specifies a desired state of affairs in the world, such a model as is
manifested in the terms of an Act of Parliament is designed carefully
to avoid internal contradictions, to be maximally explicit and unambiguous, and to be comprehensive. It is a quality product by what

are supposed to be the finest intellects of the society, stemming perhaps from many centuries of traditional craftsmanship in the phrasing of decrees — not thrown together as an intellectual exercise like so many anthropologist's models. Since it *institutes* the very objects it deals with, the ontological problem disappears; though perhaps the greatest excitement in political life is in observing how Acts work out in practice, a kind of experimental sociology. It is indeed striking how much sociological methods have come to provide quasi-scientific legitimations for modern legislature (see the Wheatley Report 1969; Kilbrandon Report 1973).

Equipped with a political model precisely specified by an Act of Parliament, the anthropologist is in an excellent position to try out various notions regarding folk models. It may seem a little cheeky to refer to Acts as "folk models" but there seem to be no obvious theoretical reasons against it. The argument presented here is that if currently fashionable notions regarding the structure of folk models are hard to apply in this context, then it is likely that in less explicit areas of custom and belief their use is no more than mystification and jargon. A series of political folk models will be presented, and the usefulness of applying such distinctions as operational:representational (Caws 1974), specific:general, descriptive:prescriptive, and ethical:pragmatic to them will be examined. More will be said about the meaning of these terms — which should be fairly familiar — in the discussion of actual folk political models later.

One aim of this paper is to produce a believable account of a particular sequence of events of public significance. The judge of credibility is the reader, obviously; what are characterized here as folk models are of course only my descriptions of hypothetical mental constructs, taken to be more-or-less shared by the actors (who do actually exist even though they are given pseudonyms in this paper). It is for the reader to decide whether to believe my inferences regarding what the actors know, to decide whether my rhetoric proclaims the requisite blend of objectivity and empathy. I will consider the point proved if my use of conceptualized folk models renders the flow of events more transparent to understanding, so that the misunderstanding which underlies the conflict to be analyzed can be seen as in some sense an inevitable consequence of the misformulation of a particular model by the institution obligated to put it into effect. If this is granted, we have a case where certain collective representations, in the form of folk models, can be seen to have determining influence in a sequence of political events, and the anthropological task of hermeneutically ordering experience has been achieved.

Part 1

The Local Government (Scotland) Act 1973 created a number of levels at which different folk models of good government can be conceived. These will be listed and discussed in order; then a conflict arising from the clash of differing models will be described in the form of a social drama, illustrating dynamical aspects of political models at the local level.

The primary level to be considered here is represented by the *Report of the Royal Commission on Local Government in Scotland 1966-69,* otherwise known as the Wheatley Report. This was itself the successor of a number of other Parliamentary Reports and White Papers, but it is not intended to delve far into political history. From this carefully worked out report it is possible to abstract a model for local government which will be denoted the *Wheatley Model.* A major emphasis of the report was something called "public participation" or "local democracy", in line with the earlier Skeffington Report (1969). Although that perceptive commentator, the late J. P. Mackintosh M. P. observed that

> there is a view held in parts of Whitehall that the purpose of local govern-
> ment is not to create strong centres of local democratic initiative, but to
> produce an efficient set of agencies, for carrying out central government
> policies (1977: 193),

these developments brought into official parlance for the first time the concept of "community".

The "Community Survey" of the Wheatley Report showed that 85% of electors recognized a "home area" to which they felt they belonged; this sociological datum was used as part of the justification for the setting-up of Community Councils, which will be the main concern of the second half of this paper.

At the next level comes the Local Government (Scotland) Act of 1973, putting into effect many of the proposals of the Wheatley Report (Masterson 1978), which was introduced by the Conservative Government of the time shortly after a similar Act for England and Wales. Separate Acts were required because of the many administrative differences between Scotland and the rest of the U.K. The model of government contained in this Act will be referred to as the *Parliament Model.*

The terms of the Act gave the newly formed, elected District Councils the responsibility of drawing up schemes creating Community Councils. This required considerable efforts at District Council level in interpreting the relevant sections of the Act; indeed

Edinburgh District Council was still not convinced at the time of writing of the desirability of Community Councils and had so far resisted its statutory duty to draw up such a scheme. Elsewhere, a variety of schemes have been put forward, have been given the Secretary of State for Scotland's blessing, and the Community Councils have been formed. The scheme operated by the District Council controlling Easthaven was set out in a document entitled *Scheme for Community Councils,* which forms the basis of another model, the *DC Model.*[1]

Next will be considered the models held at two different times by members of the Easthaven Community Council. The structure of previous models in this listing may be deduced with little difficulty from the pertinent documents; but at this level and onwards a different methodology is required. The fieldworker can never be quite sure that the people he is observing, interviewing and chatting with have anything in their minds as definite as a model. Statements about how things are get tinged with attitudes about how things ought to be; people's words and actions may by themselves transform the situation and hence the models held. It is for *ease of thinking* and *exposition* that the anthropologist systematizes his observations in the form of models; ontological priority must always be conceded to the actual events. However, because the framing (Goffman 1974) of the processes at this level is made so explicit by the models already listed, there is a good chance that insights may be gained by positing partially-corresponding models in the heads of the actors, and examining their relationship with the models at other levels. The models imputed on the basis of extensive interviews and observation to Community Council members — inferred collective representations — will be referred to as *CC Models.*

Finally there are the models held by the general public. Most people in the locality have not studied the Wheatley Report, nor the terms of the Act, nor the *Scheme for Community Councils.* Many are only dimly aware of the existence of the Community Council, if at all. For the majority local democracy is a thing of the past; the model of government which dominates their thinking is still the old system of Burgh and County Councils. The new system is judged usually unfavourably by reference to the old, in this often highly traditionalistic community. Models at this level will be referred to as *Local Models;* again they must be inferred and classified by the fieldworker. However, because it persisted with little change for 50 years the former system of local government was well understood by most local adult inhabitants, so an uncontroversial model of their view may easily be constructed.

Before the content of these models is outlined one further element should be introduced into the discussion, which bears on the social drama to be described later. This is the system of health administration. The National Health Service (Scotland) Act of 1972 set up a number of Regional Health Boards, members of which are appointed by the Secretary of State for Scotland, which control the supply and delivery of health services to the public. These Health Boards are composed of highly professional persons, often with few links to the local communities for which they are responsible. In response to the same political pressures for public participation mentioned earlier, bodies called Local Health Councils were also established, whose "general function (is) to represent the interests of the public in the health service in the area or district for which they have been established". (National Health Service (Scotland) Act 1972 II, 14-1) Once again the Parliamentary Act may be represented by a model, which in this case appears to be shared by the Regional Health Boards, though not until recently by the Health Council for the area under study. The Parliamentary health administration model has been incorporated into the *Parliament Model* already mentioned, and the slightly different version of the Local Health Council before recent events will be denoted the *LHC Model.*

Part 2

The only feasible way to distil the hundreds of pages of the Wheatley Report down to a manageable summary for the purposes of this paper is to construct a diagram. Such a diagram is, strictly speaking, a model of a model. The "original" is the patterned behaviour of millions of people envisaged by the writers of the Report; the first model is the text of the Report itself. This is *prescriptive,* in that it models a future, not an existing state of affairs; *representational,* in that it is a specification of desired institutions and not a blueprint for tactical action; *general,* in that it depicts a scheme suitable for the whole of Scotland; and primarily *ethical* in tone, based on the legitimating value of "public participation" rather than Machiavellian considerations of political expedience. In the diagram (Fig. 1), which portrays the institutions and relationships most germane to the local conflict studied, the link between Community Councils and Other Public Authorities is of the greatest interest. The Report states

the community council should also be the recognized body for public authorities of all kinds, including district and regional authorities, to consult on matters affecting that neighbourhood. (Wheatley Report 1969: 208)

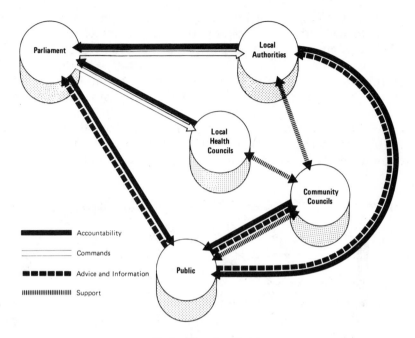

Fig.1 Wheatley Model

These diagrams, as can be seen, depict institutions and the formal relationships between them. I have classified the institutional relationships into four types: accountability, commands, advice and information, and support. Which types pertain for each pair of institutions can for some models be decided by reference to the relevant Government documents, in which such terms as "shall" or "may" are used in a technical way to minimize ambiguity. For some of the models considered here, no documents exist, and the type of relationship must be inferred from informants' descriptions.

To be specific, "accountability" here means the statutory obligation to justify or to give an account of actions or decisions. "Commands" means the right to exercise executive authority, on pain of legal sanction. "Advice and Information" means the right to be heard and to provide information on relevant concerns. "Support" means the legitimacy imparted to an institution as a result of the election by popular vote of its members.

It is of interest that accountability always turns out to be paired either with support or command in the diagrams shown here, except in the Prescriptive CC Model (Fig. 4) where the local authorities and other public authorities are held to be accountable to the Community Council. This unrealistic model resulted from the

Community Council's feeling that since it was accountable to the public, higher authorities should in turn be accountable to it.

For the purposes of this paper, the important features of the diagrams are the *types of link,* the *connectivity,* and the *degree of specification* of the institutions concerned. As the original model diffuses out into actual practice, it becomes transformed in each of these respects.

The Local Government (Scotland) Act 1973 and the National Health Service (Scotland) Act 1972 can be combined and distilled to produce the next diagram, Fig. 2, again a model of a model.

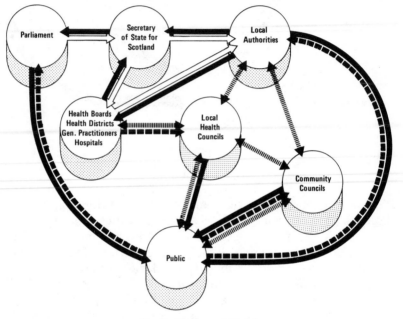

Fig. 2   Parliament Model

The Parliament Model, like the Wheatley Model, is prescriptive, representational and general, but it must be classified as pragmatic, not ethical, since it is supported by legal not moral sanctions. "Other Public Authorities" are now specified; they include Regional Health Boards, Health Districts and so forth. However, it is clearly laid down that it is the right of the Local Health Councils alone to represent public interest in health, and that Regional Health Boards are accountable only to the Secretary of State for Scotland (National Health Service (Scotland) Act 1972: 13-5). Community Councils are given no role in health matters, though Local Health Councils are left free to consult them.

Unfortunately, when the District Council responsible for East-haven came to draw up its *Scheme for Community Councils* (1976) it did not apparently examine the terms of the Act just quoted. The Scheme adopts much of the wording of the Local Government Act, asserting that "the general purpose of a Community Council shall be to ascertain, co-ordinate, and express to the local authorities for its area, *and to public authorities,* the views of the community which it represents, in relation to matters for which those bodies are responsible. . . " (my emphasis). Regional Health Boards are unquestionably public authorities. The relevant parts of the Scheme, or DC Model, are represented in Fig. 3. This model is now prescriptive and largely operational (as a blueprint for action), specific (designed for a particular District), and pragmatic.

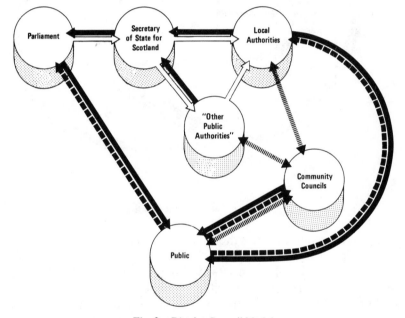

Fig. 3   District Council Model

In view of the Scheme, the Community Council in question could hardly be blamed for maintaining the model represented by Fig. 4. I have inferred this model on the basis of attendance at five Community Council meetings, and extended interviews with each of the councillors. It is, like the Wheatley Model, prescriptive, representational, general and ethical — and did not survive the dispute to be described shortly. Taking the absence of a link between the Community Council and the Local Health Council as an example of methods of inference used, the evidence for this was the lack of interest shown by councillors when copies of the Annual Report of the Local Health Council were circulated. Since there was supposed to be a direct link between the Community Council and the Regional Health Board, in any case, the Local Health Council was regarded as otiose.

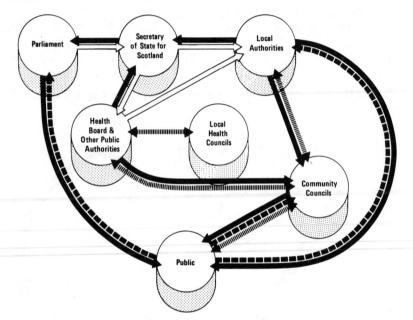

Fig. 4   CC Model – Prescriptive

The LHC Model, on the other hand, as inferred from conversations with the permanent secretary of that body, and from its Annual Reports, includes only a one-way link of advice and information from the Local Health Council to the Community Council. Since members of the Local Health Council were supposed themselves to represent local interests the Community Councils were seen as superfluous in this regard. This model is portrayed in Fig. 5; it is prescriptive, operational, general, and pragmatic.

To complete the background to this social drama, two further models should be described. These are Local Models. The first, Fig. 6, is the model for local government (including regulation of health services) characteristically held by "ordinary" Easthaven people to have been the case before local government reorganization. Almost everyone I spoke to expressed satisfaction with the former system of government; it was a matter for general pride

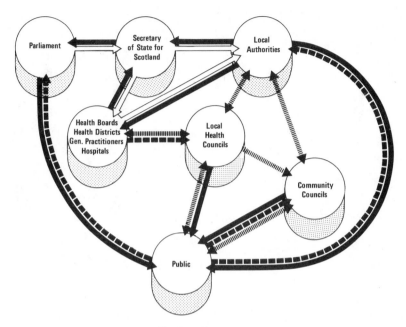

Fig. 5   LHC Model

that the burgh rates were among the lowest in Scotland. "We could look after ourselves well enough" was the usual comment. The Town Council, with elections marked by fierce competition and a 50-60% electoral turnout, was assumed to be properly informed about the activities of other public authorities, while the general attitude to health was that it was a matter requiring such expertise that it should be left to the doctors. This folk model is descriptive and prescriptive, representational and operational, specific, and pragmatic. The degree of accountability of the Town Council to the local public can be judged by the former existence of an annual "Greetin' Meetin' ", attended by a large proportion of the electorate, at which anyone was allowed and indeed encouraged to raise questions and voice complaints to the assembled Town Councillors, and even to hurl abuse at them. Apparently it was quite a festive occasion.

But since 1975, "people are in just such a state now that they just accept what they're told by the District Council," as one leading local man described it. The model of this attitude, presented in Fig. 7, is perhaps a little pessimistic but reflects quite well the views of many people interviewed. Neither Community Council nor Local Health Council appear at all as significant public bodies. Local

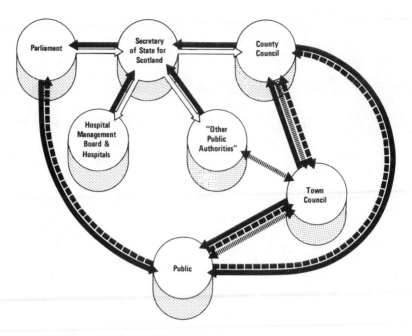

Fig. 6   Local Model – Before Re-organisation of Local Government

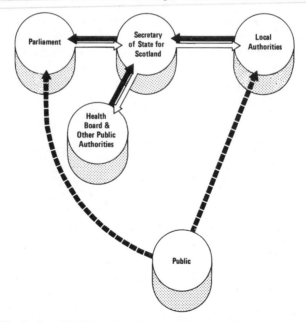

Fig. 7   Local Model – After Re-organisation of Local Government

authorities are too "far-off" to be seen as accountable. This model is descriptive, operational, specific and pragmatic. The Community Councillors are well aware of this view; which partly explains the vehemence of their reactions during the Health Centre showdown.

Part 3

Little has been said so far about the social features of Easthaven, but no convincing account can be made of the events without some historical and ethnographic background. It is not enough to specify the relevant models of local government; in order to understand the predicament of the Community Council it is essential to have some picture of the town's social structure.

Easthaven is a seaside town of about 4000 population, on the fringe of a large metropolitan area in the Scottish Lowlands. It grew up originally around a coal and salt harbour established by a powerful Earl in the 17th century, but by the end of the eighteenth century it had become primarily an oyster-fishing port, with a population of 430 in 1791 (Sinclair, 1792). The important family of local Whig lairds, which by then had replaced the traditional aristocracy, obtained a considerable income from coal mines and factories elsewhere, and were inclined to extend a benign paternalism to the fisher folk of Easthaven, whose economic values and religious outlook they shared. When organized local government was established in the village, by 1889, it was not surprisingly this family which took the leadership, lending its patrimonial legitimacy to the newly formed body of Police Commissioners, the forerunners of the Town Council. At that time home ownership was strongly encouraged, the home being a rich and evocative complex of symbols of social identity. A fishermen's housing association built some 90 houses in the second half of the 19th century.

By the beginning of World War I, Easthaven was a prosperous fishing village, having taken full advantage of the herring "boom" of the turn of the century. More than half the adult male population were fishermen — such trades as joinery, building, market gardening and coal mining accounting for the remainder. Women maintained fishing gear, baited lines, worked in the fields for local market gardeners, opened their houses as guest houses in the summer, and found jobs in mills in the nearby industrial town. Boats were owned by groups of kinsmen, and some 50% of houses were owner-occupied, a very high figure for the region. Marriage was mainly within the community; considerable social pressure was exerted to prevent girls of fishing families from marrying miners. Religious involvement was high, as it still is, with evangelistic groups both inside and outside of the established Church of Scotland. All these characteristics betoken an ethos of independence, self-reliance; of being special and different.

After the Great War the herring fishery never really recovered. But the population of Easthaven had grown at a very rapid rate, mainly because of survival of six or seven children per family. The result was that many young men from fishing families were forced to emigrate or to swallow their pride and find work in the nearby collieries, which were then expanding. This broke down to some extent the distinctiveness of the town as regards occupation, but the exclusivity of the community was now preserved by other means. The public housing programmes of the 1920s and 1930s meant that the Town Council had control of almost all the new houses in Easthaven, and allocation methods were devised such that hardly anyone who was neither a native nor married to a native could find anywhere to live there. The family of local lairds had by now died out, and the Town Council was composed mostly of the more successful shopkeeper sons of fishing families, "Independent" in political orientation. Left wing miners' representatives were always a small minority even when, in the late 1940s, it looked as though mining not fishing would dominate the town's future. Town Councillors held on to their positions largely through patronage – some were almost explicitly "church" candidates. Apparently, since most local residents were extensively linked by kinship, patronage proved fairly effective in distributing social benefits evenly.

When local government re-organization came in 1974-75, it created a great power vacuum in Easthaven. Men who one day were the cynosure of all eyes, men of worth and character, experienced in public authority, were the next day transformed into common citizens, stripped of their civic dignity. Not one former Town Councillor expressed an interest in joining the Community Council – though in other Lowland towns it is common to find ex-Town Councillors on the Community Council. But in Easthaven, such a body was universally regarded as useless. "I think it's non-existent, certainly powerless", said the owner/manager of a small but highly lucrative machine shop. A former Town Councillor explained "I've never really been particularly interested (in the Community Council) because it doesn't have any powers worth talking about . . . " In view of the preceding discussion, we may clearly identify "powers worth talking about" as powers to build and allocate houses.

By this time Easthaven had a mixed economy, most of the workforce finding employment in the nearby metropolis. Fishing still provided a focus of cultural identity, and gave well-paid jobs to some 10% of the workforce, while fish processing accounted for another 5%. The largest sector, 38%, worked in distribution and service industries, many of these women working in shops and offices in the metropolis. A power station provided about a hundred jobs for Easthaven residents, though most of these went to specialized personnel imported from other parts of Scotland, representing the largest influx of strangers at one time since 1900. 17% of the workforce were employed in manufacturing, 8% in construction, and only 3% in coal mining. This is roughly the position at present.

It is possible to distinguish four different elites in Easthaven, which play significantly different roles in public affairs. An interesting comparison may be made with the leadership structure found by Cohen (1975) in a Newfoundland outport undergoing a similar process of cultural modernization. First, there is the group of top fishing boat skippers, whose earnings may top £20,000 per annum and whose capital assets may amount to several hundred thousand pounds. Though highly respected, they traditionally take little part in local government. Several of them are elders of the Church of Scotland (often when they retire from active fishing), and their private opinions are taken very seriously by their friends more active in public life. They live surprisingly unostentatiously, in keeping with the ethos of egalitarianism that prevails among many Scottish fisherfolk. It may seem paradoxical that the wealthiest men have little public involvement, but their lives are timetabled by the tides, which makes it difficult for them to attend regular weekday meetings of official bodies. Some are, however, active in government-level negotiations over Common Market fishing policies.

Secondly, there is a number of "home-grown" professional men, sent to good schools by successful fishermen fathers. They are typically architects and industrial scientists; together with the better-off local merchants they formed the nucleus of the former Town Council in its final years. Thirdly, we find a group of immigrant professional men of 10-15 years residence, owner-occupiers mostly with local ties of some sort but not classifiable as "yin a oo" – the term used to distinguish true indigenes from "strangers". Not surprisingly, the Community Council mainly draws its membership and support from this group, which does not include the immigrant power station workers. It should not be assumed that these men are socially isolated from the majority of the population; on the contrary, most of them have wide local networks and are involved in "traditional" collective social activities such as organizing the "Old Folks' Treat".

Fourthly, there is a female elite. These women do not gain their prestige from the kind of job they do, but from their skill, enterprise and dedication as organizers and co-ordinators of the numerous local associations, such as the two church women's guilds, the Gala Day Committee, the Women's Rural Institute, and so on. They tend to be indigenes. One became a Community Councillor for a few months, but when she was appointed to senior office in a local association she found she no longer had time for the former role — a characteristic indication of local priorities. No local woman has significant political contacts with the larger world — that is left to men — while within the town women are the custodians of custom and with the aid of gossip provide much of the quite firm existing social control. Their role is symbolically represented and celebrated at the Gala Day crowning of the Easthaven Queen each year. (Turner 1979).

Cohen (1975) found a social structure in some respects surprisingly similar. Though the "politics of leadership in Focaltown is about legitimacy" (Cohen 1975: 2) in a way very different from Easthaven — since Focaltown, Newfoundland, still had some measure of political autonomy — the two rival groups he describes have much in common with two of Easthaven's elite groups. He characterizes the "People's Group" as

> associated with the traditional leadership of the community . . . identified with the status quo . . . built on the indigenous cultural disinclination to become politically involved and equally marked determination to defer to paternalistic authority, and on patronage. (1975: 50)

This group identifies with "traditional political values" and has "long established family roots in the community" (1975: 51) — and thus corresponds closely with the second elite described here, the source formerly of Town Councillors. The "Sophisticates", Cohen's other group, form

> a political elite; the bases of their ascendancy are meritocratic and organizational . . . all outsiders . . . businessmen, opposed to traditional community leadership . . . based on unlegitimated and exclusive institutions, and informed by situationally "new" values. (1975: 59)

Only in the organizational base of this group — exclusive institutions such as the Lions Club — does this differ from the third elite described in this paper, the origin of the present Community Councillors. There is no evidence that local exclusive organizations, such as the Freemasons or Rotary Club, dominate the membership of the Community Council, though there are, to be sure, open organizations such as the Sports Club which seem to attract almost exclusively that particular elite.

The fourth elite, of women, compares interestingly with the female elite described by Armstrong in an Argyll fishing village, where "women's activities are limited to protest; they do not participate in planning" (1978: 69) and where they "simply do not have the recognized political resources such as development grants or planning information to redistribute" (1978: 67).

There is a fair amount of informal social interaction between these various elites in Easthaven, and not much competition for power, since there is none to be had. Among members of all elite groups the purpose and position of the Community Council is quite well understood, and there is general approval of the character of its members, though everyone claims to have been happier with the old system. The present Community Council actually comprises: an architectural technician, an architect, an engineering draughtsman, a civil engineer, a market gardener, a middle-rank civil servant, and a high-ranking civil servant. All of them are owner-occupiers, though 70% of the population of Easthaven are Council tenants. All but one are politically Conservative, reflecting quite well Easthaven's overall Tory bias.

Within the Community Council there is a good deal of bonhomie; most of the councillors are also friends outside that context. All are between 35 and 45, married, with children still at home. Meetings are conducted with very little formality and consensus is reached in almost all decisions; in the meetings attended by the author there was never even a show of hands. The (Conservative) District Councillor for Easthaven attends the monthly meetings regularly and is punctilious in his efforts to help the Community Council to carry out its function properly. As spokesman for the District Council he is sometimes the object of sharp criticism, but on the whole he is on good terms with the Community Councillors. Comparison with community councils elsewhere in Scotland (Lothian Regional Council Committee Minutes, 1977; Masterson *et al.* 1978; Masterson 1978) reveals that Easthaven's is fairly typical — in electoral turnout (20% at the last election, 1976; not enough candidates stood for there to have been an election this year (1979) as scheduled), and in characteristic activities (organizing community events such as civic weeks, making representations to District

Council about issues such as siting of new sewage works, applying to Regional Council for funds for special projects such as planting amenity trees). A major concern of this Community Council is its shortage of legitimacy (see Fig. 7) in the eyes of local people, and many of these activities have publicity as their ultimate purpose. A reporter from the local newspaper is briefed about decisions taken in each meeting, and there is general rejoicing when such accounts hit the headlines — even though reporting inaccuracies are frequent.

Part 4

Let us turn now to the Health Centre Row. A Health Centre, to begin with, is an integrated medical building containing facilities for several G.P.s, a clinic, nurses and receptionists. In recent years the two general practices in Easthaven have languished in former shop premises, commonly regarded as inadequate and undignified. Discussions regarding provision of better premises began before local government re-organization in 1975, probably then between the Regional Health Board and the local G.P.s. A site which seemed suitable was earmarked by the Health Board and bought from the District Council in November 1976. It had previously been part of the site of an annexe to the primary school, but had come into District Council hands when a new primary school was built and the annexe found use as a public library. The building was found to be structurally unsafe in the early 1970s and was demolished.

The secretary of the Local Health Council asserts that all information regarding the use of this site as a Health Centre was passed on to the Community Council from the earliest days of that body's existence. The Councillors were fully in favour of the project in the abstract — as professional men they regarded Health Centres as the latest thing, of which Easthaven should not be deprived. Little attention was paid to the actual siting, however, mainly because no-one expected the project to proceed to the building stage in the foreseeable future (a pessimism characteristic among those who have dealings with local government in Britain). In the meantime, confusing the issue, the District Council decided to make part of the "Annexe Site" available to the Community Council as a play area for young children in view of the inadequacy of existing facilities. Unfortunately the District Council had got confused about which part of the site it owned; in 1978, when it took this action, it no longer owned the south part of the site it had made available — this being the site for the Health Centre. To make matters worse, the District Council encouraged the Community Council to apply for a

grant from the Regional Council for the purchase of play equipment — swings and the like — for this play area. The Community
Council of course went ahead. Looking at Fig. 2 — the Parliament
Model shared by the Health Board by virtue of its proximity to the
centre of power, the Secretary of State for Scotland — it is clear
that the Health Board had not the slightest statutory obligation to
tell the Community Council which part of the site it owned. Its
remoteness meant that it was hardly likely to find out until the
last moment that play equipment had been erected there.

The Community Council itself rationalized the situation by
presuming that the Health Centre would occupy only that part of
the site not recommended by the District Council as a play area —
and thus the play area could continue even when the Health Centre
was eventually built. This impression was only reinforced by the
appearance of the Local Plan in April 1978, whose relevant
sections showed a "Public Playing Field" on the site of the play
area. The two lengthy opaquely-written volumes of the local plan
were discussed briefly by the Community Council at a meeting
in June 1978, but no-one noticed that *very* careful reading of the
text would reveal that in fact the play area would be squeezed out
of existence by the developments contemplated. The Local Plan
clearly marked the *north* part of the site as a "Housing Site"; thus
implying that the Health Centre would be on the *south* part of the
site. At that stage the Community Council could have objected to
the proposed housing — sheltered houses for infirm elderly people —
since it had not yet been given final approval by the District Council;
but the Councillors were hoping that matters would sort themselves
out with time.

The penny only dropped in March 1979, when they realized quite
suddenly that nothing could be done to save the play area. They
were put in a very uncomfortable position. Any protest on their part
could easily be construed by the general public as a wicked attempt
to delay the construction of the Health Centre or the sheltered
housing. But some action had to be taken to express the Community
Council's feeling of helpless indignation at the lack of proper consultation, and to save face. The Local Model (Fig. 7) was receiving
ample confirmation, and the prescriptive CC Model (Fig. 4) needed
to be asserted as strongly as possible. What little popular legitimacy
the Community Council possessed was under grave threat.

And so the drama began. During the March Meeting of the
Community Council the District Councillor announced, in a
suspiciously casual and round-about way, that the Health Centre
had been given the final go-ahead and that it would be built on the

south end of the Annexe site. It took a little while for news of the siting to sink in, and did not provoke discussion until the meeting proceeded to "Any Other Business". Then one of the more forceful and articulate Community Councillors, Mr. A., a civil engineer, pounced on the District Councillor and claimed that he had been led to believe that the Health Centre would be built at the north end of the site. The District Councillor, by way of excuse, explained that the Health Centre planners had found that the north end was unsuitable, being too small for the larger Health Centre envisaged, so they had swapped it for the south half of the site with the Recreation Department of the District Council. However, the Regional Health Board has since informed me that no such swap ever took place; this was obviously a red herring.

At this point Mr. B., the high-rank civil servant, weighed in, a man of strong opinions, atheist, proud of his common sense, with high ideals about community and the role of the Community Councils, as in Fig. 4. He declared that the affair deserved "a storm of protest"; that the "limited public open space" was "too valuable to squander" in this way. This rhetoric met with general approval, and the District Councillor was obliged to sympathize, claiming that he too was "incensed" about the turn of events. He had not been properly informed either, he said, he had had to make a special visit to the Planning Department to see the plans. The author's own experience of District Council operating procedures, gained while renovating his house with Council grant assistance, renders this a plausible account − communications between District Council departments are generally poor, apparently, and only those councillors who happen to be on the Planning Committee, exclusively drawn from the majority political party, are well-informed about the implications of such decisions. Mr. B. now reiterated that the Community Council should have been consulted at an early stage since it was a question of using open space in short supply (an endemic problem in Easthaven since adjacent agricultural land is of very high quality and consequently hard to buy for housing and other civic purposes). The District Councillor, in a shrewd tactical move, urged that no obstacles be placed in the way of speedy development of the much-needed Health Centre, or of the sheltered housing. After further disappointed and critical murmurings from the other Community Councillors the meeting ended.

By the next meeting, in April, the Secretary of the Community Council, Mr. C., had written a "strongly-worded letter" to the Health Board complaining about the lack of consultation. He read out the reply, which stated "we are not obliged to consult the Community

Council", and that the council should refer the issue to the Local Health Council. At this point the contradiction between the CC Model, Fig. 4, in which the Health Board is accountable to the Community Council, and the Parliament Model, Fig. 2, became glaringly apparent. The reaction was unanimous: the Health Board's behaviour was seen as intolerably arrogant. "This letter is a breach of the whole ethos of local government . . . It's the only pathetic statutory function we have, to be consulted", Mr. B. exclaimed – perfectly consistent with Wheatley Model I. Had anyone on the Community Council been aware of the defects of the District Council Model, Fig. 3, he would have spoken up at this point. Mr. A. chipped in "perhaps the siting question was still not over" – the remainder of the site could still be used as a play area – a forlorn hope in view of the sheltered housing plans. It was quickly agreed that now the secretary should get as much press coverage as possible on this scandal, and that he should contact the local M.P. if a satisfactory response was not forthcoming.

This marks the first phase of the social drama, the breach of the peace (Swartz *et al.* 1966). According to the local cultural code, local administration is supposed to work efficiently and invisibly, to trouble and be troubled by nobody. Thus to seek publicity for the Health Board's actions, to excoriate them in print, was a genuine flinging down of the gauntlet by the Community Council – at its own risk since it was thereby revealing its powerlessness. If Model 4 had really been the way the power structure was defined, the result should have been some sort of crisis, as the Health Board sought to defend and justify itself. The threat of appeal to the Member of Parliament was real, as M.P.s have been known to intervene in such cases, through the well-established lines of accountability common to all the models held; questions could be asked in Parliament and civil servants' career prospects thus impaired.

However, the Health Board was more than adequately protected by statute from this attack; it declined to make any public reply to the allegations which duly appeared in the local newspaper three weeks later. The consultation issue was clearly not going to provoke any creative discord. In the meantime, among the general public of Easthaven realization was growing that the play area was about to vanish. For most people, holding Local Model 7, resignation was the only available attitude; but one woman, Mrs. D., an incomer and the wife of a social worker, had more progressive ideas. She and her husband are close friends of one of the Community Councillors and have young children who used to play in the area under dispute, so it was entirely natural that she should set in motion a petition calling for prompt action in providing a new play area. Mrs. D. is not a native of Easthaven, but she has lived in the town for several years and could be said to be on the fringe of the female elite. The Community Councillors encouraged the petition, which collected 200 names in a very short time.

The June meeting of the Community Council marks the phase of crisis in the social drama. A reporter was actually present this time, and, more important, an official representative Mr. E. of the District Council Administration Department, there to offer explanation to the Community Council for the nasty surprise it had suffered. The petition was timed to be handed in at this meeting, which Mrs. D. also attended (all such meetings are open to the public but few ever put in an appearance). Mr. E. proceeded to claim that the Local Plan (mentioned earlier) had specified the site of the Health Centre, and that the Community Council had had its chance to comment when that document appeared a year before. However, as already pointed out, the Local Plan was never explicit about the site, with the position of the Health Centre needing to be inferred from two short sentences separated by over 100 pages of text.

But it was not the consultation issue that got the big headlines, but the petition. The story appeared as the main front page news — though Mrs. D.'s Christian name was incorrectly quoted. Also apparent in this article are attempts by the District Council to redress the situation. The first was a letter from the Director of Administration to the Community Council, containing an actual apology that full investigation of the Annexe site had not been carried out before it was handed over to the Community Countil as a play area. This can be seen as an implicit acknowledgement that the District Council did not actually own the land at the time. The District Council Director of Leisure and Recreation was quoted as saying "we will just have to look around for another suitable site, that's all." But there was no suggestion that the DC Model 3 needed revision, that the ultimate cause of the problem was the conflict in the cognitive models. Perhaps when the Scheme for Community Councils is reviewed in a few years' time efforts will be made to be more explicit about who is entitled to talk to whom.

Meanwhile, the Health Board had passed on all the angry letters from the Community Council Secretary to the Local Health Council. This Council had no idea that the siting of the Health Centre was in any way problematic; in any case it regarded such details as outwith its competence. Details had been sent on to the Community Council as the Health Council had received them from the Health Board. The only problem was that when these documents were photocopied, the red cross-hatching marking the actual site had failed to reproduce properly, so that the Community Council could not have discovered the site that way. The Secretary of the Local Health Council responded to the angry letters by sending what have come to be laughingly termed "anodyne" replies to the Community Council, pointing out that consultation with the Health Board should have proceeded through the Local Health Council, and that the latter body could only know what the Health Board was willing to tell them. The reaction to these, predictably, was one of derision; the Health Council was seen to be as powerless and unrepresentative as the Community Council, if not more so.

While the Health Board did not react publicly it was quite embarrassed by the unfavourable publicity. Its members came rapidly to the conclusion, reviewing the events, that they were blameless in the matter — that the fault lay in the District Council allotting the site as a play area in the first place — but nonetheless a request for clarification was sent to the Secretary of State for Scotland. His response was a reaffirmation of Model 2, the Parliament Model: the Health Board had no obligation to talk to the Community Council. However, he went on to urge Health Boards to obtain comments in future on the actual siting of health facilities from the appropriate Local Health Councils. This forces a change in the LHC Model, Fig. 5. To provide sound advice about siting, Local Health Councils would have to consult Community Councils, making a *two-way* flow of information and advice between these bodies.

Eventually civic peace seems to have been restored. Construction of the Health Centre is now under way, clearing of the ground having been contracted out, ironically to the civil engineer member of the Community Council who fired the first shot in the dispute.

The cognitive effects of the dispute can be summarized as follows:

1) The Wheatley Model, the DC Model and the CC Model, Fig. 4, were all revealed to be in contradiction with the dominating Parliament Model. The Wheatley Model has clearly lost some of its moral force; the DC Model may be changed in future, and the CC Model has now been replaced by a new model, shown in Fig. 8. This is a pessimistic re-evaluation of the power relations; the Community Councillors realize that the Health Board need tell them nothing, and that the Local Authorities and even the Local Health Council need tell them only what they choose.

2) The Local Model, Fig. 7, appears to be gradually admitting the Community Council as a well-meaning but powerless element, and now coincides more or less with Fig. 8. It is fair to claim that the

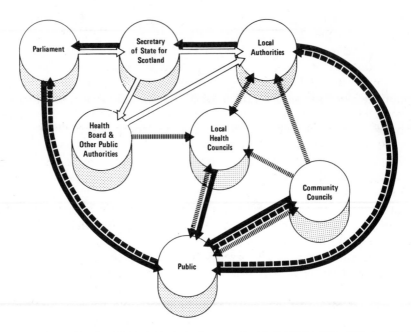

Fig. 8   CC Model-Descriptive, after Health Centre Conflict

Community Council was successful in steering a path between the dangers of not being seen to be active enough about the loss of the play area and the lack of consultation, and being seen as so active as to delay the construction of the much-desired Health Centre and sheltered housing. Thus the Community Council has marginally improved its status locally, though its self-image has deteriorated.

3) The LHC Model, Fig. 5, has been changed to include a two-way flow of information and advice between the Local Health Council and the Community Council.

4) The theoretical questions, as to who is to consult whom, and whether the Parliament Model can ever work very well, have been dropped at an early stage in favour of the practical question, more accessible to public emotional involvement and less tricky for the District Council, of how to provide a play area for the local children.

Conclusion

Returning now to the questions raised at the beginning of this paper, let us consider the adequacy of this account. We are given certain entities which endure: the political institutions, their individual members (to a degree), the government documents constituting the institutions. I have postulated, in the form of folk models characterizing what the actors know, a further collection of entities assumed to endure except insofar as they are altered by circumstance. The question is, am I entitled to do this?

There are two kinds of answer to this question, realist (as Friedman 1974; Levi Strauss 1963: 281) and instrumentalist. The realist answer argues that in a case like this, the actors really do have in their heads shared folk models representing the political frameworks with which they have to deal. They must have such models, the argument runs, because there is a cultural value (perhaps peculiar to our society) demanding consistency in a person's public conduct. How can one be accountable if one has no desire to be consistent? And consistency demands a shared mental template, or model, to be maintained by the actors. One need not look for consistency in social contexts where there is no moral or cultural payoff for it, but in this case the actors' dignity and credibility depend on it. Thus the task of the anthropologist is merely to discover, by hypothetico-deductive process, what those models are.

This pushes the problem back to ethnography. And here it is customary in the profession to take the fieldworker's account on trust, *faute de mieux,* I have endeavoured to validate those models (CC Models and Local Models) inferred from observation and interview by describing them to certain informants and taking note of their reactions. It seems that my characterizations are uncontroversial, at least; though of course they cannot include all the variations.

The second kind of answer to the question, is one entitled to postulate folk models, is instrumental in nature. One *is* entitled, if it works; that is to say, if the sequence of events has occurred "as if" people had the described models in their heads. We can say the account "makes sense from this point of view". I would argue that in the foregoing analysis, careful specification of the models has permitted precise identification of the probable origins of the cognitive conflict, namely the confusion regarding the relationship between the Community Council and "Other Public Authorities"; and that it is uncertain whether this could have been achieved in any other way. In this perspective the failure on the part of the Community Council to demand a new constitution, when its members discovered that it had no right to obtain explanations from the Regional Health Board, can be interpreted as a failure of nerve - which is neatly associated with the observation that the corresponding folk model CC Model 4, was prescriptive and representational and could not be operationalized in that form, which was the product of wishful thinking. It is worth noting in this context that it has been unnecessary to make distinctions between such types of model as "rhetorical", "strategic", or "normative". In understanding the conflict I have only needed to consider what the actors appear, in their words and actions, to reveal themselves as collectively *knowing*. It may be that certain Community Councillors (for instance) successfully *pretended* for strategic reasons not to know that the Community Council had no statutory right to be heard by the Regional Health Board, instead of really being ignorant of this; but since I have concerned myself with *institutional* constructions of reality, this is irrelevant. Matters proceeded as if all Community Councillors were unanimous in their adherence to CC Model 4. Indeed, it is hard to imagine motives for Community Councillors to dissemble to each other, or to the public.

It must be admitted that Local Models 6 and 7, particularly the latter, represent gross simplifications of the wide range of ideas held by the population of Easthaven regarding local government. What I have depicted in Model 7 is a model which corresponded to the ideas of some thirty or forty diverse informants, and represented quite well what the Community Councillors felt they were up against in establishing a legitimate political role for themselves. Whether this is a "realist" or "instrumentalist" justification of this model I leave to the reader to decide.

To sum up, I have portrayed a series of events highly significant to a small Scottish town, by describing the folk models held by actors at various levels in the political hierarchy, and by showing how certain of these models, embedded in their social context, eventually came into conflict and gave rise to a social drama which resulted in the transformation of three of the models. Pressure to transform the dominant political model ordained by the District Council was deflected by the emergency regarding provision of play space for children, and this defective model will probably persist until another contradiction arises.

I have argued that as a guide to the understanding of local political events, the formulation of these models is effective. Finally, I should comment that the qualifying terms — prescriptive, operational, and so on, suggested by Holy and Stuchlik — are easy enough to apply to these models, though they have not played a major role in the analysis.

Acknowledgements

I would like to thank members of Easthaven's Community Council for their extremely kind co-operation, and also the local District Councillor. Mr. David Guest, of the Edinburgh Community Councils Action Group has provided some useful insights and background information. I would also like to thank Mr. W. Harper, of Lothian Regional Council, for his assistance. This research has been carried out as part of a project funded by the Social Science Research Council, for which I am very grateful. Lastly I would like to thank Dr. Alan Barnard, Dr. Tony Cohen and Mr. Alan Campbell for their incisive and stimulating criticisms of the first draft of this paper.

Notes

1. Guidelines towards the formulation of such schemes were published in 1974 by a branch of the Scottish Office, the Scottish Development Department Central Research Office.

References

Armstrong, K. (1978). Rural Scottish women: politics without power. *Ethnos* **43**, 51-72.

Black, M. (1962). *Models and Metaphors*. Ithaca: Cornell University Press.

Caws, P. (1974). Operational, representational and explanatory models. *American Anthropologist* **76**, 1-10.

Cohen, A. P. (1975). *The Management of Myths*. Manchester University Press.

Friedman, J. (1974). Marxism, structuralism and vulgar materialism. *Man* **9**, 444-69.

Goffman, E. (1974). *Frame Analysis*. New York: Harper Colophon Books.

Kilbrandon Report (1973); *Royal Commission on the Constitution*. Cmnd 5460. London: HMSO.

Levi-Strauss, C. (1963). *Structural Anthropology*. London: Penguin.

Mackintosh, J. P. (1977). *The Government and Politics of Britain*. London: Hutchinson.

Masterson, M. (1978). Forming community councils — East Kilbride. *Local Government Studies* October 1978: 67-79.

Masterson, M., Masterman, E. M., Cosgrove, D. F. and Sheldon, H. N. (1978). *Community Councils Research Reports: Interim Reports*. Central Research Unit, Scottish Office.

Sinclair, Sir J. (1972). *Statistical Account of Scotland*.

Skeffington Report (1969). *People and Planning: Report of the Committee on Public Participation in Planning*. London: HMSO.

Swartz, W., Turner, V. W. and Tuden, A. (1966). *Political Anthropology*. Chicago University Press.

Turner, R. (1979). Gala Day as an Expression of Community Identity. (In press)

Wheatley Report (1969). *Royal Commission on Local Government in Scotland* 1966-69 Report. Cmnd 4150. London: HMSO.

NOTES ON CONTRIBUTORS

John BLACKING
Born 1928, England. Studied at Cambridge University, B.A., University of Witwaterstrand, PhD., D.Litt. Lecturer in Social Anthropology and African Government, University of Witwaterstrand, Johannesburg, 1959-1965; Professor and Head of Dept., and Chairman of African Studies Programme, 1966-1969; Visiting Professor at Makerere University College, Kampala, 1965; Professor of Anthropology, Western Michigan University, 1970-1972; John Danz Lecturer at the University of Washington, Seattle, 1971; Visiting Andrew Mellon Professor at the University of Pittsburgh, 1980; Professor of Social Anthropology and Head of Dept., the Queen's University of Belfast, 1970-, Main publications: *Black Background: The Childhood of an African Girl* (1964); *Venda Children's Songs: A Study in Ethnomusicological Analysis* (1967); *Process and Product in Human Society* (1969); *Man and Fellowman* (1974); *How Musical is Man?* 1973 and 1976). Editor: *The Anthropology of the Body,* ASA Monograph 15 (1977); *Aspects of Family life in Ireland* (1979); *The Performing Arts: Music and Dance,* ICAES volume (1979).

John G. GALATY
Born 1945, near Chicago. Studied at the University of Chicago, PhD. Assistant Professor, Dept. of Anthropology, McGill University, Montreal, 1977-. Has published articles on symbolic analysis of the Maasai and the Maasai group-ranch program, and is presently completing a book on the *Dialectic of Maasai Identity,* and an edited volume on *Change and Development in Nomadic Societies.*

Ladislav HOLY
Born 1933, Prague. Studied at Charles University, Prague, PhD.

Research worker, Institute for Ethnography, Czechoslovak Academy of Sciences, Prague 1956-1968; Lecturer in Social Anthropology, Charles University, Prague, 1961-1968; Director, Livingstone Museum, Zambia, 1968-1972; Lecturer and Senior Lecturer in Social Anthropology, the Queen's University, Belfast, 1972-1979; Reader in Social Anthropology, St. Andrews University, 1979-. Author of *Neighbours and Kinsmen: A Study of the Berti People of Darfur* (1974), and various articles. Editor: *Social Stratification in Tribal Africa* (1968); Knowledge and Behaviour, *The Queen's University Papers in Social Anthropology* 1, (1976); Segmentary Lineage Systems Reconsidered, *The Queen's University Papers in Social Anthropology* 4 (1979).

Richard Paul JENKINS
Born 1952, Liverpool. Studied at the Queen's University of Belfast, B.A. (1976). Research Student at the University of Cambridge 1977-1980. Research Fellow, SSRC Research Unit on Ethnic Relations, 1980-.

Graham W. McFARLANE
Born in 1951, N. Ireland. Studied at the Queen's University of Belfast, B.A. (1974), PhD. (1979). Lecturer in Social Anthropology, the Queen's University, Belfast, 1979-. Author of Gossip and Social Relations in a Northern Irish Community, *Queen's University Papers in Social Anthropology* 2, (1977); Mixed Marriages in Ballycuan, Northern Ireland, *Journ. of Comp. Family Studies* 10, 1979; co-author of *Social Change in Dunrossness, Shetland* (SSRC/North Sea Oil Panel Occas. Paper, forthc.).

Kay MILTON
Born 1951. Studied at Durham University, B.A. (1972). Lecturer in Social Anthropology, the Queen's University of Belfast, 1974-. Author of Irish Hero Tales as a Historical Source: An Anthropologist's View. In R. Thelwall (ed.), *Approaches to Oral Tradition,* (1978); Male Bias in Anthropology? *Man* (1979); and other articles.

Sutti ORTIZ
Born 1929, Argentina. Studied at the University of London, PhD. (1963). Lecturer in Social Anthropology, London School of Economics, 1963-1969; Associate Professor, Case Western Reserve, 1962-1972; Visiting Associate Professor, Oberlin College, 1975-1976; Academic Visitor, London School of Economics,

1977-1978. Author of *Uncertainties in Peasant Farming* (1973); Colombian Rural Market Organization, *Man* (1967); Reflections on the Concept of Peasant and Peasant Cognitive Systems. In T. Shanin (ed.), *Peasant and Peasant Societies* (1971); The Effect of Risk Aversion Strategies and Cash Crop Decisions. In Roumasset (ed.), *Risk and Uncertainty in Agriculture* (1967); Expectations and Forecasts in the Face of Uncertainty, *Man* (1978).

Eleanor PRESTON–WHYTE

Born 1940, South West Africa. Associate Professor of Social Anthropology in the Dept. of African Studies. at the University of Natal, Durban. Author of several papers on Zulu kinship. Co-editor (with W.J. Argyle) of *Social System and Tradition in Southern Africa* (1978).

David RICHES

Born 1947. Studied at Cambridge University, B.A. (1968), London School of Economics, PhD. (1975). Lecturer in Social Anthropology, the Queen's University of Belfast, 1973-1979; Lecturer in Social Anthropology, St. Andrews University, 1979-. Author of Cash, Credit and Gambling in a Modern Eskimo Economy. *Man* (1975); Ecological Variation on the Northwest Coast. In R. Ellen and P. Burnham (eds.), *Social and Ecological Systems* (1979). Editor of The Conceptualisation and Explanation of Processes of Social Change, *Queen's University Papers in Social Anthropology* 3, (1979).

Philip Carl SALZMAN

Born 1940, USA. Studied at Antioch Col., B.A. (1963), University of Chicago, M.A. (1966), PhD., (1972). Assistant Professor in Anthropology McGill University, 1968-1973; Associate Professor 1973-1979; Professor 1980-. Author of Political Organization among Nomadic Peoples, *Proceedings of the American Philosophical Society* (1967); National Integration of the Tribes in Modern Iran, *Middle East Journal* (1971); Adaptation and Political Organization in Iranian Baluchistan, *Ethnology* (1971); Movement and Resource Extraction among Pastoral Nomads, *Anthropological Quarterly* (1971); Multi-Resource Nomadism in Iranian Baluchistan, in Wm. Irons and N. Dyson-Hudson (eds.), *Perspectives on Nomadism* (1972); Continuity and Change in Baluchi Tribal Leadership, *International Journal of Middle East Studies* (1973); Tribal Chiefs as Middlemen: The Politics of Encapsulation in the Middle East, *Anthropological Quarterly*

(1974); Islam and Authority in Tribal Iran, *The Muslem World* (1975); The Study of "Complex Society" in the Middle East, *International Journal of Middle East Studies* (1978); The Proto-State in Iranian Baluchistan, in R. Cohen and E. Service (eds.), *Origins of the State* (1978); Does Complementary Opposition Exist? *American Anthropologist* (1978); Ideology and Change in Middle Eastern Tribal Societies, *Man* (1978); Inequality and Oppression in Nomadic Society, in *Equipe écologie et anthropologie des sociétés pastorales* (ed.); *Pastoral Production and Society* (1979); Is "Nomadism" a Useful Concept? *Nomadic Peoples* (1980). Editor of *When Nomads Settle: Processes of Sedentarization as Adaptation and Response* (1980).

Basil Leon SANSOM
Born 1938, South Africa. Studied at the University of Witwaterstrand, B.A. (1961); University of Manchester, PhD. (1970). Lecturer in Social Anthropology, University of Manchester, 1965-1974; Research Fellow in Urban Anthropology (AIAS), 1974-1977. Professor of Social Anthropology, University of Western Australia. Author of When Witches are not named: in M. Gluckman (ed.), *The Allocation of Responsibility* (1971); Traditional Economic Systems and Traditional Rulers and their Realms: in W.D. Hammond-Tooke (ed.), *The Bantu Speaking Peoples of Southern Africa* (1974). Co-editor of *Race and Social Difference* (1972). A signal Transaction and its Currency: in B. Kapferer (ed.), *Transaction and Meaning* (1976). Sex, Age and Social Control in Mobs of the Darwin Hinterland: in J.S. La Fontaine (ed.), *Sex and Age as Principles of Social Differentiation* (1978). *The Camp at Wallaby Cross* (1980).

Andrew STRATHERN
Born 1939, England. Studied at Cambridge University, B.A. (1962), M.A. (1965), PhD. (1966). Research Fellow, Trinity College, Cambridge, 1965-1968; Fellow R.S.Pac.S., 1969-72; Professor of Social Anthropology, University of Papua New Guinea, 1973-1977; Professor of Anthropology and Head of Dept., University College London, 1977–. Author of *The Rope of Moka* (1971); *One Father, One Blood* (1972); *Self-Decoration in Mount Hagen* (with M. Strathern, 1972); Why is Shame on the Skin? *Ethnology* (1975); *Ongka* (1979).

Milan STUCHLIK
Born 1932, Vienna. Studied at the Charles University, Prague, PhD. (1963). Keeper of Indonesian Ethnography, Naprstek

Museum, Prague, 1956-1968; Lecturer in Social Anthropology, Charles University, Prague, 1962-1968; Professor of Anthropology, University of Concepcion, Chile, 1969-1970; Professor of Anthropology and Head of Department, Universidad Catolica, Temuco, Chile, 1970-1973; Lecturer in Social Anthropology, the Queen's University of Belfast, 1974-1980; Reader, 1980—. Author of *Razgos de la Sociedad Mapuche Contemporanea* (1974); *Life on a Half Share: Mechanisms of Social Recruitment among the Mapuche of Southern Chile* (1976); and numerous articles. Editor of Goals and Behaviour, *Queen's University Papers in Social Anthropology* 2, (1977).

Elizabeth TONKIN

Born 1934, England. Studied at Oxford University, B.A. (1955), M.A. (1961), D.Phil. (1971). Home Civil Service 1955-1958; Education Officer (Kenya) 1958-1963; Lecturer in English, Ahmadu Bello University, Nigeria, 1963-1966; Lecturer in Social Anthropology, Centre of West African Studies, Birmingham University, 1970. Author of Some Coastal Pidgins of West Africa, in E. Ardener (ed.), *Social Anthropology and Language* (1971), ASA Monograph 10; Masks and Powers, *Man* (1979); and other papers.

Robert TURNER

Born 1946, England. Studied at Cornell University, B.A. (Maths and Physics), Simon Fraser University, PhD. (Physics), University College, London, Dipl. in Social Anthropology. Research Assistant, Cavendish Laboratory, University of Cambridge, 1972-1975; Research Fellow, Dept. of Social Anthropology, University of Edinburgh, 1978-80. Author of several research papers in Physics.

INDEX OF NAMES [*]

*This index lists the names of persons mentioned in the text only and does not include names of tribes, territories etc. Numbers within parentheses refer to the page numbers of the chapter written by that contributor.

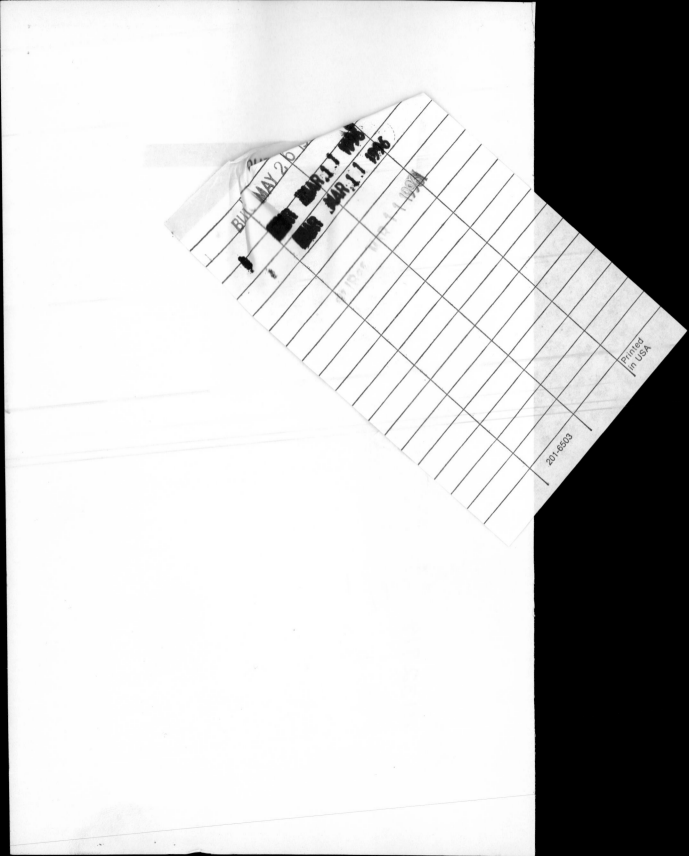